THEODORE PARKER: *An Anthology*

THEODORE PARKER:

An Anthology

Edited, with an Introduction and Notes, by

HENRY STEELE COMMAGER

Beacon Press   Boston

BX
9815
.P32
1960

Published simultaneously in Canada by
S. J. Reginald Saunders and Company, Ltd., Toronto

TO

Lewis Gannett

HEIR TO THE PARKER TRADITION

IN A LIFE DEVOTED TO

LITERATURE AND PUBLIC SERVICE

HE HAS HONORED THAT TRADITION

Contents

V Slavery and Abolition

VI A Sheaf of Letters

VII Poems

VIII "I Have Finished the Course"

Introduction

"There are two Theodore Parkers. One is dying here in Italy; the other I have planted in America. He will live there and finish my work." So said the Lexington farm boy who grew to be the greatest preacher of his day. He knew a thing or two about planting: the physical Theodore Parker died there in Italy and lies buried in the pathetic Campo Santo, now almost lost in the midst of the bustling, modern Florence, but the spiritual Parker survived and grew and flourished—and carries on still his beneficent work.

The simple headstone in that cemetery now so overgrown and neglected bears the epitaph *The Great American Preacher.* Parker was, first and last, a preacher: a man of faith and of religion, and even of the church—he who had so little use for formal religion or the organized church. He was a rebel against the Unitarianism of his own day, but almost alone of the rebels (Emerson, Ripley, Pierpont and Higginson, for example) he refused either to leave the church or to be put out. As his early friend James Russell Lowell put it, when it came to the Unitarian dissenters.

From their orthodox kind of dissent he dissented.

It was religion that permeated his life, inspired his thought, commanded his learning, directed his conduct and sustained his spirit throughout his life. For all his fascination with secular learning, he had never known a time when he did not purpose to be a minister, or when he was tempted to reconsider his function; and for all his far-flung public activities, he never consciously abandoned his clerical role. When he left his pulpit in Boston's great Music Hall, he carried an invisible pulpit with him; and from whatever platform he spoke, it was a religious platform.

Parker came early under the influence of two of the seminal minds of the New England renaissance, William Ellery Channing and Ralph Waldo Emerson. It was to be his historic role to carry Channing's religious philosophy and Emerson's Transcendentalism to their logical, or at least their practical, conclusions—to take them out of the study, where both Channing and Emerson were

1

content to confine them, and put them to work in the home, the market place and the legislative chamber. Without the delicacy or sensitiveness of Channing, or the originality and distinction of Emerson, Parker had greater vigor than either—greater physical and intellectual vigor, and possibly greater moral vigor as well. And in his own lifetime he was, it is fair to say, more widely known and more widely influential than either of them.

Parker's contribution to religion was fourfold. First, he was the most ardent and effective of those who refused to be bound by the dominant Unitarianism of the time—that curious combination of supernaturalism with rationalism which was given orthodox form by the Reverend Andrews Norton. Parker found the supernaturalism of miracles revolting, and substituted for it the miracle of intuitive truth; he found pure intellectualism uninspiring, and substituted for it the intellectualism of sociological investigation and historical analysis. Second, he brought to the study of religion what it was soon popular to call the Higher Criticism, illuminated the problems of theology with the findings of German scholarship and, in a long series of volumes, himself contributed to the scholarly and the philosophical investigation of some of the major issues of theology. Third, he stimulated the revival of religion by carrying his gospel to hundreds of thousands of men and women throughout the whole country, from Maine to Illinois; the whole North was his parish, and those he did not reach by voice, he reached with his ardent pen. As Emerson was the philosopher of those who knew no other philosopher, so Parker was the theologian of those who had no other theology, or who instinctively rejected all that traditionally went by the term theology. And fourth, more fully than any of his contemporaries, he applied what he thought were the great truths of religion to the social issues of the day.

It is not possible adequately to represent these varied contributions to religion in the present anthology. Parker's systematic explorations of religion—if Transcendentalism was ever systematic—do not lend themselves to easy abbreviation, while excerpts from more controversial theological works would do injustice to the reasonableness and the cogency of the arguments. Those larger works include substantial treatises such as *A Discourse of Matters Pertaining to Religion; Ten Sermons of Religion; Discourses of Theology; Lessons from the World of Matter and the World of Man;* and *Sermons of Theism, Atheism, and the Popular Theology,* as well as many other sermons, some collected, some published only in pamphlet form. We have confined ourselves, therefore, to Parker's considered observations on his concept of the Christian church and the Christian minister; his attempt to systematize Transcendentalism; and his appreciation of such moral and religious leaders as Channing and Emerson.

Parker's generation was deeply concerned about the position of the scholar in American society. It was eager to assert the claims of scholarship and competent to do so, but curiously uncomfortable about it, for the responsibilities of the scholar weighed upon its conscience. That discomfort took two forms. First was the feeling that scholarship was at war with Nature, the head with the heart, and that Nature and the heart were, after all, the most important because they came directly from God. There was a tendency to associate scholarship with self-indulgence or with pedantry, to feel that it too easily got out of touch with the "great heart of humanity" or with the requirements of morality. This accounts, in part at least, for that curious but ardent strain of anti-intellectualism that runs through so much of American romanticism and Transcendentalism. We can read it in Emerson's famous *American Scholar,* often mistakenly assumed to be a plea for scholarship rather than for a new kind of scholar; we can read it in Whitman's insistence on the poet as the true spokesman for the new democracy; we can read it, too, in much of Parker's somewhat labored effort to substitute for the authority of learning the authority of intuition, and to find a new and special function for the scholar in America. Americans were beset, too, by a second embarrassment, one that closely affected Parker himself and many of his contemporaries—like Bancroft and Brownell, and such disparate men as Noah Webster, Francis Wayland and Horace Greeley. This was the conviction that democracy makes new and special demands on the scholar in America, demands not valid in Old World society: that in America the scholar has a special obligation to democracy itself, an obligation not to take refuge in private learning but to spend himself and his learning in the service of the people.

Here again Parker spoke eloquently for his generation, and not only spoke but acted. He was deeply committed to scholarship and deeply immersed in it—a collector of languages, of books and of esoteric lore. His scholarship was prodigious, and so too his ability to absorb, to remember—and to use. When (as in that *Defence* which, alas, he was not permitted to argue in Court) he loosed the floodgates of his learning, the waters spilled over the entire landscape, drowning out lesser talents. But he was never entirely happy about his learning; never quite sure that he was justified in spending so many hours in his study; never sure that his accumulation of languages and learning—and books—was not a kind of dissipation.

Something of this comes out in the essay on *The Position and Duties of the American Scholar,* excerpts from which are included in this anthology; and it is implicit in much that he wrote, in his letters and sermons as in his more formal essays. It is most explicit, perhaps, in the essay celebrating the practical Benjamin Franklin, who added his learning and his science to the commonwealth, and in that long and unfair attack on Prescott's histories because they failed to denounce tyranny and champion freedom as energetically as Parker thought they should. We can give here only a few samples of Parker's scholarship and his philosophy of scholarship; a really representative selection would include generous excerpts from his New Testament studies, essays on classical and German literature, and bibliographical correspondence— and best of all, perhaps, the stirring *Defence,* with its rich ore from the quarries of English history.

Religion, philosophy and scholarship combined so harmoniously to require active participation in the affairs of society and of the nation that we may suspect it was not so much logic as temperament which led to a conclusion so inescapable. It was that; but it was heredity, too—or at least a sense of the past and of association with it, for Parker was ever conscious of his grandfather on Lexington Common and of his deep roots in the American past, and could not persuade himself that he had less responsibility for the vindication of intellectual and moral independence than his grandfather for political. "You know that I do not like fighting," he said in an impromptu talk on the Fugitive Slave Act. "But what could I do? I was born in the little town where the fight and bloodshed of the Revolution began. The bones of the men who first fell in that war are covered by the monument at Lexington. . . . These men were my kindred. My grandfather drew the first sword in the Revolution; my fathers fired the first shot; the blood which flowed there was kindred to this which courses in my veins today."

In any event, Parker could no more keep out of the social and political battleground than he could the theological. He was by nature and temperament—and soon by habit—a controversialist, even a fighter; a champion of ideas and causes that were neglected and condemned, as of men and women who were neglected and condemned.

What distinguished him, even in a generation of active reformers, was his passionate concern for what we now call the socialization of Christianity. It was a quality that Emerson seized upon in that moving elegy which he pronounced shortly after Parker's death—Emerson, who himself had been so reluctant to move out of his study and onto the clamorous field of controversy and of battle. "His commanding merit as a reformer," Emerson declared, "is this, that he insisted beyond all men in pulpits . . . that the essence of Christianity is its practical morals; it is there for use, or it is nothing; and if you combine it with sharp trading, or with ordinary city ambitions to gloze over municipal corruptions, or private intemperance, or successful fraud, or immoral politics, or unjust wars, or the cheating of Indians, or the robbery of frontier nations, or leaving your principles at home to follow on the high seas or in Europe a supple complaisance to tyrants,—it is a hypocrisy, and the truth is not in you. . . ."

Parker was, to be sure, but one of a veritable host of reformers, for in that age the stage was crowded with those who would remake the world: Phillips, Garrison, Higginson, Howe, Ripley, Alcott, Pierpont, Sumner, Greeley, Mann, Owen, Weld, Gerrit Smith, the Tappans, Dorothea Dix, Margaret Fuller—the list could go on almost indefinitely. Parker knew them all and worked with most of them. We remember him as a religious liberal and an abolitionist, but somehow he found time and energy to champion the cause of women, of labor, of the poor and neglected, of peace and temperance, and of education. He was, in short, what his religion and his philosophy required: the universal reformer.

And through all this, more clearly than most of the Transcendentalists, he confronted, though he never really resolved, some of the dilemmas of Transcendentalism implicit in his public conduct. For Transcendentalism taught that truth was intuitive and personal, and it was therefore naturally individualistic, almost atomistic. This was the way truth operated in the Old World and —had Dr. Marsh of Vermont had his way—the way it might have operated in the New as well. Parker accepted the teachings but not the conclusions; instead, he socialized intuitive ideas. And this was not too difficult, for clearly what was true for man was true for Man. Divinity inhered in all men alike; and if men were divine, it was wicked that their bodies should be confined in slavery, their minds clouded by ignorance and their souls corrupted by sin. It was a wickedness that Parker could not let go unrebuked.

Nor did the second paradox of Transcendentalism, on the surface more awkward, prove formidable. Transcendentalism relied on the deductive, or a priori, method and looked with suspicion on evidence from the senses or the laboratory; it was at war with Lockean sensationalism and with Utilitarianism; it was suspicious of science, learning and reason. Parker accepted the a priori method, but early fell into the habit of supporting its sentiments and conclusions with a vast paraphernalia of factual evidence; reversing the processes of nature, he built lofty superstructures of statistics and facts on foundations mostly theoretical. To Parker this was not indulgence in a paradox, but merely a convenient method of amalgamating the secular world and the spiritual.

Even where Parker's ideals commanded respect, his methods often did not, for on some matters he was harsh, dogmatic and violent. Passionate in his hostility to every form of injustice and superstition—to religious obscurantism, ignorance, intemperance, greed and selfishness in the rich, arrogance in the powerful, vanity in the learned—on one matter he was clearly a fanatic: slavery. Our generation finds this difficult to forgive. Yet we should not find it too difficult to understand. For slavery, more clearly than any other malpractice, violated the most cherished principle of Parker's religious faith—the principle of the divinity of man—and was therefore most clearly a sin against the light. After the passing of the Fugitive Slave Law of 1850, Parker concluded that there was no solution to the evil of slavery except by force. Who now that contemplates the intransigence of the slaveholders; the formulation of a proslavery philosophy which held slavery a blessing; the pressure for the expansion of the "peculiar institution" into the West and the Caribbean; the steady growth in the numbers of slaves and the power of the slavocracy; the implacable hostility of slaveholders not only to criticism but to inquiry and discussion— who now can be sure that Parker was wrong?

Like so many of the Victorians, in America and in England, Parker was given to thinking and writing much about himself. But his writing was manly and straightforward; it confessed little of that introspection we associate with so many of the romantics and the Transcendentalists, little of that excessive preoccupation with the state of his own soul that led Whitman to protest:

I think I could turn and live with animals, they are so placid and
    self-contain'd . . .
They do not sweat and whine about their condition;
They do not lie awake in the dark and weep for their sins;
They do not make me sick discussing their duty to God. . . .

Alas, Parker never managed to write an autobiography. But he
provided us, in his letters and in the miscellaneous jottings in his
journal, with rich and picturesque material; and his last substantial work was a review of his experience as a minister, which
was not so much a personal as an intellectual autobiography. He
was a dying man when he wrote it, but it is wonderfully fresh and
vigorous and alive. One of the most illuminating documents in our
intellectual history, it is also—for all its retrospective quality—the
most valuable of all revelations of Parker's mind and spirit. Better than anything else we have, it illuminates that character
which fascinated contemporaries and which has not yet lost its
fascination: the cascading energy, the indomitable courage, the
passion for learning, the faith in his fellow men and in progress,
the burning hatred of all forms and manifestations of injustice, and
the bursting love of life itself—the feeling for the inexhaustible
richness of life that sustained him and that he communicated so
ardently to others.

    Lowell and Emerson both emphasized that element in Parker
which was simple, muscular and forthright. Thus the description in
Lowell's *A Fable for Critics:*

    There's a background of god to each hard-working feature,
    Every word that he speaks has been fierily furnaced
    In the blast of a life that has struggled in earnest:
    There he stands, looking more like a ploughman than priest,
    If not dreadfully awkward, not graceful at least,
    His gestures all downright and same, if you will,
    As of brown-fisted Hobnail in hoeing a drill. . . .

No one of Parker's generation commanded a more vigorous style,
more sinewy, more ardent, more perfectly adapted to its purposes.
His words still fall on us

    . . . stroke after stroke,
      Like the blows of a lumberer felling an oak. . . .

He was a coiner of phrases; Lincoln borrowed one of them and
gave it immortality. He could use words like weapons; he organized them and marshaled them like a well-disciplined army and

hurled them at the walls of opposition, which crumbled under
their impact. But the army marched to music, too, and with
banners fluttering in the breeze, for with the power went beauty
and light and even poetic fancy.

Both qualities, the muscular and the poetic, proclaim themselves in that great oration on Webster, which Richard Henry
Dana called "the most touching, elevated, meaning eulogy" pronounced on the man. Listen to this example of the muscular vigor:

"Mr. Webster stamped his foot, and broke through into the
great hollow of practical atheism, which undergulfs the State and
Church. Then what a caving in was there! The firm-set base of
northern cities quaked and yawned with gaping rents. 'Penn's
sandy foundation' shook again, and black men fled from the city
of brotherly love, as doves, with plaintive cry, flee from a farmer's
barn when summer lightning stabs the roof. There was a twist in
Faneuil Hall, and the doors could not open wide enough for
Liberty to regain her ancient Cradle; only soldiers, greedy to steal
a man, themselves stole out and in. Ecclesiastical quicksand ran
down the hole amain. Metropolitan churches toppled, and pitched,
and canted, and cracked, their bowing walls all out of plumb.
Colleges, broken from the chain which held them in the stream of
time, rushed towards the abysmal rent. . . . Fossils of theology,
dead as Ezekiel's bones, took to their feet again, and stood up for
arrant wrong. 'There is no higher law of God,' quoth they, as they
went down; 'no golden rule, only the statutes of men.' "

And to this tribute of poetry: "[Webster] was a farmer, and
took a countryman's delight in country things,—in loads of hay,
in trees, in turnips, and the noble Indian corn, in monstrous swine.
He had a patriarch's love of sheep,—choice breeds thereof he had.
He took delight in cows,—short-horned Durhams, Hereford-
shires, Ayrshires, Alderneys. He tilled paternal acres with his
own oxen. He loved to give the kine fodder. It was pleasant to
hear his talk of oxen. And but three days before he left the earth;
too ill to visit them, his cattle, lowing, came to see their sick
lord; and, as he stood in his door, his great oxen were driven up,
that he might smell their healthy breath, and look his last on those
broad, generous faces, that were never false to him."

We do not have so many masters of prose that we can afford
to neglect Theodore Parker.

"Ah, my brave brother!" said Emerson in that moving ele-
giac to his friend, "it seems as if, in a frivolous age, our loss were
immense, and your place cannot be supplied." The age is no

longer frivolous but desperate, and Parker's place is still not fully supplied; for there is no one who is the conscience of our generation, who speaks to the moral sense of the community—to presidents and congressmen, to businessmen and scholars and preachers, as Parker did in his day. But, as Emerson added, "The nature of the world will affirm to all men, in all times, that which for twenty-five years you valiantly spoke; the winds of Italy murmur the same truth over your grave; the winds of America over these bereaved streets; . . . the sea which bore your mourners home affirms it, the stars in their courses, and the inspirations of youth." Even now, as problems of war and peace, of arrogance of power and pretensions of race crowd upon us, the world of nature and of man still affirms the truths that Parker preached.

The editorial principles controlling this anthology require little comment. Wherever possible, I have taken the text from Frances Cobbe's edition of *The Collected Works,* though in some instances I have drawn on the Centenary Edition published half a century ago by the American Unitarian Association. Parker's letters are taken chiefly from the pages of John Weiss's early, semiofficial biography. In part because Parker is perfectly able to speak for himself, in part because my biography of him is available, I have confined my editorial comment here to an explanation of the selections at hand, rather than making it a vehicle of interpretation. There are brief introductions to virtually all the divisions of this collection, and briefer explanations of such essays and letters as require explanation.

Anyone wanting more than this can turn to the admirable biographies of Parker by Weiss, Frothingham and Chadwick, none of them now in print, but to be found in most libraries. Alas, one can only with difficulty turn to the originals of Parker's works, for both the Cobbe and the Centenary editions are long out of print and unavailable even in many of the larger libraries. It is to be hoped that the current interest in Parker will inspire a new comprehensive edition of his writings. Meanwhile, this collection is offered in the hope that it will make familiar to a new generation the thought and character of that crusader for righteousness who may still claim to be The Great American Preacher.

Henry Steele Commager

AMHERST, MASSACHUSETTS
APRIL 1960

I

Autobiography

Theodore Parker was affluent, exuberant, introspective and articulate. He was a great preacher and a great dramatist, able to infuse almost any subject with excitement. Endlessly fascinated by the spectacle of Man and the beauty of Nature, he was enraptured with life in all its manifestations.

"To me," he wrote in his autobiographical *Experience as a Minister,* "human life in all its forms, individual and aggregate, is a perpetual wonder; the flora of the earth and sea is full of beauty and of mystery which science seeks to understand; the fauna of land and ocean is not less wonderful; the world which holds them both, and the great universe that folds it on every side, are still more wonderful, complex, and attractive, to the contemplating mind. But the universe of human life, with its peculiar worlds of outer sense and inner soul, the particular faunas and floras which therein find a home, are still more complex, wonderful, and attractive; and the laws which control it seem to me more amazing than the mathematical principles that explain the celestial mechanics of the outward world."

Clearly he had a talent for autobiography; whatever he wrote of an autobiographical nature, from his occasional recollections in letters and his jottings in journals to the more formal essay on his *Experience as a Minister,* was fresh, revealing and exciting. Had he lived to complete the autobiography which he began in the last months of his life, it would have been one of the memorable books of its kind in our literature, worthy to rank with that of another great New England dissenter, Henry Adams.

Parker cared little—so he said—for genealogy or for forebears. It was Franklin he admired most, Franklin who said that in America we ask, not who are you, but what can you do? And yet he was very conscious of his own antecedents, and proud too. He liked to remember Captain Parker on Lexington Common, liked to think of the musket hanging so incongruously over his clerical mantlepiece, liked to tell of his mother and his father and their people, so sturdy and simple and God-fearing. He liked to connect himself with the past—the past of his own community, the past of the Bay Colony, the past of the English race. For a man who looked to the future, he was immensely historical-minded. He had the self-consciousness we associate with New England; he had the Puritan conscience and the Yankee curiosity. He never got over the wonder of the world about him—or the wonder of

13

himself, either; how did it happen, he asks again and again, that the little Lexington farm boy became the Great American Preacher? All his speculations on this matter are fascinating.

We give here, at the very threshold, some fragments of autobiography culled from letters and journals. The first is a memoir which Parker began in Rome on March 16, 1860. "It is not likely I shall get very far in it," he wrote prophetically, but he got as far as he could; in less than two months, he was dead. He thought it the product of a sickbed, but in fact it has a freshness about it, a simplicity and a clarity that are rarely found in the recollections of the old.

We supplement this brief memoir of childhood with a series of fragments from letters and journals, arranged chronologically. The full-dress presentation of Parker's *Experience as a Minister* is reserved for the concluding pages of this volume.

1. Recollections of Boyhood

About 1710, my grandfather's grandfather, John Parker, then somewhat advanced in life, with a part of his grown-up children, removed from Reading, where a family of Parkers had settled about 1640, to the Cambridge Farms, since called Lexington, where he had bought a considerable quantity of land, with one small house upon it, probably of logs. The next year he built him a large and commodious house, and furnished it with the usual out-buildings necessary for a farmer's business. The situation was pleasant; a considerable valley a mile or more in length and half a mile wide, with a fresh meadow at the bottom, called in deeds of the time "the great meadow," wound among hills tall and steep on the western and northern side, while on the south and east the hills were of less height and more gradual in their slope. Indeed, it is the general character of the hills in that part of the country to be steep on their southern and eastern side, and of gradual ascent on the opposite side. A brook stole through the valley or percolated through the soft, spongy meadow; following a continuation of the valley, it falls into Charles River at length. The stream was then much larger than at present; for now the hills have nearly all been stripped of their trees and the meadows drained, and the brook is proportionally shrunk, except when a sudden melting of snow floods the meadow and restores it to more than its original size.

Near the upper end of this valley, in about the centre of his farm lot, the old settler built his house, in which children to the fourth generation were to be born to him. It stood about 80 or 100 feet above the present surface of the great meadow, on the south-east side of a high hill, which, gently sloping in front of the house, rose steep and abrupt behind. It faced as near the south as the rude science of the owner or builder could make it, and so was a perpetual sun-dial. It had but one chimney, that a huge one in the centre of the building. The large bricks, made half-a-mile off, were laid in clay as far as the ridge-pole, while the part of the chimney above the roof was *pointed* with mortar. Limestone was not found within many miles, and the want of it was a serious in-

15

convenience in building. The house, like all the others in that neighbourhood, was two storeys high in front, and only one in the rear. The rooms were few, but large and airy; the windows not numerous, of various size, but all small: originally all the latches, except that of the "fore-door," were of wood, with wooden thumb-pieces, but these had nearly all passed away before my recollection. The house, as it stood in my day, had been built at different times, the eastern end being considerably younger than the western, and not furnished with the massive oak-beams which everywhere stuck out in the older part. A New England farmer of "comfortable estate" would hesitate a good deal before setting up his household in such a cheerless shelter; but three generations of stout and long-lived men were born and grew up there; and if the fourth be more puny and sink quicker to the grave, it is from no fault of the old house, but from the consumption which such spongy meadows in New England seldom fail to produce in the course of time; even children, who have removed to healthier situations, carry with them the fatal poison in their blood, and transmit it to their sons and daughters.

As the old man at sunrise stood at the front or south door of his new house on some fine October morning of 1710, he could see but a single house, and that half or three-quarters of a mile off, the other side of the valley: two other columns of pale blue smoke in that direction might tell him of other neighbours, while not far off in the same valley were two others, hid by wooded hills; in a different direction one more house had been built earlier than his own, but on the north side of the hill which sheltered him. . . .

OF THE HUMAN SURROUNDINGS.

. . . 1. In my earliest childhood the family at home consisted (to begin in the order of age) of my father's mother, more than 80 at my birth. A tall, stately, proud-looking woman: she occupied an upper chamber, but came down-stairs to dinner—other meals she took in her own room—and sat at the head of the table on the woman side thereof, opposite my father, who kept up the ancient Puritan respect for age—always granting it precedence. She busied herself chiefly in knitting and puttering about the room, but passed the Sundays in reading the large Oxford quarto Bible of her husband, bought for the price of more than one load of hay, delivered up at Boston. She had also the original edition of the Puritan Hymn Book, printed at Cambridge, which was much in her hands. She read the newspapers, the *Columbian Centinel,* which then appeared twice a week; but common mundane literature she seldom touched. It was a part of my childish business to carry the *drink* to my venerable grandmother—twice a day, at 11 A.M and 4 P.M.; this was *flip* in cool weather, and in spring and summer was *toddy* or *punch*—the latter was, however, more commonly reserved for festive occasions.

2. Next were my father and mother: grave, thoughtful, serious, and industrious people. From an ancestry of five generations of his own name, who had died in New England, my father had inherited a strong and vigorous body; in his youth, there was but one man in town who could surpass him in physical strength, and few who were his equals. He could endure cold and heat, abstinence from food and rest, to a degree that would be impossible to men brought up in the effeminate ways which so often are thought to be the curses of civilization. He was a skilful farmer; though, as he lived not on his own land, but on "the widows' thirds," which his mother had only a life-estate in, he was debarred from making costly improvements in the way of buildings, fences, and apple-trees, which are long in returning profit to him that plants. But he yet contrived to have, perhaps, the best peach orchard in the county of Middlesex, to graft valuable kinds of fruit upon the old trees, and to adopt nearly all of the improvements in farming, as they were tested and found valuable.

He was also an ingenious mechanic: his father and grandfather were mechanics as well as farmers, and did all kinds of work in wood, from building saw-mills, cider-mills, pumps, to making flax-spinning wheels, and turning wooden bread bowls out of maple stumps. He had religiously kept the tools of his father and grandfather, and like them continued to do all kinds of ordinary jobs; indeed, both he and they were such mechanics as men must be in a new country, and should not be in one where industry is more elaborate, and able-minded men are ready to turn their hand to anything. Mechanical talent was hereditary in the family for several generations, and appeared in my remote relations, and even among women, on whose slender shoulders this mantle seldom falls. My father was a thoughtful man, turning his large and active brain and his industrious hand to the mechanical and agricultural work before him; he was an originator of new and short ways of doing many things, and made his head save his hands. In this respect his father and grandfather resembled him.

His education—his schooling ended when the Revolution begun—was of course, much neglected, but he was an uncommonly good arithmetician, often puzzling the school-masters with his original problems. Works on political economy and the philosophy of legislation were favourites with him. He had learned algebra and geometry, and was familiar with the use of logarithms. He read much on Sundays, in the long winter evenings, sometimes in the winter mornings before it was light, and in the other intervals of toil. His favourite works were history—that of New England he was quite familiar with—biography and travels; but he delighted most of all in works of philosophy which give the *rationale* of the material or the human world; of course he read much of the theology of his times, and the literature of progressive minds found its way to the farmer's kitchen. He had no fondness for poetry. In his latter years, his reading was chiefly of novels, not to instruct, but only to amuse the old man. whose mortal life was all behind him. His fathers before him had been bookish men.

My mother, a woman of slight form, flaxen hair, blue eyes, and a singularly fresh and delicate complexion, more nervous than muscular, had less education than my father. Her reading was confined mainly to the Bible, the hymn-book, stories of New England captives among the Indians, of which there were many in the neighbourhood, some in manuscript, and perhaps never printed. Ballads and other humble forms of poetry gave her a great delight. Of course the newspapers passed through her busy hands. My father often read aloud to her and the rest of the family in the long winter evenings, while her fingers were occupied with sewing or knitting, making or mending. She was industrious, as indeed were all the women of the neighbourhood, but like them found opportunities, though too rare, for social enjoyment with them. Dinner was always at noon, and after that was over and its paraphernalia put in order, the household work was done, and a more comely dress took the place of the blue check of the morning.

She was eminently a religious woman. I have known few in whom the religious instincts were so active and so profound, and who seemed to me to enjoy so completely the life of God in the soul of man. To her the Deity was an Omnipresent Father, filling every point of space with His beautiful and loving presence. She saw him in the rainbow and in the drops of rain which helped compose it as they fell into the muddy ground to come up grass and trees, corn and flowers. She took a deep and still delight in silent prayer—of course it was chiefly the more spiritual part of the Old Testament and New Testament that formed her favourite reading, the dark theology of the times seems not to have blackened her soul at all. She took great pains with the moral culture of her children—at least with mine.

3. Come the brothers and sisters, nine in number, and one in infancy laid away in the grave. Some of these were much older than I, and had already gone to seek their fortunes in the various trades and callings of the time. There was still a houseful at home; all of them but three had a decided fondness for literature; they read all the good books they could lay their hands on, and copied the better parts. At school they were always among the best scholars.

4. The uncles and aunts come next. . . .

5. The neighbours about us were farmers; a shoemaker lived a mile off on one side, and a blacksmith within two miles on the other. These were generally, perhaps universally, honest, hardworking men; they went to meeting Sundays, morning and afternoon. "Their talk was of bullocks, and they were diligent to give the kine fodder." In their houses, generally neat as good housewifery could make them, you would find the children's schoolbooks, commonly a "singing-book," Billing's Collection, or some other, perhaps a hymn-book, and always a good quarto Bible kept in the best room, sometimes another Bible inherited from some Puritanic ancestor; these, with an almanack hung in the corner of the kitchen chimney, made up the family library. Perhaps a weekly or semi-weekly newspaper was also taken and diligently read. Two families not far off were exceptions to this poverty of books. I now think of no more. Yet now and then the life of some great thief, like Stephen Burrow, or some pirate or highwayman, would show itself. In other parts of Lexington, "on the great road," in "the middle of the town," perhaps there was a better show of books. I only speak of my immediate neighbourhood.

From Birth till the Age of Eight.

On the 24th of August, 1810, early on a hot, sweltering morning, I came into this world of joys and sorrows. It seems one of my sisters thought an eleventh child improbable; for she had finished the "Family Tree" with the tenth—five years older than myself. However, a place was soon found for the new-comer both in the needle-work and the hearts of the household. As the youngest child, it may be supposed I was treated with uncommon indulgence, and probably received a good deal more than a tenth part of the affection distributed. I remember often to have heard neighbours say, "Why, Miss Parker, you're spilin' your boy! He never can take care of himself when he grows up." To which she replied "she hoped not," and kissed my flaxen curls anew.

Among the earliest things I remember is the longing I used to feel to have the winter gone, and to see the great snow-bank— sometimes, when new-fallen, as high as the top of the kitchen window—melt away in front of the house. I loved, though, to run in the snow barefoot, and with only my night-shirt on, for a few minutes at a time. When the snow was gone, the peculiar smell of the ground seemed to me delicious. The first warm days of spring, which brought the blue birds to their northern home, and tempted the bees to try short flights, in which they presently dropped on the straw my provident father had strewn for them over the snow about their hives, filled me with emotions of the deepest delight. In the winter I was limited to the kitchen, where I could build cobhouses, or form little bits of wood into fantastic shapes. Sometimes my father or one of my brothers would take me to the shop where he pursued his toilsome work, or to the barn, where the horse, the oxen, and the cows were a perpetual pleasure. But when the snow was gone, and the ground dry, I had free range. I used to sit or lie on the ground in a dry and sheltered spot, and watch the great yellow clouds of April, that rolled their huge masses far above my head, filling my eye with their strange, fantastic, beautiful, and ever-changing forms, and my mind with wonder at what they were, and how they came there.

But the winter itself was not without its in-door pleasure, even for a little fellow in brown home-spun petticoats. The uncles and aunts came in their sleighs full of cousins, some of whom were of my own age, to pass a long afternoon and evening, not without abundant good-cheer and a fire in "the other room," as the humble parlour was modestly named. They did not come without a great apple, or a little bag of shag-barks, or some other tid-bit for "Miss Parker's" baby; for so the youngest was called long after he ceased to merit the name. Nay, father and mother often returned these visits, and sometimes took the baby with them; because the mother did not like to leave the darling at home, or perhaps she wished to show how stout and strong her eleventh child had come into the world.

I must relate one example to show, as well as many more, the nice and delicate care she took of my moral culture. When a little boy in petticoats in my fourth year, one fine day in spring, my father led me by the hand to a distant part of the farm, but soon sent me home alone. On the way I had to pass a little "pond-hole" then spreading its waters wide; a rhodora in full bloom— a rare flower in my neighbourhood, and which grew only in that locality—attracted my attention and drew me to the spot. I saw a little spotted tortoise sunning himself in the shallow water at the root of the flaming shrub. I lifted the stick I had in my hand to strike the harmless reptile; for, though I had never killed any creature, yet I had seen other boys out of sport destroy birds, squirrels, and the like, and I felt a disposition to follow their wicked example. But all at once something checked my little arm, and a voice within me said, clear and loud, "It is wrong!" I held my uplifted stick in wonder at the new emotion—the consciousness of an involuntary but inward check upon my actions, till the tortoise and the rhodora both vanished from my sight. I hastened home and told the tale to my mother, and asked what was it that told me it was wrong? She wiped a tear from her eye with her apron, and taking me in her arms, said, "Some men call it conscience, but I prefer to call it the voice of God in the soul of man. If you listen and obey it, then it will speak clearer and clearer, and always guide you right; but if you turn a deaf ear or disobey, then it will fade out little by little, and leave you all in the dark and without a guide. Your life depends on heeding this little voice." She went her way, careful and troubled about many things, but doubtless pondered them in her motherly heart; while I went off to wonder and think it over in my poor, childish way. But I am sure no event in my life has made so deep and lasting an impression on me. . . .

When a little boy, an old man overtook me going to school, and walked a mile with me. He told me what it was possible for a bright boy to *do* and to *be*—what I might do and be; it had a great influence on me. I began to think I "might be somebody."

Homer and Plutarch I read before I was eight; Rollin's Ancient History about the same time; and lots of histories, with all the poetry I could find, before ten. I took to metaphysics about eleven or twelve.

We had in the family some MS. histories of the Segur family, and their captivity among the Indians; also Mrs. Rowlandson's adventures. Mother knew by heart many family histories of the old New-England times, and used to tell them to me. We had also a folio volume of travels in the Levant, which interested me much, as soon as I could read, and to this day; father and mother always read the books first, and examined me in every book I read. If I could not give a good account of it, I must not have another till I could satisfy the rigorous demands of father.

I began to write verses at eight, and could repeat at ten a poem of 500 or 1000 lines after a single reading, or a song from hearing it once. I used to commit the hymns which the minister was reading, and before the choir began to sing.

At ten I made a catalogue of all the vegetable productions, trees, and shrubs, which grew upon the farm; there were many of which I could not find the names, so I invented them—fanciful enough.

We had a copy of Morse's large Geography, which helped me a good deal, and a folio copy of Evelyn's celebrated Sylva. It was a great treasure to me; it contained bits of poetry too, which delighted me, passages from Tusser and Chaucer, which I had not seen before.

Mr. Lyman's garden, at Waltham, filled me with admiration at the rare trees, plants, and shrubs, which I did not know. I went there when twelve or thirteen. Then the foreign fruits which I saw at my first visit to Boston, the tropical husks and leaves which came wrapped around bales of merchandize, tea-chests, and other boxes, stimulated my love of nature still more.

I used to inquire after the conformation of the hills in other parts of the country, which I had never seen. In my neighbourhood they all had their steep sides towards the south and east. I always asked boys—and men when I dared—who came from a distance, if it were so in their country. I commonly got the answer, *"I den know."* An Englishman told me about the peat mounds in Britain, which I could not account for. I got together all the odd stones, &c., I could find. A neighbour once brought me in my fourteenth year a bit of brown oxide of manganese, which abounded on the farm of his son in Vermont, and wanted to know what it was. It took me a day or two to find out, with the rude chemical apparatus I had made; but I did—and told him, to the amusement of the neighbours.

At ten I began to study Latin. This continued five winters, in which time I read the usual elementary books, with Virgil,

Cicero's Select Orations and Sallust. I began Greek at eleven. Natural Philosophy, Astronomy, Chemistry and Rhetoric I studied by myself. Astronomy had always interested me much. When twelve years old I once saw the crescent of Venus with my naked eye. It amazed me. Nobody else could see it; father was not at home. Nobody knew that the planets exhibit this form. So I hunted after a book on Astronomy, and got it from the schoolmaster, and found out the fact and its reason.

2. Autobiographical Fragments

Did I ever tell you of the earliest fact of consciousness I ever felt pained at? When in my 4th year my father had a neighbour, Deacon Stearns, come to kill a calf. My father would not do it himself, as other farmers did. I was not allowed to see the butchery; but after it was all over, the Deacon, who had lost all his children, asked me who I loved best? "Papa." "What! Better than yourself?" "Yes, sir." "But," said my father, "if one of us must take a whipping, which would you rather should have the blows?" I *said* nothing, but wondered and wondered why I should prefer that he should have the blows and not I. The fact was plain, and plainly selfish, and, it seemed to me, wicked. Yet I could not help the feeling. It tormented me for weeks in my long clothes.

I drew my first breath in a little town not far off, a poor little town where the farmers and mechancs first unsheathed that Revolutionary sword which, after eight years of hewing, clove asunder the Gordian knot that bound America to the British yoke. . . . When a boy my mother left me up, one Sunday, in her religious, patriotic arms, and held me while I read the first monumental line I ever saw:—

"SACRED TO LIBERTY AND THE RIGHTS OF MANKIND."

Since then I have studied the memorial marbles of Greece and Rome in many an ancient town; nay, on Egyptian Obelisks have read what was written before the Eternal roused up Moses to lead Israel out of Egypt, but no chiselled stone has ever stirred me to such emotions as those rustic names of men who fell

"IN THE SACRED CAUSE OF GOD AND THEIR COUNTRY."

25

Gentlemen, the Spirit of Liberty, the Love of Justice, was early fanned into a flame in my boyish heart. That monument covers the bones of my own kinsfolk; it was their blood which reddened the long, green grass at Lexington. It is my own name which stands chiselled on that stone; the tall Captain who marshalled his fellow farmers and mechanics into stern array and spoke such brave and dangerous words as opened the War of American Independence,—the last to leave the field,—was my father's father. I learned to read out of his Bible, and with a musket he that day captured from the foe, I learned also another religious lesson, that

"REBELLION TO TYRANTS IS OBEDIENCE TO GOD."

I keep them both, "Sacred to Liberty and the Rights of Mankind," to use them both "In the Sacred Cause of God and my Country."

III

TO GEORGE RIPLEY

Boston, September 21, 1854

When a boy, I had an intense passion for beauty in every form. I knew all the rare flowers, wild or cultivated. When a little boy in petticoats, I used to lie all the forenoon in June, and watch the great clouds, and see the incessant play of form and color. There was a pond a mile off, whither I used to go a-fishing; but I only caught the landscape. I never fished much, but looked down into the water, and saw the shadows on the other side creep over the water, and listened to the sounds from the distant farms. When I was six or seven years old, there came a perfectly beautiful young girl to our little district-school: she was seven to eight. She fascinated my eyes from my book, and I was chid for not getting my lessons. It never happened before; never after the little witch went away. She only staid a week; and I cried bitterly when she went off. She was so handsome I did not dare speak to her, but loved to keep near her as a butterfly to a thistle-blossom. Her name was Narcissa. She fell over into the flood of time, and vanished before I was seven years old. I loved beauty of form before beauty of color. I wonder if this is usual. You know beauty of sound (not artificial, of music) filled me with ravishment. The winds in the leaves, and the rushing brooks, were a delight from the earliest boyhood till now. Fine little pieces of literary art I culled out in childhood, and committed them to memory. It was no effort: it did itself. Especially poetry was my delight. My sisters had a little bagful of clippings from the newspaper which helped nurse my little soul. They also encouraged me in my transcendental tastes for the beautiful. But hard work and the *res angustae domi* left but a poor soil for such a harvest. Yet it was hard to tear the tired body from the handsome moonlight or the evening star. Mornings, from before daylight to sunrise, when forced to be abroad, gave an acquaintance with the beauty of Nature at that hour, which was worth more to me than all my night-labors brought to my father. It was poetry to me, even if only a dull horse or heavy oxen were my only companions. The pictures of old times live now in my memory, a never-failing delight in my hours when I am too tired to do any kind of work or to sleep. This hanging-garden is always over me; and I rejoice therein as no Nebuchadnezzar, I fear, ever did.

I love children and hens; all sorts of men; and have the oddest set of intimates you will find any scholarly man to be acquainted with. But I am much less of a practical man than men think. All my ideals of life are of philosophical and literary activity, with a few friends about me, Nature and children. Good-by!

IV

TO DR. SAMUEL GRIDLEY HOWE

Rome, March 23, 1860

It is twenty-nine years to-day since I left my father's house and home and sought a new in Boston. A raw boy, with clothes made by country tailors, coarse shoes, great hands, red lips, and blue eyes, I went to serve in a private school, where, for fifteen dollars a month and my board, I taught Latin, Greek, subsequently French (!), and Spanish—both which I could read and write, though not speak—the mathematics, and all sorts of philosophy. I was not twenty-one, and hired a man for eleven dollars a month to take my place for five months at home and do the farm work. My father refused to accept this, but I insisted that it would be unjust to use me better than the other boys before me. I taught in the school six hours a day, and from May to September seven; but I always had from ten to twelve hours a day for my own private studies out of school. You may judge what sort of a boy I was from the kind of man you have known since. Life lay before me then (it is all behind me now), and I had hope where now is only remembrance. Judge if I did not work: it makes my flesh creep to think how I used to work, and how much I learned that year, and the four next. Had not I a constitution for a scholar? Oh, that I had known the art of life, or found some book or some man to tell me how to *live,* to *study,* to *take exercise,* &c. But I found none, and so here I am.

V

TO MISS LYDIA D. CABOT

Watertown, October 30, 1833

I walked to father's; he soon returned from church, and I caught him in the garden, and informed him of the "fatal" affair, if you will call it so.

The tear actually started to his aged eye. "Indeed," said he. "Indeed," I replied, "and attempted to describe *some* of your good qualities." "It is a good while to wait," he observed. "Yes, but we are young, and I hope I have your approval." "Yes, yes! I should be pleased with anyone you would select; but, Theodore," said he, and the words sank deep into my heart, "you must be a good *man* and a good *husband,* which is a great undertaking."

I promised all good fidelity; and may Heaven see it kept!

VI

TO COLUMBUS GREENE

Cambridge, July 11, 1834

Should you be pleased to know something of our ordinary course of proceedings in this institution [the Harvard Divinity School]? We have about thirty scholars, divided into three classes; one of these graduates in about a week. Some one of the senior class preaches each Sabbath evening during the year; all the school and some few strangers attend. Prayers are performed at morning of every day by Prof. Palfrey, and at evening by one of the senior class. The junior class, to which I belong, recites in Hebrew every Monday, Wednesday, and Friday afternoon; attends a lecture upon the criticism of the New Testament, Monday and Friday, when we translate the original, ask questions, and engage in discussion with the Professor. We recite and discuss the Evidences of Christianity with Dr. Ware every Wednesday. Tuesday afternoon we have an exercise in extemporaneous speaking with Prof. Ware, jun., one of the finest men I have ever known. Some subject is proposed to the class at one meeting and discussed at the next. Saturday morning Mr. Ware delivers a lecture upon composition of sermons, subjects to be treated, &c., to the whole school. Thursday we have no recitation. One-third of the school declaims every Tuesday evening. Friday evening the whole school meet for extemporaneous speaking. Thursday evening is spent in a religious meeting.

A society for the promotion of the interests of humanity, and called the "Philanthropic Society," meets once a fortnight on Wednesday evening. A report is always read upon some interesting subject, such as "Infidelity," "Temperance," "The License Laws," by a committee previously appointed to investigate the subject. Besides this, I have a fine lad who comes every morning to recite Greek and Latin, &c., and had a young gentleman who came twice a week to recite German, but I have not seen him this fortnight.

All my leisure is devoted to translating some papers of La Fayette, which I am doing for Mr. Sparks, who is going to publish them. This is his work, and not mine. I shall be constantly occupied upon this translation during the whole of vacation.

Sunday I visit the States' Prison, where I have an interesting class in the Sunday school.

VII

TO MISS LYDIA D. CABOT

June 17, 1835

When I was a boy I had always a world of my own, an ideal creation, where I could roam and luxuriate at random. Many a time have I strayed from the right path and gone far beyond my stopping-place, while I was brooding over some scheme not yet accomplished. How many times has my plough run upon a rock while I was expounding law, making speeches in the senate, or astonishing men with a display of intellectual power, fitly put forth, in my imaginary Utopia. . . .

It is delightful now to imagine myself a minister, to recount the duties of the station, and consider all the ways of performing them, and forefeel the glorious satisfaction of seeing God's work prosper in my hand. I turn to a home—to a home of beauty, of affection, of love! To a home where all noble feelings are cherished, and whence all jarring interests and strife are excluded. Calamities may fall upon that home; they come upon all men— each country has its own storms. But if it is built upon the rock of holy affection, *it will stand:* the floods may pass over it—they can never shake its fixt foundation.

VIII

The 19th of May, 1841, I preached an Ordination Sermon in Boston—"A Discourse of the Transient and Permanent in Christianity." It was the first "Ordination Sermon" I ever preached; the first separate document I ever published with my own name. It cost me my reputation in the "Christian Church;" even the Unitarian ministers, who are themselves reckoned but the tail of heresy, denounced me as "no Christian," an "Infidel." They did what they could to effect my ruin—denied me all friendly intercourse, dropped me from committees of their liberal college, in public places refused my hand extended as before in friendly salutation; mocked at me in their solemn meetings; struck my name out of their Almanac,—the only Unitarian form of excommunication,—and in every journal, almost every pulpit, denounced the young man who thought the God who creates earth and heaven had never spoken miraculously in Hebrew words bidding Abraham kill his only son and burn him for a sacrifice, and that Jesus of Nazareth was not a finality in the historical development of mankind. Scarce a Protestant meeting-house in America, not a single theological newspaper, I think, but blew its trumpet with notes of alarm and denunciation. Behold! said they, behold a minister thinking for himself afresh on religion! actually thinking! and believing his thoughts! and tell his own convictions! He tells us

God is not dead! that the Bible is not his last word; that he inspires men now as much as ever,—even more so. Surely this man is an "Infidel," a "Deist," nay, an "Atheist." Down with him! Nay, one venerable orthodox minister, still living, published a letter calling on the authorities of the commonwealth to send this young "blasphemer" to the State's prison for three years, according to law in such case made and provided!

II

The True Religion and the Christian Church

In his own day, Parker was known as "The Great American Preacher," and however varied his other activities—as scholar, editor, man of letters, reformer—he always thought of himself as a spiritual rather than a secular leader. From earliest boyhood he had felt called to the ministry; it never occurred to him, apparently, that he could be anything but a preacher. He did not go to Harvard College, but he managed to work his way through the Divinity School, and his early letters to his father and to his betrothed are eloquent of his delight in religion.

But what was religion? Was it a sentiment? an organization? a way of life? It was, to be sure, all of these things, but most clearly the last. As an ardent Transcendentalist—and an ardent romantic—Parker embraced religion as a sentiment. "The chiefest of all my delights," he wrote, "is . . . the religious. . . . What delight have I in my consciousness of God, the certainty of His protection, of His infinite love." But that was a private and therefore a selfish indulgence—and surely religion could not be a private affair. Was religion, then, an organized affair: the church? It was, to be sure; and Parker became part of the church and prepared to labor in its fold. But not easily, not uncritically. He quickly discovered what Emerson had discovered, and Ripley—that the organized church was not identical with religion, and might be antipathetic to it. With his sermon *The Transient and Permanent in Christianity,* he proclaimed his dissatisfaction with much that the church taught; the church, in turn, quickly proclaimed its dissatisfaction with what he taught. The Unitarians made clear that they would prefer Parker out of the church rather than in it. But he refused to resign, and the church, as such, could do nothing about it except ostracize him socially and professionally.

Meantime, Parker went his way, preaching religion as a way of life. To the exploration of this idea—that a church, the ministry and the Christian religion must all be a way of life—he devoted his last fifteen years. If religion did not possess a man, if it did not penetrate his whole life, his mind and heart and soul, then it somehow failed. If religion did not condition the way a man thought and the way he acted, in public and in private, then it failed. This was the theme of sermon after sermon, in Boston and elsewhere in the country. It was the theme, too, of those massive, scholarly books on religion—*A Discourse of Matters Pertaining to Religion; Theism, Atheism, and the Popular Theology;*

Lessons from the World of Matter and the World of Man; and the discourses on *The World of Matter and the Spirit of Man.*

Most of the selections in this section are addressed directly to the subject of the nature of religion and the obligations of the minister and of the church. Two of them bear indirectly upon these subjects: the moving tribute to William Ellery Channing and the vigorous presentation of the philosophy of Transcendentalism.

3. The Transient and Permanent in Christianity

1842

Emerson had precipitated the great Unitarian controversy with his Divinity School Address of July 1838. His gentle words churned the waters of the vasty deep. "It is thought," wrote Parker to his friend George Ellis, "that chaos is coming back; the world is coming to an end. Some seem to think the Christianity which has stood some storms will not be able to weather this gale and that truth, after all my Lord Bacon has said, will have to give it up now. For my part I see that the sun still shines, the rain rains, and the dogs bark, and I have great doubts whether Emerson will overthrow Christianity this time." But Andrews Norton, the pope of the Unitarians, was not willing to take a chance. Mr. Emerson's address was merely "the latest form of infidelity," and Norton asserted that "no clergy will be supported among us to teach transcendentalism, infidelity and pantheism."

Parker could no more stay out of such a quarrel than he could stay out of a library, and in almost no time he had entered the fray with an article, "The Previous Question between Mr. Andrews Norton and his Alumni . . . by Levi Blodgett." Everybody knew that Levi Blodgett was none other than Parker, and he soon suffered the same odium theologicum that was meted out to Emerson. But for him the consequences were more serious. Emerson had left the church and could not really be touched, but this Parker was not prepared to do.

Smarting under criticism he thought unfair, he took the occasion of an ordination sermon at the installation of young Charles Shackford, in South Boston, to preach a sermon on *The Transient and Permanent in Christianity* (presented here in its entirety). The sermon made a prodigious stir. Even the title was an affront: it was taken from an essay by David F. Strauss, whose *Life of Jesus* was regarded by the orthodox as blasphemous. As for Parker: "He has with justice annihilated the Transient," wrote John Weiss, who was one day to be Parker's biographer, "but where is the Permanent?" That is what many of Parker's brethren asked with mounting concern.

"Heaven and earth shall pass away; but my words shall not
pass away."—LUKE xxi, 33.

In this sentence we have a very clear indication that Jesus of
Nazareth believed the religion he taught would be eternal, that the
substance of it would last for ever. Yet there are some who are
affrighted by the faintest rustle which a heretic makes among the
dry leaves of theology; they tremble lest Christianity itself should
perish without hope. Ever and anon the cry is raised, "The Philis-
tines be upon us, and Christianity is in danger." The least doubt
respecting the popular theology, or the existing machinery of the
church; the least sign of distrust in the religion of the pulpit, or the
religion of the street, is by some good men supposed to be at
enmity with faith in Christ, and capable of shaking Christianity
itself. On the other hand, a few bad men, and a few pious men, it
is said, on both sides of the water, tell us the day of Christianity is
past. The latter, it is alleged, would persuade us that, hereafter,
piety must take a new form, the teachings of Jesus are to be passed
by, that religion is to wing her way sublime, above the flight of
Christianity, far away, toward heaven, as the fledged eaglet leaves
for ever the nest which sheltered his callow youth. Let us, therefore, devote a few moments to this subject, and consider what is
transient in Christianity, and what is *permanent* therein. The topic
seems not inappropriate to the times in which we live, or the occasion that calls us together.

Christ says his word shall never pass away. Yet, at first sight,
nothing seems more fleeting than a word. It is an evanescent im-
pulse of the most fickle element. It leaves no track where it went
through the air. Yet to this, and this only, did Jesus intrust the
truth wherewith he came laden to the earth; truth for the salvation
of the world. He took no pains to perpetuate his thoughts: they
were poured forth where occasion found him an audience—by the
side of the lake, or a well; in a cottage, or the temple; in a fisher-
man's boat, or the synagogue of the Jews. He founds no institution
as a monument of his words. He appoints no order of men to preserve his bright and glad relations. He only bids his friends give
freely the truth they had freely received. He did not even write his
words in a book. With a noble confidence, the result of his abiding
faith, he scattered them broadcast on the world, leaving the seed
to its own vitality. He knew that what is of God cannot fail, for
God keeps his own. He sowed his seed in the heart, and left it

there, to be watered and warmed by the dew and the sun which heaven sends. He felt his words were for eternity. So he trusted them to the uncertain air; and for eighteen hundred years that faithful element has held them good—distinct as when first warm from his lips. Now they are translated into every human speech, and murmured in all earth's thousand tongues, from the pine forests of the north to the palm groves of eastern Ind. They mingle, as it were, with the roar of a populous city, and join the chime of the desert sea. Of a Sabbath morn they are repeated from church to church, from isle to isle, and land to land, till their music goes round the world. These words have become the breadth of the good, the hope of the wise, the joy of the pious, and that for many millions of hearts. They are the prayers of our churches, our better devotions by fireside and fieldside; the enchantment of our hearts. It is these words that still work wonders, to which the first recorded miracles were nothing in grandeur and utility. It is these which build our temples and beautify our homes. They raise our thoughts of sublimity; they purify our ideal of purity; they hallow our prayer for truth and love. They make beauteous and divine the life which plain men lead. They give wings to our aspirations. What charmers they are! Sorrow is lulled at their bidding. They take the sting out of disease, and rob adversity of his power to disappoint. They give health and wings to the pious soul, broken-hearted and shipwrecked in his voyage through life, and encourage him to tempt the perilous way once more. They make all things ours: Christ our brother; time our servant; death our ally, and the witness of our triumph. They reveal to us the presence of God, which else we might not have seen so clearly, in the first wind-flower of spring, in the falling of a sparrow, in the distress of a nation, in the sorrow or the rapture of the world. Silence the voice of Christianity, and the world is well-nigh dumb, for gone is that sweet music which kept in awe the rulers of the people, which cheers the poor widow in her lonely toil, and comes like light through the windows of morning, to men who sit stooping and feeble, with failing eyes and a hungering heart. It is gone—all gone! only the cold, bleak world left before them.

Such is the life of these words; such the empire they have won for themselves over men's minds since they were spoken first. In the meantime, the words of great men and mighty, whose name shook whole continents, though graven in metal and stone, though stamped in institutions, and defended by whole tribes of priests and troops of followers—their words have gone to the ground, and the world gives back no echo of their voice. Meanwhile, the great works, also, of old times—castle, and tower, and town, their cities and their empires, have perished, and left scarce a mark on the bosom of the earth to show they once have been. The philosophy of the wise, the art of the accomplished, the song of the poet, the ritual of the priest, though honored as divine in their day, have gone down a prey to oblivion. Silence has closed over them; only their spectres now haunt the earth. A deluge of blood has swept over the nations; a night of darkness, more deep than the fabled darkness of Egypt, has lowered down upon that flood, to destroy or to hide what the deluge had spared. But through all this the words of Christianity have come down to us from the lips of that Hebrew youth, gentle and beautiful as the light of a star, not spent by their journey through time and through space. They have built up a new civilization, which the wisest gentile never hoped for, which the most pious Hebrew never foretold. Through centuries of wasting these words have flown on, like a dove in the storm, and now wait to descend on hearts pure and earnest, as the Father's spirit, we are told, came down on his lowly Son. The old heavens and the old earth are indeed passed away, but the word stands. Nothing shows clearer than this how fleeting is what man calls great, how lasting what God pronounces true.

Looking at the word of Jesus, at real Christianity, the pure religion he taught, nothing appears more fixed and certain. Its influence widens as light extends; it deepens as the nations grow more wise. But looking at the history of what men call Christianity, nothing seems more uncertain and perishable. While true religion is always the same thing, in each century and every land, in each man that feels it, the Christianity of the pulpit, which is the religion taught, the Christianity of the people, which is the religion that is accepted and lived out, has never been the same thing in any two centuries or lands, except only in name. The difference between what is called Christianity by the Unitarians in our times, and that of some ages past, is greater than the difference between Mahomet and the Messiah. The difference at this day between opposing classes of Christians, the difference between the Christianity of some sects, and that of Christ himself, is deeper and more vital than that between Jesus and Plato, pagan as we call him. The Christianity of the seventh century has passed away. We recognize only the ghost of superstition in its faded features, as it comes up at our call. It is one of the things which has been, and can be no more, for neither God nor the world goes back. Its terrors do not frighten, nor its hopes allure us. We rejoice that it has gone. But how do we know that our Christianity will not share the same fate? Is there that difference between the nineteenth century, and some seventeen that have gone before it since Jesus, to warrant the belief that our notion of Christianity shall last for ever? The stream of time has already beat down philosophies and theologies, temple and church, though never so old and revered. How do we know there is not a perishing element in what we call Christianity? Jesus tells us *his* word is the word of God, and so shall never pass away. But who tells us that *our* word shall never pass away? that *our notion* of his word shall stand for ever?

Let us look at this matter a little more closely. In actual Christianity—that is, in that portion of Christianity which is preached and believed—there seems to have been, ever since the time of its earthly founder, two elements, the one transient, the other permanent. The one is the thought, the folly, the uncertain wisdom, the theological notions, the impiety of man; the other, the eternal truth of God. These two bear, perhaps, the same relation to each other that the phenomena of outward nature, such as sunshine and cloud, growth, decay, and reproduction, bear to the great law of nature, which underlies and supports them all. As in that case more attention is commonly paid to the particular phenomena than to the general law, so in this case more is generally given to the transient in Christianity than to the permanent therein.

It must be confessed, though with sorrow, that transient things form a great part of what is commonly taught as religion. An undue place has often been assigned to forms and doctrines, while too little stress has been laid on the divine life of the soul, love to God and love to man. Religious forms may be useful and beautiful. They are so, whenever they speak to the soul, and answer a want thereof. In our present state some forms are perhaps necessary. But they are only the accident of Christianity, not its substance. They are the robe, not the angel, who may take another robe quite as becoming and useful. One sect has many forms; another, none. Yet both may be equally Christian, in spite of the redundance or the deficiency. They are a part of the language in which religion speaks, and exist, with few exceptions, wherever man is found. In our calculating nation, in our rationalizing sect, we have retained but two of the rites so numerous in the early Christian Church, and even these we have attenuated to the last degree, leaving them little more than a spectre of the ancient form.

Another age may continue or forsake both; may revive old forms, or invent new ones to suit the altered circumstances of the times, and yet be Christians quite as good as we, or our fathers of the dark ages. Whether the Apostles designed these rites to be perpetual, seems a question which belongs to scholars and antiquarians; not to us, as Christian men and women. So long as they satisfy or help the pious heart, so long they are good. Looking behind or around us, we see that the forms and rites of the Christians are quite as fluctuating as those of the heathens, from whom some of them have been, not unwisely, adopted by the earlier church.

Again, the doctrines that have been connected with Christianity, and taught in its name, are quite as changeable as the form. This also takes place unavoidably. If observations be made upon nature, which must take place so long as man has senses and understanding, there will be a philosophy of nature, and philosophical doctrines. These will differ as the observations are just or inaccurate, and as the deductions from observed facts are true or false. Hence there will be different schools of natural philosophy so long as men have eyes and understandings of different clearness and strength. And if men observe and reflect upon religion—which will be done so long as man is a religious and reflective being— there must also be a philosophy of religion, a theology and theological doctrines. These will differ, as men have felt much or little of religion, as they analyze their sentiments correctly or otherwise, and as they have reasoned right or wrong. Now the true system of nature, which exists in the outward facts, whether discovered or not, is always the same thing, though the philosophy of nature, which men invent, change every month, and be one thing at London and the opposite at Berlin. Thus there is but one system of nature as it exists in fact, though many theories of nature, which exist in our imperfect notions of that system, and by which we may approximate and at length reach it. Now there can be but one religion which is absolutely true, existing in the facts of human nature and the ideas of Infinite God. That, whether acknowledged or not, is always the same thing, and never changes. So far as a man has any real religion—either the principle or the sentiment thereof —so far he has that, by whatever name he may call it. For, strictly speaking, there is but one kind of religion, as there is but one kind of love, though the manifestations of this religion, in forms, doctrines, and life, be never so diverse. It is through these men approximate to the true expression of this religion. Now, while this religion is one and always the same thing, there may be numerous systems of theology or philosophies of religion. These, with their creeds, confessions, and collections of doctrines, deduced by reasoning upon the facts observed, may be baseless and false, either because the observation was too narrow in extent, or otherwise defective in point of accuracy, or because the reasoning was illogical, and therefore the deduction spurious. Each of these three faults is conspicuous in the systems of theology. Now, the solar system as it exists in fact is permanent, though the notions of Thales and Ptolemy, of Copernicus and Descartes, about this system, prove transient, imperfect approximations to the true expression. So the Christianity of Jesus is permanent, though what passes for Christianity with popes and catechisms, with sects and churches, in the first century or in the nineteenth century, prove transient also. Now it has sometimes happened that a man took his philosophy of nature at second-hand, and then attempted to make his observations conform to his theory, and nature ride in his panniers. Thus some philosophers refused to look at the moon through Galileo's telescope, for, according to their theory of vision, such an instrument would not aid the sight. Thus their preconceived notions stood up between them and nature. Now it has often happened that men took their theology thus at second-hand, and distorted the history of the world and man's nature besides, to make religion conform to their notions. Their theology stood between them and God. Those obstinate philosophers have disciples in no small number.

What another has said of false systems of science will apply equally to the popular theology: "It is barren in effects, fruitful in questions, slow and languid in its improvement, exhibiting in its generality the counterfeit of perfection, but ill filled up in its details, popular in its choice, but suspected by its very promoters, and therefore bolstered up and countenanced with artifices. Even those who have been determined to try for themselves, to add their support to learning, and to enlarge its limits, have not dared entirely to desert received opinions, nor to seek the spring-head of things. But they think they have done a great thing if they intersperse and contribute something of their own; prudently considering, that by their assent they can save their modesty, and by their contributions, their liberty. Neither is there, nor ever will be, an end or limit to these things. One snatches at one thing, another is pleased with another; there is no dry nor clear sight of anything. Every one plays the philosopher out of the small treasures of his own fancy; the more sublime wits more acutely and with better success; the duller with less success but equal obstinacy; and, by the discipline of some learned men, sciences are bounded within the limits of some certain authors which they have set down, imposing them upon old men and instilling them into young. So that now (as Tully cavilled upon Cæsar's consulship) the star Lyra riseth by an edict, and authority is taken for truth, and not truth for authority; which kind of order and discipline is very convenient for our present use, but banisheth those which are better."

Any one who traces the history of what is called Christianity, will see that nothing changes more from age to age than the doctrines taught as Christian, and insisted on as essential to Christianity and personal salvation. What is falsehood in one province passes for truth in another. The heresy of one age is the orthodox belief and "only infallible rule" of the next. Now Arius, and now Athanasius, is lord of the ascendant. Both were excommunicated in their turn, each for affirming what the other denied. Men are burned for professing what men are burned for denying. For centuries the doctrines of the Christians were no better, to say the least, than those of their contemporary pagans. The theological doctrines derived from our fathers seem to have come from Judaism, heathenism, and the caprice of philosophers, far more than they have come from the principle and sentiment of Christianity. The doctrine of the trinity, the very Achilles of theological dogmas, belongs to philosophy and not religion; its subtleties cannot even be expressed in our tongue. As old religions became superannuated, and died out, they left to the rising faith, as to a residuary legatee, their forms and their doctrines; or rather, as the giant in the fable left his poisoned garment to work the overthrow of his conqueror. Many tenets that pass current in our theology seem to be the refuse of idol temples, the off-scourings of Jewish and heathen cities, rather than the sands of virgin gold, which the stream of Christianity has worn off from the rock of ages, and brought in its bosom for us. It is wood, hay, and stubble, wherewith men have built on the corner-stone Christ laid. What wonder the fabric is in peril when tried by fire? The stream of Christianity, as men receive it, has caught a stain from every soil it has filtered through, so that now it is not the pure water from the well of life which is offered to our lips, but streams troubled and polluted by man with mire and dirt. If Paul and Jesus could read our books of theological doctrines, would they accept as their teaching what men have vented in their name? Never till the letters of Paul had faded out of his memory; never till the words of Jesus had been torn out from the book of life. It is their notions about Christianity men have taught as the only living word of God. They have piled their own rubbish against the temple of truth where piety comes up to worship; what wonder the pile seems unshapely and like to fall? But these theological doctrines are fleeting as the leaves on the trees. They—

> "are found
> Now green in youth, now withered on the ground:
> Another race the following spring supplies;
> They fall successive, and successive rise."

Like the clouds of the sky, they are here to-day; to-morrow, all swept off and vanished, while Christianity itself, like the heaven above, with its sun, and moon, and uncounted stars, is always over our head, though the cloud sometimes debars us of the needed light. It must of necessity be the case that our reasonings, and therefore our theological doctrines, are imperfect, and so perishing. It is only gradually that we approach to the true system of nature by observation and reasoning, and work out our philosophy and theology by the toil of the brain. But meantime, if we are faithful, the great truths of morality and religion, the deep sentiment of love to man and love to God, are perceived intuitively, and by instinct, as it were, though our theology be imperfect and miserable. The theological notions of Abraham, to take the story as it stands, were exceedingly gross, yet a greater than Abraham has told us Abraham desired to see my day, saw it, and was glad. Since these notions are so fleeting, why need we accept the commandment of men as the doctrine of God?

This transitoriness of doctrines appears in many instances, of which two may be selected for a more attentive consideration. First, the doctrine respecting the origin and authority of the Old and New Testament. There has been a time when men were burned for asserting doctrines of natural philosophy which rested on evidence the most incontestable, because those doctrines conflicted with sentences in the Old Testament. Every word of that Jewish record was regarded as miraculously inspired, and therefore as infallibly true. It was believed that the Christian religion itself rested thereon, and must stand or fall with the immaculate Hebrew text. He was deemed no small sinner who found mistakes in the manuscripts. On the authority of the written word man was taught to believe impossible legends, conflicting assertions; to take fiction for fact, a dream for a miraculous revelation of God, an oriental poem for a grave history of miraculous events, a collection of amatory idyls for a serious discourse "touching the mutual love of Christ and the church;" they have been taught to accept a picture sketched by some glowing eastern imagination, never intended to be taken for a reality, as a proof that the Infinite God spoke in human words, appeared in the shape of a cloud, a flaming bush, or a man who ate, and drank, and vanished into smoke; that he gave counsels to-day, and the opposite to-morrow; that he violated his own laws, was angry, and was only dissuaded by a mortal man from destroying at once a whole nation—millions of men who rebelled against their leader in a moment of anguish. Questions in philosophy, questions in the Christian religion, have been settled by an appeal to that book. The inspiration of its authors has been assumed as infallible. Every fact in the early Jewish history has been taken as a type of some analogous fact in Christian history. The most distant events, even such as are still in the arms of time, were supposed to be clearly foreseen and foretold by pious Hebrews several centuries before Christ. It is assumed at the outset, with no shadow of evidence, that those writers held a miraculous communication with God, such as he has granted to no other man. What was originally a presumption of bigoted Jews became an article of faith, which Christians were burned for not believing. This has been for centuries the general opinion of the Christian church, both Catholic and Protestant, though the former never accepted the Bible as the *only* source of religious truth. It has been so. Still worse, it is now the general opinion of religious sects of this day. Hence the attempt, which always fails, to reconcile the philosophy of our times with the poems in Genesis writ a thousand years before Christ. Hence the attempt to conceal the contradictions in the record itself. Matters have come to such a pass that even now he is deemed an infidel, if not by implication an atheist, whose reverence for the Most High forbids him to believe that God commanded Abraham to sacrifice his son, a thought at which the flesh creeps with horror; to believe it solely on the authority of an oriental story, written down nobody knows when or by whom, or for what purpose; which may be a poem, but cannot be the record of a fact, unless God is the author of confusion and a lie.

Now, this idolatry of the Old Testament has not always existed. Jesus says that none born of a woman is greater than John the Baptist, yet the least in the kingdom of heaven was greater than John. Paul tells us the law—the very crown of the old Hebrew revelation—is a shadow of good things, which have now come; only a schoolmaster to bring us to Christ; and when faith has come, that we are no longer under the schoolmaster; that it was a law of sin and death, from which we are made free by the law of the spirit of life. Christian teachers themselves have differed so widely in their notion of the doctrines and meaning of those books, that it makes one weep to think of the follies deduced therefrom. But modern criticism is fast breaking to pieces this idol which men have made out of the scriptures. It has shown that here are the most different works thrown together; that their authors, wise as they sometimes were, pious as we feel often their spirit to have been, had only that inspiration which is common to other men equally pious and wise; that they were by no means infallible, but were mistaken in facts or in reasoning—uttered predictions which time has not fulfilled; men who in some measure partook of the darkness and limited notions of their age, and were not always above its mistakes or its corruptions.

The history of opinions on the New Testament is quite similar. It has been assumed at the outset, it would seem with no sufficient reason, without the smallest pretence on its writers' part, that all of its authors were infallibly and miraculously inspired, so that they could commit no error of doctrine or fact. Men have been bid to close their eyes at the obvious difference between Luke and John—the serious disagreement between Paul and Peter; to believe, on the smallest evidence, accounts which shock the moral sense and revolt the reason, and tend to place Jesus in the same series with Hercules, and Apollonius of Tyana; accounts which Paul in the Epistles never mentions, though he also had a vein of the miraculous running quite through him. Men have been told that all these things must be taken as part of Christianity, and if they accepted the religion, they must take all these accessories along with it; that the living spirit could not be had without the killing letter. All the books which caprice or accident had brought together between the lids of the Bible were declared to be the infallible word of God, the only certain rule of religious faith and practice. Thus the Bible was made not a single channel, but the *only* certain rule of religious faith and practice. To disbelieve any of its statements, or even the common interpretation put upon those statements by the particular age or church in which the man belonged, was held to be infidelity, if not atheism. In the name of him who forbid us to judge our brother, good men and pious men have applied these terms to others, good and pious as themselves. That state of things has by no means passed away. Men, who cry down the absurdities of paganism in the worst spirit of the French "free-thinkers," call others infidels and atheists, who point out, though reverently, other absurdities which men have piled upon Christianity. So the world goes. An idolatrous regard for the imperfect scripture of God's word is the apple of Atalanta, which defeats theologians running for the hand of divine truth.

But the current notions respecting the infallible inspiration of the Bible have no foundation in the Bible itself. Which evangelist, which apostle of the New Testament, what prophet or psalmist of the Old Testament, ever claims infallible authority for himself or for others? Which of them does not in his own writings show that he was finite, and, with all his zeal and piety, possessed but a limited inspiration, the bound whereof we can sometimes discover? Did Christ ever demand that men should assent to the doctrines of the Old Testament, credit its stories, and take its poems for histories, and believe equally two accounts that contradict one another? Has he ever told you that all the truths of his religion, all the beauty of a Christian life, should be contained in the writings of those men who, even after his resurrection, expected him to be a Jewish king; of men who were sometimes at variance with one another, and misunderstood his divine teachings? Would not those modest writers themselves be confounded at the idolatry we pay them? Opinions may change on these points, as they have often changed—changed greatly and for the worse since the days of Paul. They are changing now, and we may hope for the better; for God makes man's folly as well as his wrath to praise him, and continually brings good out of evil.

Another instance of the transitoriness of doctrines taught as Christian is found in those which relate to the nature and authority of Christ. One ancient party has told us that he is the infinite God; another, that he is both God and man; a third, that he was a man, the son of Joseph and Mary—born as we are, tempted like ourselves, inspired, as we may be, if we will pay the price. Each of the former parties believed its doctrine on this head was infallibly true, and formed the very substance of Christianity, and was one of the essential conditions of salvation, though scarce any two distinguished teachers, of ancient or modern times, agree in their expression of this truth.

Almost every sect that has ever been makes Christianity rest on the personal authority of Jesus, and not the immutable truth of the doctrines themselves, or the authority of God, who sent him into the world. Yet it seems difficult to conceive any reason why moral and religious truths should rest for their support on the personal authority of their revealer, any more than the truths of science on that of him who makes them known first or most clearly. It is hard to see why the great truths of Christianity rest on the personal authority of Jesus, more than the axioms of geometry rest on the personal authority of Euclid or Archimedes. The authority of Jesus, as of all teachers, one would naturally think, must rest on the truth of his words, and not their truth on his authority.

Opinions respecting the nature of Christ seem to be constantly changing. In the three first centuries after Christ, it appears, great latitude of speculation prevailed. Some said he was God, with nothing of human nature, his body only an illusion; others, that he was man, with nothing of the divine nature, his miraculous birth having no foundation in fact. In a few centuries it was decreed by councils that he was God, thus honoring the divine element; next, that he was man also, thus admitting the human side. For some ages the Catholic church seems to have dwelt chiefly on the divine nature that was in him, leaving the human element to mystics and other heretical persons, whose bodies served to flesh the swords of orthodox believers. The stream of Christianity has come to us in two channels—one within the church, the other without the church—and it is not hazarding too much to say, that since the fourth century the true Christian life has been out of the established church, and not in it, but rather in the ranks of dissenters. From the Reformation till the latter part of the last century, we are told, the Protestant church dwelt chiefly on the human side of Christ, and since that time many works have been written to show how the two—perfect deity and perfect manhood—were united in his character. But, all this time, scarce any two eminent teachers agree on these points, however orthodox they may be called. What a difference between the Christ of John Gerson and John Calvin—yet were both accepted teachers and pious men. What a difference between the Christ of the Unitarians and the Methodists—yet may men of both sects be true Christians and acceptable with God. What a difference between the Christ of Matthew and John—yet both were disciples, and their influence is wide as Christendom and deep as the heart of man. But on this there is not time to enlarge.

Now it seems clear, that the notion men form about the origin and nature of the scriptures, respecting the nature and authority of Christ, have nothing to do with Christianity except as its aids or its adversaries; they are not the foundation of its truths. These are theological questions, not religious questions. Their connection with Christianity appears accidental: for if Jesus had taught at Athens, and not at Jerusalem; if he had wrought no miracle, and none but the human nature had ever been ascribed to him; if the Old Testament had for ever perished at his birth, Christianity would still have been the word of God; it would have lost none of its truths. It would be just as true, just as beautiful, just as lasting, as now it is; though we should have lost so many a blessed word, and the work of Christianity itself would have been, perhaps, a long time retarded.

To judge the future by the past, the former authority of the Old Testament can never return. Its present authority cannot stand. It must be taken for what it is worth. The occasional folly and impiety of its authors must pass for no more than their value; while the religion, the wisdom, the love, which make fragrant its leaves, will still speak to the best hearts as hitherto, and in accents even more divine when reason is allowed her rights. The ancient belief in the infallible inspiration of each sentence of the New Testament is fast changing, very fast. One writer, not a sceptic, but a Christian of unquestioned piety, sweeps off the beginning of Matthew; another, of a different church and equally religious, the end of John. Numerous critics strike off several epistles. The Apocalypse itself is not spared, notwithstanding its concluding curse. Who shall tell us the work of retrenchment is to stop here; that others will not demonstrate, what some pious hearts have long felt, that errors of doctrine and errors of fact may be found in many parts of the record, here and there, from the beginning of Matthew to the end of Acts? We see how opinions have changed ever since the apostles' time; and who shall assure us that they were not sometimes mistaken in historical, as well as doctrinal matters; did not sometimes confound the actual with the imaginary; and that the fancy of these pious writers never stood in the place of their recollection?

But what if this should take place? Is Christianity then to perish out of the heart of the nations, and vanish from the memory of the world, like the religions that were before Abraham? It must be so, if it rest on a foundation which a scoffer may shake, and a score of pious critics shake down. But this is the foundation of a theology, not of Christianity. That does not rest on the decision of councils. It is not to stand or fall with the infallible inspiration of a few Jewish fishermen, who have writ their names in characters of light all over the world. It does not continue to stand through the forbearance of some critic, who can cut, when he will, the thread on which its life depends. Christianity does not rest on the infallible authority of the New Testament. It depends on this collection of books for the historical statement of its facts. In this we do not require infallible inspiration on the part of the writers, more than in the record of other historical facts. To me it seems as presumptuous, on the one hand, for the believer to claim this evidence for the truth of Christianity, as it is absurd, on the other hand, for the sceptic to demand such evidence to support these historical statements. I cannot see that it depends on the personal authority of Jesus. He was the organ through which the infinite spoke. It is God that was manifested in the flesh by him, on whom rests the truth which Jesus brought to light, and made clear and beautiful in his life; and if Christianity be true, it seems useless to look for any other authority to uphold it, as for some one to support Almighty God. So if it could be proved—as it cannot—in opposition to the greatest amount of historical evidence ever collected on any similar point, that the gospels were the fabrication of designing and artful men, that Jesus of Nazareth had never lived, still Christianity would stand firm, and fear no evil. None of the doctrines of that religion would fall to the ground; for, if true, they stand by themselves. But we should lose—oh, irreparable loss!—the example of that character, so beautiful, so divine, that no human genius could have conceived it, as none, after all the progress and refinement of eighteen centuries, seems fully to have comprehended its lustrous life. If Christianity were true, we should still think it was so, not because its record was written by infallible pens, nor because it was lived out by an infallible teacher; but that it is true, like the axioms of geometry, because it is true, and is to be tried by the oracle God places in the breast. If it rest on the personal authority of Jesus alone, then there is no certainty of its truth if he were ever mistaken in the smallest matter, as some Christians have thought he was in predicting his second coming.

These doctrines respecting the scriptures have often changed, and are but fleeting. Yet men lay much stress on them. Some cling to these notions as if they were Christianity itself. It is about these and similar points that theological battles are fought from age to age. Men sometimes use worst the choicest treasure which God bestows. This is especially true of the use men make of the Bible. Some men have regarded it as the heathen their idol, or the savage his fetish. They have subordinated reason, conscience, and religion to this. Thus have they lost half the treasure it bears in its bosom. No doubt the time will come when its true character shall be felt. Then it will be seen, that, amid all the contradictions of the Old Testament—its legends, so beautiful as fictions, so appalling as facts; amid its predictions that have never been fulfilled; amid the puerile conceptions of God, which sometimes occur, and the cruel denunications that disfigure both psalm and prophecy, there is a reverence for man's nature, a sublime trust in God, and a depth of piety, rarely felt in these cold northern hearts of ours. Then the devotion of its authors, the loftiness of their aim, and the majesty of their life, will appear doubly fair, and prophet and psalmist will warm our hearts as never before. Their voice will cheer the young, and sanctify the grey-headed; will charm us in the toil of life, and sweeten the cup death gives us when he comes to shake off this mantle of flesh. Then will it be seen that the words of Jesus are the music of heaven, sung in an earthly voice, and the echo of these words in John and Paul owe their efficacy to their truth and their depth, and to no accidental matter connected therewith. Then can the word, which was in the beginning and now is, find access to the innermost heart of man, and speak there as now it seldom speaks. Then shall the Bible—which is a whole library of the deepest and most earnest thoughts and feelings, and piety and love, ever recorded in human speech—be read oftener than ever before, not with superstition, but with reason, conscience, and faith fully active. Then shall it sustain men bowed down with many sorrows; rebuke sin, encourage virtue, sow the world broadcast and quick with the seed of love, that man may reap a harvest for life everlasting.

With all the obstacles men have thrown in its path, how much has the Bible done for mankind! No abuse has deprived us of all its blessings! You trace its path across the world from the day of Pentecost to this day. As a river springs up in the heart of a sandy continent, having its father in the skies, and its birthplace in distant, unknown mountains; as the stream rolls on, enlarging itself, making in that arid waste a belt of verdure wherever it turns its way; creating palm groves and fertile plains, where the smoke of the cottager curls up at eventide, and marble cities send the gleam of their splendor far into the sky; such has been the course of the Bible on the earth. Despite of idolaters bowing to the dust before it, it has made a deeper mark on the world than the rich and beautiful literature of all the heathen. The first book of the Old Testament tells man he is made in the image of God; the first of the New Testament gives us the motto, Be perfect as your Father in heaven. Higher words were never spoken. How the truths of the Bible have blessed us! There is not a boy on all the hills of New England; not a girl born in the filthiest cellar which disgraces a capital in Europe, and cries to God against the barbarism of modern civilization; not a boy nor a girl all Christendom through—but their lot is made better by that great book.

Doubtless the time will come when men shall see Christ also as he is. Well might he still say, "Have I been so long with you, and yet hast thou not known me?" No! we have made him an idol, have bowed the knee before him, saying, "Hail, king of the Jews!" called him "Lord, Lord!" but done not the things which he said. The history of the Christian world might well be summed up in one word of the evangelist—"and there they crucified him;" for there has never been an age when men did not crucify the Son of God afresh. But if error prevail for a time and grow old in the world, truth will triumph at the last, and then we shall see the Son of God as he is. Lifted up, he shall draw all nations unto him. Then will men understand the word of Jesus, which shall not pass away. Then we shall see and love the divine life that he lived. How vast has his influence been! How his spirit wrought in the hearts of his disciples, rude, selfish, bigoted, as at first they were! How it has wrought in the world! His words judge the nations. The wisest son of man has not measured their height. They speak to what is deepest in profound men, what is holiest in good men, what is divinest in religious men. They kindle anew the flame of devotion in hearts long cold. They are spirit and life. His truth was not derived from Moses and Solomon; but the light of God shown through him, not colored, not bent aside. His life is the perpetual rebuke of all time since. It condemns ancient civilization; it condemns modern civilization. Wise men we have since had, and good men; but this Galilean youth strode before the world whole thousands of years, so much of divinity was in him. His words solve the questions of this present age. In him the godlike and the human met and embraced, and a divine life was born. Measure him by the world's greatest sons—how poor they are! Try him by the best of men— how little and low they appear! Exalt him as much as we may, we shall yet, perhaps, come short of the work. But still was he not our brother; the son of man, as we are; the Son of God, like ourselves? His excellence—was it not human excellence? His wisdom, love, piety—sweet and celestial as they were—are they not what we also may attain? In him, as in a mirror, we may see the image of God, and go on from glory to glory, till we are changed into the same image, led by the spirit which enlightens the humble. Viewed in this way, how beautiful is the life of Jesus! Heaven has come down to earth, or, rather, earth has become heaven. The Son of God, come of age, has taken possession of his birthright. The brightest revelation is this—of what is possible for all men, if not now, at least hereafter. How pure is his spirit, and how encouraging its words! "Lowly sufferer," he seems to say, "see how I bore the cross. Patient laborer, be strong; see how I toiled for the unthankful and the merciless. Mistaken sinner, see of what thou art capable. Rise up, and be blessed."

But if, as some early Christians began to do, you take a heathen view, and make him a god, the Son of God in a peculiar and exclusive sense, much of the significance of his character is gone. His virtue has no merit, his love no feeling, his cross no burden, his agony no pain. His death is an illusion, his resurrection but a show. For if he were not a man, but a god, what are all these things? what his words, his life, his excellence of achievement? It is all nothing, weighed against the illimitable greatness of him who created the worlds and fills up all time and space! Then his resignation is no lesson, his life no model, his death no triumph to you or me, who are not gods, but mortal men, that know not what a day shall bring forth, and walk by faith "dim sounding on our perilous way." Alas! we have despaired of man, and so cut off his brightest hope.

In respect of doctrines as well as forms, we see all is transitory. "Everywhere is instability and insecurity." Opinions have changed most on points deemed most vital. Could we bring up a Christian teacher of any age—from the sixth to the fourteenth century, for example, though a teacher of undoubted soundness of faith, whose word filled the churches of Christendom—clergymen would scarce allow him to kneel at their altar, or sit down with them at the Lord's table. His notions of Christianity could not be expressed in our forms, nor could our notions be made intelligible to his ears. The questions of his age, those on which Christianity was thought to depend—questions which perplexed and divided the subtle doctors—are no questions to us. The quarrels which then drove wise men mad, now only excite a smile or a tear, as we are disposed to laugh or weep at the frailty of man. We have other straws of our own to quarrel for. Their ancient books of devotion do not speak to us; their theology is a vain word. To look back but a short period, the theological speculations of our fathers during the last two centuries, their "practical divinity," even the sermons written by genius and piety, are, with rare exceptions, found unreadable; such a change is there in the doctrines.

Now, who shall tell us that the change is to stop here; that this sect or that, or even all sects united, have exhausted the river of life, and received it all in their canonized urns, so that we need draw no more out of the eternal well, but get refreshment nearer at hand? Who shall tell us that another age will not smile at our doctrines, disputes, and unchristian quarrels about Christianity, and make wide the mouth at men who walked brave in orthodox raiment, delighting to blacken the name of heretics, and repeat again the old charge, "He hath blasphemed?" Who shall tell us they will not weep at the folly of all such as fancied truth shone only in the contracted nook of their school, or sect, or coterie? Men of other times may look down equally on the heresy-hunters, and men hunted for heresy, and wonder at both. The men of all ages before us were quite as confident as we that their opinion was truth, and their notion was Christianity and the whole thereof. The men who lit the fires of persecution, from the first martyr to Christian bigotry down to the last murder of innocents, had no doubt their opinion was divine. The contest about transubstantiation, and the immaculate purity of the Hebrew and Greek texts of the scriptures, was waged with a bitterness unequalled in these days. The Protestant smiles at one, the Catholic at the other, and men of sense wonder at both. It might teach us all a lesson, at least of forbearance. No doubt an age will come in which ours shall be reckoned a period of darkness—like the sixth century—when men groped for the wall, but stumbled and fell, because they trusted a transient notion, not an eternal truth; an age when temples were full of idols set up by human folly; an age in which Christian light had scarce begun to shine into men's hearts. But while this change goes on, while one generation of opinions passes away, and another rises up, Christianity itself, that pure religion which exists eternal in the constitution of the soul and the mind of God, is always the same. The word that was before Abraham, in the very beginning, will not change, for that word is truth. From this Jesus subtracted nothing; to this he added nothing. But he came to reveal it as the secret of God, that cunning men could not understand, but which filled the souls of men meek and lowly of heart. This truth we owe to God; the revelation thereof to Jesus, our elder brother, God's chosen son.

To turn away from the disputes of the Catholics and the Protestants, of the Unitarian and the Trinitarian, of old school and new school, and come to the plain words of Jesus of Nazareth, Christianity is a simple thing, very simple. It is absolute, pure morality; absolute, pure religion; the love of man; the love of God acting without let or hindrance. The only creed it lays down is the great truth which springs up spontaneous in the holy heart—there is a God. Its watchword is, Be perfect as your Father in heaven. The only form it demands is a divine life; doing the best thing in the best way, from the highest motives; perfect obedience to the great law of God. Its sanction is the voice of God in your heart; the perpetual presence of him who made us and the stars over our head; Christ and the Father abiding within us. All this is very simple—a little child can understand it; very beautiful—the loftiest mind can find nothing so lovely. Try it by reason, conscience, and faith—things highest in man's nature—we see no redundance, we feel no deficiency. Examine the particular duties it enjoins—humility, reverence, sobriety, gentleness, charity, forgiveness, fortitude, resignation, faith, and active love; try the whole extent of Christianity, so well summed up in the command, "Thou shalt love the Lord thy God with all thy heart, and with all thy soul, and with all thy mind—thou shalt love thy neighbor as thyself;" and is there anything therein that can perish? No, the very opponents of Christianity have rarely found fault with the teachings of Jesus. The end of Christianity seems to be to make all men one with God as Christ was one with him; to bring them to such a state of obedience and goodness that we shall think divine thoughts and feel divine sentiments, and so keep the law of God by living a life of truth and love. Its means are purity and prayer; getting strength from God, and using it for our fellow-men as well as ourselves. It allows perfect freedom. It does not demand all men to *think* alike, but to think uprightly, and get as near as possible at truth; not all men to *live* alike, but to live holy, and get as near as possible to a life perfectly divine. Christ set up no pillars of Hercules, beyond which men must not sail the sea in quest of truth. He says, "I have many things to say unto you, but ye cannot bear them now. . . .

Greater works than these shall ye do." Christianity lays no rude hand on the sacred peculiarity of the individual genius and character. But there is no Christian sect which does not fetter a man. It would make all men think alike, or smother their conviction in silence. Were all men Quakers or Catholics, Unitarians or Baptists, there would be much less diversity of thought, character, and life, less of truth active in the world, than now. But Christianity gives us the largest liberty of the sons of God; and were all men Christians after the fashion of Jesus, this variety would be a thousand times greater than now: for Christianity is not a system of doctrines, but rather a method of attaining oneness with God. It demands, therefore, a good life of piety within, of purity without, and gives the promise that whoso does God's will shall know of God's doctrine.

In an age of corruption, as all ages are, Jesus stood and looked up to God. There was nothing between him and the Father of all; no old world, be it of Moses or Esaias, of a living rabbi, or sanhedrim of rabbis; no sin or perverseness of the finite will. As the result of this virgin purity of soul and perfect obedience, the light of God shone down into the very depths of his soul, bringing all of the Godhead which flesh can receive. He would have us do the same; worship with nothing between us and God; act, think, feel, live, in perfect obedience to him; and we never are *Christians* as he was the *Christ,* until we worship, as Jesus did, with no mediator, with nothing between us and the Father of all. He felt that God's word was in him; that he was one with God. He told what he saw, the truth; he lived what he felt, a life of love. The truth he brought to light must have been always the same before the eyes of all-seeing God, nineteen centuries before Christ, or nineteen centuries after him. A life supported by the principle and quickened by the sentiment of religion, if true to both, is always the same thing in Nazareth or New England. Now that divine man received these truths from God, was illumined more clearly by "the light that lighteneth every man," combined or involved all the truths of religion and morality in his doctrine, and made them manifest in his life. Then his words and example passed into the world, and can no more perish than the stars be wiped out of the sky. The truths he taught; his doctrines respecting man and God; the relation between man and man, and man and God, with the duties that grow out of that relation—are always the same, and can never change till man ceases to be man, and creation vanishes into nothing. No; forms and opinions change and perish, but the word of God cannot fail. The form religion takes, the doctrines wherewith she is girded, can never be the same in any two centuries or two men; for since the sum of religious doctrines is both the result and the measure of a man's total growth in wisdom, virtue, and piety, and since men will always differ in these respects, so religious *doctrines* and *forms* will always differ, always be transient, as Christianity goes forth and scatters the seed she bears in her hand. But the *Christianity holy men feel in the heart,* the Christ that is born within us, is always the same thing to each soul that feels it. This differs only in degree, and not in kind, from age to age, and man to man. There is something in Christianity which no sect, from the "Ebionites" to the "Latter-Day Saints," ever entirely overlooked. This is that common Christianity which burns in the hearts of pious men.

Real Christianity gives men new life. It is the growth and perfect action of the holy spirit God puts into the sons of men. It makes us outgrow any form or any system of doctrines we have devised, and approach still closer to the truth. It would lead us to take what help we can find. It would make the Bible our servant, not our master. It would teach us to profit by the wisdom and piety of David and Solomon, but not to sin their sins, nor bow to their idols. It would make us revere the holy words spoken by "godly men of old," but revere still more the word of God spoken through conscience, reason, and faith, as the holiest of all. It would not make Christ the despot of the soul, but the brother of all men. It would not tell us that even he had exhausted the fulness of God, so that he could create none greater; for with him "all things are possible," and neither Old Testament nor New Testament ever hints that creation exhausts the creator. Still less would it tell us the wisdom, the piety, the love, the manly excellence of Jesus was the result of miraculous agency alone, but that it was won, like the excellence of humbler men, by faithful obedience to him who gave his son such ample heritage. It would point to him as our brother, who went before, like the good shepherd, to charm us with the music of his words, and with the beauty of his life to tempt us up the steeps of mortal toil, within the gate of heaven. It would have us make the kingdom of God on earth, and enter more fittingly the kingdom on high. It would lead us to form Christ in the heart, on which Paul laid such stress, and work out our salvation by this. For it is not so much by the Christ who lived so blameless and beautiful eighteen centuries ago that we are saved directly, but by the Christ we form in our hearts and live out in our daily life, that we save ourselves, God working with us both to will and to do.

Compare the simpleness of Christianity, as Christ sets it forth on the mount, with what is sometimes taught and accepted in that honored name; and what a difference! One is of God; one is of man. There is something in Christianity which sects have not reached; something that will not be won, we fear, by theological battles, or the quarrels of pious men; still we may rejoice that Christ is preached in any way. The Christianity of sects, of the pulpit, of society, is ephemeral—a transitory fly. It will pass off and be forgot. Some new form will take its place, suited to the aspect of the changing times. Each will represent something of truth, but no one the whole. It seems the whole race of man is needed to do justice to the whole of truth, as "the whole church to preach the whole gospel." Truth is intrusted for the time to a perishable ark of human contrivance. Though often shipwrecked, she always comes safe to land, and is not changed by her mishap. That pure ideal religion which Jesus saw on the mount of his vision, and lived out in the lowly life of a Galilean peasant; which transforms his cross into an emblem of all that is holiest on earth; which makes sacred the ground he trod, and is dearest to the best of men, most true to what is truest in them—cannot pass away. Let men improve never so far in civilization, or soar never so high on the wings of religion and love, they can never outgo the flight of truth and Christianity. It will always be above them. It is as if we were to fly towards a star, which becomes larger and more bright the nearer we approach, till we enter and are absorbed in its glory.

If we look carelessly on the ages that have gone by, or only on the surfaces of things as they come up before us, there is reason to fear; for we confound the truth of God with the word of man. So at a distance the cloud and the mountain seem the same. When the drift changes with the passing wind an unpracticed eye might fancy the mountain itself was gone. But the mountain stands to catch the clouds, to win the blessing they bear, and send it down to moisten the fainting violet, to form streams which gladden valley and meadow, and sweep on at last to the sea in deep channels, laden with fleets. Thus the forms of the church, the creeds of the sects, the conflicting opinions of teachers, float round the sides of the Christian mount, and swell and toss, and rise and fall, and dart their lightning, and roll their thunder, but they neither make nor mar the mount itself. Its lofty summit far transcends the tumult, knows nothing of the storm which roars below, but burns with rosy light at evening and at morn, gleams in the splendors of the mid-day sun, sees his light when the long shadows creep over plain and moorland, and all night long has its head in the heavens, and is visited by troops of stars which never set, nor veil their faces so pure and high.

Let then the transient pass, fleet as it will; and may God send us some new manifestation of the Christian faith, that shall stir men's hearts as they were never stirred; some new word, which shall teach us what we are, and renew us all in the image of God; some better life, that shall fulfil the Hebrew prophecy, and pour out the spirit of God on young men and maidens, and old men and children; which shall realize the word of Christ, and give us the Comforter, who shall reveal all needed things! There are Simeons enough in the cottages and churches of New England, plain men and pious women, who wait for the consolation, and would die in gladness if their expiring breath could stir quicker the wings that bear him on. There are men enough, sick and "bowed down, in no wise able to lift up themselves," who would be healed could they kiss the hand of their Savior, or touch but the hem of his garment; men who look up and are not fed, because they ask bread from heaven and water from the rock, not traditions or fancies, Jewish or heathen, or new or old; men enough who, with throbbing hearts, pray for the spirit of healing to come upon the waters, which other than angels have long kept in trouble; men enough who have lain long time sick of theology, nothing bettered by many physicians, and are now dead, too dead to bury their dead, who would come out of their graves at the glad tidings. God send us a real religious life, which shall pluck blindness out of the heart, and make us better fathers, mothers, and children! a religious life, that shall go with us where we go, and make every home the house of God, every act acceptable as a prayer. We would work for this, and pray for it, though we wept tears of blood while we prayed.

Such, then, is the transient and such the permanent in Christianity. What is of absolute value never changes; we may cling round it and grow to it for ever. No one can say his notions shall stand. But we may all say, the truth as it is in Jesus shall never pass away. Yet there are always some, even religious men, who do not see the permanent element, so they rely on the fleeting, and, what is also an evil, condemn others for not doing the same. They mistake a defence of the truth for an attack upon the holy of holies, the removal of a theological error for the destruction of all religion. Already men of the same sect eye one another with suspicion, and lowering brows that indicate a storm, and, like children who have fallen out in their play, call hard names. Now, as always, there is a collision between these two elements. The question puts itself to each man, "Will you cling to what is perishing, or embrace what is eternal?" This question each must answer for himself.

My friends, if you receive the notions about Christianity which chance to be current in your sect or church, solely because they are current, and thus accept the commandment of men instead of God's truth, there will always be enough to commend you for soundness of judgment, prudence, and good sense, enough to call you Christian for that reason. But if this is all you rely upon, alas for you! The ground will shake under your feet if you attempt to walk uprightly and like men. You will be afraid of every new opinion, lest it shake down your church; you will fear "lest, if a fox go up, he will break down your stone wall." The smallest contradiction in the New Testament or Old Testament, the least disagreement between the law and the gospel, any mistake of the apostles, will weaken your faith. It shall be with you "as when a hungry man dreameth, and behold, he eateth; but he awaketh, and his soul is empty."

If, on the other hand, you take the true word of God, and live out this, nothing shall harm you. Men may mock, but their own mouthfuls of wind shall be blown back upon their own face. If the master of the house were called Beelzebub, it matters little what name is given to the household. The name Christian, given in mockery, will last till the world go down. He that loves God and man, and lives in accordance with that love, needs not fear what man can do to him. His religion comes to him in his hour of sadness, it lays its hand on him when he has fallen among thieves, and raises him up, heals and comforts him. If he is crucified, he shall rise again.

My friends, you this day receive, with the usual formalities, the man you have chosen to speak to you on the highest of all themes—what concerns your life on earth, your life in heaven. It is a work for which no talents, no prayerful diligence, no piety, is too great; an office that would dignify angels, if worthily filled. If the eyes of this man be holden, that he *cannot* discern between the perishing and the true, you will hold him guiltless of all sin in this; but look for light where it can be had, for his office will then be of no use to you. But if he sees the truth, and is scared by worldly motives, and *will* not tell it, alas for him! If the watchman see the foe coming, and blow not the trumpet, the blood of the innocent is on him.

Your own conduct and character, the treatment you offer this young man, will in some measure influence him. The hearer affects the speaker. There were some places where even Jesus "did not many mighty works, because of their unbelief." Worldly motives —not seeming such—sometimes deter good men from their duty. Gold and ease have, before now, enervated noble minds. Daily contact with men of low aims takes down the ideal of life, which a bright spirit casts out of itself. Terror has sometimes palsied tongues that, before, were eloquent as the voice of persuasion. But thereby truth is not holden. She speaks in a thousand tongues, and with a pen of iron graves her sentence on the rock forever. You may prevent the freedom of speech in this pulpit if you will. You may hire your servants to preach as you bid; to spare your vices, and flatter your follies; to prophesy smooth things, and say, It is peace, when there is no peace. Yet in so doing you weaken and enthral yourselves. And alas for that man who consents to think one thing in his closet and preach another in his pulpit! God shall judge him in his mercy, not man in his wrath. But over his study and over his pulpit might be writ, EMPTINESS; on his canonical robes, on his forehead and right hand, DECEIT, DECEIT.

But, on the other hand, you may encourage your brother to tell the truth. Your affection will then be precious to him, your prayers of great price. Every evidence of your sympathy will go to baptize him anew to holiness and truth. You will then have his best words, his brightest thoughts, and his most hearty prayers. He may grow old in your service, blessing and blest. He will have—

> "The sweetest, best of consolation,
> The thought that he has given,
> To serve the cause of Heaven,
> The freshness of his early inspiration."

Choose as you will choose; but weal or woe depends upon your choice.

4. A Crusading Clergyman and a Conservative Church

1842

Parker's essay on the Hollis Street Council appeared in *The Dial* of October 1842 as a review of the Proceedings of an Ecclesiastical Council in the Case of the Proprietors of Hollis Street Meeting House and the Rev. John Pierpont. One of the most energetic of Unitarian reformers, Pierpont devoted himself to crusades for peace, to antislavery and to the abolition of capital punishment and of imprisonment for debt. These enthusiasms, while irritating to his conservative parishioners, would not by themselves have brought on a crisis. What did precipitate a crisis was Pierpont's zealous advocacy of temperance and his denunciation of the liquor interests of Boston. The cellar of the Hollis Street Church was rented out to a rum merchant as a warehouse, and several liquor dealers were pew-holders (though not active members) in the church. Exasperated by their minister's attacks on intemperance, these men, along with other conservative elements, agitated to remove him from his pulpit on a series of charges that bore little relation to the real issues. A "seven-years' war" to remove Pierpont ended with his somewhat dubious vindication by a less-than-friendly Ecclesiastical Council, whose proceedings Parker here reviews with an absence of tact as pronounced as that charged against Pierpont himself. Four years later Pierpont resigned. He is remembered today chiefly as the grandfather of John Pierpont Morgan.

Parker's essay on the Hollis Street Council is interesting mainly for its autobiographical overtones and anticipations, for he himself was to be charged with most of the sins alleged against Dr. Pierpont and was to arouse just the kind of animosity inspired by the hapless minister of the Hollis Street Church. We include here, as a kind of appendix, a letter which Parker wrote to Pierpont at the time of Pierpont's resignation.

I

Let us now consider the "charges" brought against the Pastor. Every body knows, that for a minister to be useful, he must be *free*, free to *think, speak,* and *act,* and also that the parish be free to think, speak, and act. But if both are free, a collision may come between the pews and the pulpit. The preacher may be over timid, and wise men in the pews complain of that. For example, if the minister preach a sermon on temperance, and say at the end of it, "But, my beloved brethren, I would not have you think my words apply to *you;* no, God forbid that I should suspect sin of *this sober village."* Good men will say, "He is not the man for us." Then again the minister may be unduly bold, and meddle with matters too high for him. Good men will have a right to complain. If he is impertinent, sarcastic, scornful, insolent; if he abuses his pulpit by introducing personal spleen, and vents his ill-humor in sermons on laymen by profane swearing,—and cases of this kind have happened,—all good men should exclaim against it. Explanations, or a separation must follow; but neither party would lose its freedom. "Take heed how you hear," is a good rule. But in such cases of disagreement the issue that is made out to be the true one. It is unfair to contend with a minister for not preaching Anti-slavery and Temperance, when the fault is, that he has neither Zeal nor Grace. We should rejoice to see the time, when a perfect openness might prevail, and when not only the preacher did the abstract and concrete work above hinted at,—for the greater part of the clergy, no doubt, still aim at that,—but when the laity, if they did not find their minister a spiritual guide, should tell him plainly the facts of the case, and say, if it were so, "Sir, we can't bear you; we are hungry, you give us no meat; we are thirsty, you give us no drink; we are in prison of our prejudices, and sick through our sins, you do not come to us, your words don't visit us, nor comfort us. Why should we trouble one another? The world is large and wide; we wish you may be very useful to others, but you cannot be a Christian minister to us. You don't speak to our souls. Let us part in peace and good understanding." This would be fair to all parties; both would know what they were about, and the "charges," like the grand juror's bill, would make a "true presentment" of the case as it was supposed to be. The active man would not be condemned as a drone, nor the drone as one over active.

Now the "grounds of complaint," alleged against the Pastor before the Council, are in substance as follows. 1. That he has neglected his *professional* duties for mere *secular* concerns. 2. That he has preached in an *unkind manner on exciting topics,* such as *ardent spirits, imprisonment for debt,* and *slavery.* 3. That he has *not treated his opponents well.* 4. That he has shown a *want of reverence for the Scriptures.* 5. That he has made *indelicate state-ments* in the pulpit. 6. That he has not been *honest.* 7. That he has not been *true.* 8. That he has *promoted quarrels.* 9. That he has *not shown a proper ministerial decorum* in the pulpit and elsewhere.

Now there come up two questions. I. Do these charges make a true presentment of the real subject on which the parties are at issue? II. Are the charges true?

I. To look at the first question, after a careful study of the records of the Council, we confess to a general and very strong impression, that these charges, as a whole, do NOT represent the subject at issue. We must, as impartial judges, agree with the confession of the Moderator, "I HAVE NOT A DOUBT THAT TEMPER-ANCE IS THREE QUARTERS OF ALL OUR TROUBLE."—p. 204. We confess that, if much stress was *really* laid on the other offences, we should suppose the complaint would be made at the time the offence was committed. Was such the case? It does not appear. On the contrary, it does appear, that the offence in some cases was favored at the time by some of the very men who brought the present complaints. Mr. Pierpont has doubtless his faults; faults as a minister, faults as a man. They are apparent in this trial. But was he really on trial for *these faults,* or were they brought up to serve another purpose? To our mind there is no doubt of the answer which a majority of unprejudiced readers will make.

II. The next question is, are the "grounds of complaint" proven against the Pastor? Here we have not only the opinion of the Moderator, but the whole Council, in the negative. How-ever, the decision of the Council is but a *qualified* negative. They divide the charges into three classes:—those affecting the Pastor's *moral* character, his *ministerial* character, and those *growing out of the difficulties between him and his parish.* They think the *first* "are not sustained." "The Council are of opinion that he cannot be so regarded, [that is, as 'wanting in purity, integrity, and moral truth,'] and ought not to be so pronounced."—p. 378.

The *second* class of charges are also dismissed by the Council as not sustained. "They think that *few clergymen could have a ministry of more than twenty years so thoroughly scanned and investigated, and not have more instances of neglect and evidence of inattention brought forward against him.* Upon this point the Council cannot but consider the investigation had before them as honorable to the Pastor."—p. 379. This decision, however, is somewhat qualified. The Council think he has not always been "wise, prudent, and discreet." *"He might have manifested more of calmness and moderation, and through them have been more useful."* "The circumstances of his parish, and the condition of things in that quarter of the city, where his ministry was chiefly exercised, were peculiar, and such as called for a large measure and a constant exhibition of that wisdom which is from above,"&c. —p. 380. "In this wisdom the Council consider the Pastor has been somewhat deficient." "It is to be considered probable also, that, if there was sometimes a want of prudence in the Pastor, there may have been on the part of some of his hearers, unconsciously, a susceptibility to offence, and thus the difficulties have arisen from faults and failings in both parties."—*Ibid.*

In respect to the *third* class of charges, the Council find in the Pastor's conduct nothing "vindictive," nor any "intentional irreverence for the Holy Scriptures," though he has made a "use of Scripture language painful to the feelings of this Council."[!] With these exceptions, however, the Council think the charges are "in a measure sustained."—p. 381. See also pp. 382, 383.

"The Result in Council" is concluded with this resolution, "That although on such of the charges preferred against the Rev. John Pierpont, as most directly affect his moral character, the proof which has been presented has been altogether insufficient; yet on other charges such an amount of proof has been brought forward, as requires this Council to express their disapprobation of Mr. Pierpont's conduct on some occasions, and in some respects, but not sufficient, in their opinion, to furnish ground for advising a dissolution of the connexion between him and his parish."—p. 383.

This is the sum of the whole matter. With this the Council concluded their long and laborious session. We have spoken before of the pure and high moral character of individuals of that body. It is not for us to inquire what were the motives that weighed with them; not for us to ask how far prejudice or spleen choked the course of justice on the one hand, or how far a deference to public opinion, and a diplomatic fear of the popular sympathy, setting strongly in the Pastor's favor, prevented a full expression of the censure which is insinuated rather than roundly delivered. We know there was a time when ecclesiastical councils governed public opinion. "We have changed all that." Does public opinion govern ecclesiastical councils? We know not. At the time the Council, "preceded by the Moderator," first passed into the

Supreme Court Room, we heard grave men, and pious men say, "A just judgment is not to be looked for from that body; if they let him off with no censure, they condemn themselves, for God knows they have not undertaken his work. We honor and love the men, but hope no justice from them in this case." Another said, "The Council is a farce. The Boston ministers, instead of trying Mr. Pierpont, ought themselves to be brought before a council for *not* having done in a good spirit, what he is accused of *doing* in a bad one." To our mind there was no little truth in both sayings. We question no man's motive in the matter, but we take it no plain man, who reads the volume before us, will doubt which way the prejudice of the Council tended, or what would have been the decision of at least some of its members, if public opinion, the despot of the vulgar, had not so plainly favored Mr. Pierpont. In every single case, as we understand it, the weight of the Council was thrown against him; offences were sought committed months after the charges were first brought; he was rebuked for a trifle at the very least, and his opponents—members of the Council—allowed to insult him with no reproof. Facts tell their own story. It is admitted by the Council that the wrong is on both sides; but how daintily is the complaining party rebuked! In the case of the litigation, was all the "vindictive" spirit on one side? Let the candid reader decide.

What then? Is the Pastor justifiable in all things? We think not. There is something that we must censure, several things we cannot understand; sometimes he pursues, as we think, an oblique course, when a straight one would better compass the end; he allows himself an indignant eloquence, which were better let alone; he gives blow for blow, and scorn for scorn; he does not speak gently. He rebukes sin more strongly than beautifully; we would try him by no vulgar measure, but by the absolute standard of Ideal goodness. As a minister and as a man he does not come up to the measure. It may be said, "His provocation was great." Nothing more true; but what then? The courage that will not stand fire is no courage for us; the Christian virtue which is not superior to ALL temptation is no Christian virtue to our taste. For such departure from the true spirit and the true method let him be censured.

But are we speaking of angels? Let us see how other men of flesh and blood have done under similar circumstances. The Prophet Jeremiah is a man held in some estimation by the Christian Church; but when men said, "come let us devise devices against Jeremiah," what did that prophet return for answer? "Give heed to me, Oh Lord, and hearken to the voice of them that contend with me. Deliver up their children to the famine, and pour out their blood by the force of the sword, and let their wives be bereaved of their children, and be widows; and let their men be put to death. . . . Forgive not their iniquity, neither blot out their sin from thy sight, but let them be overthrown before thee." But that Prophet was a *Jew;* let us now hear how a Christian minister, an "inspired" man, the very chiefest apostle, speaks in the New Testament. The magistrate commands the bystanders to smite Paul on the mouth. What says the Apostle? "God shall smite thee, thou whited wall," &c. That was the way *flesh and blood* treated its opponents in the days of the Bible.

To take another case. There were *peculiar circumstances* in the early days of the Christian church, and "a liberal measure" of divine wisdom *was* needed; but what says "a servant of God and the Lord Jesus" to men that committed a sin? "Go to now, ye rich men, weep and howl for your miseries that shall come upon you. Your riches are corrupted and your garments are moth-eaten. Ye have heaped treasure together for the last days! Behold the hire of the laborers who have reaped down your fields, which is of you kept back by fraud, crieth; and the cries of those which have reaped are entered into the ears of the Lord of Sabaoth. Ye have lived in pleasure on the earth, and been wanton; ye have nourished your hearts as in the day of slaughter. Ye have condemned and killed the just, and he doth not resist you." Let the "Pastor of Hollis street Church" be condemned, if need is, for foulness of speech, but let it be remembered, how far the charge goes, and on what other names it shall rest. We would not excuse him, because Jewish and Christian Reformers sinned with their lips in the same way. Let the camp of Reformers be pure as the holy of holies; let no selfishness, nor violence, nor vengeance be found in it, "to make the camp of Israel a curse." Are Reformers warring on sin? Then let their hands be clean; let there be none of the "accursed thing" found in their tents. Is their cause glorious? Then the purer should be their hearts, and the holier their weapons. In the pirates' battle for gold we look for false weapons and foul play; not in the saints' battle for the souls of mankind. We expect dirt on a butcher's frock; not on the wing of the Angel, who comes down to trouble the pool of Bethesda, and make its waters healing to the impotent folk that lie in its gates.

But to speak humanly, there is no little palliation for the Pastor. Let him be weighed in an even balance; his heroic virtues be matched with his faults. He has then nothing to fear. Honor to that man, who in an age of selfishness and sin lifts up a manly voice, and cries out against the actual crimes and oppressions of his own time, his own neighborhood, till the ears of sin tingle. There is a time when few lift up the hand against vice, because sin is popular. How warily some "Temperance men" came up to beat the bush, years ago; how fearful were they of hurting the feelings of men that drank Rum, sold Rum, made Rum! They were prudent men, and it was then doubtful how the issue would terminate! Now, when the victory is won, these men do the chief part of the shouting, and almost the whole of the denunciation, and, as we believe, are driving the temperance *party* to madness and ruin. Wine is the only Devil, and wine-drinkers the only demoniacs with them! Oh the shortness of human memories! The coward forgets where he was when blows were to be got.

Mr. Pierpont came forward as a Reformer, a rare character in the Pulpit, at a time when there were no honors to be won, no victory to be rejoiced in. The "peculiar circumstances" of his parish were Rum-selling, Rum-making, Rum-drinking. The head and front of his offending, we honestly believe, is this, the crime of preaching against the actual sins of his own parish. An exciting topic, no doubt; it requires much of "the wisdom that cometh from above" to do the work well. He preached, as Paul at Ephesus, *against the Idolatry of the place he was in;* and with a similar result. "Moreover ye see and hear," said the opponents of the Apostle, "that this Paul hath persuaded and turned away much people, saying that they be no Gods which are made with hands, so that not only this our craft is in danger to be set at nought, but also that the temple of the great goddess . . . be despised." We do not place the opponents of Mr. Pierpont among idolaters. Some of them are men whose personal character is noble, beautiful, Christian; can we say more? We would go far to honor such men, and would repel any assault upon the general righteousness of their motives. But good men are sometimes deceived, wise men see not all things, it is difficult for most men to see anything wrong, in a calling which is sanctioned by the laws of the land, and which, more than all, brings money to their pocket. Certainly, a *reasonable* allowance is to be made in such instances.

Let the case of the Pastor be examined ever so minutely, by eyes howsoever partial, and it is only a few details that can be censured; the main parts of his course, when tried by the standard of Christianity, must be commended. The World and the Church have prowled about his parish; have hunted with hungry maw, through and through a ministry of twenty years' continuance; nothing was too little to escape their scrutiny; nothing too great for their assault; nothing too private for their examination. Yet after all, what have they started and run down? There has been a great beating of the bush; baying and shouting enough, for a Persian hunting in the days of Cyrus; but they who have made this cry and ado find but little game at the last. After all the "investigation," notwithstanding the Pastor was in fact tried for offences committed after the indictment was made out and presented; spite of the diligence displayed in searching for sins of omission and commission, the World and the Church have scraped together but a small amount of filth; enough to soil their own hands, not to bespatter the reputation of him at whom it has been thrown. Well says an ancient, "Gold shall be tried in the *fire,* but acceptable men in *the furnace of adversity!*" Both come out of the trial purer than before.

II

TO REV. JOHN PIERPONT

West Roxbury, October 15, 1845

DEAR SIR,—I called to see you yesterday, but unluckily missed you; and as I shall not, it is probable, have another opportunity to take you by the hand, I will now say a word to you before you leave Boston. None can regret your departure more than I. We have not been much together. You have been busy, and so have I: therefore I have not seen you so often as I could always have wished. But I have always felt encouraged and strengthened by your example, and that long before I had any "troubles" with my theological "brethren." If you had done as the other ministers, had you been as they are, you would not now have been leaving Boston. If you had flattered the follies, and winked at the sins, of the rich, you would have had, not *your* reward (that you have now), but *their* reward: I mean, the reward of the ministers you leave behind. But you have chosen another part, and have YOUR reward,—a little different from theirs. You must go in triumph;

for you have fought a good fight and a great one. For nearly thirty years, you have been foremost in all the great reforms of the day which had the welfare of men for their object. You have been fearless and free. If others didn't help you, you thought that was a reason why *you* should work the more. When your valor was called for, you did not turn round to remember your discretion. None of the great moral enterprises of the day would have stood where now they stand, if you had not opened your manly voice in their behalf. Where would *temperance* have been if John Pierpont had been silent? where many other good and noble causes? It is your zeal for the great cause which Jesus died to serve that now has brought you to your present position. Your reward is with you. The confidence that you worked faithfully, and wrought a great work, will go with you, and bless you to the end of your days. Nothing has happened for years so reflecting disgrace on the Boston clergy as your departure from the city under the present circumstances. But what is their disgrace is your glory. Go, then; and may God be with you! For *my* sake, for the sake of *many,* I could wish you were to stay; but it is better you should go. I know you will find work enough to be done, and warm hearts to welcome you in doing it. You leave behind not a few to bless you for your toils, and to pray for your future success and welfare. Your memory will live ever in their affections, and their good wishes will follow you wherever you go. I beg you to accept my thanks for all that you have done, and to believe me ever

Your friend and brother,

5. William Ellery Channing

1842

Freeman, Buckminister, Bentley and Ware had been forerunners of Unitarianism, but Channing was its true founder and father. Theologically orthodox—by Unitarian standards—and content to stay within the fold of the church, Channing was nevertheless closer to Emerson than to, let us say, Andrews Norton. His liberalism came out rather in his social consciousness, his friendliness to reform and his hostility to slavery than in theological doctrines. "Our ultimate reliance is and must be on our own reason," he said. "I am surer that my rational nature is from God than that any book is an expression of his will."

From his earliest years Parker had admired Channing, even revered him. He thought him the greatest clergyman of his time, perhaps the greatest man of his time: in all New England the man who best combined saintliness with practical reform. The Peace Society of Massachusetts had been organized in Channing's study, and there too Dorothea Dix had written her *Memorial on the Condition of the Insane*. Channing had championed penal reform, the abolition of capital punishment, public education and religious toleration; he looked with favor on Brook Farm and, at the end of his life, declared open war on slavery. "I felt," wrote Parker, "there was a broad common ground between us." And Channing in turn, when he read the controversial *Transient and Permanent in Christianity*, said, "Let the full heart pour itself forth." When he died, in October 1842, Parker preached a sermon on the meaning of his life and his philosophy. The following extracts are taken from that sermon, not elsewhere published in book form.

Dr. Channing's influence was not confined to New England; the South and the West were warmed at his fire; not to the United States, for in England his works were more read, his spirit took a stronger and deeper hold than with us. The local jealousies, the party strife, the pecuniary interests, the fanaticism of a sect, had less power over his writings abroad than at home. He was not personally mingled with their discussions, nor involved in their strife, as whoever speaks must be at home, and therefore he was heard with something of the same impartiality as a voice from remote ages. The absolute value of his works was weighed more judiciously there, because the reader stood aloof from the war of opinions that went on with us. None of our writers was so well known abroad among serious and religious men; none so well represented the morality and Religion of our land; none contributed so much to wipe off the foul but just imputation cast upon us,—of caring only for money, and if that came, not caring by what means, though we violate all laws of man or God, and break our faith, and butcher the Red-man, who will not work, and chain the Black-man, whom stripes compel to toil.

No American had such power abroad. His judgment on the great moral questions of the day was earnestly looked for by wise men, and respected when it came. We have had great men; men that did honor to their country and their kind; men of large soul and broad views, who have made a mark on their age; political men, that warded off the perils which hung over our heads, and helped us live together on better terms. But I hesitate not to say, that since Washington, no man has died amongst us whose real influence was so wide, and so beneficent, both abroad and at home.

It may be asked, what was the SECRET OF HIS POWER? It was in no uncommon gifts of mind that God gave him outright. With these, no doubt, he was sufficiently well provided; a man thoroughly well-born and amply endowed. But many of his fellow-citizens far outshone him in this respect, who have yet no influence. He had not the power of acute analysis and rapid combination of particulars; the faculty of seeing the soul of things, the one common property, which, as a law, runs through the many diverse particulars; the quality that makes a philosopher. Of this he had less than many of his contemporaries who shall go down to their grave and be forgot, leaving no mark, but a stone in the church-yard, to show they once have been. Dr. Channing's analysis seems sometimes to have halted this side of the ultimate fact.

Not possessing this quality in a very eminent degree, he could not be "original" as a philosopher or theologian. His abstract opinions, or his general laws, never struck you, therefore, as his own discoveries. His *speculations* had not the charm of even apparent novelty, which imposes on the superficial whenever some unripe apple is shaken from the tree, or some withered dogma is disquieted and brought up from its place of oblivion. In matters of pure thought, Dr. Channing was never conspicuous for originality. Others went before him in all paths of philosophy, ethics, or theology which he afterwards trod.

He had not the powers of Imagination which wheels over earth and through the sky, and comes rounding home at last, its chariot laden with spoils gathered from every flower and every star. Of this he had little, because others have more; though certainly he was not deficient when measured by the common scale. No one will contend that he had the creative faculty of Imagination as it appears in some of his contemporaries on both sides the water. Perhaps he had not the lively Fancy that passes for Imagination with the careless; which allures and disappoints you in so many writers of the present day. Certainly he never embellished meagre conceptions with a dazzling trope, nor used fine words to conceal poverty of sense.

He had not that practical turn for affairs, which often does what neither inventive nor creative powers can accomplish. He had neither skill nor boldness to put himself at the head of a mass of men and lead them on to some one particular end. He did not know the right handle of things, the only philosophy of some that have passed for great. If the world is ruled by boldness, as some fancy, he was destined at birth to have no place in its government. He was cautious and timid both in thought and action.

It was none of these things that gave him his power. No, that came from a deeper, purer, and more enduring source. It was a MORAL POWER that spoke in him; which spoke *through* him. As you read his works, or listened to his words, you felt it was not his Understanding that addressed you, but his whole character. There are some that speak bravely and in fine speech; yes, with deep thought, but you think of *them* when they speak. Their opinions seem their property; at least for the time. Others put themselves in the back-ground, their thought concealing them. It seems to be no personal thing, but the voice of Wisdom or Piety that speaks through them, not affected by the man's private will. You say, "An angel spoke; let us obey." So was it with him. When their great orator thundered, the Athenians forgot Demosthenes in thinking of Philip and the City. In hearing a sermon of Dr. Channing, men thought of Goodness, Duty, Religion, not of him.

His fidelity to his moral and religious convictions made him strong and great. What he said seemed to come from nothing partial and peculiar to this man, or that man; but from what is universal, the Soul of all our souls. He would think for himself. Nothing could pervert his moral judgment; neither the eclat of greatness; neither the antiquity of an ungodly custom become a law; nor yet the respectability of sin long wonted to the world. Timid though he was, and self-distrustful to a great degree, yet when Conscience spoke, he heeded neither the roar of the little, nor the clamor of the great which excites that roar. He saw through the shadows, and into the reality of life. Many knew more of things as they are; few men have been so true to things as they ought to be. With him, to see what is Right, was to begin to move towards it, for he made no distinction between things right and things to be done. He was single-hearted in his efforts, aiming at no personal aggrandisement. He forgot himself in finding the truth. He did not ask for the consequences of right action, or right thought, but took them when they came. He trusted God, as a child its father, and did not fear to be true to truth. This moral simplicity was beautiful above praise. . . .

Then, again, he loved mankind. He did not believe moral laws were beautiful in thought, but become deformed when applied to life, and therefore good for nothing when tried, and so he attempted not to amend the laws of God. He did not think Piety had done its work when it said grace, or rose from prayer. Though, by the peculiar and natural bent of his mind, more meditative than philosophic, more mystical than rationalistic, he was yet the last to go astray in pietistic vagaries, and revel in the flowers of sentimental devotion, bringing back nothing to the hive that sheltered and fed him. Oh, no. His love of God did not hinder him from loving man. Did love of God ever do this? No, but the love of Self often, in Religion's name. His piety helped him to a good life, of thought and action. His Religion and Reason, his Love of God and Love of man walked together and did not fall out by the way. His vine proved its planting by bearing much fruit. He loved man as man; not because he was educated, or famous, or rich, but for the immortal nature that was in him, the affections that never die, the spirit capable of unbounded growth, and infinite glory. He looked deeper than the wrappage which circumstances place about mankind. He saw the man in the beggar. To him the greatest man was he who conformed most nearly to the divine image. "The greatest man is he who chooses the Right with invincible resolution, who resists the sorest temptations from within and without, who bears the heaviest burthen cheerfully, who is calmest in storms and most fearless under menace and frowns, whose reliance on truth, on virtue, on God, is most unfaltering." Save only the words of Jesus in the Gospels, I know of nothing, in the whole compass of human literature, that partakes so largely of this love, as his eloquent works. How he plead for man against the tyranny of ages past; the tyranny of the present; the despotism of social institutions; the tyranny of the strong over the weak! Still, his pleading was not a "woe-unto-you," but a "Father-forgive-them." You turn from the writings of the few great men and the multitude of little men, that are read amongst us, and in his page you find words which come straightway out of a heart full of love —love to all. His affection was strong and manly, not that puling sentimentalism which takes a friend by the hand in a conference-room, saying, "Oh, how I love you, my brother," and after that has no more that it can do; nor, was it of that sublimated sort, which loves man as an abstraction, but treads individuals, concrete men, under foot in so doing. No, it was a love of making them greater, wiser, better. Though not found in the busy walks of men, few had so many that made him their adviser in spiritual things, and sought his sympathy in distress. He was disinterested, and forgetful of himself, to a degree rare among men. If he saw an error or a sin of society, he told of it. Distrustful of himself in many things; so mild and meek that it seemed he would not break the wing of a perished fly,—when Sin came before him, no fire was so scorching as his words; no man's indignation like his. He did not ask, What will my friends or my foes think of *me* for doing or saying this? but what he thought right to do and say, he did without fear. Living in a place where he said it was "difficult to draw a long breath;" surrounded by men of views widely different from his own; dependent upon them, in some measure, when Duty called him, he did not ask what they favored; what they feared; or what they would tolerate; or what they would think of him, knowing that the consequences of truth God will take care of. A man truly religious—of whom should he be afraid?

His self-discipline was not the less remarkable. His self-command, it is said, was not a natural gift, but bought with its price. In youth, we are told, he was hasty, impetuous. His controversial writings in theology, printed many years ago, do not discover the same philosophical composure and unconscious moderation that mark those of at least *one* of his early fellow-soldiers, and which distinguish his own later works. He knew the power of genius, but believed in industry none the less. His tranquillity of mind; his acquaintance with the world—great for a man so recluse; his clearness of insight; his skill in separating the unimportant from the essential points of any case; his accurate discriminations of character, all these were the result of diligent cultivation, far more than of natural gifts. Had he not culivated the affections and religious sentiments with the same care as the intellectual and moral faculties, to produce that piety and love so conspicuous in him?

Such, then, were the sources of his influence; a fountain of healing water fed by five perennial springs; his moral fidelity, his pious heart, his love of man, his forgetfulness of self, and the careful cultivation of his gifts,—these were the secret of his eloquence and power. As a man he must have had his faults; certainly his imperfections, which some one, I trust, will relate, for of *such* a man the faults should be portrayed, as the scars of a hero. . . .

Let us now consider more particularly the work to which he devoted himself. He engaged in the REFORM OF THEOLOGY, in common with many of his contemporaries. We all of us know something of the present state of theology, in what are called the more "liberal churches;" we know how slowly the voice of truth gets heard, or even spoken in theological matters. But it is better in our time than in days gone by. When Dr. Channing came to the pulpit, the gloomy doctrines of that austere theology which our fathers embraced, prevailed far more widely than now, and in a form more repulsive than the present. The comon doctrine of the churches respecting the character of God, the nature of man, the terms of salvation, the future condition of the greater part of mankind, were such as to make the flesh creep with horror; doctrines which, if preached to you at this day, I trust, would drive you forth to the fields to learn your Religion in the flowers and the trees. The common theology made God a King not a Father; Christ the master not the brother of us all; and man a worm, a child of God's wrath, not the Son of his love, made in the Father's image. These views still prevail in the greater part of the New England churches, but they are modified, softened here and there, and beside, there is, amongst us, a "more liberal" sect called Unitarians, who disclaim the most revolting doctrines of the old school; a sect halting, indeed, it seems, between life and death, between the liberty of the Spirit, and the thraldom of the letter, but still an auspicious and blessed sign of the times. . . .

How the old questions of theology are *now* met, it is not needful to say, nor to waste time in describing how the broad banner, once borne in the van, on which great men had emblazoned the motto, MAN'S FREEDOM AND GOD'S TRUTH, is now draggled in the dust. Let this subject pass for some other time. But this must be said of Dr. Channing, that if he was slow in coming to the principles and the method of a liberal theology, he never forsook them, but went farther than his former friends, to some conclusions logically unavoidable, but now vehemently denied. He did not—certainly not in his later years, quarrel with a theology, because its circle was wider than his own. It is not saying too much to declare, that no one of our century, in England or America, has done so much as he, to set forth the greatness of man's nature, the loveliness of Jesus, and the goodness of God. In this respect he is the father of us all. What a welcome did a "great truth" meet from him; what a cordial hand did he extend to every earnest soul struggling through the darkness and calling for aid? He did not fear inquiry, for he knew Truth not only takes care of herself but of us. He did not trust God for nothing; his trust made him fearless and strong. He did not see all the truth that will be seen in the next century. He did what was better, he helped men to see somewhat of truth in this, and blessed all that aided others to see. . . .

He turned his attention also, to another branch of the great work in the salvation of man, to the REFORM OF SOCIETY. Here his courage and influence were greater than in the theological reform. Here he was more alone. True, he had his friends, who went with him, and before him, to this work, but not men of the same stamp as in the earlier reform. Some differed from him conscientiously, and stood back; some were taking their ease in their inn; some were busy about particular concerns of man, the fishing, the manufacturing, the shipping interest, but forgot, it seems, the great interest of man, to be cared for, not by neglecting the parts, indeed, but by attending to the whole. . . .

He saw the vice of INTEMPERANCE belittling the faculties, and impoverishing the resources of man. He lifted his voice against the sin; and of all that has been written on this fertile theme, perhaps nothing is more just and wise, than his Temperance Address. It has counsel not to be neglected at the present day.

He turned, also, to the great subject of EDUCATION. He saw its value, and felt the necessity of a work very different from what is commonly conceived of. Had man great powers of mind, affection, soul? They must be developed by careful cultivation. He demanded an education, for all men, far in advance of what many deem sufficient, or even possible. He thought that the resources and talent of the country could not be better employed than in building up a nobler population, better men and women, able to understand the world, and fit to live in it. It was no one-sided culture, but the perfection of all the faculties, that he demanded.

He turned his attention to one other theme; the subject of SLAVERY, "which makes us the byword and scorn of the nations." I know it is a tender subject; one which many think must not be touched upon with us, "who have no concern,"—so it is said—"in the matter." Against this national crime, this hideous sin of a free people, whose motto is, "All are born free;" a Christian people, whose religion says, "Love your brother;" against this sin he uplifted his voice, with more than even his usual eloquence and persuasive power, but not without his customary charity and moderation. No subject, of late years, engrossed so much of his attention as this. None of his writings, I may safely say, does so much honor to his head and heart as on this theme. I know there are men, good and wise men, who scruple not to condemn his course; others, who think slavery is a "very clever thing to all parties," for the Slave is fed and clothed, lives, not among savage blacks, but Christian whites, and the master can get more sugar or cotton, with slaves, than without them! I know there are "good and wise men" who would not have any one cry out for the wrongs of two of three millions of souls, held in the foulest bondage, because, to their owners, these souls are worth some twelve hundred millions of dollars, and the dollars must be kept, though the souls be lost. I know there are men, "Christian men," as the world uses that term, who think the righting of wrongs belongs to any body but themselves. Dr. Channing was not of this number. His mind was early turned to this sin, and his zeal against it never abated. On this ground, also, he had his predecessors, men whose self-denying zeal is so well known, that their names need not be spoken here. In the warfare against slavery, he encountered the abuse—that is the true word for the treatment he met—the abuse of both parties. The one condemned him for meddling with the matter at all, and could "never forgive his speaking about slavery; that must be left to the slave-holders;" the other condemned him for not going the same length, or in the same way with themselves. But did it never happen, in times of excitement, that he who was condemned by the extremes of both parties, was not very far from the right? His opposition to this national sin brought on him more obloquy than all his theological heresies, early and late. His tracts on slavery have been widely read, and perhaps have had more influence than any other contemporary works, in turning the attention of wise and serious men to this crime; perhaps more than all others. Here, too, he was not alone; others went with him to the work, and got honorable scars. Above all others, in his esteem, there was one, united to him in the closest ties of friendship; sharing his aspirations and his sympathies. Shoulder to shoulder they went to this work, each encouraging the other; the same spirit seemed in them both, and they took sweet counsel together. In the inscrutable wisdom of Him, without whom not a sparrow falleth to the ground, that one was torn from us, leaving us, indeed, tears for his departure, but joy, also, for his life. Honor to him, honor to both. Yes, honor to all who dare lift up their voice for freedom, and for man. The tyranny of opinion is the most stifling of all tyranny; but to true men like these, it was neither let nor bar.

He aimed to IMPROVE SOCIETY in its general principles and entire framework. He saw that we live in a state unchristian and not rational; that wars prevail, and must be prepared for; that we prevent crime by remedies almost as bad as the disease; that laws do not reach all offenders, perhaps not the most heinous; that the goods of society do not always fall into the hands of their primitive owners; that some men are losers by what we call civilization; that laws and institutions do not always make us more free, but weave webs of conventionalism about us, belittling the might of man. He saw that the strong use the weak as their tools, and do not bear the burthens of the weak, as Reason and Religion demand. He saw, too, the increasing power of Covetousness, which is corrupting the whole people, individuals, legislatures, yes, the nation; a Spirit that may make the rich richer, but certainly the poor poorer; which drives the laboring man each year farther from honorable competency. Against all these he lifted up his voice, thinking we were never a rational nor a Christian people till we applied Reason and Religion to all our daily life. To dwell a moment on a single point: he loved FREEDOM, the largest liberty of the Sons of God. He asked this for himself; for all men; the liberty to feel right, think right, do right.

6. The True Idea of a Christian Church

1846

In December 1845, a group of gentlemen in Boston met and passed a resolution: "That the Rev. Theodore Parker shall have a chance to be heard in Boston," and invited him to be minister to the newly organized Twenty-Eighth Congregational Society. With some reluctance, for he loved his village parish in West Roxbury, Parker accepted. "I think I have a great work to do," he said. His Boston friends rented the old Melodeon on Washington Street, and Parker himself moved into nearby Exeter Place.

His formal installation came the first Sunday in the new year. Octavius Frothingham, who knew him well, describes the occasion: "The ceremony was of the simplest. There was no charge, the minister's good conscience being deemed sufficient pledge of his fidelity; no address to the people, they having already listened to the voice of their own heart, and being disposed to follow it; no right hand of fellowship, a hundred hands with souls in them being outstretched to give the pastor welcome. The minister preached his own sermon, and prayed his own prayer: none could do it better. The chairman of the committee made a short statement of the measures taken in founding the society, and calling Mr. Parker: then the 'exercises' went on. The preacher announced as the subject of his sermon, 'The [True] Idea of a Christian Church.' "

This memorable sermon was a summary of what Parker had preached and taught, and an anticipation of what he was to preach and teach in the coming years. "A Christian church," he announced boldly, "should be a means of reforming the world." Years later he could look back on this sermon and say, I have kept the faith.

A Christian church should be a means of reforming the world, of forming it after the pattern of Christian ideas. It should therefore bring up the sentiments of the times, the ideas of the times, and the actions of the times, to judge them by the universal standard. In this way it will learn much and be a living church, that grows with the advance of men's sentiments, ideas, and actions, and while it keeps the good of the past will lose no brave spirit of the present day. It can teach much; now moderating the fury of men, then quickening their sluggish steps. We expect the sins of commerce to be winked at in the street; the sins of the state to be applauded on election days and in a Congress, or on the fourth of July; we are used to hear them called the righteousness of the nation. There they are often measured by the avarice or the ambition of greedy men. You expect them to be tried by passion, which looks only to immediate results and partial ends. Here they are to be measured by Conscience and Reason, which look to permanent results and universal ends; to be looked at with reference to the Laws of God, the everlasting ideas on which alone is based the welfare of the world. Here they are to be examined in the light of Christianity itself. If the church be true, many things which seem gainful in the street and expedient in the senate-house, will here be set down as wrong, and all gain which comes therefrom seen to be but a loss. If there be a public sin in the land, if a lie invade the state, it is for the church to give the alarm; it is here that it may war on lies and sins; the more widely they are believed in and practised, the more are they deadly, the more to be opposed. Here let no false idea or false action of the public go without exposure or rebuke. But let no noble heroism of the times, no noble man pass by without due honour. . . .

A Christian church should be a society for promoting true sentiments and ideas. If it would lead, it must go before men; if it would be looked up to, it must stand high.

That is not all: it should be a society for the promotion of good works. . . .

Here are the needy who ask not so much your gold, your bread, or your cloth, as they ask also your sympathy, respect, and counsel; that you assist them to help themselves, that they may have gold won by their industry, not begged out of your benevolence. It is justice more than charity they ask. Every beggar, every pauper, born and bred amongst us, is a reproach to us, and condemns our civilization. For how has it come to pass that in a land of abundance here are men, for no fault of their own, born into want, living in want, and dying of want? and that, while we pretend to a religion which says all men are brothers! There is a horrid wrong somewhere.

Here too are the drunkard, the criminal, the abandoned person, sometimes the foe of society, but far oftener the victim of society. Whence come the tenants of our almshouses, jails, the victims of vice in all our towns? Why, from the lowest rank of the people; from the poorest and most ignorant! Say rather from the most neglected, and the public sin is confessed, and the remedy hinted at. What have the strong been doing all this while, that the weak have come to such a state? Let them answer for themselves.

Now for all these ought a Christian church to toil. It should be a church of good works; if it is a church of good faith it will be so. Does not Christianity say the strong should help the weak? Does not that mean something? It once did. Has the Christian fire faded out from those words, once so marvellously bright? Look round you, in the streets of your own Boston! See the ignorant, men and women with scarce more than the stature of men and women; boys and girls growing up in ignorance and the low civilization which comes thereof, the barbarians of Boston. Their character will one day be a blot and a curse to the nation, and who is to blame? Why, the ablest and best men, who might have had it otherwise if they would. Look at the poor, men of small ability, weak by nature, born into a weak position, therefore doubly weak; men whom the strong use for their purpose, and then cast them off as we throw away the rind of an orange after we have drunk its generous juice. Behold the wicked, so we call the weak men that are publicly caught in the cobweb of the law; ask why they became wicked; how we have aimed to reform them; what we have done to make them respect themselves, to believe in goodness, in man and God? and then say if there is not something for Christian men to do, something for a Christian church to do! Every almshouse in Massachusetts shows that the churches have not done their duty, that the Christians lie lies when they call Jesus "master" and men "brothers!" Every jail is a monument, on which it is writ in letters of iron that we are still heathens, and the gallows, black and hideous, the embodiment of death, the last argument a "Christian" state offers to the poor wretches it trained up to be criminals, stands there, a sign of our infamy; and while it lifts its horrid arm to crush the life out of some miserable man, whose blood cries to God against Cain in the nineteenth century, it lifts that same arm as an index of our shame.

Is that all? Oh, no! Did not Jesus say, resist not evil—with evil? Is not war the worst form of that evil; and is there on earth a nation so greedy of war; a nation more reckless of provoking it; one where the war-horse so soon conducts his foolish rider into fame and power? The "Heathen" Chinese might send their missionaries to America, and teach us to love men! Is that all? Far from it. Did not Christ say, whatsoever you would that men should do unto you, do you even so unto them; and are there not three million brothers of yours and mine in bondage here, the hopeless sufferers of a savage doom; debarred from the civilization of our age, the barbarians of the nineteenth century; shut out from the pretended religion of Christendom, the heathens of a Christian land; chained down from the liberty unalienable in man, the slaves of a Christian republic? Does not a cry of indignation ring out from every legislature in the North; does not the press war with its million throats, and a voice of indignation go up from East and West, out from the hearts of freemen? Oh, no. There is none of that cry against the mightiest sin of this age. The rock of Plymouth, sanctified by the feet which led a nation's way to freedom's large estate, provokes no more voice than the rottenest stone in all the mountains of the West. The few that speak a manly word for truth and everlasting right, are called fanatics; bid be still, lest they spoil the market! Great God! and has it come to this, that men are silent over such a sin? 'Tis even so. Then it must be that every church which dares assume the name of Christ, that dearest name to men, thunders and lightens on this hideous wrong! That is not so. The church is dumb, while the state is only silent; while the servants of the people are only asleep, "God's ministers" are dead!

In the midst of all these wrongs and sins, the crimes of men, society, and the state, amid popular ignorance, pauperism, crime, and war, and slavery too—is the church to say nothing, do nothing; nothing for the good of such as feel the wrong, nothing to save them who do the wrong? Men tell us so, in word and deed; that way alone is "safe!" If I thought so, I would never enter the church but once again, and then to bow my shoulders to their manliest work, to heave down its strong pillars, arch and dome, and roof and wall, steeple and tower, though like Samson I buried myself under the ruins of that temple which profaned the worship of God most high, of God most loved. I would do this in the name of man; in the name of Christ I would do it; yes, in the dear and blessed name of God.

It seems to me that a church which dares name itself Christian, the Church of the Redeemer, which aspires to be a true church, must set itself about all this business, and be not merely a church of theology, but of religion; not of faith only, but of works; a just church by its faith bringing works into life. It should not be a church termagant, which only peevishly scolds at sin, in its anile way; but a church militant against every form of evil, which not only censures, but writes out on the walls of the world the brave example of a Christian life, that all may take pattern therefrom. Thus only can it become the church triumphant. . . .

The church that is to lead this century will not be a church creeping on all fours; mewling and whining, its face turned down, its eyes turned back. It must be full of the brave, manly spirit of the day, keeping also the good of times past. There is a terrific energy in this age, for man was never so much developed, so much the master of himself before. Great truths, moral and political, have come to light. They fly quickly. The iron prophet of types publishes his visions, of weal or woe, to the near and far. This marvellous age has invented steam, and the magnetic telegraph, apt symbols of itself, before which the miracles of fable are but an idle tale. It demands, as never before, freedom for itself, usefulness in its institutions; truth in its teachings, and beauty in its deeds. Let a church have that freedom, that usefulness, truth, and beauty, and the energy of this age will soon be on its side. But the church which did for the fifth century, or the fifteenth, will not do for this. What is well enough at Rome, Oxford, or Berlin, is not well enough for Boston. It must have our ideas, the smell of our ground, and have grown out of the religion in our soul. The freedom of America must be there before this energy will come; the wisdom of the nineteenth century before its science will be on the churches' side, else that science will go over to the "infidels."

Our churches are not in harmony with what is best in the present age. Men call their temples after their old heroes and saints—John, Paul, Peter, and the like. But we call nothing else after the old names; a school of philosophy would be condemned if called Aristotelian, Platonic, or even Baconian. We out-travel the past in all but this. In the church it seems taught there is no progress unless we have all the past on our back; so we despair of having men fit to call churches by. We look back and not forward. We think the next saint must talk Hebrew like the old ones, and repeat the same mythology. So when a new prophet comes we only stone him.

A church that believes only in past inspiration will appeal to old books as the standard of truth and source of light; will be antiquarian in its habits; will call its children by the old names; and war on the new age, not understanding the man-child born to rule the world. A church that believes in inspiration now will appeal to God; try things by reason and conscience; aim to surpass the old heroes; baptize its children with a new spirit, and using the present age will lead public opinion, and not follow it. Had Christ looked back for counsel, he might have founded a church fit for Abraham or Isaac to worship in, not for ages to come, or the age then. He that feels he is near to God, does not fear to be far from men; if before, he helps lead them on; if above, to lift them up. Let us get all we can from the Hebrews and others of old time, and that is much; but still let us be God's free men, not the Gibeonites of the past.

Let us have a church that dares imitate the heroism of Jesus; seek inspiration as he sought it; judge the past as he; act on the present like him; pray as he prayed; work as he wrought; live as he lived. Let our doctrines and our forms fit the soul, as the limbs fit the body, growing out of it, growing with it. Let us have a church for the whole man: truth for the mind; good works for the hands; love for the heart; and for the soul, that aspiring after perfection, that unfaltering faith in God which, like lightning in the clouds[,] shines brightest when elsewhere it is most dark. Let our church fit man, as the heavens fit the earth!

7. Transcendentalism

c. 1850

Nothing is easier to describe or more difficult to define than Transcendentalism. All are familiar with Emerson's essay *The Transcendentalist* (1842) and with his lectures on *Man the Reformer* and the *New England Reformers,* largely devoted to the same subject. It was, indeed, a favorite theme. (Samples of the numerous efforts of the Transcendentalists to define themselves and their beliefs can be found in Perry Miller's anthology *The Transcendentalists.*) Parker, who counted himself an ardent Transcendentalist even though the bent of his mind was in many ways empirical, succeeded as well as anyone in the quest for a definition.

The following essay was written sometime around 1850 but not printed during Parker's lifetime. As an appendix to this more systematic interpretation of Transcendentalism, we add some passages from Parker's sermon on *The Function and Place of Conscience in Relation to the Laws of Men,* which he preached in September 1850.

I

Such is the problem of philosophy, to explain the facts of the universe; such the two departments of philosophy, physics and metaphysics; such the two methods of inquiry, deductive and inductive; such are the two forms of error,—the assumption of a false fact as the starting-point of deduction, the induction of a false fact by the inductive process. Now these methods are of use in each department of philosophy, indispensable in each, in physics and in metaphysics.

This is the problem of metaphysics,—to explain the facts of human consciousness. In metaphysics there are and have long been two schools of philosophers. The first is the sensational school. Its most important metaphysical doctrine is this: There is nothing in the intellect which was not first in the senses. Here "intellect" means the whole intellectual, moral, affectional and religious consciousness of man. The philosophers of this school claim to have reached this conclusion legitimately by the inductive method. It was at first an hypothesis; but after analyzing the facts of consciousness, interrogating all the ideas and sentiments and sensations of man, they say the hypothesis is proved by the most careful induction. They appeal to it as a principle, as a maxim, from which other things are deduced. They say that experience by one or more of the senses is the ultimate appeal in philosophy: all that I know is of sensational origin; the senses are the windows which let in all the light I have; the senses afford a sensation. I reflect upon this, and by reflection transform a sensation into an idea. An idea, therefore, is a transformed sensation. . . .

I come now to the other school. This is distinguished by its chief metaphysical doctrine, that there is in the intellect (or consciousness), something that never was in the senses, to wit, the intellect (or consciousness) itself; that man has faculties which transcend the senses; faculties which give him ideas and intuitions that transcend sensational experience; ideas whose origin is not from sensation, nor their proof from sensation. This is the transcendental school. They maintain that the mind (meaning thereby all which is not sense) is not a smooth tablet on which sensation writes its experience, but is a living principle which of itself originates ideas when the senses present the occasion; that, as there is a body with certain senses, so there is a soul or mind with certain powers which give the man sentiments and ideas. This school maintains that it is a fact of consciousness itself that there is in the intellect somewhat that was not first in the senses; and also that they have analyzed consciousness, and by the inductive method established the conclusion that there is a consciousness that never was sensation, never could be; that our knowledge is in part *a priori;* that we know, 1, certain truths of necessity; 2, certain truths of intuition, or spontaneous consciousness; 3, certain truths of demonstration, a voluntary consciousness; all of these truths not dependent on sensation for cause, origin, or proof. Facts of observation, sensational experience, it has in common with the other school.

Transcendentalism, also, reports itself in the four great departments of human activity—in physics, politics, ethics, religion.

I. In physics it starts with the maxim that the senses acquaint us actually with body, and therefrom the mind gives us the idea of substance, answering to an objective reality. Thus is the certainty of the material world made sure of. Then *a priori* it admits the uniformity of the action of nature; and its laws are *a priori* known to be universal, and not general alone. These two doctrines it finds as maxims resulting from the nature of man, facts given. Then it sets out with other maxims, first truths, which are facts of necessity, known to be such without experience. All the first truths of mathematics are of this character, *e.g.,* that the whole is greater than a part. From these, by the deductive method, it comes at other facts,—facts of demonstration; these also are transcendental, that is, transcend the senses, transcend the facts of observation. For example, the three angles of a triangle are equal to two right angles,—that is universally true; it is a fact of demonstration, and is a deduction from a first truth which is self-evident, a fact of necessity. But here the fact of demonstration transcends the fact of experience, philosophy is truer than sensation. The whole matter of geometry is transcendental. . . .

II. In politics, transcendentalism starts not from experience alone, but from consciousness; not merely from human history, but also from human nature. It does not so much quote precedents, contingent facts of experience, as ideas, necessary facts of consciousness. It only quotes the precedent to obtain or illustrate the idea. It appeals to a natural justice, natural right; absolute justice, absolute right. Now the source and original of this justice and right it finds in God—the conscience of God; the channel through which we receive this justice and right is our own moral sense, our conscience, which is our consciousness of the conscience of God. This conscience in politics and in ethics transcends experience, and *a priori* tells us of the just, the right, the good, the fair; not the relatively right alone, but absolute right also. As it transcends experience, so it anticipates history; and the ideal justice of conscience is juster than the empirical and contingent justice actually exercised at Washington or at Athens, as the ideal circle is rounder than one of the stone-cutter scratches on his rough seal. In transcendental politics the question of expediency is always subordinate to the question of natural right; it asks not merely about the cost of a war, but its natural justice. It aims to organize the ideals of man's moral and social nature into political institutions; to have a government which shall completely represent the facts of man's social consciousness so far as his nature is now developed. But as this development is progressive, so must government be; yet not progressive by revolution, by violence; but by harmonious development, progressive by growth. The transcendental politician does not merely interpret history, and look back to Magna Charta and the Constitution; but into human nature, through to divine nature; and so anticipates history, and in man and God finds the origin and primary source of all just policy, all right legislation. So looking he transcends history.

For example, the great political idea of America, the idea of the Declaration of Independence, is a composite idea made up of three simple ones: 1. Each man is endowed with certain unalienable rights. 2. In respect of these rights all men are equal. 3. A government is to protect each man in the entire and actual enjoyment of all the unalienable rights. Now the first two ideas represent ontological facts, facts of human consciousness; they are facts of necessity. The third is an idea derived from the two others, is a synthetic judgment *a priori;* it was not learned from sensational experience; there never was a government which did this, nor is there now. Each of the other ideas transcended history: every unalienable right has been alienated, still is; no two men have been actually equal in actual rights. Yet the idea is true, capable of proof by human nature, not of verification by experience; as true as the proposition that three angles of a triangle are equal to two right angles; but no more capable of a sensational proof than that. The American Revolution, with American history since, is an attempt to prove by experience this transcendental proposition, to organize the transcendental idea of politics. The idea demands for its organization a democracy—a government of all, for all, and by all; a government by natural justice, by legislation that is divine as much as a true astronomy is divine, legislation which enacts law representing a fact of the universe, a resolution of God. . . .

The transcendental politician does not say that might makes right, but that there is an immutable morality for nations as for men. Legislation must represent that, or the law is not binding on any man. By birth man is a citizen of the universe, subject to God; no oath of allegiance, no king, no parliament, no congress, no people, can absolve him from his natural fealty thereto, and alienate a man born to the rights, born to the duties, of a citizen of God's universe. Society, government, politics come not from a social compact which men made and may unmake, but from a social nature of God's making; a nation is to be self-ruled by justice. In a monarchy, the king holds power as a trust, not a right: in a democracy, the people have it as a right, the majority as a trust; but the minority have lost no right, can alienate none, delegate none beyond power of ultimate recall. A nation has a right to make just laws, binding because just. Justice is the point common to one man and the world of men, the balance-point. A nation is to seek the greatest good of all, not of the greatest number; not to violate the constitution of the universe, not sacrifice the minority to the majority, nor one single man to the whole. But over all human law God alone has eminent domain.

Here too is a danger: the transcendental politician may seek to ignore the past, and scorn its lessons; may take his own personal whims for oracles of human nature; and so he may take counsel from the selfishness of lazy men against the selfishness of active men, counsel from the selfishness of poor men against the selfishness of rich men, and think he hears the voice of justice, or the reverse, as himself is rich or poor, active or idle; there is danger that he be rash and question as hastily in politics as in physics, and reckon without his host, to find that the scot is not free when the day of reckoning comes.

III. In ethics. Transcendentalism affirms that man has moral faculties which lead him to justice and right, and by his own nature can find out what is right and just, and can know it and be certain of it. Right is to be done come what will come. I am not answerable for the consequences of doing right, only of not doing it, only of doing wrong. The conscience of each man is to him the moral standard; so to mankind is the conscience of the race. In morals conscience is complete and reliable as the eye for colors, the ear for sounds, the touch and taste for their purposes. While experience shows what has been or is, conscience shows what should be and shall.

Transcendental ethics look not to the consequences of virtue, in this life or the next, as motive, therefore, to lead men to virtue. That is itself a good, an absolute good, to be loved not for what it brings, but is. It represents the even poise or balance-point between individual and social development. To know what is right, I need not ask what is the current practice, what say the Revised Statutes, what said holy men of old, but what says conscience? what, God? The common practice, the Revised Statutes, the holy men of old are helps, not masters. I am to be co-ordinate with justice.

Conscience transcends experience, and not only explains but anticipates that, and the transcendental system of morals is to be founded on human nature and absolute justice. . . .

IV. In religion. Transcendentalism admits a religious faculty, element, or nature in man, as it admits a moral, intellectual and sensational faculty,—that man by nature is a religious being as well as moral, intellectual, sensational; that this religious faculty is adequate to its purposes and wants, as much so as the others, as the eye acquainting us with light; and that this faculty is the source of religious emotions, of the sentiments of adoration, worship. Through this we have consciousness of God as through the senses consciousness of matter. In connection with reason it gives us the primary ideas of religion, ideas which transcend experience.

Now the transcendental philosophy legitimates the ideas of religion by reference to human nature. Some of them it finds truths of necessity, which cannot be conceived of as false or unreal without violence to reason; some it finds are truths of consciousness,—of spontaneous consciousness, or intuition; some, truths of voluntary consciousness, or demonstration, inductive or deductive. Such ideas, capable of this legitimation, transcend experience, require and admit no further proof; as true before experience as after; true before time, after time, eternally; absolutely true. On that rock transcendentalism founds religion, sees its foundation, and doubts no more of religious truths than of the truths of mathematics. All the truths of religion it finds can be verified in consciousness today, what cannot is not religion. But it does not neglect experience. In human history it finds confirmations, illustrations, of the ideas of human nature, for history represents the attempt of mankind to develop human nature. So then as transcendentalism in philosophy legitimates religion by a reference to truths of necessity, to truths of consciousness, it illustrates religion by facts of observation, facts of testimony. . . .

Transcendentalism has a work to do, to show that physics, politics, ethics, religion rest on facts of necessity, facts of intuition, facts of demonstration, and have their witness and confirmation in facts of observation. It is the work of transcendentalism to give us politics which represent God's thought of a state,—the whole world, each man free; to give us morals which leave the man a complete individual, no chord rent from the human harp,—yet complete in his social character, no string discordant in the social choir; to give us religion worthy of God and man,—free goodness, free piety, free thought. That is not to be done by talking at random, not by idleness, not by railing at authority, calumniating the past or the present; not by idle brains with open mouth, who outrage common sense; but by diligent toil, brave discipline, patience to wait, patience to work. Nothing comes of nothing, foolishness of fools; but something from something, wise thought from thinking men; and of the wise thought comes a lovely deed, life, laws, institutions for mankind.

The problem of transcendental philosophy is no less than this, to revise the experience of mankind and try its teachings by the nature of mankind; to test ethics by conscience, science by reason; to try the creeds of the churches, the constitutions of the states by the constitution of the universe; to reverse what is wrong, supply what is wanting, and command the just. To do this in a nation like ours, blinded still by the sensational philosophy, devoted chiefly to material interests, its politics guided by the madness of party more than sober reason; to do this in a race like the Anglo-Saxon, which has an obstinate leaning to a sensational philosophy, which loves facts of experience, not ideas of consciousness, and believes not in the First-Fair, First-Perfect, First-Good, is no light work; not to be taken in hand by such as cannot bear the strife of tongues, the toil, the heat, the war of thought; not to be accomplished by a single man, however well-born and well-bred; not by a single age and race. It has little of history behind, for this philosophy is young. It looks to a future, a future to be made; a church whose creed is truth, whose worship love; a society full of industry and abundance, full of wisdom, virtue, and the poetry of life; a state with unity among all, with freedom for each; a church without tyranny, a society without ignorance, want, or crime, a state without oppression; yes, a world with no war among the nations to consume the work of their hands, and no restrictive policy to hinder the welfare of mankind. That is the human dream of the transcendental philosophy. Shall it ever become a fact? History says, No; human nature says, Yes.

II

There are some things which are true, independent of all human opinions. Such things we call facts. Thus it is true that one and one are equal to two, that the earth moves round the sun, that all men have certain natural unalienable rights, rights which a man can alienate only for himself, and not for another. No man made these things true; no man can make them false. If all the men in Jerusalem and ever so many more, if all the men in the world, were to pass a unanimous vote that one and one were not equal to two, that the earth did not move round the sun, that all men had not natural and unalienable rights, the opinion would not alter the fact, nor make truth false and falsehood true.

So there are likewise some things which are right, independent of all human opinions. Thus it is right to love a man and not to hate him, to do him justice and not injustice, to allow him the natural rights which he has not alienated. No man made these things right; no man can make them wrong. If all the men in Jerusalem and ever so many more, if all the men in the world, were to pass a unanimous vote that it was right to hate a man and not love him, right to do him injustice and not justice, right to deprive him of his natural rights not alienated by himself, the opinion would not alter the fact, nor make right wrong and wrong right.

There are certain constant and general facts which occur in the material world, the world of external perception, which represent what are called the laws of matter, in virtue of which things take place so and not otherwise. These laws are the same everywhere and always; they never change. They are not made by men, but only discovered by men, are inherent in the constitution of matter, and seem designed to secure the welfare of the material world. These natural laws of matter, inherent in its constitution, are never violated, nor can be, for material nature is passive, or at least contains no element or will that is adverse to the will of God, the ultimate Cause of these laws as of matter itself. The observance of these laws is a constant fact of the universe; "the most ancient heavens thereby are fresh and strong." These laws represent the infinity of God in the world of matter, His infinite power, wisdom, justice, love, and holiness.

So there are likewise certain constant and general facts which occur in what may be called the spiritual world, the world of internal consciousness. They represent the laws of spirit—that is, of the human spirit—in virtue of which things are designed to take place so and not otherwise. These laws are the same everywhere and always; they never change. They are not made by men, but only discovered by men. They are inherent in the constitution of man, and as you cannot conceive of a particle of matter without extension, impenetrability, figure, and so on, no more can you conceive of man without these laws inhering in him. They seem designed to secure the welfare of the spiritual world. They represent the infinity of God in the world of man, His infinite power, wisdom, justice, love, and holiness. But while matter is stationary, bound by necessity, and man is progressive and partially free, to the extent of a certain tether, so it is plain that there may be a will in the world of man adverse to the will of God, and thus the laws of man's spirit may be violated to a certain extent. The laws of matter depend for their execution only on the infinite will of God, and so cannot be violated. The laws of man depend for their execution also on the finite will of man, and so may be broken.

8. The Position and Duty of a Minister

1852

In the six years after Parker took up his duties in Boston, the Twenty-Eighth Congregational Society grew to be one of the largest and most flourishing in the country. Every Sunday, hundreds—and sometimes thousands—tried to throng into the old Melodeon, which was quite inadequate for a parish of such dimensions. In 1852 the congregation moved to the commodious Music Hall; on the occasion of that move, Parker gave an account of his ministry in the form of two sermons, *Some Account of My Ministry* and *Of the Position and Duty of a Minister*. The second of these is presented here.

It is relevant to note that, while many dissenting Unitarians left the church—Emerson, Ripley and Pierpont come to mind—Parker stubbornly refused to be driven out or to resign. He was a scholar, a publicist, an editor and something of a politician; but he was, above all, a minister and delighted in the ministry.

It is idle to say the minister must not meddle with practical things. If the sun is to shine in heaven, it must look into the street, and the shop, and the cellar; it must burnish with lovely light a filing of gold in the jeweller's shop, and it must illuminate the straggling straw in a farmer's yard. And just so religion, which communes with God with one hand, must lay the other on every human duty. So you see the relation which the minister must sustain to the great works of man, to political and commercial activity, to literature, and to society in general.

The State is a machine to work for the advantage of a special nation, for its material welfare alone, by means of certain restricted sentiments and ideas limited to that work, written in a Constitution, which is the norm of the statutes; by means of statute laws, which are the norm of domestic and social conduct. So the Legislature makes statutes for the material welfare of the majority of that nation; the Judiciary decides that the statutes conform to the Constitution; the Executive enforces the statutes, and the people obey. When the State has done this, it has done everything which its idea demands of it at the present day.

Now, the minister is to represent, not America, not England, not France alone, but the human nature of all mankind; and see that his nation harms no other nation; that the majority hinders no minority, however small; that it brings the weight of its foot upon no single man, never so little. He must see that the material comfort of to-day is not got at the cost of man's spiritual welfare for to-day, to-morrow, and eternity. So he is to try every statute of men by the law of God; the Constitution of America by the Constitution of the Universe. National measures he must try by universal principles; and if a measure does not square with the abstract true and the abstract right, does not conform to the will and the law of God,—then he must cry out, "Away with it!" Statesmen look at political economy; and they ask of each measure, "Will it pay, here and now?" The minister must look for political morality, and ask, "Is it right in the eyes of God?" So you see that at once the pulpit becomes a very near neighbour to the State-house; and the minister must have an eye to correct and guide the politicians. He must warn men to keep laws that are just, warn them to break laws that are wicked; and, as they reverence the dear God, never to bow before an idol of statesmen or the State.

Then he must have an eye to the business of the nation; and while the trader asks only, "What merchandise can we make?" the minister must also ask, "What men shall we become?" Both the politicians and the merchant are wont to use men as mere tools, for the purposes of politics and trade, heedless of what comes, by such conduct, to their human instruments. The minister is to see to it, that man is never subordinated to money, morality never put beneath expediency, nor eternity sacrificed to to-day. The slave-trade was once exceedingly profitable to Newport and Liverpool, and was most eminently "respectable." But the minister is to ask for its effects on men; the men that traffic, and the trafficked men. Once it was as disreputable in a certain church in this city to preach against slave-buying in Guinea and slave-selling in Cuba, as it is now to preach against slave-taking in Boston or New Orleans. The spirit of modern commerce is sometimes as hostile to the higher welfare of the people as the spirit of ancient war: both Old and New England have abundantly proved this in the present century.

The minister is to look also at the character of literature; to warn men of the bad, and guide them to the good. At this day the power of the press is exceedingly great for good or for evil. In America, thank God, it is a free press; and no wicked censor lays his hand on any writer's page. See what a great expansion the press has got: what was a private thought one night in a senator's heart, is the next day a printed page, spread before the eyes of a million men. The press is an irresponsible power, and needs all the more to be looked after; and who is there to look after it, if not the minister that reverences the great God?

Then the minister is to study nicely the general conduct of society, and seek to guide men from mere desire to the solemn counsels of duty; to check the redundance of appetite in the period of passion, and the redundance of ambition in the more dangerous period of calculation; to guard men against sudden gusts of popular frenzy.

The great concerns of education come also beneath the minister's eye; and while the press, business, and politics keep the lower understanding intensely active and excessively developed, he is to guide men to the culture of reason, imagination, conscience, the affections, and the soul; is to show them a truth far above the forum and the market's din; is to lead them to justice and to love, and to enchant their eyes with the beauty of the infinite God. The minister of absolute religion must be the schoolmaster for the loftier intellect and the conscience; the teacher of a philanthropy that knows no distinction of colour or of race; the teacher of a faith in God which never shrinks from obedience to His law.

In society, as yet, there is still a large mass of "heathenism," —I mean of scorn for that which is spiritual in the body, and immortal in the soul; a contempt for the feeble, hatred against the unpopular transgressor, a contempt for justice, a truckling to expediency, and a cringing to men of large understanding and colossal wickedness. Hence, in the nation there is a perishing class three and thirty hundred thousand strong, held as slaves. In all our great cities there is another perishing class, goaded by poverty, oppressed by crime. The minister is to be an especial guardian and benefactor of the neglected, the oppressed, the poor; eyes to the ignorant, and conscience and self-respect to the criminal. He is not to represent merely the gallows and the jail: he is to represent the spirit of the man who "came to save that which was lost," and the infinite goodness of God, who sends this sunlight on you and me, as well as on better men.

Then, in all our great cities, there is one deep, and dark, and ghastly pit of corruption, whereinto, from all New-England's hills, there flows down what was once as fair and as pure and as virgin-fresh as the breath of maiden morn. It is the standing monument which shows the actual position of woman in modern society; that men regard her as the vehicle of their comfort and the instrument of their lust,—not a person, only a thing! The minister, remembering who it was that drew Moses out of the river Nile, and who washed the feet of one greater than Moses with her own tears, and wiped them with her hair, must not forget this crime, its consequences, which contaminate society, and its cause afar off,—contempt and scorn for woman: that is its cause.

In all this you see how different is the position and function of the minister of absolute religion from that of the mere priest. In Russia the few hold down the many, and the priest says nothing against it. He is there only to appease God, to administer salvation, to communicate Scripture; not to teach morality and piety. In America the many hold down the few,—the twenty millions chain the three; and the priest says nothing against it. What does he care? He goes on appeasing the wrath of God, administering salvation, explaining and communicating Scripture, and turns round and says: "This is all just as it should be, a part of the revelation, salvation, and sacraments too; come unto me, and believe, and be baptized with water." But the minister of absolute religion is to hold a different speech. He is to say: "My brethren, hold there! Stop your appeasing of God!—wait till God is angry. Stop your imputing of righteousness! There is no salvation in that. Stop your outcry of 'Believe, believe, believe?' Turn round and put an end to this hateful oppression, and tread it under your feet; and then come before your God with clean hands, and offer your gift. That is your sacrifice." . . .

The churches decline. All over New-England they decline. They cannot draw the rich, nor drive the poor, as once they did of old. Why is it so? They have an idea which is behind the age; a theology that did very well for the seventeenth century, but is feeble in the nineteenth. Their science is not good science; you must take it on faith, not knowledge: it does not represent a fact. Their history is not good history: it does not represent man, but old dreams of miracles. They have an idea of God which is not adequate to the purposes of science or philanthropy, and yet more valueless for the purposes of piety. Hence men of science turn off with contempt from the God of the popular theology; the philanthropists can only loathe a Deity who dooms mankind to torture. And will you ask deeply pious men to love the popular idea of God? Here are in Boston a hundred ministers: you would hardly know it except by the calendar. Many of them are good, kind, well-conducted, well-mannered men, with rather less than the average of selfishness, and rather more than the average of charity. But how little do they bring to pass? Drunkenness reels through all the streets, and shakes their pulpit; the Bible rocks; but they have nothing to say, though it rock over. The kidnapper seizes his prey, and they have excuses for the stealer of men, but cannot put up a prayer for his victim; nay, would drive the fugitive from their own door. What is the reason? Blame them not. They are "ordained to appease the wrath of God," to "administer salvation" in wine or water, to "communicate and explain a miraculous revelation." They do not think that religion is piety and morality: it is belief in the Scriptures; compliance with the ritual. This is the cause which paralyzes the churches of New-England and all the North. The clergy are better than their creed. But who can work well with a poor tool?

Well, my friends, it is to this pulpit that I have come. This is my function, such are my means. There was never such a time for preaching as this nineteenth century,—so full of vigour, enterprise, activity; so full of hardy-headed men. There was never such a time to speak in, such a people to speak to. In no country could I have so fair "a chance to be heard" as you have given me.

9. The Character of the American Church

1857

Parker contributed generously to *The Dial* and to his own magazine, *The Massachusetts Quarterly Review*. After the demise of the *Review* in 1850, he lacked an organ, and most of his speeches, addresses and sermons were published as pamphlets. The newly founded *Atlantic Monthly* belonged to the Brahmin wing of Boston, rather than to what might be called the Transcendental—to Holmes, Lowell and Ticknor, rather than to Bancroft, or Alcott, or Parker. Yet Parker was not excluded, and the first volume of the new journal carried his essay on the only preacher who rivaled him in popularity and influence— Henry Ward Beecher.

Parker had long been familiar with the extraordinary Beecher family. As a student at the Harvard Divinity School, he had walked into Boston on Sundays to hear the great Lyman Beecher thunder against heterodoxy and infidelity at the Hanover Street Church. "A year of his preaching about finished all my respect for the Calvinistic scheme of theology," he wrote later. Parker was not really sympathetic to the younger Beecher either, and his interpretation of him lacks penetration or warmth. What is interesting in this essay, however, are the observations on the grand divisions of the "ministerial army"—the church militant, the church termagant and the church beneficent. Parker himself was popularly supposed to represent the first of these divisions, but he preferred to think of himself as a leader in the third.

There are more than thirty thousand preachers in the United States, whereof twenty eight thousand are Protestants, the rest Catholics,—one minister to a thousand men. They make an exceeding great army,—mostly serious, often self-denying and earnest. . . .

This ministerial army may be separated into three divisions. First, the church militant, the fighting church, as the ecclesiastical dictionaries define it. Reverend men serve devoutly in its ranks. Their work is negative, oppositional. Under various banners, with diverse and discordant war-cries, trumpets braying a certain or uncertain sound, and weapons of strange pattern, though made of trusty steel, they do battle against the enemy. What shots from antique pistols, matchlocks, from crossbows and catapults, are let fly at the foe! Now the champion attacks "New Views," "Ultraism," "Neology," "Innovation," "Discontent," "Carnal Reason"; then he lays lance in rest, and rides valiantly upon "Unitarianism," "Popery," "Infidelity," "Atheism," "Deism," "Spiritualism"; and though one by one he runs them through, yet he never quite slays the evil one;—the severed limbs unite again, and a new monster takes the old one's place. It is serious men who make up the church militant,—grim, earnest, valiant. If mustered in the ninth century, there had been no better soldiers nor elder.

Next is the church termagant. They are the scolds of the church-hold, terrible from the beginning hitherto. Their work is denouncing; they have always a burden against something. Obsta decisis is their motto,—"Hate all that is agreed upon." When the "contrary-minded" are called for, the church termagant holds up its hand. A turbulent people, and a troublesome, are these sons of thunder,—a brotherhood of universal come-outers. Their only concord is disagreement. It is not often, perhaps, that they have better thoughts than the rest of men, but a superior aptitude to find fault; their growling proves, "not that themselves are wise, but others weak." So their pulpit is a brawling-tub, "full of sound and fury, signifying nothing." They have a deal of thunder, and much lightning, but no light, nor any continuous warmth, only spasms of heat. Odi presentem laudare absentem,—the Latin tells their story. They come down and trouble every Bethesda in the world, but heal none of the impotent folk. To them,

> "Of old things, all are over old,
> Of new things, none is new enough."

They have a rage for fault-finding, and betake themselves to the pulpit as others are sent to Bedlam. Men of all denominations are here, and it is a deal of mischief they do,—the worst, indirectly, by making a sober man distrust the religious faculty they appeal to, and set his face against all mending of anything, no matter how badly it is broken. These Theudases, boasting themselves to be somebody, and leading men off to perish in the wilderness, frighten every sober man from all thought of moving out of his bad neighborhood or seeking to make it better. But this is a small portion of the ecclesiastic host. Let us be tolerant to their noise and bigotry.

Last of all is the church beneficient or constructant. Their work is positive,—critical of the old, creative also of the new. They take hold of the strongest of all human faculties,—the religious,—and use this great river of God, always full of water, to moisten hill-side and meadow, to turn lonely saw-mills, and drive the wheels in great factories, which make a metropolis of manufactures,—to bear alike the lumberman's logs and the trader's ships to their appointed place; the stream feeding many a little forget-me-not, as it passes by. Men of all denominations belong to this church catholic; yet all are of one *persuasion,* the brotherhood of humanity,—for the one spirit loves manifoldness of form. They trouble themselves little about sin, the universal but invisible enemy whom the church termagant attempts to shell and dislodge; but are very busy in attacking sins. These ministers of religion would rout drunkenness and want, ignorance, idleness, lust, covetousness, vanity, hate, and pride,—vices of instinctive passion or reflective ambition. Yet the work of these men is to build up; they cut down the forest and scare off the wild beasts only to replace them with civil crops,—cattle, corn, and men. Instead of the howling wilderness, they would have the village or the city, full of comfort and wealth and musical with knowledge and with love. How often are they misunderstood! Some savage hears the ring of the axe, the crash of falling timber, or the rifle's crack and the drop of wolf or bear, and cries out, "A destructive and dangerous man; he has no reverence for the ancient wilderness, but would abolish it and its inhabitants; away with him!" But look again at this destroyer, and in place of the desert woods, lurked in by a few wild beasts and wilder men, behold, a whole New England of civilization has come up! The minister of this Church of the Good Samaritans delivers the poor that cry, and the fatherless, and him that hath none to help him; he makes the widow's heart sing for joy, and the blessing of such as are ready to perish comes on him; he is eyes to the blind, feet to the lame; the cause of evil which he knows not he searches out; breaking the jaws of the wicked to pluck one spirit out of their teeth. In a world of work, he would have no idler in the market-place; in a world of bread, he would not eat his morsel alone while the fatherless has nought; nor would he see any perish for want of clothing. He knows the wise God made man for a good end, and provided adequate means thereto; so he looks for them where they were placed, in the world of matter and of men, not outside of either. So while he entertains every old truth, he looks out also into the crowd of new opinions, hoping to find others of their kin; and the new thought does not lodge in the street; he opens his doors to the traveler, not forgetful to entertain strangers,—knowing that some have also thereby entertained angels unawares. He does not fear the great multitude, nor does the contempt of a few families make him afraid.

10. The Religion Which Is Needed

1858

The depression years 1857 and 1858 witnessed a widespread religious revival in America—a revival that affected even the staid Unitarian church. In April 1858, Parker preached two sermons on the revival: *A False and True Revival of Religion* and *The Revival of Religion Which We Need.* In the current revival, he said, "there is much that is encouraging . . . [but] in the conduct of it there is much profoundly melancholy."

In the following selection (from the latter sermon), Parker indicates the revival that he feels is really needed, a revival which would stir the conscience of the nation with reference to the great sins of the day—slavery, crime, vice, corruption and war. Here was a program for the (by now) thirty thousand Protestant ministers and the two thousand Catholic priests: to arouse the conscience of the nation as Jesus had aroused the conscience of his time.

How much we need a real revival of religion! Not a renewal of ecclesiastic theology, but a revival of piety and morality in men's hearts.

The people *feel* this need; hence we turn off to look at all new things in religion. We are tired of that old stack of hard, dry, meadow hay, where the Christian herd has so long sought fodder, and been filled with the east wind. We long for the green pastures and sweet grass along the streams which run among the hills; hence we wish to leap over or crawl under or crowd through the bars of this old winter cowyard of the church, and at least get out of that unwholesome pen and go somewhere, with God to guide us, though we know not whither.

See the growth of Mormonism. Even that has something which mankind needs; else men, and especially women, would not cross the sea three thousand miles wide, and then travel three thousand more by river or by land for its sake. The success of Mormonism is a terrible protest against the enforced celibacy of millions of marriageable women, and the worse than celibacy of so many who are called married, but are not. Fifteen years ago

"Spiritualism" was two women making mysterious noises in Rochester, New York. Now it is I know not how many millions of persons, some of them thoughtful, many hungering after God. "Spiritualism" had something to offer which the churches could not give. Nothing comes of nothing; every something has a cause. This very revival, foolish as is the conduct of it, selfish as are the managers who pull the strings,—with the people it indicates a profound discontent in the dull death of our churches. God created man a living soul, and he continues such only by feeding on every word which freshly proceedeth out of the mouth of God. The old bibles did for those who wrote them; the old creeds for such as believed. We want the help of the old bibles, the inspiration of the new bibles, ever proceeding from God, who freshly fills the old stars in heaven, and creates new flowers every spring on earth.

I say the people feel this need; but the need itself is greater and deeper than the popular consciousness thereof. We do not know how sick we are. Look at the chaotic state of things in America, which is but like the rest of Christendom. First, there is war. Fenced with a two-fold oceanic ditch, from two to seven thousand miles wide, we yet spend more than thirty millions of dollars every year to hire fighting men, in a time of profound peace; and not one of them fixes bayonet to do mankind good.

Next consider the character of the Federal Government—it is the last place to which you would look for common honesty, for justice to our own nation; just now it is a vulture which eats the nation's vitals out; only the strong giant grows faster than this administration can tear off and swallow down. Men tell us human life is more safe in Constantinople, in Damascus, in Samarcand, in Timbuctoo, than it is in Washington. We are told that we have three murders a fortnight in the capital of the United States, all the session through. The Government is so busy fillibustering against Cuba, Mexico, Central America, planting slavery in Kansas, that it cannot protect the lives of its own Congress men in its own capital.

Next look at slavery. Every seventh man is property—a negro slave; and our Supreme Court says coloured people have no rights which we are bound to respect. The Government seeks to spread this blot across the continent, from east to west, from south to north—asks five thousand new soldiers to do it with. A new State knocks at the door seeking to join the sisterhood of freedom; the Government says, "You shall not come in free; with bondsmen you may enter."

Fourth: Look at the antagonistic character of our civilization. So much poverty in the midst of so much riches—so many idlers in so much industry. How many children in prudent, wealthy, charitable Boston, cannot go to school in winter from lack of clothes! See what fortunes are dishonestly made by men who are only the fillibusters of commerce, robbers in a peaceful way! Our industry even now is a war of business—it is competition, not co-operation. How much power is lost in the friction of our social machinery. There are savages in our civilization. In the south, many of them are slaves—in the north, they are free; but still savages. A black sea of crime lashes the white houses of wealth and comfort, where science, literature, virtue, and piety together dwell.

Fifth: Look at the condition of woman. There is no conscious antagonism betwixt men and women; each doubtless unconsciously aims to be more than fair to the other; but nowhere has woman her natural right. In the market, the state, the church, she is not counted the equal of man. Hence come monstrous evils —prostitution, dependence, lack of individual character, enforced celibacy, not more grateful to maid than to man, meant for neither him nor her; and hence come those marriages which are worse than celibacy itself.

These are the five great evils of mankind to-day, whence many lesser ones proceed—drunkenness, crime in its thousand forms. I do not speak to scold mankind, still less to scold America. In all respects save one, we have the best institutions in the world; and certainly, the human race had never so glorious a welfare as to-day. These evils, they were never before so small. History, it is not a retreat backwards, it is progress forth, upwards, on. These things are not a finality; they are to man's attainable condition what stumbling is to walking, stammering to speech, the boy's clumsy, mistaken scrawl to the clear current writing of the man. We are to outlearn these five evils—war, wicked government, slavery, selfish antagonism in society, the degradation of woman. We shall outgrow these things. God has given us the fittest of all possible means for attaining the end. One of the mightiest of man's helpers is this religious faculty in us; this, nothing else, can give us strength to do that work.

The business of the farmer is to organize the vegetative force of the ground, and raise thence the substances which shall feed and clothe mankind. The mechanic is to organize the force of metals, wood, fire, earth, water, lightning, air, and thereby shape the material things necessary to human needs—to feed, clothe, house, and heal mankind; corn he must turn to bread, cotton and wool to cloth, the clay, the forest, the rock, to houses; poison to medicine. The philosopher is to translate the facts of nature, from matter into mind, making them into thoughts, ideas of consciousness; then to show us how to use the powers of nature for the farmer's and mechanic's work. The statesman is to organize the nation's power, its matter and its mind, its bodily force, its wealth, intelligence, justice, love, charity, religion, so that men shall live in peace together at home, with peace abroad, having security for the person, the substance of manhood, and for property, the accident of manhood; so that each shall help all, and all enjoy the special genius God gives to each.

It is the business of the minister to waken, quicken, strengthen, and guide the religious faculty, and so gain for us a great general power to help the individual man in his development of body and of spirit. But man is social. The individual alone is a wild man; it is only in society that noble individualism is instantially possible. While these five evils just named continue, individual men will be as now. It is in the great social mill that men are made what they are. Here and there may be one so born, that society cannot shape, bleach, or dye him. He takes no form or colour, save from his mother's bosom; he has an impenetrable genius from his birth,—plastic to mould others, not pliant, to be shaped or dyed. But in ninety-nine hundredths of our character most men are what society makes them. . . .

It is the minister's business not only to waken, strengthen, and quicken the religious power, and point to this end, but also to diffuse the ideas which shall mould society, so that it can rear noble men, with all their natural powers developed well.

The minister is the teacher of the church; not a master; a servant to teach. A normal church is a body of men, assembling to promote religion, piety, and morality. Its business is, first, protective at home—to promote piety and morality in its own members; and, second, it is diffusive abroad—to promote piety and morality in all the world according to its strength: for duty is proportionate to power to do; and where the power is little, so is the duty, where much, there great. So a church must protest against all wrong which it knows to be wrong; promote all right which it knows to be right. It is a church for that very purpose, and nothing less. The minister is to help do that work; to lead in it. He must be in advance of mankind in what pertains to religion—to all religion, individual, social. Else he cannot teach; he is no minister to work and serve, only an idler to be worked for and ministered unto.

No doubt there must be primary churches, to teach the A B C of religion, and ministers fit for that work of nursing babies; and also academic and collegiate churches, and ministers for that grand function. Let neither despise the other. So, then, the function of a real church of religion will be partly critical, to war against the wrong, partly creative, to show us the right and guide us thither, at least thither-ward.

We have thirty thousand Protestant ministers in the United States, supported at the public charge, and to do this very work, for so the people mean. They are not rich; are not rich men's sons. As a class, they have an education which is costly, even where it is not precious; which is often paid for directly by the people's work. All education is thus paid for indirectly, for in that money all human accounts are at last settled, in the great clearing-house of mankind. Work is the only coin which is current the world over. Therein do you pay for the murders which are committed at Washington, and for the angels of mercy, who in Boston carry your beneficence from house to house, and take unlawful babies newly born, and set them in religious homes, to grow up to nobleness. In that coin we pay for all things,—the minister's education amongst others. The ministers come mainly from that class of people who are most affected by religious emotions and ideas, where human sympathies are the strongest. They seldom are borne by the miserably poor, or the ruinously rich. They have two advantages: birth in the middle class, where they touch the ground and touch the sky; and superior culture above that class. Add to this, moreover, they commonly enter the ministry with good motives, more self-denial than self-indulgence; they are usually free from gross vices, the crimes of passion; they are the most charitable of alms-giving men; they have the best opportunities to teach the churches, and to help promote the critical and creative function which belongs thereto.

But now, alas! taken as a class, they do no such thing,—they attempt none such. They do not count it their business to remove any one of those five great social evils, and so enable society to raise up noble individual men. Nay, they seldom take much pains to remove the lesser evils which have leaked out from those five great tubs of malarious poison. Let the prayers of the Protestant churches be answered to-night; let all the white men and women in the United States be converted to the ecclesiastic theology which is taught in orthodox meeting-houses; let the conversion take in all the babies who know their right hand from their left—suppose there are fifteen millions who are "brought under," and "bowed down," as they properly call it, and made to believe in the creeds of the revival ministers; let all these be added to the church next Sunday, and take their communion of baker's bread and grocer's wine,—it would not abate one of those five great evils—war, political corruption, slavery, selfish antagonism in society, nor the degradation of woman! Such a conversion is not a step towards removing any one of these evils—nay, it is a step away from that work. Such a conversion would entail inferiority on a woman; retard the progress of civilization, the moralization of mankind; add to the fetters of the slave; strengthen the tyrant's hand; increase the chances of prospective war, and add to its horrors when it broke out. For it would bless all these iniquities in the name of God, and justify them out of the Old Testament and the New—it is quite easy to do so. Nay, suppose you should convert the three millions of African slaves over ten years old, not one of them would dare thereafter to run away from his master, or strike that master down. Such conversions would unman the negro slave!

Why is all this? Two months ago I spoke of the false method of theology. The Christian church has followed that method, and while teaching many truths and doing very great service to mankind—which I should be the last to deny—it has made three monstrous errors. Here they are.

First, it has a false conception of God;—its God is a devil, who means damnation.

Second, it has a false conception of man;—its man is a worm, who is religiously good for nothing; the "natural man" fit only for damnation.

Third, it has a false conception of religion;—its religion is to save men from hell, and it is fit only for that. But it does not do even that for more than one out of a thousand; for the other nine hundred and ninety-nine it is absolutely good for nothing on earth or beneath it; and the one saved is not borne to heaven on mighty wings of piety and morality, fanning the thin, cold air of the world, but by the magic-miracle of the atonement, which turns off God's wrath, and carries man into eternal joy which he has done nothing to merit and to earn. . . .

We want a revival of religion in the American church which shall be to the church what the religion of Jesus was to heathenism and Judaism, which, though useful once, in his day had served out their time, and had no more that they could do. We do not want a religion hierarchically organized, which shall generate nothing but meeting-houses made of stone, and end at last in a priesthood. We want a religion democratically organized, generating great political, social, domestic institutions, and ending in a world full of noble men and women, all their faculties developed well, they serving God with that love which casts out fear.

How can we stir that element to emotions fit for such a work? Only by a theology which shall meet the people's want, a natural and just idea of man, of God, of the relation between them—of religion, life, duty, destination on earth and in heaven; a theology which has its evidences in the world of matter,—all science God's testimony thereto; and in the world of consciousness,—every man bearing within him the "lively oracles" the present witness of his God, his duty and destination. No sect has such a theology; no great sect aims at such, or the life it leads to. . . .

If a minister is filled with this religion, it will not let him rest. He must speak, whether men hear or whether they forbear. No fear can scare, no bribe can charm, no friends can coax him down. The church, the state, the world oppose him, all in vain. "Get thee behind me," he quietly says; and while Satan goes from this other son of man in his triumph, angels come and minister to him. He may have small talents; it matters not. The new power of his religious idea comes into him, and one such man "can chase a thousand, and two ten thousand put to flight." Nay, he gets inspiration from God. He makes the axis of his little glass parallel with the axis of God, and the perpendicular Deity shines through with concentrated light and heat.

What if there were one such minister in each of the three hundred and seventy towns in this State—what a revival would they make in Massachusetts! What an increase of economy, industry, riches! What a growth of temperance, education, justice, love, in all its forms,—filial, friendly, related, connubial, parental, patriotic, philanthropic love! What if all the thirty thousand Protestant ministers, and the two thousand Catholic priests, in the United States, had such religion—worked with such theological ideas of man, God, duty, destination! There would never be another war, staining America with blood; filibustering would be impossible; political oppression, it would not continue a week, the people would not choose a magistrate in the day time whom they must hire watchers to sit up and look after all night, lest he do mischief; a wicked ruler would be as impossible as a ghost in the day time. Slavery would end before the fourth of July, and on Independence day, the mayor of the city might tell the rear admiral of the Turks, "My dear sir, we are converted, and as good as African Mahommedans, and there is not a slave in all the United States. Boston has become almost as Christian as Tunis or Algiers!" What a change would come over the structure of society! Co-operative industry would take the place of selfish antagonism. How would that flower of womanhood expand with fairer, sweeter, and more prophetic bloom! How would the nation's wealth increase! What education of all—what welfare now, what progress for the future! What a generation of sons and daughters would this people raise up! Ay, what missionaries should we send abroad, not to preach ignorance to the heathen, who have enough of it already, but to carry the light of the gospel of life to the nations that "sit in darkness and in the shadow of death!"

11. Delight in Religion

1858

This almost ecstatic confession of delight in religion is taken from a sermon delivered to the Progressive Friends, a Quaker congregation in Chester County, Pennsylvania, in 1858.

I have swum in clear, sweet waters all my days; and if sometimes they were a little cold, and the stream ran adverse and something rough, it was never too strong to be breasted and swam through. From the days of earliest boyhood, when I went stumbling through the grass, "as merry as a May bee," up to the grey-bearded manhood of this time, there is none but has left me honey in the hive of memory that I now feed on for present delight. When I recall the years of boyhood, youth, early manhood, I am filled with a sense of sweetness and wonder that such little things can make a mortal so exceedingly rich! But I must confess that the chiefest of all my delights is still the religious. This is the lowest down, the inwardest of all—it is likewise highest up. What delight have I in my consciousness of God, the certainty of His protection, of His infinite love? God loves me as my natural mother never did, nor could, nor can, even now, with the added beatitudes of wellnigh two-score years in heaven. How the religious disposition inclines the little boy or girl to veneration and gratitude, virtues which in the child are what good-breeding is in the full-grown gentleman, giving a certain air of noble birth and well-bred superiority! There is a Jacob's ladder for our young pilgrim, whereon he goes up from his earthly mother, who manages the little room he sleeps in, to the dear Heavenly Mother, who never slumbers nor sleeps, who is never careful nor troubled about anything, but yet cares continually for the great housekeeping of all the world, giving likewise to her beloved even in their sleep. In the child it is only the faint twilight, the beginning, of religion which you take notice of, like the voice of the blue bird and the Phœbe, coming early in March, but only as a prelude to that whole summer of joyous song which, when the air is delicate, will ere long gladden and beautify the procreant nest.

117

III

Social and Moral Reform

"In the history of the world the doctrine of reform never had such scope as at the present hour," wrote Emerson in 1844. "We are to revise the whole of our social structure—the state, the school, religion, marriage, trade, science, and explore the foundations in our own nature." It was indeed a day of universal reform, of infinite hope and infinite discontent, when every institution was called before the bar of reason and of faith and required to justify itself. "A restless, prying, conscientious criticism broke out in unexpected quarters," Emerson added. This essay might almost have been written about Parker, except that it came a year or two before Parker got into his stride—and that once Parker was under way, his pulpit could by no stretch of the language be called an "unexpected" quarter. Parker was, on the contrary, the very archetype of the New England reformer.

The reform movement of which Parker was so eloquent a spokesman and so vigorous a champion was rooted in religion and philosophy, in the religion of liberal Unitarianism and the philosophy of Transcendentalism. God is benign; Nature, beneficient; man, divine—if these things are true, then every denial of God's benevolence, every violation of man's divinity, every deviation from virtue, is contrary to true religion. But if philosophy and religion taught that the imperfections of man and of society were contrary to God's will, did they also teach that these imperfections should be healed? Not in Kant's Germany, where the Idealists were not reformers. Not in Coleridge's England, where the work of reform was left to the Utilitarians. Not even in Vermont; James Marsh thought the whole of Boston Transcendentalism "a superficial affair." It was the Boston and Concord Unitarians who felt compelled, by the inner logic of their faith, to respond to the challenge defined by Lowell in *The Present Crisis:*

New occasions teach new duties; Time makes ancient good uncouth;
They must upward still, and onward, who would keep abreast of Truth.

During his West Roxbury years, Parker had confined himself largely to study and to preaching and parish duties, meanwhile accumulating the foundations of his great library, translating learned theological works from the German, contributing scholarly essays to *The Dial* and working out his theological principles and beliefs. Not until he had moved to his Boston pulpit did he launch upon a career

121

of reform. Once launched, however, he stirred the waters to their depths. He had announced, in *The True Idea of a Christian Church,* a broad program of social reform as appropriate for the church—and the minister. He devoted the rest of his life to what a later generation was to call the socialization of Christianity.

Parker's sermons ran to fifty or sixty closely printed pages and cannot be reproduced in full. Those represented here are but a small selection from the large number addressed to current social, economic and political problems which Parker preached from 1845 to the end of his ministerial life. For all their concern with what are customarily considered secular problems, all of them are deeply moral and deeply religious.

12. The Perishing Classes and Why They Perish

1846

No sooner was Parker established in Boston than he launched a broad moral inquiry into the economic and social practices and malpractices of the community and—by implication—of the nation. In the early summer he preached on the iniquity of the Mexican War. This was followed, in the fall and winter, by a series of three ambitious and closely knit sermons on the "perishing classes," the "merchant class" and the "dangerous classes" of Boston.

Taken together, these sermons constitute a large-scale sociological, as well as moral, inquiry into the economy of midcentury New England. They are part of that great humanitarian crusade which embraced the work of Dorothea Dix for the insane, S. G. Howe's labors for the blind, the campaign against capital punishment, much of the temperance movement, the campaign against war (waged by such men as William Ladd, Elihu Burritt and Charles Sumner), the new tenderness for children (exemplified by Charles Loring Brace), the interest in woman's rights and the widespread crusade for education. Parker himself was deeply involved in most of these movements. It was his peculiar merit that he saw the problems of poverty, vice and crime in social and economic, as well as in moral, terms and insisted on the ultimate responsibility of society for the violations of morality.

"It is not the will of your Father which is in heaven, that one of these little ones should perish."—MATTHEW xviii. 14.

There are two classes of men who are weak and little: one is little by nature, consisting of such as are born with feeble powers, not strongly capable of self-help; the other is little by position, comprising men that are permanently poor and ignorant. When Jesus said, "It is not God's will that one of these little ones should perish," I take it He included both these classes—men little by nature, and men little by position. Furthermore, I take it He said what is true, that it is not God's will one of these little ones should perish. Now, a man may be said to perish when he is ruined, or even when he fails to attain the degree of manhood he might attain under the average circumstances of this present age,

123

and these present men. In a society like ours, and that of all nations at this time, as hitherto, with such a history, a history of blood and violence, cunning and fraud; resting on such a basis— a basis of selfishness; a society wherein there is a preference of the mighty, and a postponement of the righteous, where power is worshipped and justice little honoured, though much talked of, it comes to pass that a great many little ones from both these classes actually perish. If Jesus spoke the truth, then they perish contrary to the will of God, and, of course, by some other will adverse to the will of God. In a society where the natural laws of the body are constantly violated, where many men are obliged by circumstances to violate them, it follows unavoidably that many are born little by nature, and they transmit their feebleness to their issue. The other class, men little by position, are often so hedged about with difficulties, so neglected, that they cannot change their condition; they bequeath also their littleness to their children. Thus the number of little ones enlarges with the increase of society. This class becomes perpetual; a class of men mainly abandoned by the Christians.

In all forms of social life hitherto devised these classes have appeared, and it has been a serious question, What shall be done with them? Seldom has it been the question, What shall be done for them? In olden time the Spartans took children born with a weak or imperfect body, children who would probably be a hinderance to the nation, and threw them into a desert place to be devoured by the wild beasts, and so settled that question. At this day, the Chinese, I am told, expose such children in the streets, and beside the rivers, to the humanity of passers by; and not only such, but sound, healthy children, none the less, who, though strong by nature, are born into a weak position. Many of them are left to die, especially the boys. But some are saved, those mainly girls. I will not say they are saved by the humanity of wealthier men. They become slaves, devoted by their masters to a most base and infamous purpose. With the exception of criminals, these abandoned daughters of the poor form, it is said, the only class of slaves in that great country.

Neither the Chinese nor the Spartan method is manly or human. It does with the little ones, not for them. It does away with them, and that is all. I will not decide which is the worst of the two modes, the Chinese or the Spartan. We are accustomed to call both these nations heathen, and take it for granted they do not know it is God's will that not one of these little ones should perish. Be that as it may, we do not call ourselves heathen; we pretend to know the will of God in this particular. Let us look, therefore, and see how we have disposed of the little ones in Boston, what we are doing for them or with them.

Let me begin with neglected and abandoned children. We all know how large and beautiful a provision is made for the public education of the people. About a fourth part of the city taxes are for the public schools. Yet one not familiar with this place is astonished at the number of idle, vagrant boys and girls, in the streets. It appears from the late census of Boston, that there are 4948 children between four and fifteen who attend no school. I am not speaking of truants, occasional absentees, but of children whose names are not registered at school, permanent absentees. If we allow that 1948 of these are kept in some sort of restraint by their parents, and have, or have had, some little pains taken with their culture at home; that they are feeble, and do not begin to attend school so early as most; or that they are precocious, and complete their studies before fifteen; or for some other good reason are taken from school, and put to some useful business, there still remain 3000 children who never attend any school, turned loose into your streets! Suppose there is some error in the counting, that the number is overstated one-third, still there are left 2000 young vagrants in the streets of Boston!

What will be the fate of these 2000 children? Some men are superior to circumstances; so well born they defy ill breeding. There may be children so excellent and strong they cannot be spoiled. Surely there are some who will learn with no school; boys of vast genius, whom you cannot keep from learning. Others there are of wonderful moral gifts, whom no circumstances can make vulgar; they will live in the midst of corruption and keep clean through the innate refinement of a wondrous soul. Out of these 2000 children there may be two of this sort; it were foolish to look for more than one in a thousand. The [rest] depend mainly on circumstances to help them; yes, to make their character. Send them to school and they will learn. Give them good precepts, good examples, they will also become good. Give them bad precepts, bad examples, and they become wicked. Send them half-clad and uncared for into your streets, and they grow up hungry savages, greedy for crime.

What have these abandoned children to help them? Nothing, literally nothing! They are idle, though their bodies crave activity. They are poor, ill-clad, and ill-fed. There is nothing about them to foster self-respect; nothing to call forth their conscience, to awaken and cultivate their sense of religion. They find themselves beggars in the wealth of a city; idlers in the midst of its work. Yes, savages in the midst of civilization. Their consciousness is that of an outcast, one abandoned and forsaken of men. In cities, life is intense amongst all classes. So the passions and appetites of such children are strong and violent. Their taste is low; their wants clamorous. Are religion and conscience there to abate the fever of passion and regulate desire? The moral class and the cultivated shun these poor wretches, or look on with stupid wonder. Our rule is that the whole need the physician, not the sick. They are left almost entirely to herd and consort with the basest of men; they are exposed early and late to the worst influences, and their only comrades are men whom the children of the rich are taught to shun as the pestilence. To be poor is hard enough in the country, where artificial wants are few, and those easily met, where all classes are humbly clad, and none fare sumptuously every day. But to be poor in the city, where a hundred artificial desires daily claim satisfaction, and where, too, it is difficult for the poor to satisfy the natural and unavoidable wants of food and raiment; to be hungry, ragged, dirty, amid luxury, wantonness and refinement; to be miserable in the midst of abundance, that is hard beyond all power of speech. Look, I will not say at the squalid dress of these children, as you see them prowling about the markets and wharves, or contending in the dirty lanes and by-places into which the pride of Boston has elbowed so much of her misery; look at their faces! Haggard as they are, meagre and pale and wan, want is not the worst thing written there, but cunning, fraud, violence and obscenity, and, worst of all, fear!

Amid all the science and refined culture of the nineteenth century, these children learn little; little that is good, much that is bad. In the intense life around them, they unavoidably become vicious, obscene, deceitful, and violent. They will lie, steal, be drunk. How can it be otherwise?

If you could know the life of one of those poor lepers of Boston, you would wonder and weep. Let me take one of them at random out of the mass. He was born, unwelcome, amid wretchedness and want. His coming increased both. Miserably he struggles through his infancy, less tended than the lion's whelp. He becomes a boy. He is covered only with rags, and those squalid with long accumulated filth. He wanders about your streets, too low even to seek employment, now snatching from a gutter half-rotten fruit which the owner flings away. He is ignorant; he has never entered a school-house; to him even the alphabet is a mystery. He is young in years, yet old in misery. There is no hope in his face. He herds with others like himself, —low, ragged, hungry, and idle. If misery loves company, he finds that satisfaction. Follow him to his home at night; he herds in a cellar; in the same stye with father, mother, brothers, sisters, and perhaps yet other families of like degree. What served him for dress by day, is his only bed by night.

Well, this boy steals some trifle, a biscuit, a bit of rope, or a knife from a shop-window; he is seized and carried to gaol. The day comes for trial. He is marched through the streets in handcuffs, the companion of drunkards and thieves, thus deadening the little self-respect which Nature left even in an outcast's bosom. He sits there chained like a beast; a boy in irons! the sport and mockery of men vulgar as the common sewer. His trial comes. Of course he is convicted. The show of his countenance is witness against him. His rags and dirt, his ignorance, his vagrant habits, his idleness, all testify against him. That face so young, and yet so impudent, so sly, so writ all over with embryo villany, is evidence enough. The jury are soon convinced, for they see his temptations in his look, and surely know that in such a condition men will steal: yes, they themselves would steal. The judge represents the law, and that practically regards it a crime even for a boy to be weak and poor. Much of our common law, it seems to me, is based on might, not right. So he is hurried off to gaol at a tender age, and made legally the companion of felons. Now the State has him wholly in her power; by that rough adoption, has made him her own child, and sealed the indenture with the gaoler's key. His handcuffs are the symbol of his sonship to the State. She shuts him in her College for the Little. What does that teach him; science, letters,—even morals and religion? Little enough of this, even in Boston, and in most counties of Massachusetts, I think nothing at all, not even a trade which he can practise when his term expires! I have been told a story, and I wish it might be falsely told, of a boy, in this city, of sixteen, sent to the house of correction for five years because he stole a bunch of keys, and coming out of that gaol at twenty-one, unable to write, or read, or calculate, and with no trade but that of picking oakum. Yet he had been five years the child of the State, and in that College for the Poor! Who would employ such a youth; with such a reputation; with the smell of the gaol in his very breath? Not your shrewd men of business, they know the risk; not your respectable men, members of churches and all that; not they! Why it would hurt a man's reputation for piety to do good in that way. Besides the risk is great, and it argues a great deal more Christianity than it is popular to have, for a respectable man to employ such a youth. He is forced back into crime again. I say, forced, for honest men will not employ him when the State shoves him out of the gaol. Soon you will have him in the court again, to be punished more severely. Then he goes to the State Prison, and then again, and again, till death mercifully ends his career!

Who is to blame for all that? I will ask the best man among the best of you, what he would have become, if thus abandoned, turned out in childhood, and with no culture, into the streets, to herd with the wickedest of men! Somebody says, there are "organic sins" in society which nobody is to blame for. But by this sin organized in society, these vagrant children are training up to become thieves, pirates, and murderers. I cannot blame them. But there is a terrible blame somewhere, for it is not the will of God that one of these little ones should perish. Who is it that organizes the sin of society?

Let us next look at the parents of these vagrants, at the adult poor. It is not easy or needed for this purpose, to define very nicely the limits of a class, and tell where the rich end, and the poor begin. However, men may, in reference to this matter, be divided into three classes. The first acts on society mainly by their capital; the second mainly by their skill, mental and manual, by educated labour; and the third by their muscles, by brute force with little or no skill, uneducated labour. The poor, I take it, come mainly from this latter class. Education of head or hand, a profession or a trade, is wealth in possibility; yes, wealth in prospect, wealth in its process of accumulation, for wealth itself is only accumulated labour, as learning is accumulated thought. Most of our rich men have come out of this class which acts by its skill, and their children in a few years will return to it. I am not now to speak of men transiently poor, who mend their condition as the hours go by, who may gain enough, and perhaps become rich; but of men permanently poor, whom one year finds wanting, and the next leaves no better off; men that live, as we say, from hand to mouth, but whose hand and mouth are often empty. Even here in Boston, there is little of the justice that removes causes of poverty, though so much of the charity which alleviates its effects. Those men live, if you can call it life, crowded together more densely, I am told, than in Naples or Paris, in London or Liverpool. Boston has its ghetto, not for the Jews as at Prague and at Rome, but for brother Christians. In the quarters inhabited mainly by the poor, you find a filthiness and squalor which would astonish a stranger. The want of comfort, of air, of water, is terrible. Cold is a stern foe in our winters, but in these places I am told that men suffer more from want of water in summer, than want of fire in winter. If your bills of mortality were made out so as to show the deaths in each ward of the city, I think all would be astonished at the results. Disease and death are the result of causes, causes too that may for a long time be avoided, and in the more favoured classes are avoided. It is not God's will that the rich be spared and the poor die. Yet the greatest mortality is always among the poor. Out of each hundred Catholics who died in Boston, from 1833 to 1838, more than sixty-one were less than five years of age. The result for the last six years is no better. Of one hundred children born amongst them, only thirty-eight live five years; only eleven become fifty! Gray-haired Irishmen we seldom see. Yet they are not worse off than others equally poor, only we can more distinctly get at the facts. In the war with disease which mankind is waging, the poor stand in front of the fire, and are mowed down without pity!

Of late years, in Boston, there has been a gradual increase in the mortality of children. I think we shall find the increase only among the children of the poor. Of course it depends on causes which may be removed, at least modified, for the average life of mankind is on the increase. I am told, I know not if the authority be good, that mortality among the poor is greater in Boston than in any city of Europe.

Of old times the rich man rode into battle, shirted with mail, covered and shielded with iron from head to foot. Arrows glanced from him as from a stone. He came home unhurt and covered with "glory." But the poor, in his leathern jerkin or his linen frock, confronted the war, where every weapon tore his unprotected flesh. In the modern, perennial battle with disease, the same thing takes place; the poor fall and die.

The destruction of the poor is their poverty. They are ignorant, not from choice but necessity. They cannot, therefore, look round and see the best way of doing things, of saving their strength, and sparing their means. They can have little of what we call thrift, the brain in the hand for which our people are so remarkable. Some of them are also little by nature, ill-born; others well born enough, were abandoned in childhood, and have not since been able to make up the arrears of a neglected youth. They are to fight the great battle of life, for battle it is to them, with feeble arms. Look at the houses they live in, without comfort or convenience, without sun, or air, or water; damp, cold, filthy, and crowded to excess. In one section of the city there are thirty-seven persons on an average in each house.

Consider the rents paid by this class of our brothers. It is they who pay the highest rate for their dwellings. The worth of the house is often little more than nothing, the ground it covers making the only value. I am told that twelve or fifteen per cent. a year on a large valuation is quite commonly paid, and over thirty per cent. on the actual value, is not a strange thing. I wish this might not prove true.

But the misery of the poor does not end with their wretched houses and exorbitant rent. Having neither capital nor store-room, they must purchase articles of daily need in the smallest quantities. They buy, therefore, at the greatest disadvantage, and yet at the dearest rates. I am told it is not a rare thing for them to buy inferior qualities of flour at six cents a pound, or $11.88 a barrel, while another man buys a month's supply at a time for $4 or $5 a barrel. This may be an extreme case, but I know that in some places in this city, an inferior article is now retailed to them at $7.92 the barrel. So it is with all kinds of food; they are bought in the smallest quantities, and at a rate which a rich man would think ruinous. Is not the poor man, too, most often cheated in the weight and the measure? So it is whispered. "He has no friends," says the sharper; "others have broken him to fragments, I will grind him to powder!" And the grinding comes.

Such being the case, the poor man finds it difficult to get a cent beforehand. I know rich men tell us that capital is at the mercy of labour. That may be prophecy; it is not history; not fact. Uneducated labour, brute force without skill, is wholly at the mercy of capital. The capitalist can control the market for labour, which is all the poor man has to part with. The poor cannot combine as the rich. True, a mistake is sometimes made, and the demand for labour is greater than the supply, and the poor man's wages are increased. This result was doubtless God's design, but was it man's intention? The condition of the poor has hitherto been bettered, not so much by the design of the strong, as by God making their wrath and cupidity serve the weak.

Under such circumstances, what marvel that the poor man becomes unthrifty, reckless and desperate? I know how common it is to complain of the extravagance of the poor. Often there is reason for the complaint. It is a wrong thing, and immoral, for a man with a dependent family to spend all his earnings, if it be possible to live with less. I think many young men are much to be blamed, for squandering all their wages to please a dainty palate, or to dress as fine as a richer man, making only the heart of their tailor foolishly glad. Such men may not be poor now, but destine themselves to be the fathers of poor children. After making due allowance, it must be confessed that much of the recklessness of the poor comes unavoidably from their circumstances; from their despair of ever being comfortable, except for a moment at a time. Every one knows that unmerited wealth tempts a man to squander, while few men know, what is just as true, that hopeless poverty does the same thing. As the tortured Indian will sleep, if his tormentor pause but a moment, so the poor man, grown reckless and desperate, forgets the future storms, and wastes in revel the solitary gleam of sunlight which falls on him. It is nature speaking through his soul.

Now consider the moral temptations before such men. Here is wealth, food, clothing, comfort, luxury, gold, the great enchanter of this age, and but a plank betwixt it and them. Nay, they are shut from it only by a pane of glass, thin as popular justice, and scarcely less brittle! They feel the natural wants of man; the artificial wants of men in cities. They are indignant at their social position, thrust into the mews and the kennels of the land. They think some one is to blame for it. A man in New England does not believe it God's will he should toil for ever, stinting and sparing only to starve the more slowly to death, overloaded with work, with no breathing time but the blessed Sunday. They see others doing nothing, idle as Solomon's lilies, yet wasting the unearned bread God made to feed the children of the poor. They see crowds of idle women elegantly clad, a show of loveliness, a rainbow in the streets, and think of the rag which does not hide their daughter's shame. They hear of thousands of baskets of costly wine imported in a single ship, not brought to recruit the feeble, but to poison the palate of the strong. They begin to ask if wealthy men and wise men have not forgotten their brothers, in thinking of their own pleasure! It is not the poor

alone who ask that. In the midst of all this, what wonder is it
if they feel desirous of revenge; what wonder that stores and
houses are broken into, and stables set on fire! Such is the
natural effect of misery like that; it is but the voice of our brother's
blood crying to God against us all. I wonder not that it cries in
robbery and fire. The gaol and the gallows will not still that voice,
nor silence the answer. I wonder at the fewness of crimes, not
their multitude. I must say that, if goodness and piety did not
bear a greater proportion to the whole development of the poor
than the rich, their crimes would be tenfold. The nation sets the
poor an example of fraud, by making them pay highest on all
local taxes; of theft, by levying the national revenue on persons,
not property. Our navy and army set them the lesson of violence;
and, to complete their schooling, at this very moment we are
robbing another people of cities and lands, stealing, burning, and
murdering, for lust of power and gold. Everybody knows that the
political action of a nation is the mightiest educational influence
in that nation. But such is the doctrine the State preaches to
them, a constant lesson of fraud, theft, violence, and crime. The
literature of the nation mocks at the poor, laughing in the popular
journals at the poor man's inevitable crime. Our trade deals with
the poor as tools, not men. What wonder they feel wronged!
Some city missionary may dawdle the matter as he will; tell them
it is God's will they should be dirty and ignorant, hungry, cold
and naked. Now and then a poor woman, starving with cold and
hunger, may think it true. But the poor know better; ignorant as
they are, they know better. Great Nature speaks when you and I
are still. They feel neglected, wronged, and oppressed. What
hinders them from following the example set by the nation, by
society, by the strong? Their inertness, their cowardice, and, what
does not always restrain abler men, their fear of God! With
cultivated men, the intellect is often developed at the expense of
conscience and religion. With the poor this is more seldom the
case.

The misfortunes of the poor do not end here. To make their
degradation total, their name infamous, we have shut them out
of our churches. Once in our Puritan meeting-houses, there were
"body seats" for the poor; for a long time free galleries, where
men sat and were not ashamed. Now it is not so. A Christian
society about to build a church, and having $50,000, does not
spend $40,000 for that, making it a church for all, and keep
$10,000 as a fund for the poor. No; it borrows $30,000 more,

and then shuts the poor out of its bankrupt aisles. A high tower, or a fine-toned bell, yes, marble and mahogany, are thought better than the presence of these little ones whom God wills not to perish. I have heard ministers boast of the great men, and famous, who sat under their preaching; never one who boasted that the poor came into his church, and were fed, body and soul! You go to our churches—the poor are not in them. They are idling and lounging away their day of rest, like the horse and the ox. Alas me, that the apostles, that the Christ himself could not worship in our churches, till he sold his garment and bought a pew! Many of our houses of public worship would be well named, "Churches for the affluent." Yet religion is more to the poor man than to the rich. What wonder, then, if the poor lose self-respect, when driven from the only churches where it is thought respectable to pray!

This class of men are perishing; yes, perishing in the nineteenth century; perishing in Boston, wealthy, charitable Boston; perishing soul and body, contrary to God's will; and perishing all the worse because they die slow, and corrupt by inches. . . .

What shall become of the children of such men? They stand in the fore-front of the battle, all unprotected as they are; a people scattered and peeled, only a miserable remnant reaches the age of ten! Look about your streets, and see what does become of such as live, vagrant and idle boys. Ask the police, the constables, the gaols; they shall tell you what becomes of the sons. Will a white lily grow in a common sewer; can you bleach linen in a tan-pit? Yes, as soon as you can rear a virtuous population, under such circumstances. Go to any State Prison in the land, and you shall find that seven-eights of the convicts came from this class, brought there by crimes over which they had no control; crimes which would have made you and me thieves and pirates. The characters of such men are made for them, far more than by them. There is no more vice, perhaps, born into that class; they have no more "inherited sin" than any other class in the land; all the difference, then, between the morals and manners of rich and poor, is the result of education and circumstances.

The fate of the daughters of the poor is yet worse. Many of them are doomed to destruction by the lust of men, their natural guardians and protectors. . . . It seems to me as if I saw the genius of this city stand before God, lifting his hands in agony to heaven, crying for mercy on woman, insulted and trodden down, for vengeance on man, who treads her thus infamously into the dust. The vengeance comes, not the mercy. Misery in woman is the strongest inducement to crime. Where self-respect is not fostered; where severe toil hardly holds her soul and body together amid the temptations of a city, and its heated life, it is no marvel to me that this sin should slay its victims, finding woman an easy prey.

Let me follow the children of the poor a step further—I mean to the gaol. Few men seem aware of the frightful extent of crime amongst us, and the extent of the remedy, more awful yet. In less than one year, namely, from the 9th of June, 1845, to the 2nd of June, 1846, there were committed to your House of Correction, in this city, 1228 persons, a little more than one out of every fifty-six in the whole population that is more than ten years old. Of these 377 were women; 851 men. Five were sentenced for an indefinite period, and forty-seven for an additional period of solitary imprisonment. In what follows I make no account of that. But the whole remaining period of their sentences amounts to more than 544 years, or 198,568 days. In addition to this, in the year ending with June 9, 1846, we sent from Boston to the State Prison, thirty-five more, and for a period of 18,595 days, of which 205 were solitary. Thus it appears that the illegal and convicted crime of Boston, in one year, was punished by imprisonment for 217,163 days. Now as Boston contains but 114,366 persons of all ages, and only 69,112 that are over ten years of age, it follows that the imprisonment of citizens of Boston for crime in one year, amounts to more than one day and twenty-one hours, for each man, woman, and child, or to more than three days and three hours, for each one over ten years of age. This seems beyond belief, yet in making the estimate, I have not included the time spent in gaol before sentence; I have left out the solitary imprisonment in the House of Correction; I have said nothing of the 169 children, sentenced for crime to the House of Reformation in the same period.

What is the effect of this punishment on society at large? I will not now attempt to answer that question. What is it on the criminals themselves? Let the gaol-books answer. Of the whole number, 202 were sentenced for the second time; 131 for the third; 101 for the fourth; 38 for the fifth; 40 for the sixth; 29 for the seventh; 23 for the eighth; 12 for the ninth; 50 for the tenth time, or more; and of the criminals punished for the tenth time, thirty-one were women! Of the thirty-five sent to the State prison, fourteen had been there before; of the 1228 sent to the House of Correction, only 626 were sent for the first time.

There are two classes,—the victims of society, and the foes of society: the men that organize its sins, and then tell us nobody is to blame. May God deal mercifully with the foes; I had rather take my part with the victims. Yet, is there one who wishes to be a foe to mankind?

Here are the sons of the poor, vagrant in your streets, shut out by their misery from the culture of the age; growing up to fill your gaols, to be fathers of a race like themselves, and to be huddled into an infamous grave. Here are the daughters of the poor, cast out and abandoned, the pariahs of our civilization, training up for a life of shame and pollution, and coming early to a miserable end. Here are the poor, daughters and sons, excluded from the refining influences of modern life, shut out of the very churches by that bar of gold,—ignorant, squalid, hungry and hopeless, wallowing in their death! Are these the results of modern civilization; this in the midst of the nineteenth century, in a Christian city full of churches and gold; this in Boston, which adds $13,000,000 a year to her actual wealth? Is that the will of God? Tell it not in China; whisper it not in New Holland, lest the heathen turn pale with horror, and send back your missionaries, fearing they shall pollute the land!

There is yet another class of little ones. I mean the intemperate. Within the last few years it seems that drunkenness has increased. I know this is sometimes doubted. But if this fact is not shown by the increased number of legal convictions for the crime, it is by the sight of drunken men in public and not arrested. I think I have not visited the city five times in the last ten months without seeing more or less men drunk in the streets. The cause of this increase, it seems to me, is not difficult to discover. All great movements go forward by undulations, as the waves of the rising tide come up the beach. Now comes a great wave reaching far up the shore, and then recedes. The next, and the next, and the next falls short of the highest mark; yet the tide is coming in all the while. You see this same undulation in other popular movements; for example, in politics. Once the great wave of Democracy broke over the central power, washing it clean. Now the water lies submissive beneath that rock, and humbly licks its feet. In some other day the popular wave shall break with purifying roar clean over that haughty stone and wash off the lazy barnacles, heaps of corrupting drift-weed, and deadly monsters of the deep. By such seemingly unsteady movements do popular affairs get forward. The reformed drunkards, it is said, were violent, ill-bred, theatrical, and only touched the surface. Many respectable men withdrew from the work soon as the Washingtonians came to it. It was a pity they did so; but they did. I think the conscience of New England did not trust the reformed men; that also is a pity. They seem now to have relaxed their efforts in a great measure, perhaps discouraged at the coldness with which they have in some quarters been treated. I know not why it is, but they do not continue so ably the work they once begun. Besides, the State, it was thought, favoured intemperance. It was for a long time doubted if the licence-laws were constitutional; so they were openly set at nought, for wicked men seize on doubtful opportunities. Then, too, temperance had gone, a few years ago, as far as it could be expected to go until certain great obstacles were removed. Many leading men in the land were practically hostile to temperance, and, with some remarkable exceptions, still are. The sons of the pilgrims, last Forefathers' day, could not honour the self-denial of the Puritans without wine! The Alumni of Harvard University could never, till this season, keep their holidays without strong drink. If rich men continue to drink without need, the poor will long continue to be drunk. Vices, like decayed furniture, go down. They keep their shape, but become more frightful. In this way the refined man who often drinks, but is never drunk, corrupts hundreds of men whom he never saw, and, without intending it, becomes a foe to society. . . .

Let me mention some of the statistics of this trade before I speak of its effects. If there are one thousand drink-shops, and each sells liquor to the amount of only six dollars a day, which is the price of only one hundred drams, or two hundred at the lowest shops, then we have the sum of $2,190,000 paid for liquor to be drunk on the spot every year. This sum is considerably more than double the amount paid for the whole public education of the people in the entire State of Massachusetts! In Boston alone, last year, there were distilled, 2,873,623 gallons of spirit. In five years, from 1840 to 1845, Boston exported 2,156,990, and imported 2,887,993 gallons. They burnt up a man the other day, at the distillery in Merrimack-street. You read the story in the daily papers, and remember how the bystanders looked on with horror to see the wounded man attempting with his hands to fend off the flames from his naked head! Great

Heaven! It was not the first man that distillery has burnt up! No, not by thousands. You see men about your streets, all on fire; some half-burnt down; some with all the soul burnt out, only the cinders left of the man, the shell and wall, and that tumbling and tottering, ready to fall. Who of you has not lost a relative, at least a friend, in that withering flame, that terrible *auto-da-fé,* that hell-fire on earth?

Let us look away from that. I wish we could look on something to efface that ghastly sight. But see the results of this trade. Do you wonder at the poverty just now spoken of; at the vagrant children? In the poor-house at Albany, at one time, there were 633 persons, and of them 615 were intemperate! Ask your city authorities how many of the poor are brought to their alms-house directly or remotely by intemperance! Do you wonder at the crime which fills your gaols, and swells the tax of county and city? Three-fourths of the petty crime in the State comes from this source directly or remotely. Your gaols were never so full before! When the parents are there, what is left for the children? In Prussia, the Government which imprisons the father takes care of the children, and sends them to school. Here they are forced into crime.

As I gave some statistics of the cause, let me also give some of the effects. Two years ago your grand jury reports that one of the city police, on Sunday morning, between the hours of twelve and two, in walking from Cornhill Square to Cambridge Street, passed more than one hundred persons more or less drunk! In 1844 there were committed to your House of Correction, for drunkenness, 453 persons; in 1845, 595; in 1846, up to the 24th of August, that is, in seven months and twenty-four days, 446. Besides, there have been already in this year, 396 complained of at the police court and fined, but not sent to the house of correction. Thus, in seven months and twenty-four days, 842 persons have been legally punished for public drunkenness. In the last two months and a half 445 persons were thus punished. In the first twenty-four days of this month, ninety-four! In the last year there were 4643 persons committed to your watchhouses, more than the twenty-fifth of the whole population. The thousand drink-shops levy a direct tax of more than $2,000,000. That is only the first outlay. The whole ultimate cost, in idleness, sickness, crime, death, and broken-hearts—I leave you to calculate that! The men who live in the lower courts, familiar with the sinks of iniquity, speak of this crime as "most awful!" Yet in this month and the last, there were but nine persons indicted for the illegal sale of the poison which so wastes the people's life! The head of your police and the foreman of your last grand jury are prominent in that trade.

Does the Government know of these things; know of their cause? One would hope not. The last grand jury, in their public report, after speaking manfully of some actual evils, instead of pointing at drunkenness and barrooms, direct your attention "to the increased number of omnibuses and other large carriages in the streets."

These are sad things to think of in a Christian church. What shall we do for all these little ones that are perishing? "Do nothing," say some. "Am I my brother's keeper?" asked the first Cain, after killing that brother. He thought the answer would be, "No! you are not." But he was his brother's keeper, and Abel's blood cried from the ground for justice, and God heard it. Some say we can do nothing. I will never believe that a city which in twelve years can build near a thousand miles of railroad, hedge up the Merrimack and the lakes of New Hampshire; I will never believe that a city, so full of the hardiest enterprise and the noblest charity, cannot keep these little ones from perishing. Why, the nation can annex new States and raise armies at uncounted cost. Can it not extirpate pauperism, prevent intemperance, pluck up the causes of the present crime? All that is lacking is the prudent will!

It seems as if something could easily be done to send the vagrant children to school; at least to give them employment, and so teach them some useful art. If some are Catholics, and will not attend the Protestant schools, perhaps it would be as possible to have a special and separate school for the Irish as for the Africans. It was recently proposed in a Protestant assembly to found Sunday schools, with Catholic teachers for Catholic children. The plan is large and noble and indicates a liberality which astonishes one even here, where some men are ceasing to be sectarian and becoming human. Much may be done to bring many of the children to our Sunday and week-day schools, as they now are, and so brands be snatched from the burning. The State Farm School for Juvenile Offenders, which a good man last winter suggested to your Legislature, will doubtless do much for these idle boys, and may be the beginning of a greater and better work. Could the State also take care of the children when it locks the parents in a gaol, there would be a nearer approach to justice and greater likelihood of obtaining its end. Still the laws act cumbrously and slow. The great work must be done by good men, acting separately or in concert, in their private way. You are your brother's keeper; God made you so. If you are rich, intelligent, refined and religious, why you are all the more a keeper to the poor, the weak, the vulgar, and the wicked. In the pauses of your work there will be time to do something. In the unoccupied hours of the Sunday there is yet leisure to help a brother's need. If there are times when you are disposed to murmur at your own hard lot, though it is not hard; or hours when grief presses heavy on your heart, go and look after these children, find them employment, and help them to start in life; you will find your murmurings are ended, and your sorrow forgot.

It does not seem difficult to do something for the poor. It would be easy to provide comfortable and convenient houses, and at a reasonable rate. The experiment has been tried by one noble-hearted man, and thus far works well. I trust the same plan, or one better, if possible, will soon be tried on a larger scale, and so repeated, till we are free from that crowding together of miserable persons, which now disgraces our city. It seems to me that a store might be established where articles of good quality should be furnished to the poor at cost. Something has already been done in this way, by the "Trades' Union," who need it much less. A practical man could easily manage the details of such a scheme. All reform and elevation of this class of men must begin by mending their circumstances, though of course it must not end there. Expect no improvement of men that are hungry, naked, and cold. Few men respect themselves in that condition. Hope not of others what would be impossible for you!

You may give better pay when that is possible. I can hardly think it the boast of a man, that he has paid less for his labour than any other in his calling. But it is a common boast, though to to me it seems the glory of a pirate! I cannot believe there is that sharp distinction between weekday religion and Sunday religion, or between justice and charity, that is sometimes pretended. A man both just and charitable would find his charity run over into his justice, and the mixture improve its quality. When I remember that all value is the result of work, and see likewise that no man gets rich by his own work, I cannot help thinking that labour is often wickedly underpaid, and capital sometimes as grossly over-fed. I shall believe that capital is at the mercy of labour, when the two extremes of society change places. Is it Christian or manly to reduce wages in hard times, and not raise them in fair times? and not raise them again in extraordinary times? Is it God's will that large dividends and small wages should be paid at the same time? The duty of the employer is not over, when he has paid "the hands" their wages. Abraham is a special providence for Eliezer, as God, the universal providence, for both. The usages of society make a sharp distinction between the rich and poor; but I cannot believe the churches have done wisely, by making that distinction appear through separating the two, in their worship. The poor are, undesignedly, driven out of the respectable churches. They lose self-respect; lose religion. Those that remain, what have they gained by this expulsion of their brothers? A beautiful and costly house, but a church without the poor. The Catholics were wiser and more humane than that. I cannot believe the mightiest abilities and most exquisite culture were ever too great to preach and apply Christianity among the poor; and that "the best sermons would be wasted on them." Yet such has not been the practical decision here; I trust we shall yet be able to say of all our churches, however costly, "There the rich and poor meet together." They are now equally losers by the separation. The seventy ministers of Boston—how much they can do for this class of little ones, if they will! . . .

However, a reform in this matter will be permanent only through a deeper and wider reform elsewhere. Drunkenness and theft in its various illegal forms, are confined almost wholly to the poorest class. So long as there is unavoidable misery, like the present, pauperism and popular ignorance; so long as thirty-seven are crowded into one house, and that not large; so long as men are wretched and without hope, there will be drunkenness. I know much has been done already; I think drunkenness will never be respectable again, or common amongst refined and cultivated men; it will be common among the ignorant, the outcast, and the miserable, so long as the present causes of poverty, ignorance, and misery continue. For that continuance, and the want, the crime, the unimaginable wretchedness and death of heart which comes thereof, it is not these perishing little ones, but the strong that are responsible before God! It will not do for your grand juries to try and hide the matter by indicting "omnibuses and other large carriages;" the voice of God cries, "Where is thy brother?"—and that brother's blood answers from the ground.

What I have suggested only palliates effects; it removes no

cause;—of that another time. These little ones are perishing here in the midst of us. Society has never seriously sought to prevent it, perhaps has not been conscious of the fact. It has not so much legislated for them as against them. Its spirit is hostile to them. If the mass of able-headed men were in earnest about this, think you they would allow such unthrifty ways, such a waste of man's productive energies? Never! no, never. They would repel the causes of this evil as now an invading army. The removal of these troubles must be brought about by a great change in the spirit of society. Society is not Christian in form or spirit. So there are many who do not love to hear Christianity preached and applied, but to have some halting theology set upon its crutches. They like, on Sundays, to hear of the sacrifice, not to have mercy and goodness demanded of them. A Christian State after the pattern of that divine man, Jesus—how different it would be from this in spirit and in form!

Taking all this whole State into account, things, on the whole, are better here, than in any similar population, after all these evils. I think there can be no doubt of that; better now, on the whole, than ever before. A day's work will produce a greater quantity of needful things than hitherto. So the number of little ones that perish is smaller than heretofore, in proportion to the whole mass. I do not believe the world can show such examples of public charity as this city has afforded in the last fifty years. Alas! we want the justice which prevents causes no less than the charity which palliates effects. See yet the unnatural disparity in man's condition: bloated opulence and starving penury in the same street! See the pauperism, want, licentiousness, intemperance and crime, in the midst of us; see the havoc made of woman; see the poor deserted by their elder brother, while it is their sweat which enriches your ground, builds your railroads, and piles up your costly houses. The tall gallows stands in the back-ground of society, overlooking it all; where it should be the blessed gospel of the living God.

What we want to remove the cause of all this is the application of Christianity to social life. Nothing less will do the work. Each of us can help forward that by doing the part which falls in his way. Christianity, like the eagle's flight, begins at home. We can go further, and do something for each of these classes of little ones. Then we shall help others do the same. Some we may encourage to practical Christianity by our example; some we may perhaps shame. Still more, we can ourselves be pure, manly,

Christian; each of us that, in heart and life. We can build up a company of such, men of perpetual growth. Then we shall be ready not only for this special work now before us, to palliate effects, but for every Christian and manly duty when it comes. Then, if ever some scheme is offered which is nobler and yet more Christian than what we now behold, it will find us booted, and girded, and road-ready.

I look to you to do something in this matter. You are many; most of you are young. I look to you to set an example of a noble life, human, clean, and Christian, not debasing these little ones, but lifting them up. Will you cause them to perish; you? I know you will not. Will you let them perish? I cannot believe it. Will you not prevent their perishing? Nothing less is your duty.

Some men say they will do nothing to help liberate the slave, because he is far off, and "our mission is silence!" Well—here are sufferers in a nearer need. Do you say, I can do but little to Christianize society! Very well, do that little, and see if it does not amount to much, and bring its own blessing—the thought that you have given a cup of cold water to one of the little ones. Did not Jesus say, "Inasmuch as ye have done it unto one of the least of these, ye have done it unto me?"

13. The Power of the Merchant Class

1846

Here are some extracts from the second of Parker's great sermons of 1846 on the economic and social conditions of Boston—an inquiry into what we today call the power elite. Parker's approach was not only moral, but also sociological and even psychological.

Criticism of the rich was to be a commonplace in the literature of Christian socialism of the 1890s, but in the forties it was unfamiliar and unexpected: the eccentric Orestes Brownson had indulged in it temporarily, and the hapless John Pierpont, but few others. Much of Utopianism was, of course, an implied criticism of the social order of the day; but it is suggestive that while Parker was sympathetic to the Brook Farm experiment, he did not join it. He thought it essential to face the problems of the day and to attack them, not to escape from them.

I ask your attention to a "Sermon of Merchants: their Position, Temptations, Opportunities, Influence, and Duty." . . .

Here in America the position of this class is the most powerful and commanding in society. They own most of the property of the nation. The wealthy men are of this class; in practical skill, administrative talent, in power to make use of the labour of other men, they surpass all others. Now, wealth is power, and skill and power—both to a degree unknown before. This skill and wealth are more powerful with us than any other people, for there is no privileged caste, priest, king, or noble, to balance against them. The strong hand has given way to the able and accomplished head. Once head armour was worn on the outside, and of brass; now it is internal, and of brains.

To this class belongs the power both of skill and of wealth, and all the advantages which they bring. It was never so before in the whole history of man. It is more so in the United States than in any other place. . . .

Now the merchants in America occupy the place which was once held by the fighters, and next by the nobles. In our country

143

we have balanced into harmony the centripetal power of the Government, and the centrifugal power of the people: so have national unity of action, and individual variety of action—personal freedom. Therefore a vast amount of talent is active here which lies latent in other countries, because that harmony is not established there. Here the army and navy offer few inducements to able and aspiring young men. They are fled to as the last resort of the desperate, or else sought for their traditional glory, not their present value. In Europe, the army, the navy, the parliament or the court, the church and the learned professions, offer brilliant prizes to ambitious men. Thither flock the able and the daring. Here such men go into trade. It is better for a man to have set up a mill than to have won a battle. I deny not the exceptions. I speak only of the general rule. Commerce and manufactures offer the most brilliant rewards—wealth, and all it brings. Accordingly, the ablest men go into the class of merchants. The strongest men in Boston, taken as a body, are not lawyers, doctors, clergymen, book-wrights, but merchants. I deny not the presence of distinguished ability in each of those professions; I am now again only speaking of the general rule. I deny not the presence of very weak men, exceedingly weak in this class; their money their only source of power.

The merchants, then, are the prominent class; the most respectable, the most powerful. They know their power, but are not yet fully aware of their formidable and noble position at the head of the nation. Hence they are often ashamed of their calling; while their calling is the source of their wealth, their knowledge, and their power, and should be their boast and their glory. . . .

This class controls the State. The effects of that control appear in our legislation. I know there are some noble men in political life, who have gone there with the loftiest motives, men that ask only after what is right. I honour such men—honour them all the more because they seem exceptions to a general rule; men far above the spirit of any class. I must speak of what commonly takes place. Our politics are chiefly mercantile, politics in which money is preferred, and man postponed. When the two come into collision, the man goes to the wall and the street is left clear for the dollars. A few years ago, in monarchical France, a report was made of the condition of the working population in the large manufacturing towns—a truthful report, but painful to read, for it told of strong men oppressing the weak. I do not believe that such an undisguised statement of the good and ill could be tolerated in Democratic America; no, not of the condition of men in New England; and what would be thought of a book setting forth the condition of the labouring men and women of the South? I know very well what is thought of the few men who attempt to tell the truth on this subject. I think there is no nation in Europe, except Russia and Turkey, which cares so little for the class which reaps down its harvests and does the hard work. . . .

This same preference of money over men appears in many special statutes. In most of our manufacturing companies the capital is divided into shares so large that a poor man cannot invest therein! This could easily be avoided. A man steals a candlestick out of a church, and goes to the State prison for a year and a day. Another quarrels with a man, maims him for life, and is sent to the common gaol for six months. A bounty is paid, or was until lately, on every gallon of intoxicating drink manufactured here and sent out of the country. If we begin with taking care of the rights of man, it seems easy to take care of the rights of labour and of capital. To begin the other way is quite another thing. A nation making laws for the nation is a noble sight. The government of all, by all, and for all, is a Democracy. When that government follows the eternal laws of God, it is founding what Christ called the kingdom of heaven. But the predominating class making laws not for the nation's good, but only for its own, is a sad spectacle; no reasoning can make it other than a sorry sight. To see able men prostituting their talents to such a work, that is one of the saddest sights! I know all other nations have set us the example, yet it is painful to see it followed, and here.

Our politics, being mainly controlled by this class, are chiefly mercantile, the politics of pedlers. So political management often becomes a trick. Hence we have many politicians, and raise a harvest of them every year, that crop never failing, party-men who can legislate for a class; but we have scarce one great statesman who can step before his class, beyond his age, and legislate for a whole nation, leading the people and giving us new ideas to incarnate in the multitude, his word becoming flesh. We have not planters, but trimmers! A great statesman never came of mercantile politics, only of politics considered as the national application of religion to life. Our political morals, you all know what they are, the morals of a huckster. This is no new thing; the same game was played long ago in Venice, Pisa, Florence, and the result is well known. A merely mercantile politician is very sharp-sighted, and perhaps far-sighted; but a dollar will cover the whole field of his vision, and he can never see through it. The number of slaves in the United States is considerably greater than our whole population when we declared Independence, yet how much talk will a tariff make, or a public dinner: how little the welfare of three million men! Said I not truly, our most famous politicians are, in the general way, only mercantile party-men? Which of these men has shown the most interest in those three million slaves? The man who in the Senate of a Christian Republic valued them at twelve hundred million dollars! Shall respectable men say, "We do not care what sort of a Government the people have, so long as we get our dividends." Some say so; many men do not say that, but think so, and act accordingly! The Government, therefore, must be so arranged that they get their dividends.

This class of men buys up legislators, consciously or not, and pays them, for values received. Yes, so great is its daring and its conscious power, that we have recently seen our most famous politician bought up, the stoutest understanding that one finds now extant in this whole nineteenth century, perhaps the ablest head since Napoleon. None can deny his greatness, his public services in times past, nor his awful power of intellect. I say we have seen him, a senator of the United States, pensioned by this class, or a portion thereof, and thereby put mainly in their hands! When a whole nation rises up and publicly throws its treasures at the feet of a great man who has stood forth manfully contending for the nation, and bids him take their honours and their gold as a poor pay for noble works, why that sight is beautiful, the multitude shouting hosanna to their King, and spreading their garments underneath his feet! Man is loyal, and such honours so paid, and to such, are doubly gracious; becoming alike to him that takes and those who give. Yes, when a single class, to whom some man has done a great service, goes openly and makes a memorial thereof in gold and honours paid to him, why that also is noble and beautiful. But when a single class, in a country where political doings are more public than elsewhere in the whole world, secretly buys up a man, in high place and world-famous, giving him a retaining fee for life, why the deed is one I do not wish to call by name! Could such men do this without a secret shame? I will never believe it of my countrymen. A gift blinds a wise man's eyes, perverts the words even of the righteous, stopping his mouth with gold so that he cannot reprove a wrong! But there is an absolute justice which is neither bought nor sold! I know other nations have done the same, and with like effect. "Fight with silver weapons," said the Delphic oracle, "and you'll conquer all." It has always been the craft of despots to buy up aspiring talent; some with a title, some with gold. Allegiance to the sovereign is the same thing on both sides of the water, whether the sovereign be an eagle or a guinea. Some American, it is said, wrote the Lord's Prayer on one side of a dime, and the Ten Commandments on the other. The Constitution and a considerable commentary might perhaps be written on the two sides of a dollar!

This class controls the Churches, as the State. Let me show the effect of that control. I am not to try men in a narrow way, by my own theological standard, but by the standard of manliness and Christianity. As a general rule, the clergy are on the side of power. All history proves this, our own most abundantly. The clergy also are unconsciously bought up, their speech paid for, or their silence. As a class, did they ever denounce a public sin? a popular sin? Perhaps they have. Do they do it now and here? Take Boston for the last ten years, and I think there has been more clerical preaching against the abolitionists than against Slavery; perhaps more preaching against the temperance movement than in its favour. With the exception of disbelieving the popular theology, your evangelical alliance knows no sin but "original sin," unless indeed it be "organic sins," which no one is to blame for; no sinner but Adam and the devil; no saving righteousness but the "imputed." I know there are exceptions, and I would go far to do them honour, pious men who lift up a warning—yes, bear Christian testimony against public sins. I am speaking of the mass of the clergy. Christ said the priests of His time had made a den of thieves out of God's house of prayer. Now they conform to the public sins, and apologize for popular crime. It is a good thing to forgive an offence: who does not need that favour and often? But to forgive the theory of crime, to have a theory which does that, is quite another thing. Large cities are alike the court and camp of the mercantile class, and what I have just said is more eminently true of the clergy in such towns. Let me give an example. Not long ago the Unitarian clergy published a protest against American Slavery. It was moderate, but firm and manly. Almost all the clergy in the country signed it. In the large towns few: they mainly young men and in the least considerable churches. The young men seemed not to understand their contract, for the essential part of an ecclesiastical contract is sometimes written between the lines and in sympathetic ink. Is a steamboat burned or lost on the waters, how many preach on that affliction! Yet how few preached against the war? A preacher may say he hates it as a man, no words could describe his loathing at it; but as a minister of Christ, he dares not say a word! What clergymen tell of the sins of Boston, —of intemperance, licentiousness; who of the ignorance of the people; who of them lays bare our public sin as Christ of old; who tells the causes of poverty, and thousand-handed crime; who aims to apply Christianity to business, to legislation, politics, to all the nation's life! Once the church was the bride of Christ, living by His creative, animating love; her children were apostles, prophets, men by the same spirit, variously inspired with power to heal, to help, to guide mankind. Now she seems the widow of Christ, poorly living on the dower of other times. Nay, the Christ is not dead, and it is her alimony, not her dower. Her children—no such heroic sons gather about her table as before. In her dotage she blindly shoves them off, not counting men as sons of Christ. Is her day gone by? The clergy answer the end they were bred for, paid for. Will they say, "We should lose our influence were we to tell of this and do these things?" It is not true. Their ancient influence is already gone! Who asks, "What do the clergy think of the tariff, or free trade, of annexation, or the war, of Slavery, or the education movement?" Why, no man. It is sad to say these things. Would God they were not true. Look round you, and if you can, come tell me they are false. . . .

Here trade takes the place of the army, navy, and court in other lands. That is well, but it takes also the place in great measure of science, art, and literature. So we become vulgar, and have little but trade to show. The rich man's son seldom devotes himself to literature, science, or art; only to getting more money, or to living in idleness on what he has inherited. When money is the end, what need to look for anything more? He degenerates into the class of consumers, and thinks it an honour. He is ashamed of his father's blood, proud of his gold. A good deal of scientific labour meets with no reward, but itself. In our country this falls almost wholly upon poor men. Literature, science, and art are mainly in their hands, yet are controlled by the prevalent spirit of the nation. Here and there an exceptional man differs from that, but the mass of writers conform. In England, the national literature favours the church, the crown, the nobility, the prevailing class. Another literature is rising, but is not yet national, still less canonized. We have no American literature which is permanent. Our scholarly books are only an imitation of a foreign type; they do not reflect our morals, manners, politics, or religion, not even our rivers, mountains, sky. They have not the smell of our ground in their breath. The real American literature is found only in newspapers and speeches, perhaps in some novel, hot, passionate, but poor and extemporaneous. That is our national literature. Does that favour man—represent man? Certainly not. All is the reflection of this most powerful class. The truths that are told are for them, and the lies. Therein the prevailing sentiment is getting into the form of thought. Politics represent the morals of the controlling class, the morals and manners of rich Peter and David on a large scale. Look at that index, you would sometimes think you were not in the Senate of a great nation, but in a board of brokers, angry and higgling about stocks. Once, in the nation's loftiest hour, she rose inspired, and said: "All men are born equal, each with unalienable rights; that is self-evident." Now she repents her of the vision and the saying. It does not appear in her literature, nor church, nor state. Instead of that, through this controlling class, the nation says: "All dollars are equal, however got; each has unalienable rights. Let no man question that!" This appears in literature and legislation, Church and State. The morals of a nation, of its controlling class, always get summed up in its political action. That is the barometer of the moral weather. The voters are always fairly represented.

The wicked baron, bad of heart, and bloody of hand, has past off with the ages which gave birth to such a brood, but the bad merchant still lives. He cheats in his trade; sometimes against the law, commonly with it. His truth is never wholly true, nor his lie wholly false. He over-reaches the ignorant; makes hard bargains with men in their trouble, for he knows that a falling man will catch at red-hot iron. He takes the pound of flesh, though that bring away all the life-blood with it. He loves private contracts, digging through walls in secret. No interest is illegal if he can get it. He cheats the nation with false invoices, and swears lies at the custom-house; will not pay his taxes, but moves out of town on the last of April. He oppresses the men who sail his ships, forcing them to be temperate, only that he may consume the value of their drink. He provides for them unsuitable bread and meat. He would not engage in the African slave trade, for he might lose his ships, and perhaps more; but he is always ready to engage in the American slave trade, and calls you a "fanatic" if you tell him it is the worse of the two. He cares not whether he sells cotton or the man who wears it, if he only gets the money; cotton or negro, it is the same to him. He would not keep a drink-hole in Ann Street, only own and rent it. He will bring or make whole cargoes of the poison that deals "damnation round the land." He thinks it vulgar to carry rum about in a jug, respectable in a ship. He makes paupers, and leaves others to support them. Tell not him of the misery of the poor, he knows better; nor of our paltry way of dealing with public crime, he wants more gaols, and a speedier gallows. You see his character in letting his houses, his houses for the poor. He is a stone in the lame man's shoe. He is the poor man's devil. The Hebrew devil that so worried Job is gone; so is the brutal devil that awed our fathers. Nobody fears them; they vanish before cock-crowing. But this devil of the nineteenth century is still extant. He has gone into trade, and advertises in the papers; his name is "good" in the street. He "makes money;" the world is poorer by his wealth. He spends it as he made it, like a devil, on himself, his family alone, or, worse yet, for show. He can build a church out of his gains, to have his morality, his Christianity preached in it, and call that the gospel, as Aaron called a calf— God. He sends rum and missionaries to the same barbarians, the one to damn, the other to "save;" both for his own advantage, for his patron saint is Judas, the first saint who made money out of Christ. Ask not him to do a good deed in private, "men would not know it," and "the example would be lost;" so he never lets a dollar slip out between his thumb and finger without leaving his mark on both sides of it. He is not forecasting to discern effects in causes, nor skilful to create new wealth, only spry in the scramble for what others have made. It is easy to make a bargain with him, hard to settle. In politics he wants a Government that will insure his dividends; so asks what is good for him, but ill for the rest. He knows no right, only power; no man but self; no God but his calf of gold.

What effect has he on young men? They had better touch poison. If he takes you to his heart, he takes you in. What influence on society? To taint and corrupt it all round. He contaminates trade; corrupts politics, making abusive laws, not asking for justice, but only dividends. To the church he is the antichrist. Yes, the very devil, and frightens the poor minister into shameful silence, or, more shameless yet, into an apology for crime; makes him pardon the theory of crime! Let us look on that monster—look and pass by, not without prayer.

The good merchant tells the truth, and thrives by that; is upright and downright; his word good as his Bible oath. He pays for all he takes; though never so rich he owns no wicked dollar; all is openly, honestly, manfully earned, and a full equivalent paid for it. He owns money and is worth a man. He is just in business with the strong; charitable in dealing with the weak. His counting-room or his shop is the sanctuary of fairness, justice, a school of uprightness as well as thrift. Industry and honour go hand in hand with him. He gets rich by industry and forecast, not by slight of hand and shuffling his cards to another's loss. No men become the poorer because he is rich. He would sooner hurt himself than wrong another, for he is a man, not a fox. He entraps no man with lies, active or passive. His honesty is better capital than a sharper's cunning. Yet he makes no more talk about justice and honesty than the sun talks of light and heat; they do their own talking. His profession of religion is all practice. He knows that a good man is just as near heaven in his shop as in his church, at work as at prayer; so he makes all work sacramental: he communes with God and man in buying and selling—communion in both kinds. He consecrates his week-day and his work. Christianity appears more divine in this man's deed than in the holiest words of apostle or saint. He treats every man as he wishes all to treat him, and thinks no more of that than of carrying one for every ten. It is the rule of his arithmetic. You know this man is a saint, not by his creed, but by the letting of his houses, his treatment of all that depend on him. He is a father to defend the weak, not a pirate to rob them. He looks out for the welfare of all that he employs; if they are his help he is theirs, and as he is the strongest so the greater help. His private prayer appears in his public work, for in his devotion he does not apologize for his sin, but asking to outgrow that, challenges himself to new worship and more piety. He sets on foot new enterprises which develop the nation's wealth and help others while they help him. He wants laws that take care of man's rights, knowing that then he can take care of himself and of his own, but hurt no man by so doing. He asks laws for the weak, not against them. He would not take vengeance on the wicked, but correct them. His justice tastes of charity. He tries to remove the causes of poverty, licentiousness, of all crime, and thinks that is alike the duty of Church and State. Ask not him to make a statesman a party-man, or the churches an apology for his lowness. He knows better; he calls that infidelity. He helps the weak help themselves. He is a moral educator, a church of Christ gone into business, a saint in trade. The Catholic saint who stood on a pillar's top, or shut himself into a den and fed on grass, is gone to his place—that Christian Nebuchadnezzar. He got fame in his day. No man honours him now; nobody even imitates him. But the saint of the nineteenth century is the good merchant; he is wisdom for the foolish, strength for the weak, warning to the wicked, and a blessing to all. Build him a shrine in bank and church, in the market and the exchange, or build it not, no saint stands higher than this saint of trade. There are such men, rich and poor, young and old; such men in Boston. I have known more than one such, and far greater and better than I have told of, for I purposely under-colour this poor sketch. They need no word of mine for encouragement or sympathy. Have they not Christ and God to aid and bless them? Would that some word of mine might stir the heart of others to be such; your hearts, young men. They rise there clean amid the dust of commerce and the mechanic's busy life, and stand there like great square pyramids in the desert amongst the Arabians' shifting tents. Look at them, ye young men, and be healed of your folly. It is not the calling which corrupts the man, but the men the calling. The most experienced will tell you so. I know it demands manliness to make a man, but God sent you here to do that work.

The duty of this class is quite plain. They control the wealth, the physical strength, the intellectual vigour of the nation. They now display an energy new and startling. No ocean is safe from their canvas; they fill the valleys; they level the hills; they chain the rivers; they use the willing soil to double harvests. Nature opens all her stores to them; like the fabled dust of Egypt, her fertile bosom teems with new wonders, new forces to toil for man. No race of men in times of peace ever displayed so manly an enterprise, an energy so vigorous as this class here in America. Nothing seems impossible to them. The instinct of production was never so strong and creative before. They are proving that peace can stimulate more than war.

Would that my words could reach all of this class. Think not I love to speak hard words, and so often; say not that I am setting the poor against the rich. It is no such thing. I am trying to set the strong in favour of the weak. I speak for man. . . .

It is for you who own the machinery of society, to see that no class appropriates to itself what God meant for all. Remember, it is as easy to tyrannize by machinery as by armies, and as wicked; that it is greater now to bless mankind thereby, than it was of old to conquer new realms. Let men not curse you, as the old nobility, and shake you off, smeared with blood and dust. Turn your power to goodness, its natural transfiguration, and men shall bless your name, and God bless your soul. If you control the nation's politics, then it is your duty to legislate for the nation,—for man. You may develop the great national idea, the equality of all men; may frame a government which shall secure man's unalienable rights. It is for you to organize the rights of man, thus balancing into harmony the man and the many, to organize the rights of the hand, the head, and the heart. If this be not done, the fault is yours. If the nation play the tyrant over her weakest child, if she plunder and rob the feeble Indian, the feebler Mexican, the Negro, feebler yet, why the blame is yours. Remember there is a God who deals justly with strong and weak. The poor and the weak have loitered behind in the march of man; our cities yet swarm with men half-savage. It is for you, ye elder brothers, to lead forth the weak and poor! If you do the national duty that devolves on you, then are you the saviours of your country, and shall bless not that alone, but all the thousand million sons of men. Toil, then, for that. If the Church is in your hands, then make it preach the Christian truth. Let it help the free development of religion in the self-consciousness of man, with Jesus for its pattern. It is for you to watch over this work, promote it, not retard. Help build the American Church. The Roman Church has been, we know what it was, and what men it bore; the English Church yet stands, we know what it is. But the Church of America—which shall represent American vigour aspiring to realize the ideas of Christianity, of absolute religion,—that is not yet. No man has come with pious genius fit to conceive its litany, to chant its mighty creed, and sing its beauteous psalm. The church of America, the church of freedom, of absolute religion, the church of mankind, where Truth, Goodness, Piety, form one trinity of beauty, strength, and grace— when shall it come? Soon as we will. It is yours to help it come.

14. A Program of Reform for Boston

1849

"What can we do to make things better?" This was the constant inquiry that Parker hurled at his congregation and, through them, at the citizenry of Boston and of the whole country. What can we do about poverty, about ignorance, about intemperance, about crime, about juvenile delinquency—about all the things that prevent men from realizing the full potential that God has implanted in them? There were a dozen sermons of this kind, all calling for action; that call was what chiefly distinguished them from the sermons that floated out of most of the pulpits of the day. Of particular interest in the following extract are Parker's suggestions of "a moral police" to deal with juvenile offenders, and of playgrounds and recreation centers as weapons against crime.

What can we do to make things better?

I have so recently spoken of poverty that I shall say little now. A great change will doubtless take place before many years in the relations between capital and labour; a great change in the spirit of society. I do not believe the disparity now existing between the wealth of men has its origin in human nature, and therefore is to last for ever; I do not believe it is just and right that less than one-twentieth of the people in the nation should own more than ten-twentieths of the property of the nation, unless by their own head, or hands, or heart, they do actually create and earn that amount. I am not now blaming any class of men; only stating a fact. There is a profound conviction in the hearts of many good men, rich as well as poor, that things are wrong; that there is an ideal right for the actual wrong; but I think no man yet has risen up with ability to point out for us the remedy of these evils, and deliver us from what has not badly been named the feudalism of capital. Still, without waiting for the great man to arise, we can do something with our littleness even now; the truant children may be snatched from vagrancy, beggary, and ruin; tenements can be built for the poor, and rented at a reasonable rate. It seems to me that something more can be done in the way of providing employment for the poor, or helping them to employment.

In regard to intemperance, I will not say we can end it by direct efforts. So long as there is misery there will be continued provocation to that vice, if the means thereof are within reach. I do not believe there will be much more intemperance amongst well-bred men; among the poor and wretched it will doubtless long continue. But if we cannot end, we can diminish it, fast as we will. If rich men did not manufacture, nor import, nor sell; if they would not rent their buildings for the sale of intoxicating liquor for improper uses; if they did not by their example favour the improper use thereof, how long do you think your police would arrest and punish one thousand drunkards in the year? how long would twelve hundred rum-shops disgrace your town? Boston is far more sober, at least in appearance, than other large cities of America; but it is still the head-quarters of intemperance for the State of Massachusetts. In arresting intemperance, two-thirds of the poverty, three-fourths of the crime of this city would end at once, and an amount of misery and sin which I have not the skill to calculate. Do you say we cannot diminish intemperance, neither by law, nor by righteous efforts without law? Oh, fie upon such talk! Come, let us be honest, and say we do not wish to, not that we cannot. It is plain that in sixteen years we can build seven great railroads radiating out of Boston, three or four hundred miles long; that we can conquer the Connecticut and the Merrimack, and all the lesser streams of New England; can build up Lowell, and Chicopee, and Lawrence; why, in four years Massachusetts can invest eight-and-fifty millions of dollars in railroads and manufactures, and cannot prevent intemperance! cannot diminish it in Boston! So there are no able men in this town! I am amazed at such talk, in such a place, full of such men, surrounded by such trophies of their work! When the churches preach and men believe that Mammon is not the only God we are practically to serve; that it is more reputable to keep men sober, temperate, comfortable, intelligent, and thriving, than it is to make money out of other men's misery; more Christian, than to sell and manufacture rum, to rent houses for the making of drunkards and criminals, then we shall set about this business with the energy that shows we are in earnest, and by a method which will do the work.

In the matter of crime, something can be done to give efficiency to the laws. No doubt a thorough change must be made in the idea of criminal legislation; vengeance must give way to justice, policemen become moral missionaries, and gaols moral hospitals, that discharge no criminal until he is cured. It will take long to get the idea into men's minds. You must encounter many a doubt, many a sneer, and expect many a failure, too. Men who think they "know the world," because they know that most men are selfish, will not believe you. We must wait for new facts to convince such men. After the idea is established, it will take long to organize it fittingly.

Much can be done for juvenile offenders, much for discharged convicts, even now. We can pull down the gallows, and with it that loathsome theological idea on which it rests—the idea of a vindictive God. A remorseless court, and careful police, can do much to hinder crime; but they cannot remove the causes thereof.

Last year a good man, to whom the State was deeply indebted before, suggested that a moral police should be appointed to look after offenders; to see why they committed their crime; and if only necessity compelled them, to seek out for them some employment, and so remove the causes of crime in detail. The thought was worthy of the age and of the man. In the hands of a practical man, this thought might lead to good results. A beginning has already been made in the right direction, by establishing the State Reform School for Boys. It will be easy to improve on this experiment, and conduct prisons for men on the same scheme of correction and cure, not merely of punishment, in the name of vengeance. But, after all, so long as poverty, misery, intemperance, and ignorance continue, no civil police, no moral police, can keep such causes from creating crime. What keeps you from a course of crime? Your morality, your religion? Is it? Take away your property, your home, your friends, the respect of respectable men; take away what you have received from education, intellectual, moral, and religious; and how much better would the best of us be than the men who will to-morrow be huddled off to gaol, for crimes committed in a dram-shop to-day? The circumstances which have kept you temperate, industrious, respectable, would have made nine-tenths of the men in gaol as good men as you are.

It is not pleasant to think that there are no amusements which lie level to the poor in this country. In Paris, Naples, Rome, Vienna, Berlin, there are cheap pleasures for poor men, which yet are not low pleasures. Here there are amusements for the comfortable and the rich, not too numerous, rather too rare, perhaps, but none for the poor, save only the vice of drunkenness; that is hideously cheap; the inward temptation powerful; the outward occasion always at hand. Last summer, some benevolent men treated the poor children of the city to a day of sunshine, fresh air, and frolic in the fields. Once a year the children, gathered together by another benevolent man, have a floral procession in the streets; some of them have charitably been taught to dance. These things are beautiful to think of; signs of our progress from "the good old times," and omens of a brighter day, when Christianity shall bear more abundantly flowers, and fruit even yet more fair.

The morals of the current literature, of the daily press— you can change when you will. If there is not in us a demand for low morals there will be no supply. The morals of trade, and of politics, the handmaid thereof, we can make better soon as we wish.

It has been my aim to give suggestions, rather than propose distinct plans of action; I do not know that I am capable of that. But some of you are rich men, some able men; many of you, I think, are good men. I appeal to you to do something to raise the moral character of this town. All that has been done in fifty years, or a hundred and fifty, seems very little, while so much still remains to do; only a hint and an encouragement. You cannot do much, nor I much; that is true. But, after all, everything must begin with individual men and women. You can at least give the example of what a good man ought to be and to do to-day; to-morrow you will yourself be the better man for it. So far as that goes, you will have done something to mend the morals of Boston. You can tell of actual evils, and tell of your remedy for them; can keep clear from committing the evils yourself; that also is something.

Here are two things that are certain: We are all brothers, rich and poor, American and foreign; put here by the same God, for the same end, and journeying towards the same heaven, owing mutual help. Then, too, the wise men and good men are the natural guardians of society, and God will not hold them guiltless, if they leave their brothers to perish. I know our moral condition is a reproach to us; I will not deny that, nor try to abate the shame and grief we should feel. When I think of the poverty and misery in the midst of us, and all the consequences thereof, I hardly dare feel grateful for the princely fortunes some men have gathered together. Certainly it is not a Christian society, where such extremes exist; we are only in the process of conversion; proselytes of the gate, and not much more. There are noble men in this city, who have been made philanthropic, by the sight of wrong, of intemperance, and poverty, and crime. Let mankind honour great conquerors, who only rout armies, and "plant fresh laurels where they kill;" I honour most the men who contend against misery, against crime and sin; men that are the soldiers of humanity, and in a low age, amidst the mean and sordid spirits of a great trading town, lift up their serene foreheads, and tell us of the right, the true, first good, first perfect, and first fair. From such men I hear the prophecy of the better time to come. In their example I see proofs of the final triumph of good over evil. Angels are they who keep the tree of life, not with flaming sword, repelling men, but, with friendly hand, plucking therefrom, and giving unto all the leaves, the flower, and the fruit of life, for the healing of the nations. A single good man, kindling his early flame, wakens the neighbours with his words of cheer; they, at his lamp, shall light their torch and household fire, anticipating the beamy warmth of day. Soon it will be morning, warm and light; we shall be up and a doing, and the lighted lamp, which seemed at first too much for eyes to bear, will look ridiculous, and cast no shadow in the noonday sun. A hundred years hence, men will stand here as I do now, and speak of the evils of these times as things past and gone, and wonder that able men could ever be appalled by our difficulties, and think them not to be surpassed. Still, all depends on the faithfulness of men—your faithfulness and mine.

The last election has shown us what resolute men can do on a trifling occasion, if they will. You know the efforts of the three parties—what meetings they held, what money they raised, what talent was employed, what speeches made, what ideas set forth; not a town was left unattempted; scarce a man who had wit to throw a vote, but his vote was solicited. You see the revolution which was wrought by that vigorous style of work. When such men set about reforming the evils of society, with such a determined soul, what evil can stand against mankind? We can leave nothing to the next generation worth so much as ideas of truth, justice, and religion, organized into fitting institutions; such we can leave, and, if true men, such we shall.

15. The Welfare of a Nation

1856

In May 1856, Parker visited New York to give two lectures before the American Anti-Slavery Society on *The Great Battle Between Slavery and Freedom*. William Lloyd Garrison introduced him with a characteristic phrase: "The fanaticism and infidelity and treason which are hateful to the traffickers in slaves and the souls of men must be well-pleasing to God, and are indications of true loyalty to the cause of liberty. I have the pleasure of introducing to you a very excellent fanatic, a very good infidel, and a first-rate traitor, in the person of Theodore Parker."

The second of these speeches, *The Present Crisis in American Affairs,* addressed itself to the struggle for Kansas. As always, Parker tried to put the particular issue in a large historical and moral frame; here that frame is the "welfare of a nation."

In this speech, Parker defines democracy as "government over all the people by all the people, and for the sake of all." This is only one of several speeches and papers in which he used the phrase, which William Herndon picked up and called to the attention of his friend Lincoln, and which Lincoln immortalized in the Gettysburg Address.

To understand this present emergency, you must go a long ways back, and look a little carefully at what lies deep down in the foundation of States.

The welfare of a nation consists in these three things; namely: first, possession of material comfort, things of use and beauty; second, enjoyment of all the natural rights of body and spirit; and, third, the development of the natural faculties of body and spirit in their harmonious order, securing the possession of freedom, intelligence, morality, philanthropy, and piety. It ought to be the aim of a nation to obtain these three things in the highest possible degree, and to extend them to all persons therein. That nation has the most welfare which is the furthest advanced in the possession of these three things.

Next, the progress of a nation consists in two things: first, in the increasing development of the natural faculties of body and

161

spirit,—intellectual, moral, affectional, and religious,—with the consequent increasing enjoyment thereof; and, second, in the increasing acquisition of power over the material world, making it yield use and beauty, an increase of material comfort and elegance. Progress is increase of human welfare for each and for all. That is the most progressive nation which advances fastest in this development of human faculties, and the consequent acquisition of material power. There is no limit to this progress.

That is the superior nation, which, by nature, has the greatest amount of bodily and spiritual faculties, and, by education, has developed them to the highest degree of human culture, and, consequently, is capacious of the greatest amount of power over the material world, to turn it into use and beauty, and so of the greatest amount of universal welfare for all and each. The superior nation is capable of most rapid progress; for the advance of man goes on with accelerated velocity; the further he has gone, the faster he goes.

The disposition in mankind to acquire this increase of human development and material power, I will call the instinct of progress. It exists in different degrees in various nations and races: some are easily content with a small amount thereof, and so advance but slowly; others desire the most of both, and press continually forward.

Of all races, the Caucasian has hitherto shown the most of this instinct of progress, and, though perhaps the youngest of all, has advanced furthest in the development of the human faculties, and in the acquisition of power over the material world; it has already won the most welfare, and now makes the swiftest progress.

Of the various families of the Caucasian race, the Teutonic, embracing all the Germanic people kindred to our own, is now the most remarkable for this instinct of progress. Accordingly, in the last four hundred years, all the great new steps of peaceful Caucasian development have been first taken by the Teutonic people, who now bear the same relation to the world's progress that the Greeks did a thousand years before Christ, the Romans eight hundred years later, and the Romanized Celts of France at a day yet more recent.

Of the Teutons, the Anglo-Saxons, or that portion thereof settled in the Northern States of America, have got the furthest forward in certain important forms of welfare, and now advance the most rapidly in their general progress. With no class of capitalists or scholars equal to the men of great estates and great learning in Europe, the whole mass of the people have yet attained the greatest material comfort, enjoyment of natural rights, and development of the human faculties. They feel most powerfully the general instinct of progress, and advance swiftest to future welfare and development. Here the bulk of the population is Anglo-Saxon; but this powerful blood has been enriched by additions from divers other sources,—Teutonic and Celtic.

The great forces which in the last four hundred years have most powerfully and obviously helped this welfare and progress, may be reduced to two marked tendencies, which I will sum up in the form of ideas, and name the one Christianity and the other Democracy.

By Christianity, I mean that form of religion which consists of piety—the love of God, and morality—the keeping of His laws. That is not the Christianity of the Christian Church, nor of any sect; it is the ideal religion which the human race has been groping after, if happily we might find it. It is yet only an ideal, actual in no society.

By Democracy, I mean government over all the people by all the people, and for the sake of all. Of course, it is government according to the natural law of God, by justice, the point common to each man and all men, to each nation and all mankind, to the human race and to God. In a democracy, the people reign with sovereign power; their elected servants govern with delegated trust. There is national unity of action, represented by law; this makes the nation one, a whole; it is the centripetal force of society. But there is also individual variety of action, represented by the personal freedom of the people who ultimately make the laws; this makes John John, and not James, the individual a free person, discreet from all other men; this is the centrifugal force of society, which counteracts the excessive solidification that would else go on. Thus, by justice, the one and the many are balanced together, as the centripetal and centrifugal forces in the solar system.

This is not the democracy of the parties, but it is that ideal government, the reign of righteousness, the kingdom of justice, which all noble hearts long for, and labour to produce, the ideal whereunto mankind slowly draws near. No nation has yet come so close to it as the people of some of the Northern States, who are yet far beneath ideals of government now known, that are yet themselves vastly inferior to others which mankind shall one day voyage after, discover, and annex to human possession.

In this Democracy, and the tendency towards it, two things come to all; namely, labour and government.

Labour for material comfort, the means of use and beauty, is the duty of all, and not less the right, and practically the lot, of all; so there is no privilege for any, where each has his whole natural right. Accordingly, there is no permanent and vicariously idle class, born merely to enjoy and not create, who live by the unpurchased toil of others; and, accordingly, there is no permanent and vicariously working-class, born merely to create and not enjoy, who toil only for others. There is mutuality of earning and enjoying: none is compelled to work vicariously for another, none allowed to rob others of the natural fruit of their toil. Of course, each works at such calling as his nature demands: on the *mare liberum,* the open sea of human industry, every personal bark sails whither it may, and with such freight and swiftness as it will or can.

Government, in social and political affairs, is the right of all, not less their duty, and practically the lot of each. So there is no privilege in politics, no lordly class born to command and not obey, no slavish class born to serve and not command: there is mutuality of command and obedience. And as there is no compulsory vicarious work, but each takes part in the labour of all, and has his share in the enjoyment thereof; so there is no vicarious government, but each takes part in the making of laws and in obedience thereunto.

Such is the ideal Democracy, nowhere made actual.

IV

The American Scholar

All his life Parker was torn between the claims of the pulpit, the delights of the study and the allurements of the public arena. From his earliest youth it was clear to him that he wanted to be a clergyman; but from his early youth too, he found the attractions of scholarship irresistible. Even in the Divinity School, his learning was something of a legend, and the legend grew with the years. He read everything, so it seemed, and everything he read he remembered. He ranged over the whole area of theology, mastered all systems of philosophy, knew all languages—anyway, almost all. His early friendships, and his closest, were with scholars—men like Convers Francis, for example, or Dr. Follen, and all his life he delighted in his contacts with scholars in Germany and Switzerland, and not with theologians alone. As a student at the Divinity School, he earned money by translating letters of Lafayette for Professor Sparks; a few years later, he was translating and annotating Wilhelm De Wette's stout volumes, *A Critical and Historical Introduction to the Canonical Scriptures of the Old Testament.* "I meant it," he wrote, "for a labor of love."

With Parker scholarship was always a labor of love. He had been so starved in boyhood and youth that he was greedy and voracious. He couldn't read enough books, or buy enough, or—for that matter—write enough. He couldn't speak or read enough languages: three or four were insufficient; he had to cut his linguistic teeth on Scandinavian languages, Portuguese and a dozen others. Theology and philosophy and history were not enough; he had to be familiar with geology and archeology and law too. Thus his library—it was rumored to be the largest private library in Boston—included not only the *English State Trials,* Campbell's *Lives of the Chief Justices* and the *Parliamentary History of England* in many volumes, but the writings of the German jurist Savigny, a shelf of the *Jurisprudence Musselmane* and another of the *Corpus Juris Germanici Publici ac Privati* as well.

He travelled incessantly, and wherever he went, he carried with him a green bag bulging with books; even his simplest sermons read like erudite monographs. His pen too was tireless, and (as this compilation makes clear) he wrote on the most varied subjects. German literature, the authenticity of the Scriptures, the morality of Prescott's histories, Buckle's theories of civilization, Homeric criticism, politics, economics, sociology—all were grist to his literary mill.

Yet, however passionate his sense of responsibility to learning, it

167

was not as strong as his sense of moral responsibility. It was all very well, he felt, for German scholars to immure themselves in their studies eighteen hours a day and devote their lives to exhaustive research in Homeric studies or philological questions, but that would never do for the American scholar. He had other and serious responsibilities. Scholarship was not a private but a public affair; and in America the scholar was under a deep moral obligation to instruct and elevate the people.

So we have in Parker—perhaps more fully than in any other figure of the New England renaissance—the scholar in action, the scholar bringing the resources of his learning to bear on education, labor, politics, war, slavery and all the other great public issues of the day. Only in this way could he justify his scholarship.

16. The American Character

1848

Parker was something of an intellectual gourmand. He could write with learning, and sometimes with wit, on German literature, the Inca and Aztec civilizations, biblical criticism, the history of English law, philology, comparative religion and a score of learned subjects. Above all, he fancied himself an historian. He wrote and lectured on historic Americans, on the history of English liberty, on the philosophy of civilization. His philosophy of history was simple and clear: history is a branch of ethics, and the function of history is to point a moral, exalt good, rebuke evil, teach the errors of the past and provide sound principles for the future. "In telling what has been," he wrote in a scathing review of Prescott, "the historian is also to tell what ought to be, for he is to pass judgment on events, and try counsels by their causes first and their consequences not less . . . [History is] philosophy teaching by experience."

Nowhere was Parker happier than in his long essay *The Political Destination of America and the Signs of the Times.* "Every nation," he announced, "has a peculiar character, in which it differs from all others"; what is the American? The genius of America is for liberty. If this were true—and who could doubt it after reading Mr. Parker?—slavery violated the genius and the character of the American people. But the essay is more than an argument for freedom; it is an analysis of the American character scarcely less fascinating than that of Tocqueville. Here is a commentary on our American impatience with authority, precedent and tradition; our sense of newness and independence; our habit of change and desire for novelty; our tendency to broad general notions; our exaggeration, haste, humor, energy, spontaneity, intensity and superficiality. Here too is an expression of confidence that the habits of democracy and of freedom will, in the end, triumph.

Every nation has a peculiar character, in which it differs from all others that have been, that are, and possibly from all that are to come; for it does not yet appear that the Divine Father of the nations ever repeats himself and creates either two nations or two men exactly alike. However, as nations, like men, agree in more things than they differ, and in obvious things too, the special peculiarity of any one tribe does not always appear at first sight. But if we look through the history of some nation which has passed off from the stage of action, we find certain prevailing traits which continually reappear in the language and laws thereof; in its arts, literature, manners, modes of religion—in short, in the whole life of the people. . . .

The most marked characteristic of the American nation is Love of Freedom; of man's natural rights. This is so plain to a student of American history, or of American politics, that the point requires no arguing. We have a genius for liberty: the American idea is freedom, natural rights. Accordingly, the work providentially laid out for us to do seems this,—to organize the rights of man. This is a problem hitherto unattempted on a national scale, in human history. Often enough attempts have been made to organize the powers of priests, kings, nobles, in a theocracy, monarchy, oligarchy, powers which had no foundation in human duties or human rights, but solely in the selfishness of strong men. Often enough have the mights of men been organized, but not the rights of man. Surely there has never been an attempt made on a national scale to organize the rights of man as man; rights resting on the nature of things; rights derived from no conventional compact of men with men; not inherited from past generations, nor received from parliaments and kings, nor secured by their parchments; but rights that are derived straightway from God, the Author of Duty and the Source of Right, and which are secured in the great charter of our being.

At first view it will be said, the peculiar genius of America is not such, nor such her fundamental idea, nor that her destined work. It is true that much of the national conduct seems exceptional when measured by that standard, and the nation's course as crooked as the Rio Grande; it is true that America sometimes seems to spurn liberty, and sells the freedom of three million men for less than three million annual bales of cotton; true, she often tramples, knowingly, consciously, tramples on the most unquestionable and sacred rights. Yet, when one looks through the whole character and history of America, spite of the exceptions, nothing comes out with such relief as this love of freedom, this idea of liberty, this attempt to organize right. There are numerous subordinate qualities which conflict with the nation's idea and work, coming from our circumstances, not our soul, as well as many others which help the nation perform her providential work. They are signs of the times, and it is important to look carefully among the most prominent of them, where, indeed, one finds striking contradictions.

The first is an impatience of authority. Every thing must render its reason, and show cause for its being. We will not be commanded, at least only by such as we choose to obey. Does some one say, "Thou shalt," or "Thou shalt not," we ask, "Who are you?" Hence comes a seeming irreverence. The shovel hat, the symbol of authority, which awed our fathers, is not respected unless it covers a man, and then it is the man we honour, and no longer the shovel hat. "I will complain of you to the government!" said a Prussian nobleman to a Yankee stage-driver, who uncivilly threw the nobleman's trunk to the top of the coach. "Tell the government to go to the devil!" was the symbolical reply.

Old precedents will not suffice us, for we want something anterior to all precedents; we go beyond what is written, asking the cause of the precedent and the reason of the writing. "Our fathers did so," says some one. "What of that?" say we. "Our fathers— they were giants, were they? Not at all, only great boys, and we are not only taller than they, but mounted on their shoulders to boot, and see twice as far. My dear wise man, or wiseacre, it is we that are the ancients, and have forgotten more than all our fathers knew. We will take their wisdom joyfully, and thank God for it, but not their authority, we know better; and of their nonsense not a word. It was very well that they lived, and it is very well that they are dead. Let them keep decently buried, for respectable dead men never walk."

Tradition does not satisfy us. The American scholar has no folios in his library. The antiquary unrolls his codex, hid for eighteen hundred years in the ashes of Herculaneum, deciphers its fossil wisdom, telling us what great men thought in the bay of Naples, and two thousand years ago. "What do you tell of that for?" is the answer to his learning. "What has Pythagoras to do with the price of cotton? You may be a very learned man; you can read the hieroglyphics of Egypt, I dare say, and know so much about the Pharaohs, it is a pity you had not lived in their time, when you might have been good for something; but you are too old-fashioned for our business, and may return to your dust." An eminent American, a student of Egyptian history, with a scholarly indignation declared, "There is not a man who cares to know whether Shoophoo lived one thousand years before Christ, or three."

The example of other and ancient States does not terrify or instruct us. If slavery were a curse to Athens, the corruption of Corinth, the undoing of Rome, and all history shows it was so, we will learn no lesson from that experience, for we say, "We are not Athenians, men of Corinth, nor pagan Romans, thank God, but free republicans, Christians of America. We live in the nineteenth century, and though slavery worked all that mischief then and there, we know how to make money out of it, twelve hundred millions of dollars, as Mr. Clay counts the cash."

The example of contemporary nations furnishes us little warning or guidance. We will set our own precedents, and do not like to be told that the Prussians or the Dutch have learned some things in the education of the people before us, which we shall do well to learn after them. So when a good man tells us of their schools and their colleges, "patriotic" schoolmasters exclaim, "It is not true; our schools are the best in the world! But if it were true, it is unpatriotic to say so; it aids and comforts the enemy." Jonathan knows little of war; he has heard his grandfather talk of Lexington and Saratoga; he thinks he should like to have a little touch of battle on his own account: so when there is difficulty in setting up the fence betwixt his estate and his neighbours, he blusters for awhile, talks big, and threatens to strike his father; but, not having quite the stomach for that experiment, falls to beating his other neighbour, who happens to be poor, weak, and of a sickly constitution; and when he beats her at every step,—

> "For 'tis no war, as each one knows,
> When only one side deals the blows,
> And t'other bears 'em,"—

Jonathan thinks he has covered himself with "imperishable honours," and sets up his general for a great king. Poor Jonathan—he does not know the misery, the tears, the blood, the shame, the wickedness, and the sin he has set a-going, and which one day he is to account for with God, who forgets nothing!

Yet while we are so unwilling to accept the good principles, to be warned by the fate, or guided by the success, of other nations, we gladly and servilely copy their faults, their follies, their vice and sin. Like all upstarts, we pique ourselves on our imitation of aristocratic ways. How many a blusterer in Congress,—for there are two denominations of blusterers, differing only in degree, your great blusterer in Congress and your little blusterer in a bar-room, —has roared away hours long against aristocratic influence, in

favour of the "pure democracy," while he played the oligarch in
his native village, the tyrant over his hired help, and though no
man knows who his grandfather was, spite of the herald's office,
conjures up some trumpery coat of arms! Like a clown, who, by
pinching his appetite, has bought a gaudy cloak for Sabbath wear-
ing, we chuckle inwardly at our brave apery of foreign absurdities,
hoping that strangers will be astonished at us—which, sure
enough, comes to pass. Jonathan is as vain as he is conceited, and
expects that the Fiddlers, and the Trollopes, and others, who visit
us periodically as the swallows, and likewise for what they can
catch, shall only extol, or at least stand aghast at the brave spectacle we offer, of "the freest and most enlightened nation in the
world;" and if they tell us that we are an ill-mannered set, raw and
clownish, that we pick our teeth with a fork, loll back in our chairs,
and make our countenance hateful with tobacco, and that with all
our excellences we are a nation of "rowdies,"—why, we are
offended, and our feelings are hurt. There was an African chief,
long ago, who ruled over a few miserable cabins, and one day received a French traveller from Paris, under a tree. With the exception of a pair of shoes, our chief was as naked as a pestle, but
with great complacency he asked the traveller, "What do they say
of me at Paris?"

Such is our dread of authority, that we like not old things;
hence we are always a-changing. Our house must be new, and our
book, and even our church. So we choose a material that soon wears
out, though it often outlasts our patience. The wooden house is an
apt emblem of this sign of the times. But this love of change appears
not less in important matters. We think "Of old things all are over
old, of new things none are new enough." So the age asks of all
institutions their right to be: What right has the government to
existence? Who gave the majority a right to control the minority,
to restrict trade, levy taxes, make laws, and all that? If the nation
goes into a committee of the whole and makes laws, some little
man goes into a committee of one and passes his counter resolves.
The State of South Carolina is a nice example of this self-reliance,
and this questioning of all authority. That little brazen State, which
contains only about half so many free white inhabitants as the
single city of New York, but which none the less claims to have
monopolized most of the chivalry of the nation, and its patriotism,
as well as political wisdom—that chivalrous little State says, "If
the nation does not make laws to suit us; if it does not allow us
to imprison all black seamen from the North; if it prevents the

extension of Slavery wherever we wish to carry it—then the State of South Carolina will nullify, and leave the other nine-and-twenty States to go to ruin!"

Men ask what right have the churches to the shadow of authority which clings to them—to make creeds, and to bind and to loose! So it is a thing which has happened, that when a church excommunicates a young stripling for heresy, he turns round, fulminates his edict, and excommunicates the church. Said a sly Jesuit to an American Protestant at Rome, "But the rites and customs and doctrines of the Catholic church go back to the second century, the age after the apostles!" "No doubt of it," said the American, who had also read the Fathers, "they go back to the times of the apostles themselves; but that proves nothing, for there were as great fools in the first century as the last. A fool or a folly is no better because it is an old folly or an old fool. There are fools enough now, in all conscience. Pray don't go back to prove their apostolical succession."

There are always some men who are born out of due season, men of past ages, stragglers of former generations, who ought to have born before Dr. Faustus invented printing, but who are unfortunately born now, or, if born long ago, have been fradulently and illegally concealed by their mothers, and are now, for the first time, brought to light. The age lifts such aged juveniles from the ground, and bids them live, but they are sadly to seek in this day; they are old-fashioned boys; their authority is called in question; their traditions and old-wives' fables are laughed at, at any rate disbelieved; they get profanely elbowed in the crowd—men not knowing their great age and consequent venerableness; the shovel hat, though apparently born on their head, is treated with disrespect. The very boys laugh pertly in their face when they speak, and even old men can scarce forbear a smile, though it may be a smile of pity. The age affords such men a place, for it is a catholic age, large-minded, and tolerant,—such a place as it gives to ancient armour, Indian Bibles, and fossil bones of the mastodon; it puts them by in some room seldom used, with other old furniture, and allows them to mumble their anilities by themselves; now and then takes off its hat; looks in, charitably, to keep the mediæval relics in good heart, and pretends to listen, as they discourse of what comes of nothing and goes to it; but in matters which the age cares about, commerce, manufactures, politics, which it cares much for, even in education, which it cares far too little about, it trusts no such counsellors, nor tolerates nor ever affects to listen.

Then there is a philosophical tendency, distinctly visible; a groping after ultimate facts, first principles, and universal ideas. We wish to know first the fact, next the law of that fact, and then the reason of the law. A sign of this tendency is noticeable in the titles of books; we have no longer "treatises" on the eye, the ear, sleep, and so forth, but in their place we find works professing to treat of the "philosophy" of vision, of sound, of sleep. Even in the pulpits, men speak about the "philosophy" of religion; we have philosophical lectures, delivered to men of little culture, which would have amazed our grandfathers, who thought a shoemaker should never go beyond his last, even to seek for the philosophy of shoes. "What a pity," said a grave Scotchman, in the beginning of this century, "to teach the beautiful science of geometry to weavers and cobblers." Here nothing is too good or high for any one tall and good enough to get hold of it. What audiences attend the Lowell lectures in Boston—two or three thousand men, listening to twelve lectures on the philosophy of fish! It would not bring a dollar or a vote, only thought to their minds! Young ladies are well versed in the philosophy of the affections, and understand the theory of attraction, while their grandmothers, good easy souls, were satisfied with the possession of the fact. The circumstance, that philosophical lectures get delivered by men like Walker, Agassiz, Emerson, and their coadjutors, men who do not spare abstruseness, get listened to, and even understood, in town and village, by large crowds of men, of only the most common culture; this indicates a philosophical tendency, unknown in any other land or age. Our circle of professed schoalrs, men of culture and learning, is a very small one, while our circle of thinking men is disproportionately large. The best thought of France and Germany finds a readier welcome here than in our parent land: nay, the newest and the best thought of England finds its earliest and warmest welcome in America. It was a little remarkable, that Bacon and Newton should be reprinted here, and La Place should have found his translator and expositor coming out of an insurance office in Salem! Men of no great pretensions object to an accomplished and eloquent politician: "That is all very well; he made us cry and laugh, but the discourse was not philosophical; he never tells us the reason of the thing; he seems not only not to know it, but not to know that there is a reason for the thing, and if not, what is the use of this bobbing on the surface?" Young maidens complain of the minister, that he has no philosophy in his sermons, nothing but precepts, which they could read in the Bible as well as he; perhaps in heathen Seneca. He does not feed their souls. . . .

Then, again, there is great intensity of life and purpose. This displays itself in our actions and speeches; in our speculations; in the "revivals" of the more serious sects; in the excitements of trade; in the general character of the people. All that we do we overdo. It appears in our hopefulness; we are the most aspiring of nations. Not content with half the continent, we wish the other half. We have this characteristic of genius: we are dissatisfied with all that we have done. Somebody once said we were too vain to be proud. It is not wholly so; the national idea is so far above us that any achievement seems little and low. The American soul passes away from its work soon as it is finished. So the soul of each great artist refuses to dwell in his finished work, for that seems little to his dream. Our fathers deemed the Revolution a great work; it was once thought a surprising thing to found that little colony on the shores of New England; but young America looks to other revolutions, and thinks she has many a Plymouth colony in her bosom. If other nations wonder at our achievements, we are a disappointment to ourselves, and wonder we have not done more. Our national idea out-travels our experience, and all experience. We began our national career by setting all history at defiance—for that said, "A republic on a large scale cannot exist." Our progress since has shown that we were right in refusing to be limited by the past. The political ideas of the nation are transcendant, not empirical. Human history could not justify the Declaration of Independence and its large statements of the new idea: the nation went behind human history and appealed to human nature.

We are more spontaneous than logical; we have ideas, rather than facts or precedents. We dream more than we remember, and so have many orators and poets, or poetasters, with but few antiquaries and general scholars. We are not so reflective as forecasting. We are the most intuitive of modern nations. The very party in politics which has the least culture, is richest in ideas which will one day become facts. Great truths—political, philosophical, religious—lie a-burning in many a young heart which cannot legitimate nor prove them true, but none the less feels, and feels them true. A man full of new truths finds a ready audience with us. Many things which come disguised as truths under such circumstances pass current for a time, but by and by their bray discovers them. The hope which comes from this intensity of life and intui-

tion of truths is a national characteristic. It gives courage, enterprise, and strength. They can who think they can. We are
confident in our star; other nations may see it or not, we know it
is there above the clouds. We do not hesitate at rash experiments—
sending fifty thousand soldiers to conquer a nation with eight or
nine millions of people. We are up to everything, and think ourselves a match for anything. The young man is rash, for he only
hopes, having little to remember; he is excitable, and loves excitement; change of work is his repose; he is hot and noisy, sanguine
and fearless, with the courage that comes from warm blood and
ignorance of dangers; he does not know what a hard, tough, sour
old world he is born into. We are a nation of young men. We
talked of annexing Texas and northern Mexico, and did both; now
we grasp at Cuba, Central America,—all the continent,—speak
of a railroad to the Pacific as a trifle for us to accomplish. Our
national deeds are certainly great, but our hope and promise far
outbrags them all.

If this intensity of life and hope has it good side, it has also
its evil; with much of the excellence of youth we have its faults—
rashness, haste, and superficiality. Our work is seldom well done.
In English manufactures there is a certain solid honesty of performance; in the French a certain air of elegance and refinement:
one misses both these in American works. It is said America invents the most machines, but England builds them best. We lack
the phlegmatic patience of older nations. We are always in a hurry,
morning, noon, and night. We are impatient of the process, but
greedy of the result; so that we make short experiments but long reports, and talk much though we say little. We forget that a sober
method is a short way of coming to the end, and that he who, before he sets out, ascertains where he is going and the way thither,
ends his journey more prosperously than one who settles these
matters by the way. Quickness is a great desideratum with us. It
is said an American ship is known far off at sea by the quantity of
canvas she carries. Rough and ready is a popular attribute. Quick
and off would be a symbolic motto for the nation at this day, representing one phase of our character. We are sudden in deliberation; the "one-hour rule" works well in Congress. A committee of
the British Parliament spends twice or thrice our time in collecting
facts, understanding and making them intelligible, but less than
our time in speech-making after the report; speeches there commonly being for the purpose of facilitating the business, while here
one sometimes is half ready to think, notwithstanding our earnest-

ness, that the business is to facilitate the speaking. A State revises her statutes with a rapidity that astonishes a European. Yet each revision brings some amendment, and what is found good in the constitution or laws of one State gets speedily imitated by the rest; each new State of the North becoming more democratic than its predecessor.

We are so intent on our purpose that we have no time for amusement. We have but one or two festivals in the year, and even then we are serious and reformatory. Jonathan thinks it a very solemn thing to be merry. A Frenchman said we have but two amusements in America—theology for the women and politics for the men; preaching and voting. If this be true, it may help to explain the fact that most men take their theology from their wives, and women politics from their husbands. No nation ever tried the experiment of such abstinence from amusement. We have no time for sport, and so lose much of the poetry of life. All work and no play does not always make a dull boy, but it commonly makes a hard man.

We rush from school into business early; we hurry while in business; we aim to be rich quickly, making a fortune at a stroke, making or losing it twice or thrice in a lifetime. "Soft and fair, goes safe and far," is no proverb to our taste. We are the most restless of people. How we crowd into cars and steamboats; a locomotive would well typify our fuming, fizzing spirit. In our large towns life seems to be only a scamper. Not satisfied with bustling about all day, when night comes we cannot sit still, but alone of all nations have added rockers to our chairs.

All is haste, from the tanning of leather to the education of a boy, and the old saw holds its edge good as ever—"the more haste the worse speed." The young stripling, innocent of all manner of lore, whom a judicious father has barrelled down in a college, or law-school, or theological seminary, till his beard be grown, mourns over the few years he must spend there awaiting that operation. His rule is, "to make a spoon or spoil a horn;" he longs to be out in the world "making a fortune," or "doing good," as he calls what his father better names "making noisy work for repentance, and doing mischief." So he rushes into life not fitted, and would fly towards heaven, this young Icarus, his wings not half fledged. There seems little taste for thoroughness. In our schools as our farms, we pass over much ground, but pass over it poorly.

In education the aim is not to get the most we can, but the

least we can get along with. A ship with over-much canvas and over-little ballast were no bad emblem of many amongst us. In no country is it so easy to get a reputation for learning—accumulated thought, because so few devote themselves to that accumulation. In this respect our standard is low. So a man of one attainment is sure to be honoured, but a man of many and varied abilities is in danger of being undervalued. A Spurzheim would be warmly welcomed, while a Humboldt would be suspected of superficiality, as we have not the standard to judge him by. Yet in no country in the world is it so difficult to get a reputation for eloquence, as many speak, and that well. It is surprising with what natural strength and beauty the young American addresses himself to speak. Some hatter's apprentice, or shoemaker's journeyman, at a temperance or anti-slavery meeting, will speak words like the blows of an axe, that cut clean and deep. The country swarms with orators, more abundantly where education is least esteemed —in the West or South.

We have secured national unity of action for the white citizens, without much curtaining individual variety of action, so we have at the North pretty well solved that problem which other nations have so often boggled over; we have balanced the centripetal power, the government and laws, with the centrifugal power, the mass of individuals, into harmonious proportions. If one were to leave out of sight the three million slaves, one-sixth part of the population, the problem might be regarded as very happily solved. As the consequences of this, in no country is there more talent, or so much awake and active. In the South this unity is attained by sacrificing all the rights of three million slaves, and almost all the rights of the other coloured population. In despotic countries this unity is brought about by the sacrifice of freedom, individual variety of action, in all except the despot and his favourites; so, much of the nation's energy is stifled in the chains of the State, while here it is friendly to institutions which are friendly to it, goes to its work, and approves itself in the vast increase of wealth and comfort throughout the North, where there is no class of men which is so oppressed that it cannot rise. One is amazed at the amount of ready skill and general ability which he finds in all the North, where each man has a little culture, takes his newspaper, manages his own business, and talks with some intelligence of many things—especially of politics and theology. In respect to this general intellectual ability and power of self-help, the mass of people seem far in advance of any other nation. But at the same time our scholars, who always represent the nation's higher modes of consciousness, will not bear comparison with the scholars of England, France, and Germany, men thoroughly furnished for their work. This is a great reproach and mischief to us, for we need most accomplished leaders, who by their thought can direct this national intensity of life. Our literature does not furnish them; we have no great men there; Irving, Channing, Cooper, are not names to conjure with in literature. One reads thick volumes devoted to the poets of America, or her prose writers, and finds many names which he wonders he never heard of before; but when he turns over their works, he finds consolation and recovers his composure.

American literature may be divided into two departments: the permanent literature, which gets printed in books, that sometimes reach more than one edition; and the evanescent literature, which appears only in the form of speeches, pamphlets, reviews, newspaper articles, and the like extempore productions. Now our permanent literature, as a general thing, is superficial, tame, and weak; it is not American; it has not our ideas, our contempt of authority, our philosophical turn, nor even our uncertainty as to first principles, still less our national intensity, our hope, and fresh intuitive perceptions of truth. It is a miserable imitation. Love of freedom is not there. The real national literature is found almost wholly in speeches, pamphlets, and newspapers. The latter are pretty thoroughly American: mirrors in which we see no very flattering likeness of our morals or our manners. Yet the picture is true: that vulgarity, that rant, that bragging violence, that recklessness of truth and justice, that disregard of right and duty, are a part of the nation's everyday life. Our newspapers are low and "wicked to a fault;" only in this weakness are they un-American. Yet they exhibit, and abundantly, the four qualities we have mentioned as belonging to the signs of our times. As a general rule, our orators are also American, with our good and ill. Now and then one rises who has studied Demosthenes in Leland or Francis, and got a second-hand acquaintance with old models: a man who uses literary common-places, and thinks himself original and classic because he can quote a line or so of Horace, in a Western House of Representatives, without getting so many words wrong as his reporter; but such men are rare, and after making due abatement for them, our orators all over the land are pretty thoroughly American, a little turgid, hot, sometimes brilliant, hopeful, intuitive, abounding in half truths, full of great ideas; often inconsequent; sometimes coarse; patriotic, vain, self-confident, rash, strong, and young-mannish. Of course the most of our speeches are vulgar, ranting, and worthless; but we have produced some magnificent specimens of oratory, which are fresh, original, American, and brand new.

The more studied, polished, and elegant literature is not so; that is mainly an imitation. It seems not a thing of native growth. Sometimes, as in Channing, the thought and the hope are American, but the form and the colouring old and foreign. We dare not be original; our American pine must be cut to the trim pattern of the English yew, though the pine bleed at every clip. This poet tunes his lyre at the harp of Goethe, Milton, Pope, or Tennyson. His songs might be better sung on the Rhine than the Kennebec. They are not American in form or feeling; they have not the breath of our air; the smell of our ground is not in them. Hence our poet seems cold and poor. He loves the old mythology; talks about Pluto—the Greek devil, the fates and furies—witches of old time in Greece, but would blush to use our mythology, or breathe the name in verse of our devil, our own witches, lest he should be thought to believe what he wrote. The mother and sisters, who with many a pinch and pain sent the hopeful boy to college, must turn over the classical dictionary before they can find out what the youth would be at in his rhymes. Our poet is not deep enough to see that Aphrodite came from the ordinary waters, that Homer only hitched into rhythm and furnished the accomplishment of verse to street-talk, nursery tales, and old men's gossip in the Ionian towns; he thinks what is common is unclean. So he sings of Corinth and Athens, which he never saw, but has not a word to say of Boston, and Fall River, and Baltimore, and New York, which are just as meet for song. He raves of Thermopylæ and Marathon, with never a word for Lexington and Bunker Hill, for Cowpens, and Lundy's Lane, and Bemis's Heights. He loves to tell of the Ilyssus, of "smooth-sliding Mincius, crowned with vocal reeds," yet sings not of the Petapsco, the Susquehanna, the Aroostook, and the Willimantick. He prates of the narcissus and the daisy, never of American dandelions and blue-eyed grass; he dwells on the lark and the nightingale, but has not a thought for the brown thrasher and the bobolink, who every morning in June rain down such showers of melody on his affected head. What a lesson Burns teaches us, addressing his "rough burthistle," his daisy, "wee crimson tippit thing," and finding marvellous poetry in the mouse whose nest his plough turned over! Nay, how beautifully has even our sweet poet sung of our own Green river, our waterfowl, of the blue and fringed gentian, the glory of autumnal days.

Hitherto, spite of the great reading public, we have no permanent literature which corresponds to the American idea. Perhaps it is not time for that; it must be organized in deeds before it becomes classic in words; but as yet we have no such literature which reflects even the surface of American life, certainly nothing which portrays our intensity of life, our hope, or even our daily doings and drivings, as the Odyssey paints old Greek life, or Don Quixote and Gil Blas portray Spanish life. Literary men are commonly timid; ours know they are but poorly fledged as yet, so dare not fly away from the parent tree, but hop timidly from branch to branch. Our writers love to creep about in the shadow of some old renown, not venturing to soar away into the unwinged air, to sing of things here and now, making our life classic. So, without the grace of high culture, and the energy of American thought, they become weak, cold, and poor; are "curious, not knowing, not exact, but nice." Too fastidious to be wise, too unlettered to be elegant, too critical to create, they prefer a dull saying that is old to a novel form of speech, or a natural expression of a new truth. In a single American work,—and a famous one too,—there are over sixty similes, not one original, and all poor. A few men, conscious of this defect, this sin against the Holy Spirit of Literature, go to the opposite extreme, and are American-mad; they wilfully talk rude, write innumerous verse, and play their harps all jangling, out of tune. A yet fewer few are American without madness. One such must not here be passed by, alike philosopher and bard, in whose writings "ancient wisdom shines with new-born beauty," and who has enriched a genius thoroughly American in the best sense, with a cosmopolitan culture and literary skill, which were wonderful in any land. But of American literature in general, and of him in special, more shall be said at another time. . . .

An American State is a thing that must also be; a State of free men who give over brawling, resting on industry, justice, love, not on war, cunning, and violence—a State where liberty, equality, and fraternity are deeds as well as words. In its time the American Church must also appear, with liberty, holiness, and love for its watchwords, cultivating reason, conscience, affection, faith, and leading the world's way in justice, peace, and love. The Roman Church has been all men know what and how; the American

Church, with freedom for the mind, freedom for the heart, freedom for the soul, is yet to be, sundering no chord of the human harp, but tuning all to harmony. This also must come; but hitherto no one has risen with genius fit to plan its holy walls, conceive its columns, project its towers, or lay its corner-stone. Is it too much to hope all this? Look at the arena before us—look at our past history. Hark! there is the sound of many million men, the trampling of their freeborn feet, the murmuring of their voice; a nation born of this land that God reserved so long a virgin earth, in a high day married to the human race,—rising, and swelling, and rolling on, strong and certain as the Atlantic tide; they come numerous as ocean waves when east winds blow, their destination commensurate with the continent, with ideas vast as the Mississippi, strong as the Alleghanies, and awful as Niagara; they come murmuring little of the past, but, moving in the brightness of their great idea, and casting its light far on to other lands and distant days—come to the world's great work, to organize the rights of man.

17. The American Scholar

1849

European scholars customarily take not only their scholarship but their positions for granted; the nineteenth-century English and German scholar indulged in very little soul-searching. But then—and since—the American scholar has been self-conscious. "Am I not too protected a person?" asked Emerson in his *New England Reformers.* "Is there not a wide disparity between the lot of me and the lot of thee, my poor brother, my poor sister? Am I not defrauded of my best culture in the loss of those gymnastics which manual labor and the emergencies of poverty constitute?"

Surely the position of the scholar in a republic was different from that of the scholar in Old World society. Surely here it was not enough that he immerse himself in philosophical or scientific research; he had a peculiar obligation to the society which supported him, to the principles of republicanism, of democracy, of freedom. And surely, too, the scholar in America breathed an air different from—and purer than—that in the Old World. This was the theme of a score of orations and addresses on this perennial subject. Bancroft demonstrated it; Verplanck argued it; Emerson at least hinted at it. Nowhere is the question canvassed more thoroughly than in Parker's elaborate oration, *The Position and Duties of the American Scholar.*

The scholar "is to represent the higher facts of human consciousness to the people . . . to think with the sage and saint, but talk with common men." His duties were moral as well as scholarly; his interests were popular rather than abstract. His speech should be simple and vernacular; his manner, homely; his matter, democratic. It all added up to a self-portrait, but it was not the less impressive for that.

In America . . . there are no royal or patrician patrons, no plebeian clients in literature, no immoveable aristocracy to withstand or even retard the new genius, talent, or skill of the scholar. There is no class organized, accredited, and confided in, to resist a new idea; only the unorganized inertia of mankind retards the circulation of thought and the march of men. Our historical men do not found historical families; our famous names of to-day are all new names in the State. American aristocracy is bottomed on money which no unnatural laws make steadfast and immoveable. To exclude a scholar from the company of rich men, is not to exclude him from an audience that will welcome and appreciate.

Then the government does not interfere to prohibit the free exercise of thought. Speaking is free, preaching free, printing free. No administration in America could put down a newspaper or suppress the discussion of an unwelcome theme. The attempt would be folly and madness. There is no "tonnage and poundage" on thought. It is seldom that lawless violence usurps the place of despotic government. The chief opponent of the new philosophy is the old philosophy. The old has only the advantage of a few years; the advantage of possession of the ground. It has no weapons of defence which the new has not for attack. What hinders the growth of the new democracy of to-day?—only the old democracy of yesterday, once green, and then full-blown, but now going to seed. Everywhere else walled gardens have been built for it to go quietly to seed in, and men appointed, in God's name or the State's, to exterminate as a weed every new plant of democratic thought which may spring up and suck the soil or keep off the sun, so that the old may quietly occupy the ground, and undisturbed continue to decay, and contaminate the air. Here it has nothing but its own stalk to hold up its head, and is armed with only such spines as it has grown out of its own substance. . . .

Not much more is the scholar impeded by the ignorance of the people, not at all in respect to the substance of his thought. There is no danger that he will shoot over the heads of the people by thinking too high for the multitude. We have many authors below the market; scarce one above it. The people are continually looking for something better than our authors give. No American author has yet been too high for the comprehension of the people, and compelled to leave his writings "to posterity, after some centuries shall have passed by." If he has thought with the thinkers, and has something to say, and can speak it in plain speech, he is sure to be widely understood. There is no learned class to whom he may talk Latin or Sanscrit, and who will understand him if he write as ill as Immanuel Kant; there is not a large class to buy costly editions of ancient classics, however beautiful, or magnificent works on India, Egypt, Mexico—the class of scholars is too poor for that, the rich men have not the taste for such beauty; but there is an intelligent class of men who will hear a man if he has what is worth listening to, and says it plain. It will be understood and appreciated, and soon reduced to practice.

Let him think as much in advance of men as he will, as far removed from the popular opinion as he may, if he arrives at a great truth he is sure of an audience, not an audience of fellow-scholars, as in Germany, but of fellow-men; not of the children of distinguished or rich men—rather of the young parents of such, an audience of earnest, practical people, who, if his thought be a truth, will soon make it a thing. They will appreciate the substance of his thought, though not the artistic form which clothes it.

This peculiar relation of the man of genius to the people comes from American institutions. Here the greatest man stands nearest to the people, and without a mediator speaks to them face to face. This is a new thing: in the classic nations oratory was for the people, so was the drama, and the ballad; that was all their literature. But this came to the people only in cities: the tongue travels slow and addresses only the ear, while swiftly hurries on the printed word and speaks at once to a million eyes. Thucydides and Tacitus wrote for a few; Virgil sang the labours of the shepherd in old Ascræan verse, but only to the wealthy wits of Rome. "I hate the impious crowd, and stave them off," was the scholar's maxim then. All writing was for the few. The best English literature of the sixteenth and seventeenth and eighteenth centuries is amenable to the same criticism, except the dramatic and the religious. It is so with all the permanent literature of Europe of that time. The same must be said even of much of the religious literature of the scholars then. The writings of Taylor, of Barrow and South, of Bossuet, Massillon, and Bourdaloue, clergymen though they were, speaking with a religious and therefore a universal aim, always presuppose a narrow audience of men of nice culture. So they drew their figures from the schoolmen, from the Greek anthology, from heathen classics and the Christian Fathers. Their illustrations were embellishments to the scholar, but only palpable darkness to the people. This fact of writing for a few nice judges was of great advantage to the form of the literature thus produced, but a disadvantage to the substance thereof; a misfortune to the scholar himself, for it belittled his sympathies and kept him within a narrow range. Even the religious literature of the men just named betrays a lack of freedom, a thinking for the learned and not for mankind; it has breathed the air of the cloister, not the sky, and is tainted with academic and monastic diseases. So the best of it is over-sentimental, timid, and does not point to hardy, manly life. Only Luther and Latimer preached to the million hearts of their contemporaries. The dramatic literature, on the other hand, was for box, pit, and gallery; hence the width of poetry in its great masters; hence many of its faults of form; and hence the wild and wanton luxuriance of beauty which flowers out all over the marvellous field of art where Shakespeare walked and sung. In the pulpit, excellence was painted as a priest, or monk, or nun, loving nothing but God; on the stage, as a soldier, magistrate, a gentleman or simpleman, a wife and mother, loving also child and friend. Only the literature of the player and the singer of ballads was for the people.

Here all is changed, everything that is written is for the hands of the million. In three months Mr. Macaulay has more readers in America than Thucydides and Tacitus in twelve centuries. Literature, which was once the sacrament of the few, only a shew-bread to the people, is now the daily meat of the multitude. The best works get reprinted with great speed; the highest poetry is soon in all the newspapers. Authors know this, and write accordingly. It is only scientific works which ask for a special public. But even science, the proudest of the day, must come down from the clouds of the academy, lay off its scholastic garb, and appear before the eyes of the multitude in common work-day clothes. To large and mainly unlearned audiences Agassiz and Walker set forth the highest teachings of physics and metaphysics, not sparing difficult things, but putting them in plain speech. Emerson takes his majestic intuitions of truth and justice, which transcend the experience of the ages, and expounds them to the mechanics' apprentices, to the factory girls at Lowell and Chicopee, and to the merchants' clerks at Boston. The more original the speaker, and the more profound, the better is he relished; the beauty of the form is not appreciated, but the original substance welcomed into new life over the bench, the loom, and even the desk of the counting-house. Of a deep man the people ask clearness also, thinking he does not see a thing wholly till he sees it plain.

From this new relation of the scholar to the people, and the direct intimacy of his intercourse with men, there comes a new modification of his duty; he is to represent the higher facts of human consciousness to the people, and express them in the speech of the people; to think with the sage and saint, but talk with common men. It is easy to discourse with scholars, and in the old academic carriage drive through the broad gateway of the cultivated class; but here the man of genius is to take the new thought on his shoulders and climb up the stiff, steep hill, and find his way where the wild asses quench their thirst, and the untamed eagle builds his nest. Hence our American scholar must cultivate the dialectics of speech as well as thought. Power of speech without thought, a long tongue in an empty head, calls the people together once or twice, but soon its only echo is from an audience of empty pews. Thought without power of speech finds little welcome here; there are not scholars enough to keep it in countenance. This popularity of intelligence gives a great advantage to the man of letters, who is also a man. He can occupy the whole space between the extremes of mankind; can be at once philosopher in his thought and people in his speech, deliver his word without an interpreter to mediate, and, like King Mithridates in the story, talk with the fourscore nations of his camp each in his own tongue.

Further still, there are some peculiarities of the American mind, in which we differ from our English brothers. They are more inclined to the matter of fact, and appeal to history; we, to the matter of ideas, and having no national history but of a revolution, may appeal at once to human nature. So while they are more historical, fond of names and precedents, enamoured of limited facts and coy towards abstract and universal ideas, with the maxim, "Stand by the fixed," we are more metaphysical, ideal; do not think a thing right because actual, nor impossible because it has never been. The Americans are more metaphysical than the English; have departed more from the old sensational philosophy, have welcomed more warmly the transcendental philosophy of Germany and France. The Declaration of Independence, and all the State Constitutions of the North, begin with a universal and abstract idea. Even preaching is abstract and of ideas. Calvinism bears metaphysical fruit in New England.

This fact modifies still more the function of the duty of the scholar. It determines him to ideas, to facts for the ideas they cover, not so much to the past as the future, to the past only that he may guide the present and construct the future. He is to take his run in the past to acquire the momentum of history, his stand in the present, and leap into the future.

In this manner the position and duty of the scholar in America are modified and made peculiar; and thus is the mode determined for him, in which to pay for his education in the manner most profitable to the public that has been at the cost of his training. . . .

The permanent literature of America is poor and meagre; it does not bear the mark of manly hands, of original, creative minds. Most of it is rather milk for babes than meat for men, though much of it is neither fresh meat nor new milk, but the old dish often served up before. In respect to its form, this portion of our literature is an imitation. . . .

But the substance of our permanent literature is as faulty as its form. It does not bear marks of a new, free, vigorous mind at work, looking at things from the American point of view, and, though it put its thought in antique forms, yet thinking originally and for itself. It represents the average thought of respectable men, directed to some particular subject, and their average morality. It represents nothing more; how could it, while the ablest men have gone off to politics or trade? It is such literature as almost anybody might get up if you would give him a little time to make the preliminary studies. There is little in it that is national; little individual and of the writer's own mind; it is ground out in the public literary mill. It has no noble sentiments, no great ideas; nothing which makes you burn; nothing which makes you much worse or much better. You may feed on this literature all your days, and whatsoever you may gain in girth, you shall not take in thought enough to add half an inch to your stature.

Out of every hundred American literary works printed since the century began, about eighty will be of this character. Compare the four most conspicuous periodicals of America with the four great Quarterlies of England, and you see how inferior our literature is to theirs—in all things, in form and in substance too. The European has the freedom of a well-bred man—it appears in the movement of his thought, his use of words, in the easy grace of his sentences, and the general manner of his work; the American has the stiffness and limitations of a big, raw boy, in the presence of his schoolmaster. They are proud of being English, and so have a certain lofty nationality which appears in their thought and the form thereof, even in the freedom to use and invent new words. Our authors of this class seem ashamed that they are Americans, and accordingly are timid, ungraceful, and weak. They dare not be original when they could. . . . Yet it is curious to observe the praise which such men receive, how soon they are raised to the House of Lords in English literature. I have known three American Sir Walter Scotts, half a dozen Addisons, one or two Macaulays—a historian that was Hume and Gibbon both in one, several Burnses, and Miltons by the quantity, not "mute," the more is the pity, but "inglorious" enough; nay, even vain-glorious at the praise which some penny-a-liner or dollar-a-pager foolishly gave their cheap extemporary stuff. In sacred literature it is the same: in a single winter at Boston we had two American Saint Johns, in full blast for several months. Though no Felix trembles, there are now extant in the United States not less than six American Saint Pauls, in no manner of peril except the most dangerous —of idle praise.

A living, natural, and full-grown literature contains two elements. One is of mankind in general; that is human and universal. The other is of the tribe in special, and of the writer in particular. This is national and even personal: you see the idiosyncracy of the nation and the individual author in the work. . . . It is so in the *Iliad*. You see how the sea looked from Homer's point of view, and know how he felt the west wind, cold and raw. The human element has an Ionian form and a Homeric hue. The ballads of the people in Scotland and England are national in the same way; the staple of human life is wrought into the Scottish form. Before the Germans had any permanent national literature of this character, their fertile mind found vent in legends, popular stories, now the admiration of the learned. These had at home the German dress, but as the stories travelled into other lands, they kept their human flesh and blood, but took a different garb, and acquired a different complexion from every country which they visited; and, like the streams of their native Swabia, took the colour of the soil they travelled through.

The permanent and instantial literature of America is not national in this sense. It has little that is American; it might as well be written by some bookwright in Leipsic or London, and then imported. The individuality of the nation is not there, except in the cheap, gaudy binding of the work. The nationality of America is only stamped on the lids, and vulgarly blazoned on the back.

Is the book a history?—it is written with no such freedom as you should expect of a writer, looking at the breadth of the world from the lofty stand-point of America. There is no new philosophy of history in it. You would not think it was written in a democracy that keeps the peace without armies or a national gaol. Mr. Macaulay writes the history of England as none but a North Briton could do. Astonishingly well-read, equipped with literary skill at least equal to the masterly art of Voltaire, mapping out his subject like an engineer, and adorning it like a painter, you yet see, all along, that the author is a Scotchman and a Whig. Nobody else could have written so. It is of Mr. Macaulay. But our American writer thinks about matters just as everybody else does; that is, he does not think at all, but only writes what he reads, and then, like the good-natured bear in the nursery story, "thinks he has been thinking." It is no such thing, he has been writing the common opinion of common men, to get the applause of men as common as himself.

Is the book of poetry?—the substance is chiefly old, the form old, the allusions are old. It is poetry of society, not of nature. You meet in it the same everlasting mythology, the same geography, botany, zoology, the same symbols; a new figure of speech suggested by the sight of nature, not the reading of books, you could no more find than a fresh shad in the Dead Sea. You take at random eight or ten "American poets" of this stamp, you see at once what was the favourite author with each new bard; you often see what particular work of Shelley, or Tennyson, or Milton, or George Herbert, or, if the man has culture enough, of Goethe, or Uhland, Jean Paul, or Schiller, suggested the "American original." His inspiration comes from literature, not from the great universe of nature or of human life. . . .

Is it a volume of sermons?—they might have been written at Edinburgh, Madrid, or Constantinople, as well as in New England; as well preached to the "Homo Sapiens" of Linnæus, or the man in the moon, as to the special audience that heard, or heard them not, but only paid for having the things preached. There is nothing individual about them; the author seems as impersonal as Spinoza's conception of God. The sermons are like an almanack calculated for the meridian of no place in particular, for no time in special. There is no allusion to anything American. The author never mentions a river this side of the Jordan; knows no mountain but Lebanon, Zion, and Carmel, and would think it profane to talk of the Alleghanies and the Mississippi, of Monadnock and the Androscoggin. He mentions Babylon and Jerusalem, not New York and Baltimore; you would never dream that he lived in a church without a bishop, and a State without a king, in a democratic nation that held three million slaves, with ministers chosen by the people. He is surrounded, clouded over, and hid by the traditions of the "ages of faith" behind him. He never thanks God for the dew and snow, only for "the early and the latter rain" of a classic sacred land; a temperance man, he blesses God for the wine because the great Psalmist did so thousands of years ago. He speaks of the olive and the fig-tree which he never saw, not of the apple-tree and the peach before his eyes all day long, their fruit the joy of his children's heart. If you guessed at his time and place, you would think he lived, not under General Taylor, but under King Ahab, or Jeroboam; that his audience rode on camels or in chariots, not in steam-cars; that they fought with bows and arrows against the children of Moab; that their favourite sin was the worship of some graven image, and that they made their children pass through the fire unto Moloch, not through the counting-house unto Mammon. You would not know whether the preacher was married or a bachelor, rich or poor, saint or sinner; you would probably conclude he was not much of a saint, nor even much of a sinner.

The authors of this portion of our literature seem ashamed of America. . . .

Next is the transient literature, composed chiefly of speeches, orations, state papers, political and other occasional pamphlets, business reports, articles in the journals, and other productions designed to serve some present purpose. These are commonly the work of educated men, though not of such as make literature a profession. Taking this department as a whole, it differs much from the permanent literature; here is freshness of thought and newness of form. If American books are mainly an imitation of old models, it would be difficult to find the prototype of some American speeches. They "would have made Quintilian stare and gasp." Take the State papers of the American government during the administration of Mr. Polk, the speeches made in Congress at the same time, the State papers of the several States—you have a much better and more favourable idea of the vigour and originality of the American mind, than you would get from all the bound books printed in that period. The diplomatic writings of American politicians compare favourably with those of any nation in the world. In eloquence no modern nation is before us, perhaps none is our equal. Here you see the inborn strength and manly vigour of the American mind. You meet the same spirit which fells the forest, girdles the land with railroads, annexes Texas, and covets Cuba, Nicaragua, all the world. You see that the authors of this literature are workers also. Others have read of wild beasts; here are the men that have seen the wolf. . . .

The leading journals of America, political and commercial, or literary, are poor and feeble; our reviews of books afford matter for grave consideration. You would often suppose them written by the same hand which manufactures the advertisements of the grand caravan, or some patent medicine; or, when unfavourable, by some of the men who write defamatory articles on the eve of an election.

But a large part of this transient literature is very different in its character. Its authors have broken with the traditions of the past; they have new ideas, and plans for putting them in execution; they are full of hope; are national to the extreme, bragging and defiant. They put the majority before institutions; the rights of the majority before the privilege of a few; they represent the onward tendency and material prophecy of the nation. The new activity of the American mind here expresses its purpose and its prayer. Here is strength, hope, confidence, even audacity; all is American. But the great idea of the absolute right does not appear, all is more national than human; and in what concerns the nation, it is not justice, the point where all interests are balanced, and the welfare of each harmonizes with that of all, which is sought; but the "greatest good of the greatest number;" that is, only a privilege had at the cost of the smaller number. Here is little respect for universal humanity; little for the eternal laws of God, which override all the traditions and contrivances of men; more reverence for a statute, or constitution, which is indeed the fundamental law of the political State, but is often only an attempt to compromise between the fleeting passions of the day and the immutable morality of God.

18. Emerson

1850

As a young man, Parker was drawn emotionally to Channing but intellectually to Emerson, and it was Emerson's influence that proved the stronger and the more permanent. Parker had not heard the lectures on Nature; but when he read them, he was carried away by enthusiasm. "Blessed is the man who stoops and tastes of them," he wrote. "He erects himself in new vigor and freshness, and becomes a man divine." Two years later he listened, enraptured, to Emerson's Divinity School Address. "It was the noblest of all his performances," he wrote George Ellis, "the noblest and most inspiring strain I ever listened to." To his journal he confided that the lecture was "so beautiful, so just, so true, and terribly sublime." Soon the youthful Parker had entered the lists in the great controversy that raged around the Divinity School Address. Parker's own contribution, *The Previous Question,* made explicit what Emerson had left implicit and permitted the younger scholar to share something of the odium which was directed against the Concord sage.

Parker came to know Emerson well during the West Roxbury years. He was a faithful contributor to *The Dial* and a faithful member, too, of the group who sometimes met for discussion in Mr. Emerson's parlor. A few years later, when Parker founded *The Massachusetts Quarterly Review*—"The Dial with a Beard," he called it, but it was really more like the old *North American*—he tried hard to get Mr. Emerson to serve as editor, or at least to lend the dignity of his name, but in vain.

Emerson's admiration for his young friend was lively but qualified. It is not hard to understand why he sometimes found Parker a bit hard to take—the boyish enthusiasm, the volcanic energy, the tempestuous self-assurance, the indiscriminate learning, the passion for action: "Why so hot, my little man?", the excessive admiration for those who were with him and the excessive hostility to those who were against him. Yet Emerson could not withhold either admiration or affection from this Boston Savonarola with his passion for righteousness, his zeal in good causes, his prodigious learning, his eloquence, his moral earnestness. He called Parker one of the three great men of his time, and paid touching tribute to him in his memorial address of June 1860: "a son of the soil, charged with the energy of New England, strong, eager, inquisitive of knowledge, of a diligence that never tired, upright, of a haughty independence, yet the gentlest of companions; a man of study, fit for a man of the world . . . rapidly pushing his studies so far as to leave few men qualified to sit as his critics. . . . We have few such men to lose; amiable and blameless at home, feared abroad as the standard-bearer of liberty, taking all the duties he could grasp, and more, refusing to spare himself, he has gone down in early glory to his grave, to be a living and enlarging power, wherever learning, wit, honest valor and independence are honored."

We give here some extracts from one of the first—and still one of the best—of all interpretations of Emerson. It appeared first in *The Massachusetts Quarterly Review* for 1850 as a review of several of Emerson's essays. Characteristically, Parker tried to find some failings in Emerson; but he was forced to acknowledge himself frustrated, and his conclusion is hardly less than lyrical: "Emerson is a man of genius such as does not often appear, such as has never appeared before in America, and but seldom in the world."

It is now almost fourteen years since Mr. Emerson published his first book: Nature. A beautiful work it was, and will be deemed for many a year to come. In this old world of literature, with more memory than wit, with much tradition and little invention, with more fear than love, and a great deal of criticism upon very little poetry, there came forward this young David, a shepherd, but to be a king, "with his garlands and singing robes about him;" one note upon his new and fresh-strung lyre was "worth a thousand men." Men were looking for something original, they always are; when it came some said it thundered, others that an angel had spoke. How men wondered at the little book! It took nearly twelve years to sell the five hundred copies of Nature. Since that time Mr. Emerson has said much, and if he has not printed many books, at least has printed much; some things far surpassing the first essay, in richness of material, in perfection of form, in continuity of thought; but nothing which has the same youthful freshness, and the same tender beauty as this early violet, blooming out of Unitarian and Calvinistic sand or snow. Poems and Essays of a later date are there, which show that he has had more time and woven it into life; works which present us with thought deeper, wider, richer, and more complete, but not surpassing the simplicity and loveliness of that maiden flower of his poetic spring. . . .

All of Mr. Emerson's literary works, with the exception of the Poems, were published before they were printed; delivered by word of mouth to audiences. In frequently reading his pieces, he had an opportunity to see any defect of form and amend it. Mr. Emerson has won by his writings a more desirable reputation than any other man of letters in America has yet attained. It is not the reputation which bring him money or academic honours, or membership of learned societies; nor does it appear conspicuously in the literary journals as yet. But he has a high place among thinking men, on both sides of the water; we think no man who writes the English tongue has now so much influence in forming the opinions and character of young men and women. His audience steadily increases, at home and abroad, more rapidly in England than America. It is now with him as it was, at first, with Dr. Channing; the fairest criticism has come from the other side of the water; the reason is that he, like his predecessor, offended the sectarian and party spirit, the personal prejudices of the men about him; his life was a reproach to them, his words an offence, or his doctrines alarmed their sectarian, their party, or their personal pride, and they accordingly condemned the man. A writer who should bear the same relation to the English mind as Emerson to ours, for the same reason would be more acceptable here than at home. Emerson is neither a sectarian nor a partisan, no man less so; yet few men in America have been visited with more hatred,—private personal hatred, which the authors poorly endeavoured to conceal, and perhaps did hide from themselves. The spite we have heard expressed against him, by men of the common morality, would strike a stranger with amazement, especially when it is remembered that his personal character and daily life are of such extraordinary loveliness. This hatred has not proceeded merely from ignorant men, in whom it could easily be excused; but more often from men who have had opportunities of obtaining as good a culture as men commonly get in this country. Yet while he has been the theme of vulgar abuse, of sneers and ridicule in public and in private; while critics, more remarkable for the venom of their poison than the strength of their bow, have shot at him their little shafts, barbed more than pointed, he has also drawn about him some of what old Drayton called "the idle smoke of praise." Let us see what he has thrown into the public fire to cause this incense; what he has done to provoke the immedicable rage of certain other men; let us see what there is in his works, of old or new, true or false, what American and what cosmopolitan; let us weigh his works with such imperfect scales as we have, weigh them by the universal standard of beauty, truth, and love, and make an attempt to see what he is worth. . . .

Mr. Emerson is the most American of our writers. The idea of America, which lies at the bottom of our original institutions, appears in him with great prominence. We mean the idea of personal freedom, of the dignity and value of human nature, the superiority of a man to the accidents of a man. Emerson is the most republican of republicans, the most protestant of the dissenters. Serene as a July sun, he is equally fearless. He looks everything in the face modestly, but with earnest scrutiny, and passes judgment upon its merits. Nothing is too high for his examination; nothing too sacred. On earth only one thing he finds which is thoroughly venerable, and that is the nature of man; not the accidents, which make a man rich or famous, but the substance, which makes him a man. The man is before the institutions of man; his nature superior to his history. All finite things are only appendages of man, useful, convenient, or beautiful. Man is master, and nature his slave, serving for many a varied use. The results of human experience—the State, the Church, society, the family, business, literature, science, art—all of these are subordinate to man: if they serve the individual, he is to foster them, if not, to abandon them and seek better things. He looks at all things, the past and the present, the State and the Church, Christianity and the market-house, in the daylight of the intellect. Nothing is allowed to stand between him and his manhood. Hence there is an apparent irreverence; he does not bow to any hat which Gessler has set up for public adoration, but to every man, canonical or profane, who bears the mark of native manliness. He eats show-bread, if he is hungry. While he is the most American, he is almost the most cosmopolitan of our writers, the least restrained and belittled by the popular follies of the nation or the age.

In America, writers are commonly kept in awe and subdued by fear of the richer class, or that of the mass of men. Mr. Emerson has small respect for either; would bow as low to a lackey as a lord, to a clown as a scholar, to one man as a million. He spurns all constitutions but the law of his own nature, rejecting them with manly scorn. The traditions of the churches are no hindrances to his thought; Jesus or Judas were the same to him, if either stood in his way and hindered the proportionate development of his individual life. The forms of society and the ritual of scholarship are no more effectual restraints. His thought of to-day is no barrier to freedom of thought tomorrow, for his own nature is not to be subordinated, either to the history of man, or his own history. "To-morrow to fresh fields and pastures new," in his motto.

Yet, with all this freedom, there is no wilful display of it. He is so confident of his freedom, so perfectly possessed of his rights, that he does not talk of them. They appear, but are not spoken of. With the hopefulness and buoyant liberty of America, he has none of our ill-mannered boasting. He criticises America often; he always appreciates it; he seldom praises, and never brags of our country. The most democratic of democrats, no disciple of the old régime is better mannered, for it is only the vulgar democrat or aristocrat who flings his follies in your face. While it would be difficult to find a writer so uncompromising in his adhesion to just principles, there is not in all his works a single jeer or ill-natured sarcasm. None is less addicted to the common forms of reverence, but who is more truly reverential?

While his idea is American, the form of his literature is not less so. It is a form which suits the substance, and is modified by the institutions and natural objects about him. You see that the author lives in a land with free institutions, with town-meetings and ballot-boxes; in the vicinity of a decaying church; amongst men whose terrible devils are poverty and social neglect, the only devils whose damnation is much cared for. His geography is American. Katskill and the Alleghanies, Monadnock, Wachusett, and the uplands of New Hampshire, appear in poetry or prose; Contocook and Agiochook are better than the Ilyssus, or Pactolus, or "smooth-sliding Mincius, crowned with vocal reeds." New York, Fall River, and Lowell have a place in his writings, where a vulgar Yankee would put Thebes or Pæstum. His men and women are American—John and Jane, not Coriolanus and Persephone. He tells of the rhodora, the club-moss, the blooming clover, not of the hibiscus and the asphodel. He knows the humblebee, the blackbird, the bat, and the wren, and is not ashamed to say or sing of the things under his own eyes. He illustrates his high thought by common things out of our plain New-England life— the meeting in the church, the Sunday school, the dancing-school, a huckleberry party, the boys and girls hastening home from school, the youth in the shop, beginning an unconscious courtship with his unheeding customer, the farmers about their work in the fields, the bustling trader in the city, the cattle, the new hay, the voters at a town-meeting, the village brawler in a tavern full of tipsy riot, the conservative who thinks the nation is lost if his ticket chance to miscarry, the bigot worshipping the knot hole through which a dusty beam of light has looked in upon his darkness, the radical who declares that nothing is good if established, and the patent reformer who screams in your ears that he can finish the world with a single touch,—and out of all these he makes his poetry, or illustrates his philosophy. Now and then he wanders off to other lands, reports what he has seen, but it is always an American report of what an American eye saw. Even Mr. Emerson's recent exaggerated praise of England is such a panegyric as none but an American could bestow.

We know an American artist who is full of American scenery. He makes good drawings of Tivoli and Subiaco, but, to colour them, he dips his pencil in the tints of the American heaven, and over his olive trees and sempervives, his asses and his priests, he sheds the light only of his native sky. So is it with Mr. Emerson. Give him the range of the globe, it is still an American who travels.

Yet with this indomitable nationality, he has a culture quite cosmopolitan and extraordinary in a young nation like our own. Here is a man familiar with books, not with many, but the best books, which he knows intimately. He has kept good company. Two things impress you powerfully and continually—the man has seen nature, and been familiar with books. His literary culture is not a varnish on the surface; not a mere polish of the outside; it has penetrated deep into his consciousness. The salutary effect of literary culture is more perceptible in Emerson than in any American that we know, save one, a far younger man, and of great promise, of whom we shall speak at some other time. . . .

With Emerson . . . learning appears not in his quotations, but in his talk. It is the wine itself, and not the vintner's brand on the cask, which shows its quality. In his reading and his study, he is still his own master. He has not purchased his education with the loss of his identity, not of his manhood; nay, he has not forgotten his kindred in getting his culture. He is still the master of himself; no man provokes him even into a momentary imitation. He keeps his individuality with maidenly asceticism, and with a conscience rarely found amongst literary men. Virgil Homerizes, Hesiodizes, and plays Theocritus now and then. Emerson plays Emerson, always Emerson. He honours Greece, and is not a stranger with her noblest sons; he pauses as a learner before the lovely muse of Germany; he bows low with exaggerating reverence before the practical skill of England; but no one, nor all of these, have power to subdue that serene and upright intellect. He rises from the oracle he stooped to consult just as erect as before. His reading gives a certain richness to his style, which is more literary than that of any American writer that we remember; as much so as that of Jeremy Taylor. He takes much for granted in his reader, as if he were addressing men who had read everything, and wished to be reminded of what they had read. In classic times, there was no reading public, only a select audience of highly cultivated men. It was so in England once; the literature of that period indicates the fact. Only religious and dramatic works were designed for pit, box, and gallery. Nobody can speak more clearly and more plainly than Emerson, but take any one of his essays or orations, and you see that he does not write in the language of the mass of men, more than Thucydides or Tacitus. His style is allusive, as an ode of Horace or Pindar, and the allusions are to literature which is known to but few. Hence, while his thought is human in substance, and American in its modifications, and therefore easily grasped, comprehended, and welcomed by men of the commonest culture, it is but few who understand the entire meaning of the sentences which he writes. His style reflects American scenery, and is dimpled into rare beauty as it flows by, and so has a pleasing fascination, but it reflects also the literary scenery of his own mind, and so half of his thought is lost on half his readers. Accordingly no writer or lecturer finds a readier access for his thoughts to the mind of the people at large, but no American author is less intelligible to the people in all his manifold meaning and beauty of allusion. He has not completely learned to think with the sagest sages and then put his thoughts into the plain speech of plain men. Every word is intelligible in the massive speech of Mr. Webster, and has its effect, while Emerson has still something of the imbecility of the scholar, as compared to the power of the man of action, whose words fall like the notes of the wood-thrush, each in its time and place, yet without picking and choosing. "Blacksmiths and teamsters do not trip in their speech," says he, "it is a shower of bullets. It is Cambridge men who correct themselves, and begin again at every half sentence; and moreover, will pun and refine too much, and swerve from the matter to the expression." But of the peculiarities of his style we shall speak again.

Emerson's words do not betray any exact scholarship, which has a certain totality, as well as method about it. It is plain to see that his favourite authors have been Plutarch, especially that outpouring of his immense common-place book, his "Moral Writings," Montaigne, Shakspeare, George Herbert, Milton, Wordsworth, Coleridge, and Carlyle. Of late years, his works contain allusions to the ancient oriental literature, from which he has borrowed some hard names and some valuable thoughts, but is occasionally led astray by its influence, for it is plain that he does not understand that curious philosophy he quotes from. Hence his oriental allies are brought up to take a stand which no man dreamed of in their time, and made to defend ideas not known to men till long after these antediluvian sages were at rest in their graves.

In Emerson's writings you do not see indications of exact mental discipline, so remarkable in Bacon, Milton, Taylor, and South, in Schiller, Lessing, and Schleiermacher; neither has he the wide range of mere literature noticeable in all other men. He works up scientific facts in his writings with great skill, often penetrating beyond the fact, and discussing the idea out of which it and many other kindred facts seem to have proceeded: this indicates not only a nice eye for facts, but a mind singularly powerful to detect latent analogies, and see the one in the many. Yet there is nothing to show any regular and systematic discipline in science which appears so eminently in Schiller and Hegel. He seems to learn his science from occasional conversation with men of science, or from statements of remarkable discoveries in the common Journals, not from a careful and regular study of facts or treatises.

With all his literary culture he has an intense love of nature, a true sight and appreciation thereof; not the analytic eye of the naturalist, but the synthetic vision of the poet. A book never clouds his sky. His figures are drawn from nature, he sees the fact. No chart of nature hangs up in his windows to shut out nature herself. . . .

He is evenly balanced and at repose. A more tranquil spirit cannot be found in literature. Nothing seems to fret or jar him, and all the tossings of the literary world never jostle him into anger or impatience. He goes on like the stars above the noise and dust of earth, as calm yet not so cold. No man says things more terribly severe than he on many occasions; few in America have encountered such abuse, but in all his writings there is not a line which can be referred to ill-will. Impudence and terror are wasted on him; "upstart wealth's averted eye," which blasts the hope of the politician, is powerless on him as on the piles of granite in New Hampshire hills. Misconceived and misreported, he does not wait to "unravel any man's blunders: he is again on his road, adding new powers and honours to his domain, and new claims on the heart." He takes no notice of the criticism from which nothing but warning is to be had, warning against bigotry and impudence, and goes on his way, his only answer a creative act. Many shafts has he shot, not an arrow in self-defence; not a line betrays that he has been treated ill. This is small praise, but rare; even cool egotistic Goethe treated his "Philistine" critics with haughty scorn, comparing them to dogs who bark in the court-yard when the master mounts to ride:

> "Es will der Spitz aus unserm Stall
> Mit Bellen uns begleiten;
> Allein der Hundes lauter Schall
> Beweist nur dass wir reiten."

He lacks the power of orderly arrangement to a remarkable degree. Not only is there no obvious logical order, but there is no subtle psychological method by which the several parts of an essay are joined together; his deep sayings are jewels strung wholly at random. This often confuses the reader; this want appears the greatest defect of his mind. Of late years there has been a marked effort to correct it, and in regard to mere order there is certainly a great improvement in the first series of Essays on Nature, or rather formless book.

Then he is not creative like Shakspeare and Goethe, perhaps not inventive like many far inferior men; he seldom or never undertakes to prove anything. He tells what he sees, seeing things by glimpses, not by steady and continuous looking, he often fails of seeing the whole object; he does not always see all of its relations with other things. Hence comes an occasional exaggeration. But this is commonly corrected by some subsequent statement. Thus he has seen books imprison many a youth, and speaking to men, desirous of warning them of their danger, he undervalues the worth of books themselves. But the use he makes of them in his own writings shows that this statement was an exaggeration which his practical judgment disapproves. Speaking to men whose chief danger was that they should be bookworms, or mechanical grinders at a logic-mill, he says that ecstasy is the method of nature, but himself never utters anything "poor and extemporaneous;" what he gets in his ecstatic moments of inspiration, he examines carefully in his cool, reflective hours, and it is printed as reflection, never as the simple result of ecstatic inspiration, having not only the stamp of Divine truth, but the private mark of Emerson. He is never demonized by his enthusiasm; he possesses the spirit, it never possesses him; if "the God" comes into his rapt soul "without bell," it is only with due consideration that he communicates to the world the message that was brought. Still he must regret that his extravagant estimate of ecstasy, intuitive unconsciousness, has been made and has led some youths and maids astray. . . .

From what has been said, notwithstanding the faults we have found in Emerson, it is plain that we assign him a very high rank in the literature of mankind. He is a very extraordinary man. To no English writer since Milton can we assign so high a place; even Milton himself, great genius though he was, and great architect of beauty, has not added so many thoughts to the treasury of the race; no, nor been the author of so much loveliness. Emerson is a man of genius such as does not often appear, such as has never appeared before in America, and but seldom in the world. He learns from all sorts of men, but no English writer, we think, is so original. We sincerely lament the want of logic in his method, and his exaggeration of the intuitive powers, the unhappy consequences of which we see in some of his followers and admirers. They will be more faithful than he to the false principle which he lays down, and will think themselves wise because they do not study, learned because they are ignorant of books, and inspired because they say what outrages common sense. In Emerson's poetry there is often a ruggedness and want of finish which seems wilful in a man like him. This fault is very obvious in those pieces he has put before his several essays. Sometimes there is a seed-corn of thought in the piece, but the piece itself seems like a pile of rubbish shot out of a cart which hinders the seed from germinating. His admirers and imitators not unfrequently give us only the rubbish and probably justify themselves by the example of their master. Spite of these defects, Mr. Emerson, on the whole, speaks with a holy power which no other man possesses who now writes the English tongue. Others have more readers, are never sneered at by respectable men, are oftener praised in the journals, have greater weight in the pulpits, the cabinets, and the councils of the nation; but there is none whose words so sink into the mind and heart of young men and maids; none who work so powerfully to fashion the character of the coming age. Seeing the power which he exercises, and the influence he is likely to have on generations to come, we are jealous of any fault in his matter, or its form, and have allowed no private and foolish friendship to hinder us from speaking of his faults.

This is his source of strength: his intellectual and moral sincerity. He looks after Truth, Justice, and Beauty. He has not uttered a word that is false to his own mind or conscience; has not suppressed a word because he thought it too high for men's comprehension, and therefore dangerous to the repose of men. He never compromises. He sees the chasm between the ideas which come of man's nature and the institutions which represent only his history; he does not seek to cover up the chasm, which daily grows wider between Truth and Public Opinion, between Justice and the State, between Christianity and the Church; he does not seek to fill it up, but he asks men to step over and build institutions commensurate with their ideas. He trusts himself, trusts man, and trusts God. He has confidence in all the attributes of infinity. Hence he is serene; nothing disturbs the even poise of his character, and he walks erect. Nothing impedes him in his search for the true, the lovely, and the good; no private hope, no private fear, no love of wife or child, or gold, or ease, or fame. He never seeks his own reputation; he takes care of his Being, and leaves his seeming to take care of itself. Fame may seek him; he never goes out of his way a single inch for her.

He has not written a line which is not conceived in the interest of mankind. He never writes in the interest of a section, of a party, of a church, of a man, always in the interest of mankind. Hence comes the ennobling influence of his works. Most of the literary men of America, most of the men of superior education, represent the ideas and interest of some party: in all that concerns the welfare of the human race, they are proportionably behind the mass who have only the common culture; so while the thought of the people is democratic, putting man before the accidents of a man, the literature of the nation is aristocratic, and opposed to the welfare of mankind. Emerson belongs to the exceptional literature of the times—and while his culture joins him to the history of man, his ideas and his whole life enable him to represent also the nature of man, and so to write for the future. He is one of the rare exceptions amongst our educated men, and helps redeem American literature from the reproach of imitation, conformity, meanness of aim, and hostility to the progress of mankind. No faithful man is too low for his approval and encouragement; no faithless man too high and popular for his rebuke.

A good test of the comparative value of books, is the state they leave you in. Emerson leaves you tranquil, resolved on noble manhood, fearless of the consequences; he gives men to mankind, and mankind to the laws of God. His position is a striking one. Eminently a child of Christianity and of the American idea, he is out of the Church and out of the State. In the midst of Calvinistic and Unitarian superstition, he does not fear God, but loves and trusts Him. He does not worship the idols of our time—wealth and respectability, the two calves set up by our modern Jeroboam. He fears not the damnation these idols have the power to inflict— neither poverty nor social disgrace. In busy and bustling New-England comes out this man serene and beautiful as a star, and shining like "a good deed in a naughty world." Reproached as an idler, he is active as the sun, and pours out his radiant truth on Lyceums at Chelmsford, at Waltham, at Lowell, and all over the land. Out of a cold Unitarian Church rose this most lovely light. Here is Boston, perhaps the most humane city in America, with its few noble men and women, its beautiful charities, its material vigour, and its hardy enterprise; commercial Boston, where honour is weighed in the public scales, and justice reckoned by the dollars it brings; conservative Boston, the grave of the Revolution, wallowing in its wealth, yet grovelling for more, seeking only money, careless of justice, stuffed with cotton yet hungry for tariffs, sick with the greedy worm of avarice, loving money as the end of life, and bigots as the means of preserving it; Boston with toryism in its parlours, toryism in its pulpits, toryism in its press, itself a tory town, preferring the accidents of man to man himself—and amidst it all there comes Emerson, graceful as Phœbus-Apollo, fearless and tranquil as the sun he was supposed to guide, and pours down the enchantment of his light, which falls where'er it may, on dust, on diamonds, on decaying heaps to hasten their rapid rot, on seeds new sown to quicken their ambitious germ, on virgin minds of youths and maids to waken the natural seed of nobleness therein, and make it grow to beauty and to manliness. Such is the beauty of his speech, such the majesty of his ideas, such the power of the moral sentiment in men, and such the impression which his whole character makes on them, that they lend him, everywhere, their ears, and thousands bless his manly thoughts.

19. The Interpretation of American History

1850

Richard Hildreth's *History of the United States,* the first three volumes of which appeared in 1849, was anything but philosophical, but that did not prevent Parker from reviewing it. If there was little philosophy showing in the *History,* a great deal of philosophy could be wrung out of it.

Hildreth himself was, to be sure, something of a philosopher, but not the kind Parker approved of: he was a Utilitarian and had even translated Pierre Dumont's book on Bentham's theory of legislation. Yet he had also written the first important antislavery novel in our literature, *The Slave, or Memoirs of Archy Moore,* and he had joined in the assault on that scourge of the Transcendentalists, Andrews Norton. So, on balance, Parker approved of him: Hildreth's political philosophy might not always be sound, and his formal philosophy might be clearly unsound, but his heart was in the right place.

Parker introduced his review of Hildreth with a short but penetrating analysis of the American character. It was a subject that fascinated that whole generation, and one to which Parker himself returned again and again. He tried his hand at analyses of the English character, the German, the Jewish; but he wrote voluminously on the American. And in his insistence on the crucial significance of democracy and freedom in the American character, he is not too far from Tocqueville.

At the present day the United States present one of the most interesting and important political phenomena ever offered in the history of mankind. England has planted her colonies in New Holland, in New Zealand, in the East and the West Indies, at Cape Good Hope, and at Labrador; at Mauritius, Gibraltar, and in the Islands of the Pacific. She has forced an entrance into China; she longs to get firm footing in Borneo and Nicaragua. Wheresoever her children wander they carry the seed out of which British institutions are sure to grow; institutions, however, which never produce their like, but nobler and better on another soil. Omitting all mention of Ireland, America was the oldest of these colonies, the first to detach itself from the parent stem, and is perhaps the prophecy of what most of the others are destined to become.

It must be a vigorous tribe of men which can hold so vast a portion of the earth while themselves are so few in numbers. Three hundred years ago, in the reign of Edward VI., England was a third-rate power in Europe. Her population was less than three millions, her exports were trifling, and consisted of the raw materials of her clumsy agriculture and her mineral treasures, which the Tyrians had traversed the ocean to purchase two thousand years before. Her soil could hardly raise a salad. Scotland was independent, Ireland not wholly subject to English rule, Wales had but lately been added to her realm. She was remarkable chiefly for the stormy seas which girt the isle, and the chalky cliffs along her shore, for the fogs that cover it, for the rudeness of her inhabitants and the tough valor of her soldiers. Now, in three hundred years, England contains some seventeen millions of inhabitants, Scotland and Ireland ten millions more. Russia, Austria, and France are the only nations in Europe that outnumber her in population. Turkey, with nine millions, and Spain, with twelve, are powerless beside her. Her ships are in all the oceans of the world, the sun never sets on her flag; her subjects capture the whale at Baffin's Bay, and the elephant in India; they sport at hunting lions in South Africa. Her navigators, with scientific hardihood, explore each corner of the Northern Sea, or locked in ice wait the slow hand of death, or the slower sun of an arctic summer. She has climes too cold for reindeer; climes too hot almost for the sugar-cane and the pine-apple; the lean larch of Scotland, and the banyan-tree of Hindoostan, both grow in the same empire. Esquimaux, Gaboon, and Sanscrit are tongues subject to Britain. At least an eighth part of the men now living in the world owe allegiance to the queen of that little island.

Her children came to America when the nation was in all the vigor of its most rapid growth. The progress of their descendants in population and in wealth has been without parallel. Two hundred and fifty years ago there was not an English settler in the United States; now the population is not far from two-and-twenty millions; two thirds of the people are of English origin. The increase of property has been more rapid than that of numbers. In fifty years Boston has multiplied her inhabitants nearly five-fold, and her property more than twenty-five fold in the same time. The increase of intelligence is very remarkable, and probably surpasses that of property.

The Americans are now trying a political experiment which has hitherto been looked on with great suspicion and even horror. Here is a democracy on a large scale, a church without a bishop, a state without a king; society (in the free states) without the theoretical distinction of patrician and plebian. What is more surprising, the experiment succeeds better than its most sanguine friends ever dared to hope. The evils which were apprehended have not yet befallen us. The "Red Republic," which hostile prophets foretold, has not come to pass; there are "red" monarchies, enough of them, the other side of the world, born red; doomed, we fear, to die in that sad livery of woe; but in America the person of the citizen is still respected quite as much as in Austria and England; and nowhere in the world is property safer or so much honored, the lovers of liberty here are lovers of order as its condition. Even Mr. Carlyle, accustomed to speak of America with bitterness and contempt, and of the ballot-box with loathing and nausea, confesses to the success of the experiment so far as wealth and numbers are concerned. Indeed, it is a matter of rejoicing to warm-hearted men, that we have cotton to cover and corn to feed the thousands of exiles who yearly are driven by hunger from England, to seek a home or a grave on the soil of America. It is interesting to study the growth of the American people; to observe the progress of the idea on which the government rests, and the attempts to make the idea an institution.

This is one of the few great nations which can trace its history back to certain beginnings. . . .

To be rightly appreciated, American history requires to be written by a democrat. A theocrat would condemn our institutions for lacking an established church with its privileged priesthood; an aristocrat, for the absence of conventional nobility. Military men might sneer at the smallness of the army and navy; and æsthetic men deplore the want of a splendid court, the lack of operatic and other spectacles in the large towns. The democrat looks for the substantial welfare of the people, and studies America with reference to that point. At present, America is not remarkable for her literature or her art; she has made respectable advances in science, but her industrial works and her political institutions are by far her most remarkable achievments hitherto. We are not sanguine enough to suppose that all the advantages of all the other forms of government are to be secured in this, but yet trust that the most valuable things will be preserved here. In due time, we doubt not, the higher results of civilization will appear, and we shall estimate the greatness of the nation not merely by its numbers, its cotton, its cattle, and its corn. But "that is not first which is spiritual." First of all, the imperious wants of the body must be attended to,—the woods are to be felled, the log-cabins built, the corn got into the ground, the wild beasts destroyed, the savages kept at peace. There must be many generations between the woodsman who erects the first shanty of logs, and the poet who sheds immortal beauty on logs and lumberers. Were there not ages between the wooden hut of Arcadian Pelasgos in Greece and the Parthenon? From mythical Cecrops to Aristophanes the steps are many, each a generation. The genius of liberty only asks two things—time and space. Space enough she has, all America is before her; time she takes possession of fast enough, only a second at once; and in the course of ages we think she will make her mark on the world. Up to this time the achievements of America are, taken as a whole, such as we need not blush at. Some things there were and are to be ashamed of—not of the whole. That dreadful blot of slavery remains yet, an Ireland in America; among the whites, on the one hand, causing the most shameful poltroonery which modern times can redden at, and on the other, calling forth heroism that seems almost enough to redeem the wickedness which has brought it to light. But, turning to that half of the nation free from direct personal contact with this sin of the state, forgetting for a moment the foolishness of "political sages," the cowardice of those leaders who never dare enact justice as a statute, but take the responsibility of making iniquity a law, and omitting the defalcation of men who forsake their habitual worship of a calf of gold, to bow down before a face of dough,—there is certainly a gratifying spectacle. Here are some fifteen millions of free men trying the voluntary system in church and state, richer than any other people of the same numbers in the world, and with the aggregate wealth of the nation more equally distributed; a nation well fed, well clothed, well housed, industrious, temperate, well governed, and respecting one another and themselves; that certainly is something. In all that territory there are probably more muskets in the hands of private men than there are habitations, yet not one is kept for actual defense; and through the free states no soldier walks abroad with loaded gun; only in the large towns is there a visible police. There are not two thousand soldiers of the state in all that territory, and they are as inoffensive to the citizens as the scare-crows in the field, only not so useful, nor so well paying for their keep. Of this

population some three millions are in the public schools, academies, and colleges. Nowhere are churches so numerous or so well
attended; nowhere such indications of happiness, comfort, intelligence, morality among the mass of men. This, we repeat, is something. We have no very great men; we have never had such. An
Alexander, a Cæsar, a Charlemagne, a Napoleon, we have not had.
Perhaps we never shall; but it is hardly worth while to go into
mourning yet for the absence of such. Great artists, poets, philosophers, men of letters, we have not had, hitherto. We have shown
no great respect for such, to our shame be it spoken; but in due
time we may trust that they also will come and shine for ages, with
the halo of genius around their brow. However, it does seem a
little remarkable that in America everything seems to be done
democratically—by the combined force of many men with moderate abilities, and not by one man of Herculean powers. It was
so in the early periods of the nation; so in the Revolution, and so
now. It has always been so with the Teutonic tribes of men, much
more than with the nations from the Semitic stock. With them
there comes a Moses or a Mahomet who overrides a nation for
one or two thousand years, and its progress seems to be by a
series of leaps; while the western nations, with less nationalism,
and more individualism, accomplish less in that way, but slope upwards by a more gradual ascent. In the English Revolution there
was no one great man who condensed the age into himself, and
created the institutions of coming generations, as Moses and
Mahomet have done; spite of the great abilities and great services
of Cromwell, no just historian will claim that for him. It was so in
the American Revolution, so in the French. Washington led our
armies, and Napoleon the legions of France, but neither gave the
actors the idea which was slowly or suddenly to be realized in institutions.

It is an interesting work to trace the growth of the American
people from their humble beginnings to their present condition; to
discover and point out the causes which have helped that growth,
and the causes which have hindered it. To a philosophical historian this is no unpromising field; the facts are well known; it is
easy to ascertain the ideas out of which the general political institutions of America have grown; it is not difficult to see the historical causes which have modified these institutions, giving them
their present character and form. None but a democrat can thoroughly appreciate that history. As the history of Christianity must
be written by a Christian who can write from within, and the his-

tory of art by a man with an artistic soul, so must the history of America be written by a democrat—we mean one who puts man before the accidents of man, valuing his permanent nature more than the transient results of his history.

American history up to the adoption of the Federal Constitution forms a whole, and has a certain unity which is not obvious at first sight. The several colonies were getting established, learning to stand alone; they were quite unlike in their origin, form of government, ecclesiastical and other institutions. Very different ideas prevailed in Georgia and New Hampshire. Looked at carelessly they seem only divergent; but when studied carefully it seems as if there was a regular plan, and as if the whole was calculated to bring about the present result. No doubt there was such a cancatenation of part with part, only the plan lay in God, not in the mind of Oglethorpe and Captain Smith, of Carver and Roger Williams.

Considering this history as an organic whole, to treat it philosophically it seems to us it is necessary to describe the material theatre on which this historic drama is to be acted out; to describe the American continent, telling of its extent and peculiarities in general, its soil, climate, and natural productions, and its condition at the time when the white men first landed on its shores; this, of course, comprises a description of the inhabitants at that time in possession of its soil.

Then the historian is to tell us of the men who came here to found this empire; of their origin, their character, and their history in general. He is to tell the external causes which brought them here or the motives which impelled them, and the ideas which they brought, as well as those which sprung up under their new circumstances. Next, he is to show speculatively by the idea, and practically by the facts, how these ideas worked under the new conditions of the people; how they acted on circumstances and circumstances on them, and what institutions came thereof. The historian very poorly performs his duty who merely relates the succession of rulers, the increase or diminution of wealth and numbers, the coming on of wars, and the termination thereof, the rise of great men, with their decline and fall, and the presence of institutions, without telling of the ideas they represented. Showing the continual growth of the ideas which create the institutions is little more than the work of an annalist or chronicler.

20. Franklin

1858

If history is philosophy teaching by experience, it is important that the people be familiar with the right experience. In 1858, when the clouds were drawing over the southern horizon and darkening the national skies, Parker wrote four lectures on historic Americans, to be delivered to lyceum audiences. Franklin, Washington, John Adams and Jefferson were the four historic Americans he selected as illustrations of the American character. It was natural that while he was at home with all of them, he was most comfortable with Franklin.

Much that Parker wrote was autobiographical; nowhere, perhaps, did he confess more of his own character than in this warm and affectionate tribute to that earlier Boston boy who had become a scholar and a statesman.

At the beginning of the last century a hardy man, Josiah Franklin by name, born in England, the son of a blacksmith, himself a tallow-chandler, was living in a small house, in an obscure way, in Boston, then a colonial town of eight or ten thousand inhabitants, in the colony of Massachusetts Bay.

On the 17th of January, at the Blue Ball, in Hanover Street, 1706, his tenth son was born into this world, and, it being Sunday, he was taken to the meeting-house and publicly baptized the same day, according to the common custom of those times; for then it was taught by the ministers that the devil watched about every cradle, ready to seize the souls of all babies dying before they got ecclesiastically sprinkled with water, and that the ceremony of baptism would save them from his clutches until they could discern good from evil. The minister had a wig on his head, and Geneva bands about his neck. There was no Bible upon the desk of the pulpit, and he thought it a sin to repeat the Lord's Prayer. When he said, 'This child's name is Benjamin,' how all those grim puritanic Bostonians looked on the tenth boy, the fifteenth child of the tallow-chandler! and prudent aunts doubtless wondered what he would do with such a family in those hard times. That little baby, humbly cradled, has turned out to be the greatest man that America ever bore in her bosom or set eyes upon. Beyond all question, as I think, Benjamin Franklin had the largest mind that has shone this side of the sea,—widest in its comprehension, most deep-looking, thoughtful, far-seeing, of course the most original and creative child of the New World.

For the last four generations no man has shed such copious good influence on America; none added so much new truth to the popular knowledge; none has so skilfully organized its ideas into institutions; none has so powerfully and wisely directed the nation's conduct, and advanced its welfare in so many respects. No man now has so strong a hold on the habits and manners of the people. Franklin comes home to the individual business of practical men in their daily life. His homely sayings are the PROVERBS OF THE PEOPLE now. Much of our social machinery, academic, literary, philosophic, is of his device. . . .

Look, now, at the CHARACTER of Dr. Franklin. . . .

I. He had an intellect of a very high order,—inventive, capacious, many-sided, retentive. His life covers nearly the whole of the eighteenth century. Ten years he was the contemporary of Leibnitz, twenty-one of Sir Isaac Newton. He was sixty-three years old when Alexander Humboldt and Cuvier were born. He embraced Voltaire. His orbit was intersected by that of Berkeley, Montesquieu, Hume, Kant, Priestley, Adam Smith. But in the eighty-four years to which his life extended, I find no mind which, on the whole, seems so great. I mean so generally able, various, original, and strong. Others were quite superior to him in specialties of intellect,—metaphysical, mathematical, and poetical. Many surpassed him in wide learning, of literature, or science, and in careful and exact culture; but none equalled him in general largeness of power, and great variety and strength of mind. In an age of encyclopædias, his was the most encyclopedic head in all Christendom. In the century of revolution, his was the most revolutionary and constructive intellect. He had no nonsense, was never eccentric. The intellectual faculties may be thus conveniently distributed:—

1. The understanding, the practical power, which seeks economic use as the end. 2. The imagination, the poetic power, which seeks ideal beauty as the end. 3. The reason, the philosophic power, which seeks scientific truth as the end, which is parent alike of use and beauty, the Martha and Mary of the family.

Franklin had a great understanding, a moderate imagination, and a great reason. He could never have become an eminent poet or orator. With such, the means is half the end. He does not seem to have attended to any of the fine arts, with the single exception of music. He was not fond of works of imagination, and in his boyhood he sold Bunyan's Pilgrim's Progress to buy Burton's Historical Collections. Perhaps he underrated the beautiful and the sublime. I do not remember, in the ten volumes of his writings, a line containing a single reference to either. This defect in his mental structure continually appears in his works and in his life. Hence, there is a certain homeliness and lack of elegance in his writings, and sometimes a little coarseness and rudeness. Hence, also, comes the popular judgment that he was not a high-minded man. Kant, Kepler, Descartes, Leibnitz, Schelling, where men of great imagination, which gives a particular poetic charm to their works that you do not find in the Saxon philosophers. Bacon, Locke, Newton, Adam Smith, were men of vast ability, but not imaginative or poetic. Franklin thinks, investigates, theorizes, invents, but never does he dream. No haze hangs on the sharp outline of his exact idea to lend it an added charm. Besides this immense understanding, Franklin had an immense reason, which gave him great insight and power in all practical, philosophic, and speculative matters. He was a man of the most uncommon common sense. He saw clearly into the remote causes of things, and had great power of generalization to discuss the universal laws, the one eternal principle, or the manifold and floating facts. He did not come to his philosophic conclusions and discoveries by that poetic imagination which creates hypothesis after hypothesis, until some one fits the case; nor did he seem to reach them by that logical process which is called induction. But he rather perfected his wonderful inventions by his own simple greatness of understanding and of reason, a spontaneous instinct of causality, which led him to the point at once. He announced his discoveries with no parade. He does the thing, and says nothing about it, as if it were the commonest thing in the world. His simplicity appears not only in his manners and in his life, but also in his intellectual method. Accordingly, he was a great inventor of new ideas in science, the philosophy of matter, and in politics, the philosophy of States; in both running before the experience of the world. If only his philosophic writings had come down to us, we should say, 'Here was a mind of the first order,—a brother of Leibnitz, Newton, Cuvier, Humboldt.' If nought but his political writings were preserved, his thoughts on agriculture, manufactures, commerce, finance, the condition and prospect of the colonies, the effect of certain taxes on them, the historical development of America and her ultimate relation to England, then we should say, 'Here was one of the greatest political thinkers of the age or of the world.' For while he anticipated the scientific discoveries of future philosophers, he does the same in the departments of the politician and the statesman. He understood easily the complicated affairs of a Nation, and saw clearly the great general laws which determine the welfare of the individual or of the State. Yet he made occasional mistakes; for the swift forethought of genius, on the whole, is not so wise as the slow experience of the human race. Nobody is as great as everybody. Constructive as well as inventive, he was a great organizer. He knew how to make his thought a thing, to put his scientific idea into matter—making a machine, his social idea into men—creating an institution. He could produce the maximum of result with the minimum outlay of means. His contrivances, mechanical and social, are many and surprising. He improved the printing press, invented stereotyping, and manifold letter-writers. He cured smoky chimneys of their bad habits. He amended the shape and the rig of ships. He showed the sailors how they might take advantage of the Gulf-stream to shorten their eastward transit of the Atlantic, and how to steer so as to avoid it on the westward passage. He told them how a few men might haul a heavy boat, and how they might keep fresh provisions at sea. He suggested improvements in the soup-dishes of sailors, and in the water-troughs of horses. He introduced new kinds of seeds, grass, turnips, broom-corn, curious beans from England, vines from France, and many other vegetables and plants. He drained lands skilfully, and gathered great crops from them. He reformed fireplaces, and invented the Franklin stove. First of all men he warmed public buildings. He had a fan on his chair, moved by a treadle, so as to drive away the flies. He made him spectacles, with two sets of glasses, for far and near sight. He invented a musical instrument, and improved the electrical machine. He discovered that lightning and electricity are the same, proving it in the simplest and deepest and most satisfactory manner, by catching the actual lightning. He first discerned the difference between positive and negative electricity.

He taught men to protect buildings from lightning, and would use electricity to kill animals without pain, and to make tough meat tender and digestible. 'There are no bounds,' says he, in 1751, 'to the force men may raise and use in the electrical way; for little may be added to little, *ad infinitum,* and so accumulated, and then, afterwards, discharged 'together at once.' He invented a phonographic alphabet, which does not now look so strange as in 1768. He improved the wheels of carriages, the form of wind-mills and water-mills, and the covering of roofs. First of all men, he induced the citizens of Philadelphia to construct foot pavements (which we call sidewalks), and to place crossing-stones in their most frequented streets. In London, he first proved that streets could be swept in dry weather as well as hoed and scraped in wet weather. He demonstrated this fact, by hiring an old woman to sweep the street in front of his house. Thus this Yankee printer taught the Londoners a useful lesson, now universally known.

At the age of twenty-two, in 1728, Franklin founded the first American Club for mutual improvement. It was called a 'Junto.' In 1744 he was the founder of 'the American Philosophical Society,' the first scientific association on this continent. He established, in 1751, the first American free school outside of New England, and he originated the first social library in the world. He organized the first fire company in America, and the first night-watch in Philadelphia. In 1741 he started the first magazine in America,—the General Magazine,—the forerunner of the North American, Examiner, New England Review, and a great host more. In the Quaker State of Pennsylvania, in 1744, he first organized the military force, getting ten thousand subscribers to maintain a volunteer militia. The women provided silken banners, which Franklin supplied with appropriate mottoes. He was himself colonel of the Philadelphia regiment.

He first enrolled men for the military defence of the Quaker city, in 1744, when Spanish pirates came up the river, and threatened to burn the town. He planned the admirable military organization for the whole colony of Pennsylvania, in 1754, for defence against the French and Indians, and in 1755 furnished the commissariat trains of General Braddock. He first proposed the union of all the provinces, in 1754, and in 1775 he first made the plan of a confederacy of them all, which could not be adopted till 1778, though then with improvements. Such was the distracted condition of all things in America at that time, that this organizing skill seemed most of all things needful; and Franklin's great power was not only in invention, but in organization quite as much. He had a genius for creation and administration. He easily saw what things belonged together, and found the true principle which would make many coalesce and become an association, affording freedom to each individual, and social unity to all.

Yet his plan for the Constitution of the State of Pennsylvania did not work well; nor would his scheme, that the Federal officers should serve without salary, have proved to be desirable or practicable. His design for the excitement of the ambition of children at school I think was a great mistake. If he had lived in 1857, instead of in 1776, he would not have left a hundred pounds to be expended in medals of silver or gold, which, while they stir the ambition of few, dishearten and discourage many, and leave heart-burnings amongst all. He could not foresee what it is no merit in schoolmasters and schoolmistresses to perceive after him. He founded many societies, which still continue, and his schemes have been extended far and wide. The people understood this genius for all kinds of practical and social arrangement, and put his name to many institutions of which he was but remotely the founder. Churches are called after Paul, Peter, James, John, but fire companies, debating societies, book clubs, libraries, hospitals, and the like, are named for Franklin. Institutions for theology have the name of theologic apostles, but institutions for humanity bear the name of this great apostle of benevolence. Administrative as well as constructive, he was a most able manager. He knew how to deal with men, leading them to accept his conclusions, and accomplish his purposes. Here he was helped by his great shrewdness and knowledge of the world, and also by his admirable geniality and kindness of manner, good-humour, mirth, and reserve. He did not drive men, but led them, and that often with a thread so delicate that they did not see it. He did not affect to lead, but only to follow. So the wise mother conducts her refractory boy to school for the first time, not dragging him by the hand or by the ear, and hauling him there, school-mother fashion, but by throwing something forward, and letting little Master Wilful run and pick it up; then varying the experiment, and so conquering without a battle. He knew

> 'Men should be taught as if you taught them not,
> And things unknown proposed as things forgot.'

He took care not to wound the vanity of men, or hurt their self-esteem, by exhibiting his own immense superiority of knowledge, insight, and skill. He had tact,—that admirable art of hitting the nail on the head at the first strike, and not bruising the fingers while it is driven home. He was one of the most adroit of diplomatists, fully equal to the European practitioners, whose fathers, from generation to generation, had been accustomed 'to lie abroad for the advantage of their country.' Candid and open with the honest, none knew better than he how to manage a cunning man. He knew how to conciliate. When others made a speech, he told a story, or invented a parable, and so cheaply drew the thunder out of the hostile cloud. If he could not help knowing the faults of the men he was obliged to work with, he forbore from letting them see what he knew. He could speak at the right time, none more silvery; but he knew when silence was golden, and had a wise reserve. Hence he was often thought to dissemble and feign, because he said nothing. He knew how to work, and when to wait. When his iron was cold he heated it, and only struck it when it was hot; and he could make his chimney burn its own smoke.

Singularly modest, he claimed very little for himself of merit, honour, or originality. He let others, when it helped the common cause, use his political or philosophical thought as if it were common property, or the private estate of any claimant; knowing, as he said, that it would all come right in the end, without his wasting any words now. With abundance of private enemies, he had no private quarrels, which it always takes two to make. Calumnies against him he left time to answer. Where are they now? Assaulted by some of the wiliest, craftiest, and most insidious, he never broke a private friendship. Some he convinced, some he wooed, others he gently drew, and some he took up in his great fatherly arms, and carried, and kissed, and set them down just where he would. He quarrelled only with the public enemies of his country, but took the mildest ways of allaying trouble. When the Constitutional Convention was excited and inharmonious, Franklin suggested that their meetings should be opened with prayers. And so he shed oil on the troubled waters, and all tumult ceased. He knew how to use the auspicious moment, and to make hay while the sun shone. All men have fits of easy benevolence. He could take advantage of them.

Thus he procured the cannon from Governor Clinton, of New York, for the armament of the fort below Philadelphia, against a threatened invasion of French and Spaniards. Franklin, Colonel Lawrence, Messrs. Allen and Taylor, were sent to New York to borrow cannon of Governor Clinton. At first the Governor met them with a flat refusal. But after a dinner, where there was great drinking of Madeira wine, he softened by degrees, and said he would lend six. After a few more bumpers he advanced ten, and at length he very good-naturedly granted eighteen. They were fine cannon, eighteen pounders, with their proper carriages, and were soon transported, and mounted on the fort.

In like manner, seizing the opportunity when the news of General Burgoyne's surrender at Saratoga reached Paris, he at once made the treaty of alliance between the United States of America and France. It could not have been done a moment sooner.

II. Franklin's moral powers were certainly great; his moral perceptions quick, distinct, and strong. His moral character was high, though by no means without defects. He uniformly sought justice in the relation between nation and nation, government and people, man and man, and did not stop at the letter of treaties and statutes, or at habits and customs never so old, but went back to the natural rights of man. He loved peace, public and private, and hated all that was sectional and personal. He was the enemy of all slavery, called by whatever political or ecclesiastical name. Yet his moral sense does not appear to have been so active as were his affections and intellect in his early days. This is not uncommon. The faculty of conscience which sees the eternal right, is often dormant at the beginning of life. Hence he made 'errata,' as he technically calls them, which he afterwards pointed out himself, that he might warn others. He stumbled many times in learning to walk, and, as he was a tall youth, and moved fast, so he fell hard. At the last there is a little lack of that nice womanly delicacy which you find in a moral character of the very highest elevation. His was the morality of a strong, experienced person, who had seen the folly of wise men, the meanness of proud men, the baseness of honourable men, and the littleness of great men, and made liberal allowances for the failures of all men. If the final end to be reached were just, he did not always inquire about the provisional means which led thither. He knew that the right line is the shortest distance between two points, in morals as in mathematics, but yet did not quarrel with such as attained the point by a crooked line. Such is the habit of politicians, diplomatists, statesmen, who look on all men as a commander looks on his soldiers, and does not ask them to join the church or keep their hands clean, but to stand to their guns and win the battle.

Thus, in the legislature of Pennsylvania, Franklin found great difficulty in carrying on the necessary measures for military defence because a majority of the Assembly were Quakers, who, though friendly to the success of the revolution, founded contrary to their principles, refused to vote the supplies of war. So he caused them to vote appropriations to purchase bread, flour, wheat, *or other grain*. The Governor said, 'I shall take the money,' for 'I understand very well their meaning,—other grain is gunpowder.' He afterwards moved the purchase of a fire-engine, saying to a friend, 'Nominate me on the committee, and I will nominate you; we will buy a great gun, which is certainly a fire-engine; the Quakers can have no objection to that.'

Such was the course of policy that Franklin took, as I think, to excess; but yet I believe that no statesman of that whole century did so much to embody the eternal rules of right in the customs of the people, and to make the constitution of the universe the common law of all mankind; and I cannot bestow higher praise than that on any man whose name I can recall. He mitigated the ferocities of war. He built new hospitals and improved old ones. He first introduced this humane principle into the Law of Nations, that in time of war private property on land shall be unmolested, and peaceful commerce continued, and captive soldiers treated as well as the soldiers of the captors. Generous during his lifetime, his dead hand still gathers and distributes blessings to the mechanics of Boston and their children. True it is that

> 'Him only pleasure leads and peace attends,
> Whose means are pure and spotless as his ends.' . . .

No man ever rendered so great services to American education. They began forty years before the Revolution, and are not ended yet. His newspapers and pamphlets were of immense value to the cause of humanity; for he was able, wise, just, and benevolent. At twenty years of age he wrote as well as Addison or Goldsmith. His English is fresh, idiomatic, vigorous, and strong, like the language of Dean Swift. His style is direct and often beautiful as a fringed gentian in the meadows of September. He had great skill in making an abstract style popular. He reduced many things to a common denominator, that is to say, to their lowest terms, and so he made them easy for all to handle and comprehend, having in this respect the rare excellence of Socrates and Bacon. Believing sincerity to be the last part of eloquence, he has not left a line of sophistry in his ten volumes. For twenty-five years he published, annually, ten thousand copies of 'Poor Richard's Almanac,' full of thrifty maxims and virtuous counsel. It was one of the most valuable allies of the Nation. For it made popular throughout the Nation that thrift which enabled Congress to keep the Revolutionary army together for nearly seven years. I have often thought that the battles of the Revolution could not have been fought between 1775 and 1783 had not the Almanac been published from 1730 to 1755. It was the People's classic volume, hanging in the kitchens from the Penobscot to the Alleghany Mountains, and from Buffalo Creek to the mouth of the Savannah River. It was the Bible of the shop and of the barn. Poor Richard became the American saint, especially the saint of New England—a saint devoted to the almighty dollar.

His scientific labours were for the Human Race. Yet science was only an incident in his life, which was devoted intensely to practical studies. In his early days he had no training in school or college, but he had a nature that was more college than the university that could not let him in. He had no acquaintance with the higher mathematics, nor any companionship with learned men until his great discoveries were all made. The magnificent works of Newton, Leibnitz, Haller, Blumenbach, Priestley, Cuvier, Von Humboldt, fill me with less surprise than the grand generalizations of Franklin, made with no help from society or from any intellectual atmosphere about him, and in the midst of laborious duties. He pursued science under the greatest of difficulties, and how magnificent were the prizes that he won!

21. Horace Mann

1859

Horace Mann, who was to education in New England what Parker was to the church, was part of that interlocking directorate of reform that dominated the New England—or at least the Boston—scene in the 1840s and 1850s. Famous as an educator, he was also active in the law, in politics, in the struggle for temperance and peace —and in the work for the dangerous and the perishing classes as well. His marriage to one of the Peabody sisters brought him into the inner circle of the Transcendentalists, though he was never very comfortable there. Between him and Parker there was admiration, but never quite warmth. Mann died in August 1859. Parker, then in Switzerland waging a losing fight for life, heard of his death and sat down to write their mutual friend, the "Chevalier" Samuel Gridley Howe, his estimate of the great educator. The letter is a characteristic blend of eulogy and rebuke.

I knew nothing of Mann's illness till your letter told me of his death. The last time I saw him—last autumn, I was ill, and he came to see me. He looked almost healthy, with more flesh and more color than I had seen before, and in admirable spirits. Who will do full justice to his great merits as a philanthropist and a statesman? Nobody in America. I have known him since 1836: very well since 1848. I think I understand him as well as I admire, esteem, and love him. But, alas! I am not there to preach his funeral sermon at the Music Hall, to appreciate his great services, to honor his great virtues, to point out his faults, and so let the dead man warn by his failings and instruct by his great merits, and thus continue the lesson of his life, though we can directly see its practical works no more. If you thought of him, in some respects, more highly than I did, I never wished your admiration to be less. If I qualified, I did not diminish it. I think there is but one man in America who has done the nation such great service—that is Garrison; the two were much alike in their philanthropy and hatred of all oppression, in their asceticism and puritanic austerity, in their cleanness of life and readiness to sacrifice their own interests for a general good, in their steadiness of purpose and tenacity of work, and in the severity of their speech and the strength of their personal dislikes. But Garrison had more destructiveness and more courage, and also more moral directness in his modes of executing his plans. Mann did not know that "a straight line is the shortest distance between two points," in morals as in mathematics; Garrison knows no other line in abstract morals or in concrete politics. Mann had benevolence in the heroic degree. I have known none who more deeply and heartily wished for the welfare of mankind; he was also singularly enlightened as to certain modes of carrying out his philanthropy, *e.g.* towards the insane, the poor, the ignorant, and the drunken. But I think his ideas of education were not the most enlightened and comprehensive; that his estimate of woman was unphilosophic and obsolete; and his schemes of penal legislation were quite behind the foremost philanthropy of the day, especially his adhesion to the gallows.

In his intellectual composition he lacked the ideal element to an extraordinary degree, yet his mind was as rich in figures and as vivid as a New England meadow in June. Still, there was little poetry in the man; the useful left no corner for the beautiful. He loved strongly, and idealized the objects of his affection, making them quite other than they were; he also hated terribly, and never, I think, forgave a public or a private foe. His hatred idealized men downwards, and he could see no good in them, or if any, it was deformed by the evil motive he saw (or fancied that he saw), prompting and controlling it all. Like other lawyers and politicians, he judged men ungenerously, and thought their motives mean. He loved few, and liked not many. By nature he had great love of approbation, but in all his life I remember no act in which this mean passion got the better of his conscience, and bent him away from the path of right. His sense of duty was overwhelming. Bred in the worst form of Calvinism, he never quite wiped off the dreadful smooch it makes on the character—nay, he did not extract the dark colors it *bites in* to the spiritual nature of the unlucky child. Hence his low estimate of men, hence his unforgiving disposition. For if he had much justice in the abstract, he had little mercy in the concrete. In his reactionary swing from Dr. Emmon's Calvinism he went about as near Atheism as an intellectual man can go; and, as you say, under such circumstances, "that is pretty near." But his confidence in duty and philanthropy never failed him. He took phrenology for his scheme of metaphysics, and knew no psychology but physiology. This materialism was a great hindrance to him in his educational schemes. It narrowed his views of human nature. He had not great confidence in the moral, and still less in the religious instincts of mankind; so after he had broken with the substance of the popular theology, and rejected its miraculous claims to the uttermost, spurning all "revelation" and all "miracles," he yet clung to the hollow form, and used the language of theology, not as figures of speech, but as symbols of a fact. He did this because he lacked confidence in man's power to walk without that crutch. I know no politician who so hated Calvinism; none who used its language so much, or who, to the public, appeared so much the friend of the ecclesiastic theology of which it is the poison-flower. There was a certain duplicity in the man, as strange variance with the austere purity of his personal life, and the lofty elevation of his purpose. This appears in his work as Secretary of the Board of Education, as Member of Congress, and as President of Antioch College—perhaps more conspicuous in the last office. Had the little narrow, bigoted sect of Christians known his profound convictions, and the moral contempt he felt for their absurd and debasing theology, they would never have made him even a teacher in their school, much less its head. If he had lived he must have felt great embarrassment from this cause, to be met by yet farther duplicity. I like not his taking of bread and wine in the meeting-houses of his sect, nor his having prayers three times a-day at his table. It was an official, not a personal act, and savors of hypocrisy. It was done for example—but it was an instance of falseness to his own convictions. He would not have made a good president of a college, he was too austere; and besides, he could not shut his eyes. Still more, lads at college at once detect all insincerity in their teachers, and judge with terrible justice.

> "Him only pleasure leads and peace attends,
> Him, only him, the shield of God defends,
> Whose means are pure and spotless as his ends."

Mann did not know this, or knowing did not heed.

These are his great public works:—

1. He opposed intemperance, I mean drunkenness. The State had no more efficient laborer directly in this great reform. Of course he was an extremist, and went for total abstinence, and ultimately for the entire suppression of all trade in every intoxicating drink, as an article of pleasure or of diet. In 1836 he induced the Legislature to pass a law making it a crime to be drunk

in public; the State had had no such law for 150 years, I think. He put the stamp of felony on the hideous vice. As a Temperance lecturer he had great power, for he appealed both to the understanding and the conscience with masterly skill.

2. He worked for the insane. I think no one, or two, or five men in the State did them such wise service as he. But of this you know much more than I.

3. He took up the common schools of Massachusetts in his arms and blessed them. Here was the great work of his life. It was a piece of heroic self-denial to take the secretaryship of the Board of Education. He gave up his profession, and 2500 or 3000 dollars a-year; he abandoned the Presidency of the Senate, and the fairest chance of political honors, for he was one of the most popular and influential men in the Legislature, to work for the public education of the people of Massachusetts fifteen hours a-day, pay his own travelling expenses, and become the butt of all the democratic politicians—Rantoul was the only Democrat in Massachusetts who cared anything for the public schools—of all the lazy schoolmasters that were unfit for their office, and of all the little miserable orthodox ministers who complained of his want of *ng-pâi-et-ty* (you know how to *pronounce* that word). How he did work! how he did fight! how he licked the schoolmasters! If one of the little mosquitoes bit him, Mann thought he had never taken quite notice enough of the creature till he had smashed it to pieces with a 48-pound cannon-shot which rung throughout the land. He was the father of Normal Schools. His good work here will live; one hundred years hence three generations will have tasted its blessed influence, the last the deepest of all. His influence went to all New England, and her fair daughter States. It is not often that a man has such an opportunity to serve his kind; in our century I know none who used it better, almost none so well. Massachusetts had but one man fit for the work: he went in at the call of duty; the State is not yet wise enough to honor him for such heroism; it is alike incomprehensible to the Suffolk Bar and the Suffolk Pulpit.

4. He went to Congress at a most trying period. There was a little indirection in his mode of getting there, which I never liked. But when there he proved himself the ablest, the most high-minded and far-sighted, the most moral and statesmanlike man Massachusetts has sent there in the nineteenth century. In point of intellectual ability for the post, only J. Q. Adams was his superior —his long life of politics gave him that superiority; in all other matters I assign the palm to Mann. I did not agree with all his

measures, nor accept all his principles, but I honored his integrity and reverenced his power. When Daniel Webster committed the great sin which immediately doubled his popularity in Boston with the Hunkers who had bought him, and have now given him his post on that stone of shame in the State House Yard, whence Massachusetts will one day cast him down and break it to powder, Horace Mann exposed the wickedness of the deed: none in Congress, I think, did the work so ably. He smote the champion of slavery a blow which sent him reeling home: it was the heaviest Webster ever had. He never recovered from it.

In his public life I find no aims but the noblest of all. Of how many others can you or I say that? He had a great mind, though one of a quite peculiar structure. He was a formidable debater, with, however, the faults that are generic with lawyers. None that I have known could more skilfully expose the weakness of an opponent: of course, he did not always do justice to his opponent; he was combative to an extraordinary degree, and loved the *gaudium certaminis* like an old Goth. His great excellence was moral, not intellectual. He did love his kind; he did hate their oppressors. Philanthropy is the key-note of all his music.

As a lawyer I am told he never took a case that he did not conscientiously think he ought to win. I should be surprised if it was not true. But I don't think he was always quite scrupulous enough as to the means of achieving his end. His policy sometimes bordered on deceit.

As a relative, neighbor, husband, father, his character was admirable, perhaps spotless. Young men loved him—all the door-keepers at Washington and the other servants of the Capitol; and old men of noble mark looked on him with admiration and esteem. I shall always place him among the noblest men of New England, and thank God I had the privilege of his acquaintance, perhaps of his esteem and friendship; and sometimes the opportunity of doing him some little favor. There are but two men living —Emerson and Garrison—whom I have in public praised so much or ranked so high. How different the three, yet how great their public services to the cause of humanity! None could comprehend the other, though each might admire. When Mann moved out of Massachusetts he left a gap none since has filled. I don't think Ohio was worthy of him, or could appreciate his worth. Yet Boston had little claim on such a soul as his. But, dear old puritanic town, with all its faults the noblest of human cities, it yet gave money for his college! The very men, I think, whose political idols he broke to fragments, and ground to powder, and trod into the mire of the street, gave him dollars for his college!

Oh, Chev. there never was such a city, and though I shall walk in it no more, and my voice never again be heard in its halls or its meeting-houses, perhaps never in its parlors, it still lives in my prayers and my songs of thanksgiving and of praise. Few men have had more delight in it for a dozen years than I; and I murmur not that it is over now and ended. God grant that some nobler man may do better what I attempted!

V

Slavery and Abolition

No chapter of Parker's life is more difficult to understand today than that which recounts his antislavery sentiments and activities. It is easy enough to sympathize with, and to share, his hatred of slavery; it is almost impossible to sympathize with or share his expression of that hatred. For here the Reverend Theodore Parker, who ordinarily preached the gospel of love, was rancorous, unforgiving and un-Christian. Not content to attack slavery as a monstrous evil, he pursued the slave-owners—and all those who, to his mind, gave the slave-owners aid or comfort with relentless fury. He preached against one kind of intemperance; but where slavery was at issue, he was the most intemperate of men. He hated violence and war, but was prepared to palliate a slave uprising, and thought a war for freedom holy. He loved the Union, but was prepared to break it up if that would somehow advance the cause of freedom for the Negro; and he excoriated men like Daniel Webster who were not prepared to follow him down this labyrinthine way. In his speeches and sermons on slavery, Parker appears at his worst: dogmatic, overbearing and ruthless.

Yet we must try to understand him. This attitude toward slavery was, in a sense, a function of Transcendentalism and was shared by many otherwise gentle and kindly men of that persuasion. Truth, they believed, was known intuitively, not experimentally; and truth was absolute. Parker *knew* that freedom was an ultimate good; this was one of those truths he found rooted in the nature of things. He *knew* that slavery was an evil. And he *knew* that these were absolute truths. Now you cannot trifle with absolute truth; you cannot hesitate or remain silent in the choice between absolute good and absolute evil. Furthermore, the slave power was so strong, so pervasive, so arrogant and triumphant that no halfway measures would do, no mere tepid rebukes, no naive appeals to reason or to good will—above all, no compromises. This immense evil of slavery, the greatest evil of the century, could be uprooted only by the most vigorous and relentless force. On this matter, therefore, Parker was implacable; he was prepared to countenance, if not to bless, violence and bloodshed.

Where's the man for Massachusetts? Where's the voice to speak her free?
Where's the hand to light up bonfires from her mountains to the sea?
Beats her Pilgrim pulse no longer? Sits she dumb in her despair?
Has she none to break the silence? Has she none to do and dare?

So asked Whittier, in 1845, and Parker took the questions as a personal challenge. He was just the man to light up bonfires, and he proceeded to do so. He came late to the antislavery crusade; but within five years of his first appearance on the platform of historic Faneuil Hall, he was, with Garrison and Phillips, one of the leading abolitionists of New England. In one great sermon after another, in a hundred addresses throughout the North, Parker attacked the slave power and sought to arouse public opinion to the present crisis. Nor did he confine himself to the spoken word, or the written. He organized Vigilance Committees; harbored fugitive slaves and helped them escape; fomented organized resistance to the law; supported the Kansas crusade and Ossawatomie Brown. He was incessantly active, too, in politics—something of a conscience for Senators Sumner, Wilson and Hale; counsellor to Seward in New York, to Chase in Ohio and, through his friend Herndon, to Lincoln in Illinois.

These attacks on slavery reveal one pervasive characteristic of Parker's thought: the curious blend of the a priori and the experimental, the deductive and the inductive. This can be found in most of his arguments outside the realm of religion, but nowhere more conspicuously than in the arguments on slavery. He judged slavery by ideal, or intuitive, standards and found it morally wrong. Not content with that, he judged it by experimental standards and found it a failure. He denounced slavery as an absolute wrong, which should have ended the matter, then piled up evidence to prove that it was unprofitable and inefficient. Redundant as all this might be, one thing was made ineluctably clear: slavery was a wrong so great that no moral man could countenance it.

22. The Effect of Slavery on Education

1848

Parker had preached a sermon against slavery as early as 1841, but not until he moved to Boston did he plunge deeply into the anti-slavery crusade. The first of his major contributions was a massive *Letter to the People of the United States* on slavery; it covers almost every aspect of the "peculiar institution"—the statistics and history of slavery, the condition and treatment of slaves and the effects of slavery on the population, the economy, education, law, politics and morals. It reveals Parker's characteristic technique of authenticating the truths of morality by an appeal to the census statistics. We include here a section analyzing the effect of slavery on education.

Let us now look at the effects of slavery on the intellectual, moral, and religious development of the people. The effect on the intellectual, moral, and religious condition of the slave is easily understood. He is only continued in slavery by restraining him from the civilization of mankind in this age. His mind, conscience, soul—all his nobler powers—must be kept in a state of inferior development, otherwise he will not be a slave in the nineteenth century, and in the United States. In comparison with the intellectual culture of their masters the slaves are a mass of barbarians; still more emphatically, when compared with the free institutions of the North, they are savages. This is not a mere matter of inference, the fact is substantiated by the notorious testimony of slave-holders themselves. In 1834 the Synod of South Carolina and Georgia reported that the slaves "may justly be considered the heathen of this country, and will bear comparison with the heathen of any part of the world." "They are destitute of the privileges of the Gospel, and ever will be under the present state of things." "In all the slave States," says the Synod, "there are not twelve men exclusively devoted to the religious instruction of the Negroes." Of the regular ministers "but a very small portion pay any attention to them." "We know but of five churches in the slave-holding States built exclusively for their use," and "there is no sufficient

room for them in the white churches for their accommodation."
"They are unable to read, as custom, or law, and generally both,
prohibit their instruction. They have no Bible—no family altars;
and when in affliction, sickness, or death, they have no minister
to address to them the consolations of the Gospel, nor to bury
them with solemn and appropriate services." They may sometimes
be petted and caressed as children and toys, they are never treated
as men.

"Heathenism," says another Southern authority, "is as real
in the slave States as in the South Sea Islands." "Chastity is no
virtue among them [the slaves]; its violation neither injures female character in their own estimation nor that of their mistress."
Where there is no marriage recognized by the State or Church as
legal or permanent between slaves; where the female slave is
wholly in her master's power—how can it be otherwise? Said the
Roman proverb, "Nothing is unlawful for the master to his slave."
When men are counted as things, instruments of husbandry, sep-
arable limbs of the master, and retained in subjugation by external
force and the prohibition of all manly culture, the effect of slavery
on its victim is so obvious that no more need be said thereof.

The effect of slavery on the intellectual, moral, and religious
condition of the free population of the South is not so obvious
perhaps at first sight. But a comparison with the free States will
render that also plain.

All attempts at the improvement of the humbler and more
exposed portions of society, the perishing and dangerous classes
thereof, originate in the free States. It is there that men originate
societies for the Reform of Prisons, the Prevention of Crime,
Pauperism, Intemperance, Licentiousness, and Ignorance. There
spring up Education Societies, Bible Societies, Peace Societies, Societies for teaching Christianity in foreign and barbarous lands.
There, too, are the learned and philosophical societies, for the
study of Science, Letters, and Art. Whence come the men of superior education who occupy the pulpits, exercise the professions
of Law and Medicine, or fill the chairs of the Professors in the
Colleges of the Union? Almost all from the North, from the free
States. There is preaching everywhere. But search the whole
Southern States for the last seven-and-forty years, and it were hard
to show a single preacher of any eminence in any pulpit of a slave-
holding State; a single clergyman remarkable for ability in his calling, for great ideas, for eloquence, elsewhere so cheap—or even
for learning! Even Expositions and Commentaries on the Bible,

the most common clerical productions, are the work of the North alone.

Whence come the distinguished authors of America? the Poets—Bryant, Longfellow, Whittier; Historians—Sparks, Prescott, Bancroft; Jurists—Parsons, Wheaton, Story, Kent! Whence Irving, Channing, Emerson;—whence all the scientific men, the men of thought, who represent the nation's loftier consciousness? All from the free States; north of Mason and Dixon's line!

Few works of any literary or scientific value have been written in this country in any of the slave States; few even get reprinted there. Compare the works which issue from the press of New Orleans, Savannah, Charleston, Norfolk, Baltimore, with such as come from Philadelphia, New York, and Boston—even from Lowell and Cincinnati; compare but the booksellers' stock in those several cities, and the difference between the cultivation of the more educated classes of the South and North is apparent at a glance.

But leaving general considerations of this sort, let us look at facts. In 1671, Sir William Berkely, Governor of Virginia, said, "I thank God that there are no free schools nor printing-presses [in Virginia], and I hope we shall not have them these hundred years." In 1840, in the fifteen slave States and territories there were at the various primary schools 201,085 scholars; at the various primary schools of the free States 1,626,028. The State of Ohio alone had 218,609 scholars at her primary schools, 17,524 more than all the fifteen slave States. South Carolina had 12,520 such scholars, and Rhode Island 17,355. New York alone had 502,367.

In the higher schools there were in the South, 35,935 "scholars at the public charge," as they are called in the census; in the North, 432,388 similar scholars. Virginia, the largest of the slave States, had 9791 such scholars; Rhode Island, the smallest of the free States, 10,749. Massachusetts alone had 158,351, more than four times as many as all the slave States.

In the slave States, at academies and grammar schools, there were 52,906 scholars; in the free states, 97,174. But the difference in numbers here does not represent the difference of fact, for most of the academies and grammar schools of the South are inferior to the "schools at public charge" of the North; far inferior to the better portion of the northern "district schools."

In 1840 there were at the various colleges in the South, 7106 pupils, and in the free States, 8927. Here, too, the figures fail to indicate the actual difference in the numbers of such as receive a superior education; for the greater part of the eighty-seven "Universities and Colleges" of the South are much inferior to the better Academies and high schools of the North.

In the libraries of all the Universities and Colleges of the South there are 223,416 volumes; in those of the North, 593,897. The libraries of the Theological schools of the South contain 22,800 volumes; those of the North, 102,080. The difference in the character and value of these volumes does not appear in the returns.

In the slave States there are 1,368,325 free white children between the ages of five and twenty; in the free States, 3,536,689 such children. In the slave States, at schools and colleges, there are 301,172 pupils; in the free States, 2,212,444 pupils, at schools or colleges. Thus, in the slave States, out of twenty-five free white children between five and twenty, there are not quite five at any school or college; while out of twenty-five such children in the free States, there are more than fifteen at school or college.

In the slave States, of the free white population that is over twenty years of age, there is almost one tenth part that are unable to read and write; while in the free States there is not quite one in one hundred and fifty-six who is deficient to that degree.

In New England there are but few born therein and more than twenty years of age, who are unable to read and write; but many foreigners arrive there with no education, and thus swell the number of the illiterate, and diminish the apparent effect of her free institutions. The South has few such emigrants; the ignorance of the Southern States therefore is to be ascribed to other causes. The Northern men who settle in the slave-holding States, have perhaps about the average culture of the North, and more than that of the South. The South therefore gains educationally from immigration as the North loses.

Among the Northern States, Connecticut, and among the Southern States, South Carolina, are to a great degree free from disturbing influences of this character. A comparison between the two will show the relative effects of the respective institutions of the North and South. In Connecticut, there are 163,843 free persons over twenty years of age; in South Carolina but 111,663. In Connecticut, there are but 526 persons over twenty who are unable to read and write, while in South Carolina there are 20,615 free white persons over twenty years of age unable to read and write. In South Carolina, out of each 626 free whites more than twenty years of age, there are more than 58 wholly unable to read or write; out of that number of such persons in Connecticut, not quite two! More than the sixth part of the adult freemen of South Carolina are unable to read the vote which will be deposited at the next election. It is but fair to infer that at least one third of the adults of South Carolina, if not of much of the South, are unable to read and understand even a newspaper. Indeed, in one of the slave States, this is not a matter of mere inference, for in 1837 Gov. Clarke, of Kentucky, declared, in his message to the legislature, that "one third of the adult population were unable to write their names;" yet Kentucky has a "school-fund," valued at $1,221,819, while South Carolina has none.

One sign of this want of ability even to read, in the slave States, is too striking to be passed by. The staple reading of the least cultivated Americans is the newspapers, one of the lowest forms of literature, though one of the most powerful, read even by men who read nothing else. In the slave States there are published but 377 newspapers, and in the free 1135. These numbers do not express the entire difference in the case, for as a general rule the circulation of the Southern newspapers is 50 to 75 per cent. less than that of the North. Suppose, however, that each Southern newspaper has two thirds the circulation of a Northern journal, we have then but 225 newspapers for the slave States! The more valuable journals—the monthlies and quarterlies—are published almost entirely in the free States.

The number of churches, the number and character of the clergy who labour for these churches, are other measures of the intellectual and moral condition of the people. The scientific character of the Southern clergy has been already touched on. Let us compare the more external facts.

In 1830, South Carolina had a population of 581,185 souls; Connecticut, 297,675. In 1836, South Carolina had 364 ministers; Connecticut, 498.

In 1834, there were in the slave States but 82,532 scholars in the Sunday schools; in the free States but 504,835; in the single State of New York, 161,768. . . .

The effect of slavery on the industrial, numerical, intellectual, and moral developments of the people may be best shown by a comparison of the condition and history of the two largest States, one slave, the other free. Virginia contains more than 64,000 square miles, or 13,370 more than England. The climate is delightful. The State is intersected by "the finest bay in the world," watered by long and abundant rivers; this inviting navigation, and allowing numerous and easy communications with the interior; that waiting to turn the wheels of the manufacturer, to weave and spin. The soil is rich in minerals. Iron, lead, and limestone are abundant. Nitre is found in her caverns. Salt abounds on the Great Kenawha and the Holston. Fields of coal, anthracite and bituminous, are numerous, rich, and of easy access. The soil is fertile, the sky genial, the air salubrious. She is the oldest State in the Union; long the most important in wealth, population, and political power. The noble array of talent and virtue found there in the last century has already been mentioned. Abundantly blessed with bays, harbours, rivers, mines, no State in the Union had such natural advantages as Virginia in 1790. New York has 49,000 square miles, and was settled somewhat later than Virginia, and under circumstances less propitious. Numerous causes retarded her growth before the Revolution. Though favoured with an excellent harbour, she has but one natural channel of communication with the interior. In 1790 Virginia contained 748,348 inhabitants; New York but 340,120. In 1840 Virginia had 1,239,797; New York 2,428,-921, and in 1845, 2,604,495. In fifty years Virginia had not doubled her population, while New York had increased more than four-fold. In 1790, Virginia had more than eleven inhabitants to each square mile, and New York not quite eight; but in 1840, Virginia had only nineteen, and New York fifty-three persons to the square mile. In 1798, the houses and lands of Virginia were valued at $71,225,127, those of New York at $100,380,707; in 1839 the real estate in Virginia was worth but $211,930,538, while that of New York had increased to $430,751,273. In 1840 the annual earnings of Virginia were $76,769,032; of New York $193,806,433. The population of New York is not quite double that of Virginia, but her annual earnings nearly three times as great. In 1840, at her various colleges and schools, Virginia had 57,302 scholars, and also 58,787 adult free whites unable to read and write—1484 more than the entire number of her children at school or college. New York had 44,452 illiterate adults, and 565,442 children at school or college. Besides that, in Virginia there were 448,987 slaves, with no literary culture at all, shut out from communication with the intelligence of the age. In 1844, in New York, 709,156 children, between four and sixteen, attended the common public schools of the State, and the common school libraries contained over a million of volumes; while in Virginia there were over 100,000 free white children between four and sixteen, who attended no school at all, perpetual vagrants from learning, year out and year in. Shall it always be so? The effect follows the cause. A man loses half his manhood by slavery, said Homer, and it is as true of a State as a man.

23. Daniel Webster

1852

On the seventh of March, 1850, Daniel Webster had pledged his support to Clay's compromise measures, including a more stringent Fugitive Slave Law, and New England had rocked on its foundations. Overnight the "Godlike Daniel" was transformed into *Ichabod:*

> So fallen! so lost! the light withdrawn
> >Which once he wore!
> The glory from his gray hairs gone
> >Forevermore! . . .
>
> Of all we loved and honored, naught
> >Save power remains;
> A fallen angel's pride of thought,
> >Still strong in chains. . . .

Parker at once entered the battle. (When was he ever willing to stay out?) That same month of March 1850, he "replied" to Webster at Boston's historic Faneuil Hall; instead of the biblical parallel of Ichabod, he chose the historical parallel of Benedict Arnold! Two years later, Webster was dead at his beloved Marshfield. Parker retired to the country for four days to collect his thoughts and to write what was not so much a funeral oration as a declaration of war. "Of all my public trials," he said, "this is my most trying day," and he proceeded to review the whole of Webster's life and to place him in historical and moral perspective. It was a *tour de force*—a tribute, a biography, a polemic, a history, all rolled into one. All of Parker's feeling for what New England should be and what it was becoming, all his love of freedom and hatred of slavery, all his idealism and his anguish poured forth like a cataract, tumbling and swirling and foaming until it seemed to drown out all else that was said that day. "It was," wrote Parker in his journal, "a dreadful day." Most of Boston agreed, but for other reasons. Parker had attacked one of the great idols of New England; he had defied the principle that one speaks no evil of the dead; and he had used the pulpit for a political polemic. All respectable Boston echoed with disapproval. Almost all—for Richard Henry Dana wrote: "Strange that the best commendation that has appeared yet, the most touching, elevated, meaning eulogy, should have come from Theodore Parker."

241

My friends, you all know the speech of the 7th of March: you remember how men felt when the telegraph brought the first news, they thought there must be some mistake! They could not believe the lightning. You recollect how the Whig party, and the Democratic party, and the newspapers, treated the report. When the speech came in full, you know the effect. One of the most conspicuous men of the State, then in high office, declared that Mr. Webster "seemed inspired by the devil to the extent of his intellect." You know the indignation men felt, the sorrow and anguish. I think not a hundred prominent men in all New-England acceded to the speech. But such was the power of that gigantic understanding, that, eighteen days after his speech, nine hundred and eighty-seven men of Boston sent him a letter, telling him that he had pointed out "the path of duty, convinced the understanding and touched the conscience of a nation;" and they expressed to him their "entire concurrrence in the sentiments of that speech," and their "heartfelt thanks for the inestimable aid it afforded to the preservation" of the Union. . . .

The fountains of his great deep were broken up—it rained forty days and forty nights, and brought a flood of slavery over this whole land; it covered the market, and the factory, and the court-house, and the warehouse, and the college, and rose up high over the tops of the tallest steeples! But the Ark of Freedom went on the face of the waters,—above the market, above the factory, above the court-house, above the college, high over the tops of the tallest steeples, it floated secure; for it bore the Religion that is to save the world, and the Lord God of Hosts had shut it in. . . .

To secure his purposes, he left no stone unturned; he abandoned his old friends, treating them with rage and insolence. He revolutionized his own politics and his own religion. The strong advocate of liberty, of justice to all men, the opponent of slavery, turned round to the enemy and went square over! But his old speeches did not follow him: a speech is a fact; a printed word becomes immoveable as the Alps. His former speeches, set all the way from Hanover to Washington, were a line of fortresses grim with cannon, each levelled at his new position.

How low he stooped to supplicate the South, to cringe before the Catholics, to fawn upon the Methodists at Faneuil Hall! O, what a prostitution of what a kingly power of thought, of speech, of will!

The effect of Mr. Webster's speech on the 7th of March was

amazing: at first Northern men abhorred it; next they accepted it. Why was this? He himself has perhaps helped us understand the mystery:—"The enormity of some crimes so astonishes men as to subdue their minds, and they lose the desire for justice in a morbid admiration of the great criminal and the strangeness of the crime."

Slavery, the most hideous snake which Southern regions breed, with fifteen unequal feet, came crawling North; fold on fold, and ring on ring, and coil on coil, the venomed monster came: then Avarice, the foulest worm which Northern cities gender in their heat, went crawling South; with many a wriggling curl, it wound along its way. At length they met, and, twisting up in their obscene embrace, the twain became one monster, Hunkerism; theme unattempted yet in prose or song: there was no North, no South; they were one poison! The dragon wormed its way along,— crawled into the church of Commerce, wherein the minister baptized the beast, "Salvation." From the ten commandments the dragon's breath effaced those which forbid to kill and covet, with the three between; then with malignant tooth, gnawed out the chief commandments whereon the law and prophets hang. This amphisbæna of the Western World then swallowed down the holiest words of Hebrew or of Christian speech, and in their place it left a hissing at the Higher Law of God. Northward and Southward wormed the thing along its track, leaving the stain of its breath in the people's face; and its hissing against the Lord rings yet in many a speech:—

> "Religion, blushing, veils her sacred fires,
> And, unawares, morality expires."

Then what a shrinking was there of great consciences, and hearts, and minds! So Milton, fabling, sings of angels fallen from their first estate, seeking to enter Pandemonium:—

> "They but now who seemed
> In bigness to surpass Earth's giant-sons,
> Now less than smallest dwarfs, in narrow room
> Throng numberless, ...
> . . . . to smallest forms
> Reduced their shapes immense, and were at large,
> Though without number still, amidst the hall
> Of that infernal court."

Mr. Webster stamped his foot, and broke through into the great hollow of practical atheism, which undergulfs the State and Church. Then what a caving in was there! The firm-set base of northern cities quaked and yawned with gaping rents. "Penn's sandy foundation" shook again, and black men fled from the city of brotherly love, as doves, with plaintive cry, flee from a farmer's barn when summer lightning stabs the roof. There was a twist in Faneuil Hall, and the doors could not open wide enough for Liberty to regain her ancient Cradle; only soldiers, greedy to steal a man, themselves stole out and in. Ecclesiastic quicksand ran down the hole amain. Metropolitan churches toppled, and pitched, and canted, and cracked, their bowing walls all out of plumb. Colleges, broken from the chain which held them in the stream of time, rushed towards the abysmal rent. Harvard led the way, *"Christo et Ecclesiæ"* in her hand. Down plunged Andover, "Conscience and the Constitution" clutched in its ancient, failing arm. New Haven began to cave in. Doctors of Divinity, orthodox, heterodox with only a doxy of doubt, "no settled opinion," had great alacrity in sinking, and went down quick, as live as ever, into the pit of Korah, Dathan, and Abiram, the bottomless pit of lower law,— one with his mother, cloaked by a surplice, hid beneath his sinister arm, and an acknowledged brother grasped by his remaining limb. Fossils of theology, dead as Ezekiel's bones, took to their feet again, and stood up for most arrant wrong. "There is no higher law of God," quoth they, as they went down; "no golden rule, only the statutes of men." A man with mythologic ear might fancy that he heard a snickering laugh run round the world below, snorting, whinnying, and neighing, as it echoed from the infernal spot pressed by the fallen monsters of ill-fame, who, thousands of years ago, on the same errand, had plunged down the self-same way. What tidings the echo bore, Dante nor Milton could not tell. Let us leave that to darkness, and to silence, and to death.

But spite of all this, in every city, in every town, in every college, and in each capsizing church, there were found Faithful Men, who feared not the monster, heeded not the stamping;—nay, some doctors of divinity were found living. In all their houses there was light, and the destroying angel shook them not. The word of the Lord came in open vision to their eye; they had their lamps trimmed and burning, their loins girt; they stood road-ready. Liberty and Religion turned in thither, and the slave found bread and wings. "When my father and my mother forsake me, then the Lord will hold me up!"

After the 7th of March, Mr. Webster became the ally of the worst of men, the forefront of kidnapping. The orator of Plymouth Rock was the advocate of slavery; the hero of Bunker Hill put chains around Boston Court House; the applauder of Adams and Jefferson was a tool of the slave-holder, and a keeper of slavery's dogs, the associate of the kidnapper, and the mocker of men who loved the right. Two years he lived with that rabble-rout for company, his name the boast of every vilest thing.

"Oh, how unlike the place from whence he fell!"

In early life, Mr. Hill, of New Hampshire, pursued him with unrelenting bitterness. Of late years Mr. Webster had complained of this, declaring that "Mr. Hill had done more than any other man to debauch the character of New Hampshire, bringing the bitterness of politics into private life." But after that day of St. Judas, Mr. Webster pursued the same course which Mr. Hill had followed forty years before, and the two enemies were reconciled. The Herod of the Democrats and the Pilate of Federalism were made friends by the Fugitive Slave Bill, and rode in the same "Omnibus,"—"a blue-light Federalist" and "a genuine Democrat dyed in the wool."

Think of him!—the Daniel Webster of Plymouth Rock advocating the "Compromise Measures!" the Daniel Webster of Faneuil Hall, who once spoke with the inspiration of Samuel Adams and the tongue of James Otis, honouring the holy dead with his praise! —think of him at Buffalo, Albany, Syracuse, scoffing at modern men, who "perilled their lives, their fortunes, and their sacred honour," to visit the fatherless and the widows in their affliction, and to keep themselves unspotted fro mthe world!—think of him threatening with the gallows such as clothed the naked, fed the hungry, visited the prisoner, and gave a cup of cold water to him that was ready to perish! Think of Daniel Webster become the assassin of Liberty in the Capitol! Think of him, full of the Old Testament and dear Isaac Watts, scoffing at the Higher Law of God, while the mountains of Virginia looked him in the face! . . .

Did men honour Daniel Webster? So did I. I was a boy ten years old when he stood at Plymouth Rock, and never shall I forget how his clarion-words rang in my boyish heart. I was but a little boy when he spoke those brave words in behalf of Greece. I was helped to hate slavery by the lips of that great intellect; and now that he takes back his words, and comes himself to be slavery's slave, I hate it tenfold harder than before, because it made a bondman out of that proud, powerful nature.

Did men love him? So did I. Not blindly, but as I loved a

great mind, as the defender of the Constitution and the Unalienable Rights of Man.

Sober and religious men of Boston yet mourn that their brothers were kidnapped in the city of Hancock and Adams—it was Daniel Webster who kidnapped them. Massachusetts has wept at the deep iniquity which was wrought in her capital—it was done by the man whom she welcomed to her bosom, and long had loved to honour. Let history, as

> "Sad as angels at the good man's sin,
> Blush to record, and weep to give it in!"

Do men mourn for him? See how they mourn! The streets are hung with black. The newspapers are sad coloured. The shops are put in mourning. The Mayor and Aldermen wear crape. Wherever his death is made known, the public business stops, and flags drop half-mast down. The courts adjourn. The courts of Massachusetts—at Boston, at Dedham, at Lowell, all adjourn; the courts of New Hampshire, of Maine, of New York; even at Baltimore and Washington, the courts adjourn; for the great lawyer is dead, and Justice must wait another day. Only the United States Court, in Boston, trying a man for helping Shadrach out of the furnace of the kidnappers,—the court which executes the Fugitive Slave Bill,—that does not adjourn; that keeps on; its worm dies not, and the fire of its persecution is not quenched, when death puts out the lamp of life! Injustice is hungry for its prey, and must not be balked. It was very proper! Symbolical court of the Fugitive Slave Bill—it does not respect life, why should it death? and, scorning liberty, why should it heed decorum? Did the judges deem that Webster's spirit, on its way to God, would look at Plymouth Rock, then pause on the spots made more classic by his eloquence, and gaze at Bunker Hill, and tarry his hour in the august company of noble men at Faneuil Hall, and be glad to know that injustice was chanting his requiem in that court? They greatly misjudge the man. I know Daniel Webster better, and I appeal for him against his idly judging friends.

Do men now mourn for him, the great man eloquent? I put on sackcloth long ago; I mourned for him when he wrote the Creole letter, which surprised Ashburton, Briton that he was. I mourned when he spoke the speech of the 7th of March. I mourned when the Fugitive Slave Bill passed Congress, and the same cannons which have just fired minute-guns for him fired also one hundred rounds of joy at the forging of a new fetter for the fugitive's foot. I mourned fo him when the kidnappers first came to Boston,—hated then, now "respectable men," "the companions of princes," enlarging their testimony in the court. I mourned when my own parishioners fled from the "stripes" of New-England to the "stars" of Old-England. I mourned when Ellen Craft fled to my house for shelter and for succour, and for the first time in all my life I armed this hand. I mourned when I married William and Ellen Craft, and gave them a Bible for their soul, and a sword to keep that soul living in a living frame. I mourned when the Court House was hung in chains; when Thomas Sims, from his dungeon, sent out his petition for prayers, and the churches did not dare to pray. I mourned when that poor outcast in yonder dungeon sent for me to visit him, and when I took him by the hand which Daniel Webster was chaining in that hour. I mourned for Webster when we prayed our prayer and sang our psalm on Long Wharf in the morning's gray. I mourned then: I shall not cease to mourn. The flags will be removed from the streets, the cannon will sound their other notes of joy; but, for me, I shall go mourning all my days; I shall refuse to be comforted; and at last I shall lay down my gray hairs with weeping and with sorrow in the grave. O Webster! Webster! would God that I had died for thee!

He was a powerful man physically, a man of a large mould, —a great body and a great brain he seemed made to last a hundred years. Since Socrates, there has seldom been a head so massive huge, save the stormy features of Michael Angelo,—

> "The hand that rounded Peter's dome,
> And groined the aisles of Christian Rome;"

he who sculptured Day and Night into such majestic forms,— looked them in his face before he chiselled them in stone. The cubic capacity of his head surpassed nearly all former measurements of mind. Since Charlemagne, I think there has not been such a grand figure in all Christendom. A large man, decorous in dress, dignified in deportment, he walked as if he felt himself a king. Men from the country, who knew him not, stared at him as he passed through our streets. The coal-heavers and porters of London looked on him as one of the great forces of the globe. They recognized a native king. In the Senate of the United States, he looked an emperor in that council. Even the majestic Calhoun seemed common, compared with him. Clay looked vulgar, and Van Buren but a fox. His countenance, like Strafford's, was "manly black." His mind—

> "Was lodged in a fair and lofty room.
>   On his brow
> Sat terror, mixed with wisdom; and, at once,
> Saturn and Hermes in his countenance."

What a mouth he had! It was a lion's mouth. Yet there was a sweet grandeur in his smile, and a woman's softness when he would. What a brow it was! what eyes! like charcoal fires in the bottom of a deep, dark well! His face was rugged with volcanic flames,— great passions and great thoughts.

> "The front of Jove himself;
> An eye like Mars to threaten and command."

24. Anthony Burns: The New Crime Against Humanity

1854

Nothing in all his career stirred Parker more deeply than the rendition of the Negro Anthony Burns. From the beginning, Parker had been deeply involved in the case—from the moment the hapless Burns had been arrested and threatened with return to the South. Parker wrote the handbills calling on the people of Boston to rescue the fugitive; he was active on the Vigilance Committee that planned a rescue by force; he organized the great protest meeting at Faneuil Hall and was the principal speaker on that occasion. He hoped to take part in the actual rescue, but the committee got its signals mixed, and the attempt failed. Judge Edward Loring ruled that Burns was a fugitive slave and restored him to his master; President Fillmore sent soldiers to keep the peace; and to the tolling of church bells, Burns was marched through crepe-blackened streets down to the Long Wharf and put on the steamer that would take him back to Virginia.

That Sunday—June 8, 1854—Parker preached a sermon, *The New Crime Against Humanity;* it was one of his most ambitious and most stirring efforts. Four months later, he was arrested for obstructing enforcement of the Fugitive Slave Law. Out on bail, happy in his martyrdom, he dashed off a tremendous *Defence* of some three hundred pages, designed to blast Judge Loring and his colleague Judge Curtis right off their benches. Alas, Parker did not get a chance to use it. Faced with a rising tide of public indignation, the court quashed Parker's indictment on technicalities. Parker whipped the *Defence* into shape for publication and, the next summer, hurled it at his persecutors.

On Wednesday night, the 24th of May, a young man, without property, without friends—I will continue to call his name Anthony Burns—was returning home from his usual lawful and peaceful work in the clothing shop of Deacon Pitts, in Brattle Street. He was assaulted by six ruffians, who charged him with having broken into a jeweller's shop. They seized him, forced him to the Court House, thrust him into an upper chamber therein, where he was surrounded by men, armed, it is said, with bludgeons and revolvers. There he was charged with being a fugitive slave. A man from Virginia, claiming to be his owner, and another man, likewise from Virginia, confronted the poor victim, and extorted from him a confession, as they allege, that he was the claimant's fugitive slave—if, indeed, the confession was not purely an invention of his foes, who had made the false charge of burglary; for they who begin with a lie are not to be trusted after that lie has been told. He was kept all night, guarded by ruffians hired for the purpose of kidnapping a man. No friend was permitted to see him; but his deadliest foes, who clutched at what every one of us holds tenfold dearer than life itself, were allowed access. They came and went freely, making their inquisition, extorting or inventing admissions to be used for Mr. Burns's ruin.

At nine o'clock the next morning, Thursday (May 25th), the earliest hour at which the courts of Massachusetts ever open, he was brought to the court-room and arraigned before Edward Greeley Loring, Judge of Probate, one of the Fugitive Slave Bill Commissioners of the city of Boston, and immediately put on trial. "Intimidated" by the mob about him, and stupefied with terror and fear, he makes no defence. "As a lamb before his shearers is dumb, so he opened not his mouth." How could he dare make a defence, treated as he had been the night before?—confronted as he was by men clutching at his liberty?—in a court-room packed with ruffians, where the slaveholders' counsel brought pistols in their breasts? He had been in duress all night, with inquisitors about him. His claimant was there, with documents manufactured in Alexandria; with a witness brought from Richmond; with two lawyers of Boston to aid them.

What a scene it was for a Massachusetts court! A merchant from Richmond, so Mr. Brent called himself; another from Alexandria, who was a sheriff and member of the Virginia Legislature —for such Colonel Suttle has been—they were there to steal a man! They had him already in gaol; they went out and came in as they liked, and shut from his presence everybody who was not one of the minions hired to aid them in their crime.

Further, they had two lawyers of Boston giving them the benefit of their education and their knowledge of the law; and, in addition to that, the senior lawyer, Seth J. Thomas, brought considerable experience, acquired on similar occasions—for he has been the kidnappers' counsel from the beginning. The other lawyer was a young man of good culture and amiable deportment, I think with no previous stain on his reputation. This is his first offence. I trust it will be also his last—that he will not bring shame on his own and his mother's head. I know not how the kidnappers enticed the young man to do so base a deed; nor what motive turned him to a course so foul as this. He is a young man, sorely penitent for this early treason against humanity. Generous emotions are commonly powerful in the bosoms of the young. A young man with only cruel calculation in his heart is a rare and loathsome spectacle. Let us hope better things of this lawyer; that a generous nature only sleeps in him. It is his first offence. I hope he will bring forth "fruits meet for repentance." Judge of him as charitably as you can. Of Mr. Thomas I have only this to add:—that he is chiefly known in the courts as the associate of Mr. Curtis in attempts like this; the regular attorney of the stealers of men, and apparently delighted with his work. He began this career by endeavouring to seize William and Ellen Craft. He is a member of the Democratic party who has not yet received his reward.

On the side of the kidnapper there were also the district marshal, the district attorney, the Fugitive Slave Bill Commissioner, and sixty-five men whom I counted as the marshal's "guard." When the company was ordered to disperse, and the guard to remain, I tarried late, and counted them. I reckoned sixty-five in the court-room, and five more outside. I may have been mistaken in the count.

On the other side there was a poor, friendless negro, sitting between two bullies, his wrists chained together by stout handcuffs of steel—a prisoner without a crime, chained; on trial for more than life, and yet there was no charge against him, save that his mother had been a slave!

Mr. Burns had no counsel. The kidnapper's lawyers presented their documents from Alexandria, claiming him as a slave of Colonel Suttle, who had escaped from "service." They brought a Virginia merchant to identify the prisoner. He was swiftly sworn, and testified with speed. The claimant's lawyers declared that Mr. Burns had acknowledged already that he was Colonel Suttle's slave, and willing to go back. So they demanded a "certificate;" and at first it seemed likely to be granted at once. Why should a Fugitive Slave Bill Commissioner delay? Why does he want evidence? Injustice is swift of foot. You know what was done in New York, the very same week:—three men were seized, carried before a commissioner, and, without even a mock trial, without any defence, hurried to bondage, pitiless and for ever! Only an accident, it seems, saved Boston from that outrage. . . .

You remember what followed. You have seen the streets crowded with armed men. You have read the newspapers, the handbills, and the posters. You remember the Faneuil Hall meeting, when all the influence of the platform scarce kept the multitude from tearing the Court House that night to the ground. You remember the attack on the Court House—a man killed and twelve citizens in gaol, charged with crimes of an atrocious character. You recollect the conventions—Free Soil and Anti-Slavery. You call to mind the aspect of Court Square last Monday. Boston never saw such an Anniversary week. There were meetings of theological societies, philanthropic societies, reformatory societies, literary societies: and Boston was in a state of siege—the Court House full of United States soldiers—marines from the navy yard, troops from the forts, from New York, from Portsmouth, from Rhode Island. The courts sat with muskets at their backs, or swords at their bosoms; drunken soldiers charged bayonet on the witnesses, on counsel, and on strangers, who had rights where the soldier had none. The scene last Friday you will never forget— business suspended, the shops shut, the streets blocked up, all the "citizen-soldiery" under arms. Ball cartridges were made for the city government on Thursday afternoon in Dock Square, to be fired into your bosoms and mine; United States soldiers loaded their pieces in Court Square, to be discharged into the crowd of Boston citizens whenever a drunken officer should give command; a six-pound cannon, furnished with forty rounds of canister shot, was planted in Court Square, manned by United States soldiers, foreigners before they enlisted. The town looked Austrian. And, at high change, over the spot where, on the 5th of March, 1770, fell the first victim in the Boston Massacre,—where the negro blood of Christopher Attucks stained the ground,—over that spot Boston authorities carried a citizen of Massachusetts to Alexandria as a slave; "and order reigns in Boston"—or Warsaw, call it which you will.

So much for a brief statement of facts. . . .

Now, let me say another word—it must be a brief one—of this particular case. When Mr. Burns was kidnapped, a public meeting was called in Faneuil Hall. Who went there? Not one of the men who are accustomed to control public opinion in Boston. If ten of them had appeared on that platform, Mr. Phillips and myself would not have troubled the audience with our speech. We would have yielded the place—to citizens of "eminent gravity" giving their counsel, and there would have been no man carried out of Boston. I could mention ten men, known to every man here, who, if they had been there, would have so made such public opinion, that the Fugitive Slave Bill Commissioner never would have found "evidence" or "law" enough to send Anthony Burns back to Alexandria. There was not one of them there. They did not wish to be there. They cared nothing for freedom!

In general, the blame of this wickedness rests on the city of Boston, much of it on Massachusetts, on New England, and on all the North. But here I must single out some of the individuals who are personally responsible for this outrage. . . .

Look at the Marshal's conduct. Of his previous character I say nothing. But his agents arrested Mr. Burns on a false charge; threatened violence if he should cry out; they kept him in secret. Nobody came nigh unto him.

The trial was unfairly conducted on the Marshal's part. The public was excluded from the Court House. His servants lined the stairways, insulting the people. Southerners were freely admitted, but Northern gentlemen kept out. Rude, coarse, and insolent fellows found no check. Clergymen and lawyers were turned back, and Southern students of law let in. Two gentlemen were refused admission; but when one declared he was from Virginia, the other from South Carolina, they were both admitted on the instant. The whole Court House seemed to be the property of the slave power.

He crowded the Court House with soldiers. Some of them were drunk, and charged bayonet upon the counsel and witnesses for Burns, and thrust them away. He employed base men for his guard. I never saw such a motley crew as this kidnapper's gang collected together, save in the darkest places of London and Paris, whither I went to see how low humanity might go down, and yet bear the semblance of man. He raked the kennels of Boston. He dispossessed the stews, bawding the courts with unwonted infamy. He gathered the spoils of brothels; prodigals not penitent, who upon harlots had wasted their substance in riotous living; pimps, gamblers, the *succubus* of Slavery; men which the gorged gaols had cast out into the streets scarred with infamy; fighters, drunkards, public brawlers; convicts that had served out their time, waiting for a second conviction; men whom the subtlety of counsel, or the charity of the gallows, had left unhanged. "No eye hath seen such scarecrows." The youngest of the Police Judges found ten of his constituents there. Gaoler Andrews, it is said, recognised forty of his customers among them. It is said that Albert J. Tirrell was invited to move in that leprous gang, and declined! "The wicked walk on every side when the vilest men are exalted!" The publican who fed those locuts of Southern tyranny, said that out of the sixty-five, there was but one respectable man, and he kept aloof from all the rest. I have seen courts of justice in England, Holland, Belgium, Germany, France, Italy, and Switzerland, and I have seen just such men. But they were always in the dock, not the servants of the Court. The Marshal was right; "the statute is so cruel and wicked that it should not be executed by good men." He chose fit tools for fitting work. I do not think Herod sent the guardian of orphans to massacre the innocents of Bethlehem. I doubt that Pontius Pilate employed a Judge of Probate to crucify Jesus between two thieves! . . .

The conduct of the Governor requires some explanation. The law of Massachusetts was cloven down by the sword of the Marshal; no officer could be found to serve the writ of personal replevin, designed by the Massachusetts Legislature to meet exactly such cases, and bring Mr. Burns before a Massachusetts court. The Governor could not be induced to attend to it: Monday he was at the meeting of the Bible Society; Thursday at the meeting of the Sunday Schools. If the United States Marshal had invaded the sovereignty of South Carolina, where do you think her Governor would have been?

The conduct of the Mayor of Boston deserves to be remembered. He had the police of the city in Court Square, aiding the kidnapper. It was not their fault. They served against their will. Captain Hayes, of the police, that day magnanimously resigned his charge. The Mayor called out the soldiers at great cost, to some one. He did this on his own responsibility. Five Aldermen have publicly protested against the breach of honour and justice. After the wicked deed was over, he attended a meeting of Sunday School children in Faneuil Hall. When he was introduced to the audience, "Out of the mouth of babes and sucklings" came a hiss! At night, the "citizen soldiery" had a festival. The Mayor was at the supper, and toasted the military—eating and drinking and making merry. What did they care, or he, that an innocent citizen of Boston was sent into bondage for ever, and by their hands! The agony of Mr. Burns only flavoured their cup. So the butcher's dog can enjoy himself in the shambles, while the slaughter of the innocent goes on around him, "battening on garbage!"

Thus, on the 2nd of June, Boston sent into bondage the second victim. It ought to have been fifteen days later—the 17th of June. What a spectacle it was! The day was brilliant; there was not a cloud; all about Boston there was a ring of happy summer loveliness; the green beauty of June; the grass, the trees, the heaven, the light; and Boston itself was the theatre of incipient civil war!

What a day for Boston! Citizens applauding that a man was to be carried into bondage! Drunken soldiers, hardly able to stand in the street, sung their ribald song—"Oh, carry me back to old Virginia!"

Daniel Webster lies buried at Marshfield; but his dead hand put the chain on Anthony Burns. Last winter it was proposed to build him a monument. He needs it not. Hancock has none; Samuel Adams sleeps in a nameless grave; John Adams has not a stone. We are their monuments; the homage of the people is their epitaph. Daniel Webster also had his monument last Friday. It was the Court House crowded with two hundred and twenty United States soldiers and flanked with a cannon. His monument reached all the way from John Hancock's house in Court Street to the T Wharf; nay, it went far out to sea in the Revenue Cutter, and is borne seaward or shoreward. Conquer your prejudices! No higher law! On the brass cannon you could read, I STILL LIVE. . . .

The liberty of America was never in greater peril than now. Hessian bayonets were not half so dangerous as the gold of the National treasury in the hands of this Administration. Which shall conquer, Slavery or Freedom? That is the question. The two cannot long exist side by side. Think of the peril; remember the rapacity of this Administration; its reckless leaders: think of Douglas, Cushing, and the rest. They aimed at the enslavement of Nebraska. The Northern majority in Congress yielded that.

Now they aim at Hayti and Cuba. Shall they carry that point? Surely, unless we do our duty. Shall Slavery be established at the North, at the West, and the East; in all the free States? Mr. Toombs told Mr. Hale—"Before long the master will sit down at the foot of Bunker Hill Monument with his slaves." Will do it. He has done it already, and not an officer in the State of Massachusetts made the least resistance. Our laws were trod down by insolent officials, and Boston ordered out her soldiers to help the disgraceful deed. Strange that we should be asked to make the fetters which are to chain us. Mr. Suttle is only a feeler. Soon there will be other Suttles in Boston. Let them come!

It is not only wicked; it is costly. The kidnapping of Mr. Burns must have cost in all at least one hundred thousand dollars, including the loss of time and travelling expenses of our friends from the country. The publican's bill for feeding the Marshal's crew is already more than six thousand dollars!

Consider the demoralization of the people produced by such a deed. Mr. Dana was knocked down in the street by one of the Marshal's posse—as it is abundantly proved. The blow might easily have been fatal. It is long since a bully has attacked a respectable citizen in Boston before. Hereafter I fear it will be more common. You cannot employ such a body-guard as the Marshal had about him in such business without greatly endangering the safety of the persons and the property of the town. We shall hear from them again. What a spectacle it was; the army of the United States, the soldiers of Boston, sending an innocent man into Slavery! What a lesson to the children in the Sunday Schools—to the vagrant children in the streets, who have no school but the Sights of the City! What a lesson of civilization to the Irish population of Boston! Men begin to understand this. There never was so much Anti-Slavery feeling in Boston before—never so much indignation in my day. If a law aims at justice, though it fail of the mark we will respect the law—not openly resist it or with violence: wait a little, and amend it or repeal it. But when the law aims at injustice, open, manifest, palpable wickedness, why, we must be cowards and fools too, if we submit.

Massachusetts has never felt so humiliated before. Soldiers of the Government enforcing a law in peaceful Boston, the most orderly of Christian cities! We have had no such thing since the Declaration of Independence! The rendition of Mr. Burns fills New England with sorrow and bitter indignation. The people tolled the bells at Plymouth. The bones of the forefathers gave that response to the kidnappers in Boston. At Manchester and several other towns they did the same. To-day, ministers are preaching as never before. What will it all come to?

25. John Brown and the Philosophy of Freedom

1859

When John Brown visited Boston in 1856, he found his way at once to Parker's home in Exeter Place; it was there that William Lloyd Garrison first met him—and tried to argue him into nonresistance! Parker was an active member of the Massachusetts Kansas Committee, which provided arms and money for "Old Osawatomie," and knew that Brown was prepared to use violence to free slaves. When Brown and his little band attacked Harper's Ferry, Parker was in Rome; it is impossible to doubt that, had he still been in Boston, he would have been hand-in-glove with Brown; and it is hard to believe that he would have run for cover, as did Gerrit Smith and the Chevalier Howe and young Frank Sanborn. As soon as Parker got news of John Brown's raid, he hurried off a long letter to his old friend Francis Jackson. "I could not help wishing I was at home again," he wrote sadly, "to use what poor remnant of power is left to me in defence of the True and the Right."

This long letter, chiefly a defence of the right of slaves to fight for their freedom, contains two interesting predictions: "Brown will die . . . like a martyr, and also like a saint" and "The American people will have to march to rather severe music . . . and it is better for them to face it in season."

TO FRANCIS JACKSON

Rome, November 24, 1859

MY DEAR FRIEND,—I see by a recent telegraph which the steamer of Nov. 2nd brought from Boston, that the Court found Capt. Brown guilty, and passed sentence upon him. It is said Friday, Dec. 2nd, is fixed as the day for hanging him. So, long before this reaches you, my friend will have passed on to the reward of his magnanimous public services, and his pure, upright private life. I am not well enough to be the minister to any congregation, least of all to one like that which, for so many years, helped my soul while it listened to my words. Surely, the 28th Congregational Society in Boston needs a minister, not half dead, but alive all over; and yet, while reading the accounts of the affair at Harper's Ferry, and of the sayings of certain men at Boston, whom you and I know only too well, I could not help wishing I was at home again *to use what poor remnant of power is left to me in defence of the True and the Right.*

America is rich in able men, in skilful writers, in ready and accomplished speakers. But few men dare treat public affairs with reference to the great principles of justice and the American Democracy; nay, few with reference to any remote future, or even with a comprehensive survey of the present. Our public writers ask what effect will this opinion have on the Democratic party, or the Republican party? how will it affect the Presidential election? what will the great State of Pennsylvania, or Ohio, or New York say to it? This is very unfortunate for us all, especially when the people have to deal practically, and that speedily, with a question concerning the very existence of Democratic institutions in America; for it is not to be denied that we must give up DEMOCRACY if we keep SLAVERY, or give up SLAVERY if we keep DEMOCRACY.

I greatly deplore this state of things. Our able men fail to perform their natural function, to give valuable instruction and advice to the people; and at the same time they debase and degrade themselves. The hurrahs and the offices they get are poor compensation for falseness to their own consciences.

In my best estate, I do not pretend to much political wisdom, and still less now while sick; but I wish yet to set down a few thoughts for your private eye, and, it may be, for the ear of the Fraternity. They are, at least, the result of long meditation on the subject; besides, they are not at all new nor peculiar to me, but are a part of the public knowledge of all enlightened men.

1. A MAN HELD AGAINST HIS WILL AS A SLAVE HAS A NATURAL RIGHT TO KILL EVERY ONE WHO SEEKS TO PREVENT HIS ENJOYMENT OF LIBERTY. This has long been recognized as a self-evident proposition, coming so directly from the primitive instincts of human nature that it neither required proofs nor admitted them.

2. IT MAY BE A NATURAL DUTY OF THE SLAVE TO DEVELOPE THIS NATURAL RIGHT IN A PRACTICAL MANNER, AND ACTUALLY KILL ALL THOSE WHO SEEK TO PREVENT HIS ENJOYMENT OF LIBERTY. For if he continue patiently in bondage—First, he entails the foulest of curses on his children; and, second, he encourages other men to commit the crime against nature which he allows his own master to commit. It is my duty to preserve my own body from starvation. If I fail thereof through sloth, I not

only die, but incur the contempt and loathing of my acquaintances while I live. It is not less my duty to do all that is in my power to preserve my body and soul from slavery; and if I submit to that through cowardice, I not only become a bondman and suffer what thraldom inflicts, but I incur also the contempt and loathing of my acquaintance. Why do freemen scorn and despise a slave? Because they think his condition is a sign of his cowardice, and believe that he ought to prefer death to bondage. The Southerners hold the Africans in great contempt, though mothers of their children. Why? Simply because the Africans are slaves; that is, because the Africans fail to perform the natural duty of securing freedom by killing their oppressors.

3. THE FREEMAN HAS A NATURAL RIGHT TO HELP THE SLAVES RECOVER THEIR LIBERTY, AND IN THAT ENTERPRISE TO DO FOR THEM ALL WHICH THEY HAVE A RIGHT TO DO FOR THEMSELVES.

This statement, I think, requires no argument or illustration.

4. IT MAY BE A NATURAL DUTY FOR THE FREEMAN TO HELP THE SLAVES TO THE ENJOYMENT OF THEIR LIBERTY, AND AS MEANS TO THAT END, TO AID THEM IN KILLING ALL SUCH AS OPPOSE THEIR NATURAL FREEDOM.

If you were attacked by a wolf, I should not only have a *right* to aid you in getting rid of that enemy, but it would be my DUTY to help you in proportion to my power. If it were a MURDERER, and not a wolf, who attacked you, the duty would be still the same. Suppose it is not a murderer who would kill you, but a KIDNAPPER who would enslave, does that make it less my duty to help you out of the hands of your enemy? Suppose he is not a kidnapper who would make you a bondman, but a SLAVE-HOLDER who would keep you one, does that remove my obligation to help you?

5. THE PERFORMANCE OF THIS DUTY IS TO BE CONTROLLED BY THE FREEMAN'S POWER AND OPPORTUNITY TO HELP THE SLAVES. (The impossible is never the obligatory). I cannot help the slaves in Dahomey or Bornou, and am not bound to try. I can help those who escape to my own neighborhood, and I ought to do so. My duty is commensurate with my power; and as my power increases my duty enlarges along with it. If I *could* help the bondmen in Virginia to their freedom as easy and effectually as I can aid the runaway at my own door, then I OUGHT to do so.

These five maxims have a direct application to America at this day, and the people of the Free States have a certain dim perception thereof, which, fortunately, is becoming clearer every year.

Thus, the people of Massachusetts *feel* that they ought to protect the fugitive slaves who come into our State. Hence come first, the irregular attempts to secure their liberty, and the declarations of noble men, like Timothy Gilbert, George W. Carnes, and others, that they will do so even at great personal risk; and, secondly, the statute laws made by the Legislature to accomplish that end.

Now, if Massachusetts had the power to do as much for the slaves in Virginia as for the runaways in her own territory, we should soon see those two sets of measures at work in *that* direction also.

I find it is said in the Democratic newspapers that "Capt. Brown had many friends at the North, who sympathized with him in general, and in special approved of this particular scheme of his; they furnished him with some twelve or twenty thousand dollars, it would seem." I think much more than that is true of us. If he *had* succeeded in running off one or two thousand slaves to Canada, even at the expense of a little violence and bloodshed, *the majority of men in New England would have rejoiced, not only in the end, but also in the means.* The first successful attempt of a considerable number of slaves to secure their freedom by violence will clearly show how deep is the sympathy of the people for them, and how strongly they embrace the five principles I mentioned above. A little success of that sort will serve as *priming* for the popular cannon; it is already *loaded*.

Of course, I was not astonished to hear that an attempt had been made to free the slaves in a certain part of Virginia, nor should I be astonished if another "insurrection" or "rebellion" took place in the State of ———, or a third in ———, or a fourth in ———. Such things are to be expected; for they do not depend merely on the private will of men like Capt. Brown and his associates, but on the great general causes which move all human kind to hate Wrong and love Right. Such "insurrections" will continue as long as Slavery lasts, and will increase, both in frequency and in power just as the people become intelligent and moral. Virginia may hang John Brown and all that family, but she cannot hang the HUMAN RACE; and until that is done noble men will rejoice in the motto of that once magnanimous State— "*Sic semper Tyrannis!*" "Let such be the end of every oppressor."

It is a good Anti-Slavery picture on the Virginia shield—a

man standing on a tyrant and chopping his head off with a sword; only I would paint the sword-holder *black* and the tyrant *white,* to show the *immediate application* of the principle. The American people will have to march to rather severe music, I think, and it is better for them to face it in season. A few years ago it did not seem difficult first to check Slavery, and then to end it without any bloodshed. I think this cannot be done now, nor ever in the future. All the great charters of HUMANITY have been writ in blood. I once hoped that of American Democracy would be engrossed in less costly ink; but it is plain, now, that our pilgrimage must lead through a Red Sea, wherein many a Pharaoh will go under and perish. Alas! that we are not wise enough to be just, or just enough to be wise, and so gain much at small cost!

Look, now, at a few notorious facts:

I. There are four million slaves in the United States violently withheld from their natural right to life, liberty, and the pursuit of happiness. Now, they are our fellow-countrymen—yours and mine, just as much as any four million *white* men. Of course, you and I owe them the duty which one man owes another of his own nation,—the duty of instruction, advice, and protection of natural rights. If they are starving, we ought to help feed them. The color of their skins, their degraded social condition, their ignorance, abates nothing from their natural claim on us, or from our natural duty toward them.

There are men in all the Northern States who feel the obligation which citizenship imposes on them—the duty to help those slaves. Hence arose the ANTI-SLAVERY SOCIETY, which seeks simply to excite the white people to perform their natural duty to their dark fellow-countrymen. Hence comes CAPT. BROWN'S EXPEDITION—an attempt to help his countrymen enjoy their natural right to life, liberty, and the pursuit of happiness.

He sought by violence what the Anti-Slavery Society works for with other weapons. The two agree in the end, and differ only in the means. Men like Capt. Brown will be continually rising up among the white people of the Free States, attempting to do their *natural duty* to their black countrymen—that is, help them to freedom. Some of these efforts will be successful. Thus, last winter Capt. Brown himself escorted eleven of his countrymen from bondage in Missouri to freedom in Canada. He did not snap a gun, I think, although then, as more recently, he had his fighting tools at hand, and would have used them, if necessary. Even now, the Underground Railroad is in constant and beneficent operation.

By-and-bye, it will be an Overground Railroad from Mason and Dixon's line clear to Canada: the only *tunneling* will be in the Slave States. Northern men applaud the brave conductors of that Locomotive of Liberty.

When Thomas Garrett was introduced to a meeting of polit- ical Free-Soilers in Boston, as "the man who had helped 1800 slaves to their natural liberty," even that meeting gave the righteous Quaker *three times three.* All honest Northern hearts beat with admiration of such men; nay, with love for them. Young lads say, "I wish that Heaven would make me such a man." The wish will now and then be father to the fact. You and I have had opportunity enough, in twenty years, to see that this philanthropic patriotism is on the increase at the North, and the special direction it takes is toward the liberation of their countrymen in bondage.

Not many years ago, Boston sent money to help the Greeks in their struggle for *political freedom* (they never quite lost their *personal liberty*), but with the money she sent what was more valuable and far more precious, one of her most valiant and heroic sons, who stayed in Greece to fight the great battle of Humanity. Did your friend, Dr. Samuel G. Howe, lose the esteem of New England men by that act? He won the admiration of Europe, and holds it still.

Nay, still later, the same dear old Boston—Hunkers have never been more than rats and mice in her house, which she suffers for a time, and then drives out twelve hundred of them at once on a certain day of March, 1776,—that same dear old Boston sent the same Dr. Howe to carry aid and comfort to the Poles, then in deadly struggle for their political existence. Was he disgraced because he lay seven-and-forty days in a Prussian gaol in Berlin? Not even in the eyes of the Prussian King, who after- wards sent him a gold medal, whose metal was worth as many dollars as that philanthropist lay days in the despot's gaol. It is said, "Charity should begin at home." The American began a good ways off, but has been working homeward ever since. The Dr. Howe of to-day would and ought to be more ready to help an American to *personal liberty,* than a Pole or a Greek to mere political freedom, and would find more men to furnish aid and comfort to our own countrymen, even if they were black. It would not surprise me if there were other and well-planned attempts in other States to do what Captain Brown heroically, if not success- fully, tried in Virginia. Nine out of ten may fail—the tenth will succeed. The victory over Gen. Burgoyne more than made up for all the losses in many a previous defeat; it was the beginning of the end. Slavery will not die a dry death, it may have as many lives as a cat; at last, it will die like a mad dog in a village, with only the enemies of the human kind to lament its fate, and they too cowardly to appear as mourners.

II. But it is not merely white men who will fight for the liberty of Americans; the negroes will take their defence into their own hands, especially if they can find white men to lead them. No doubt, the African race is greatly inferior to the Caucasian in general intellectual power, and also in that instinct for Liberty which is so strong in the Teutonic family, and just now obvious in the Anglo-Saxons of Britain and America; besides, the African race have but little desire for vengeance—the lowest form of the love of justice. Here is one example out of many: In Santa Cruz, the old slave laws were the most horrible, I think, I ever read of in modern times, unless those of the Carolinas be an exception. If a slave excited others to run away, for the first offence his right leg was to be cut off; for the second offence, his other leg. This mutilation was not to be done by a surgeon's hand; the poor wretch was laid down on a log, and his legs chopped off with a plantation axe, and the stumps plunged into boiling pitch to stanch the blood, and to save the *property* from entire destruction; for the live *Torso* of a slave might serve as a warning. No action of a Court was requisite to inflict this punishment; any master could thus mutilate his bondman. Even from 1830 to 1846, it was common for owners to beat their offending victims with "tamarind rods" six feet long and an inch in thickness at the bigger end—rods thick set with ugly thorns. When that process was over, the lacerated back was washed with a decoction of the Manchineel, a poison tree, which made the wounds fester, and long remain open.

In 1846, the negroes were in "rebellion," and took possession of the island; they were 25,000, the whites 3000. But the blacks did not hurt the hair of a white man's head; they got their freedom, but they took no revenge! Suppose 25,000 Americans, held in bondage by 3000 Algerines on a little island, should get their masters into their hands, how many of the 3000 would see the next sun go down?

No doubt, it is through the absence of this desire of natural vengeance, that the Africans have been reduced to bondage, and kept in it.

But *there is a limit even to the negro's forbearance.* San

Domingo is not a great way off. The revolution which changed its black inhabitants from tame slaves into wild men, took place after you had ceased to call yourself a boy.

It shows what may be in America, with no white man to help. In the Slave States, there is many a possible San Domingo, which may become actual any day; and, if not in 1860, then in some other "year of our Lord." Besides, America offers more than any other country to excite the slave to love of Liberty, and the effort for it. We are always talking about "Liberty," boasting that we are "the freest people in the world," declaring that "a man would die, rather than be a slave." We continually praise our Fathers "who fought the Revolution." We build monuments to commemorate even the humblest beginning of that great national work. Once a year, we stop all ordinary work, and give up a whole day to the noisiest kind of rejoicing for the War of Independence. How we praise the "champions of Liberty"! How we point out the "infamy of the British oppressors"! "They would make our Fathers slaves," say we, "and we slew the oppressor— Sic semper Tyrannis!"

Do you suppose this will fail to produce its effect on the black man, one day? The South must either give up keeping "Independence Day," or else keep it in a little more thorough fashion. Nor is this all: the Southerners are continually taunting the negroes with their miserable nature. "You are only half human," say they, "not capable of freedom." "Hay is good for horses, not for hogs," said the *philosophic* American who now "represents the great Democracy" at the Court of Turin. *So, liberty is good for white men, not for negroes.* Have they souls? I don't know that—*non mi recordo.* "Contempt," says the proverb, "will cut through the shell of the tortoise." And, one day, even the sluggish African will wake up under the three-fold stimulus of the Fourth of July cannon, the whip of the slaveholder, and the sting of his heartless mockery. Then, if "oppression maketh wise men mad," what do you think it will do to African slaves, who are familiar with scenes of violence, and all manner of cruelty? Still more: if the negroes have not general power of mind, or instinctive love of liberty, equal to the whites, they are much our superiors in *power of cunning,* and in *contempt for death*—rather formidable qualities in a servile war. There already have been several risings of slaves in this century; they spread fear and consternation. The future will be more terrible. Now, in case of an insurrection, not only is there, as Jefferson said, "no attribute of the Almighty" which can take sides with the master, but *there will be many white men who will take part with the slave.* Men, like the Lafayettes of the last century, and the Dr. Howes of this, may give the insurgent negro as effectual aid as that once rendered to America and Greece; and the public opinion of an enlightened world will rank them among its heroes of noblest mark.

If I remember rightly, some of your fathers were in the battle of Lexington, and that at Bunker Hill. I believe, in the course of the war which followed, every able-bodied man in your town (Newton) was in actual service. Now-a-days, their descendants are proud of the fact. One day, it will be thought not less heroic for a negro to fight for his personal liberty, than for a white man to fight for political independence, and against a tax of threepence a pound on tea. Wait a little, and things will come round.

III. The existence of Slavery endangers all our Democratic institutions. It does this if only tolerated as an exceptional measure—a matter of present convenience, and still more when proclaimed as an instantial principle, a rule of political conduct for all time and every place. Look at this: In 1790, there were (say) 300,000 slaves; soon they make their first doubling, and are 600,000; then their second, 1,200,000; then their third, 2,400,000. They are now in the process of doubling the fourth time, and will soon be 4,800,000; then comes the fifth double, 9,600,000; then the sixth, 19,200,000. Before the year of our Lord nineteen hundred, there will be twenty million slaves!

An Anglo-Saxon with common sense does not like this Africanization of America; he wishes the superior race to multiply rather than the inferior. Besides, it is plain to a one-eyed man that Slavery is an irreconcilable enemy of the progressive development of Democracy; that, if allowed to exist, it must be allowed to spread, to gain political, social, and ecclesiastical power; and all that it gains for the slaveholders is just so much taken from the freemen.

Look at this—there are twenty Southern Representatives who represent nothing but property in man, and yet their vote counts as much in Congress as the twenty Northerners who stand for the will of 1,800,000 freemen. Slavery gives the South the same advantage in the choice of President; consequently the slave-holding South has long controlled the Federal Power of the nation.

Look at the recent acts of the Slave Power! The Fugitive Slave Bill, the Kansas-Nebraska Bill, the Dred Scott decision, the filibustering against Cuba (till found too strong), and now against Mexico and other feeble neighbors, and, to crown all, the actual re-opening of the African slave-trade!

The South has kidnapped men in Boston, and made the Judges of Massachusetts go under her symbolic chain to enter the courts of justice (!). She has burned houses and butchered innocent men in Kansas, and the perpetrators of that wickedness were rewarded by the Federal Government with high office and great pay! Those things are notorious; they have stirred up some little indignation at the North, and freemen begin to think of defending their liberty. Hence came the Free-Soil party, and hence the Republican party—it contemplates no direct benefit to the slave, only the defence of the white man in his national rights, or his conventional privileges. It will grow stronger every year, and also bolder. It must lay down principles as a platform to work its measures on; the principles will be found to require much more than what was at first proposed, and even from this platform Republicans will promptly see that *they cannot defend the natural rights of freemen without destroying that Slavery which takes away the natural rights of a negro.* So, first, the wise and just men of the party will sympathize with such as seek to liberate the slaves, either peacefully or by violence; next, they will declare their opinions in public; and, finally, the whole body of the party will come to the same sympathy and the same opinion. Then, of course, they will encourage men like Captain Brown, give him money and all manner of help, and also encourage the slaves whenever they shall rise to take their liberty, at all hazards. When called to help put down an insurrection of the slaves, they will go readily enough and do the work by removing the cause of insurrection—that is—*by destroying Slavery itself.*

An Anti-Slavery party, under one name or another, will before long control the Federal Government, and will exercise its Constitutional Rights, and perform its Constitutional Duty, and "guarantee a Republican form of Government to every State in the Union." That is a work of time and peaceful legislation. But the short work of violence will be often tried, and each attempt will gain something for the cause of Humanity, even by its dreadful process of blood.

IV. But there is yet another agency that will act against Slavery. There are many mischievous persons who are ready for any wicked work of violence. They abound in the city of New York (a sort of sink where the villainy of both hemispheres settles

down, and genders that moral pestilence which steams up along
the columns of the *New York Herald* and the *New York Ob-
server,* the great escape-pipes of secular and ecclesiastical wickedness), they commit the great crimes of violence and robbery
at home, plunder emigrants, and engage in the slave-trade, or
venture on fillibustering expeditions. This class of persons is
comon in all the South. One of the legitimate products of her
"peculiar institution," they are familiar with violence, ready and
able for murder. Public opinion sustains such men. Bully Brooks
was but one of their representatives in Congress. Now-a-days
they are fond of Slavery, defend it, and seek to spread it. But
the time must come one day—it may come any time—when the
lovers of mischief will do a little fillibustering at home, and rouse
up the slaves to rob, burn, and kill. Prudent carpenters sweep up
all the shavings in their shops at night, and remove this food of
conflagration to a safe place, lest the spark of a candle, the end
of a cigar, or a friction-match should swiftly end their wealth,
slowly gathered together. The South takes pains to strew her car-
penter's shop with shavings, and fill it full thereof. She encourages men to walk abroad with naked candles in their hands and
lighted cigars in their mouths; then they scatter friction-matches on
the floor, and dance a fillibustering jig thereon. She cries, "Well
done! Hurrah for Walker!" "Hurrah for Brooks!" "Hurrah for the
barque *Wanderer* and its cargo of slaves! Up with the bowie-knife!
Down with justice and humanity!" The South must reap as she
sows; where she scatters the wind, the whirlwind will come up.
It will be a pretty crop for her to reap. Within a few years the
South has BURNED ALIVE eight or ten negroes. Other black men
looked on, and learned how to fasten the chain, how to pile the
green wood, how to set this Hell-fire of Slavery agoing. The apprentice may be slow to learn, but he has had teaching enough
by this time to know the art and mystery of torture; and, depend
upon it, the negro will one day apply it to his old tormentors. The
Fire of Vengeance may be waked up even in an African's heart,
especially when it is fanned by the wickedness of a white man:
then it runs from man to man, from town to town. What shall
put it out? *The white man's blood!*

Now, Slavery is a wickedness so vast and so old, so rich and
so respectable, supported by the State, the Press, the Market, and
the Church, that all those agencies are needed to oppose it with—
those, and many more which I cannot speak of now. You and I
prefer the peaceful method; but I, at least, shall welcome the

violent if no other accomplish the end. So will the great mass of thoughtful and good men at the North; else why do we honor the Heroes of the Revolution, and build them monuments all over our blessed New England? I think you gave money for that of Bunker Hill: I once thought it a folly; now I recognize it as a great sermon in stone, which is worth not only all the money it cost to build it, but all the blood it took to lay its corner-stones. Trust me, its lesson will not be in vain—at the North, I mean, for the LOGIC OF SLAVERY will keep the South on its lower course, and drive it on more swiftly than before. "Capt. Brown's expedition was a failure," I hear it said. I am not quite sure of that. True, it kills fifteen men by sword and shot, and four or five men by the gallows. But it shows the weakness of the greatest Slave State in America, the worthlessness of her soldiery, and the utter fear which Slavery genders in the bosoms of the masters. Think of the condition of the City of Washington while Brown was at work!

Brown will die, I think, like a martyr, and also like a saint. His noble demeanor, his unflinching bravery, his gentleness, his calm, religious trust in God, and his words of truth and soberness, cannot fail to make a profound impression on the hearts of Northern men; yes, and on Southern men. For "every human heart is human," &c. I do not think the money wasted, nor the lives thrown away. Many acorns must be sown to have one come up; even then, the plant grows slow; but it is an oak at last. None of the Christian martyrs died in vain; and from Stephen, who was stoned at Jerusalem, to Mary Dyer, whom our fathers hanged on a bough of "the great tree" on Boston Common, I think there have been few spirits more pure and devoted than John Brown's, and none that gave up their breath in a nobler cause. Let the American State hang his body, and the American Church damn his soul; still, the blessing of such as are ready to perish will fall on him, and the universal justice of the Infinitely Perfect God will take him welcome home. The road to heaven is as short from the gallows as from the throne; perhaps, also, as easy.

I suppose you would like to know something about myself. Rome has treated me to bad weather, which tells its story in my health, and certainly does not mend me. But I look for brighter days and happier nights. The sad tidings from America—my friends in peril, in exile, in jail, killed, or to be hung—have filled me with grief, and so I fall back a little, but hope to get forward again. God bless you and yours, and comfort you!

Ever affectionately yours,

VI

A Sheaf of Letters

26. A Sheaf of Letters

Somehow, amid the exacting demands of a large parish, incessant travel, constant lecturing, voracious reading in one of Boston's largest libraries, and voluminous writing (the printed works come to fourteen stout volumes, plus volumes of translations, a three-hundred-page *Defence* and scores of sermons and addresses), Parker found time for a large correspondence, public and private. In that age, the term "men of letters" was meant almost literally: almost every literary and political figure managed to carry on a large correspondence, and letters were more than mere formalities.

We have, alas, few samples of Parker's private correspondence; that has disappeared, along with many of his letters to his clerical or scholarly brethren. Yet the letters given us by the pious, but not very critical, John Weiss, and by Frothingham, suggest something of the richness and variety of Parker's correspondence. Sometimes—like Theodore Roosevelt half a century later—he would employ the device of a private letter for a message designed for the public, or for history; two or three of these, such as the letters on Horace Mann and John Brown, are quoted elsewhere in this anthology. Those in the following section are for the most part personal letters, which reveal the character of the man rather than his philosophical or political ideas. For that reason, they are arranged chronologically rather than topically.

TO REV. CONVERS FRANCIS

Rome, March 18, 1844

MY DEAR FRIEND,—I owe you many thanks for all your kindness in writing to me when I am a stranger in a strange land. You tell me good tidings also. I am rejoiced to know of the doings of Ripley, Channing, and Brownson. But I hear that the latter has done what he advised the Unitarians to do, "re-establish the *Boston Quarterly*." I suppose he will devote it to the overturn of the principles established in the first series. I rejoice very much in the *Fourier* movement, not that I accept the statements of F., but because I think our present form of society is irrational and un-christian; that society makes criminals, and then hangs them; that trade (in the main) is robbery, and "justice" catches only at petty

271

rogues—never forgiving their offences, gradually makes them worse, and at last hangs them. Men are born in Boston into a condition far worse than that of the Esquimaux. Strong men build their castles by the hands of the weak and out of the property of the weak. The feudalism of money is not so bad as the feudalism of birth, nor that so bad as the feudalism of the sword, but too bad to be borne in a Christian land, it seems to me. I do not believe the Socialists see very clearly what they would be at, yet they will help open men's eyes, it seems to me. Three things are needed to make a complete revolution—the sentiment, the idea, the action. I fancy their sentiment is not far from right, but if their idea be wrong, so must their action be. I see no cure for the evil but this, to give each individual clear views of the right, and then leave it to him to do what he thinks best. A complex evil has a simple cure, it seems to me. England is the richest country in the world, perhaps, but that in which there is the most misery. It is the paradise of the rich, the purgatory of the wise, and the hell of the poor. In Italy there is much begging, but less starving. One million of the English are fine men; what are the nineteen millions?

Now, we, the Yankee nation, are going in just the same way as the English, and, unless we change our whole system, radically, in regard to the pursuit of wealth and the pursuit of power, we shall come to just the same result, and have the Christian feudalism of gold in Boston as in London. But of this when we meet face to face.

TO JOHN B. PARKER

West Roxbury, August 29, 1846

MY DEAR JOHN,—I told you I despised the study of heraldry: I have yet wasted some little time over Guillim and other writers on that theme. I am quite up to giving any information about the noble family of *Kettles*. The motto is,

"NE CALL THE POT BLACK."

It is a most ancient family. It is related to the *Pots*, the *Skillets*, the *Patty-Pans*, the *Porringers*, and divers other great and noble families in all civilized countries. Lord *Copper-Kettle*, Baron *Stew-Pan*, and his Grace the Duke of *Brass-Kettle*, are all branches of this family: so is that famous champion, Sir *Kettle-Drum;* and he is soon to be elevated to the peerage. The family of *Boilers* is of the same descent, but were for a long time in obscurity, devoted mainly to agriculture and domestic economy. But lately some of the family have entered the marine service, and have done great honor to their family; while others have become famous on land. Lord *Steamboat-Boiler* and Sir *Fizaway-Locomotive* are of this latter class. It is thought this branch of the family will surpass all others. Indeed, some of them have been so elated by success, that they have actually *burst;* and this, by the way, is the great danger to which this family is subject. You will find all about the stock, &c., in Burke's "Peerage" or "Commoners," &c.

What you say of Salem is pretty true, but not wholly. There are, as I know very well, some noble exceptions to what you state as the general rule.

If you want any books from time to time, let me know, and I think I can procure them for you. But Emmeline tells me you sit up late. Now, that is quite—nay, almost—as bad as lying late. Be sure you will repent it. If your eyes are sore, go to bed; go to sleep. You must mind me. There is no excuse for violating a law of Nature. The laws God wrote on the body are quite as binding as the ten commands which Moses wrote on stone. KEEP THE COMMANDMENTS.

And believe me truly yours,

TO REV. SAMUEL JOSEPH MAY

November 1846

I think Jesus was a perfect man—perfect in morality and religion. A religious genius, as Homer a poetical genius. I can't say there never will be a *greater* man in morality and religion, though I can conceive of none now. Who knows what is possible for man? If Jesus had lived now, I think he would have been greater; yes, if he had lived to be forty, fifty, sixty, or seventy years old —why not? I think him human, not superhuman—the manliest of men. I think him inspired directly, but not miraculously; not unnaturally, but naturally—inspired in proportion to his genius and his use thereof. I think God is immanent in man; yes, in *men*—most in the greatest, truest, best men. How much of the excellence of Jesus came from organization, I don't know. Artists are true to nature, it seems to me, and give him an organization exquisitely human—noble, intellectual, and heavenly. But I have seen no full embodiment of the Christ in art—none of *my* Christ, though enough of the Church's Christ. I doubt not, that as men follow the laws of nature, we shall have nobler forms, features, heads, and so nobler men. We have loved force hitherto, and bred *draught cattle*—men for war. May we not one day have a man with the philanthropic genius of a Socrates, the poetic of a Homer, the practical of a Napoleon, and the religious of a Christ? Even Dr. P. knows not that *it cannot be!*

How did Jesus become so great? Who can tell? Why do you turn to peace, to reform, to Christianity, and————to eating and drinking, and————to money-making? What made Homer the poet, Bacon the philosopher? Much is due to *birth;* much to *breeding;* how much to SELF? Who made us to differ? I doubt not many men go out of brothels, and jails, and from the gallows, with more merit than I have, and will take a higher place at last in heaven; for they have better worn *their* birth and breeding than I mine. I think God alone has absolute freewill; we only relative and partial—a conditional freedom—one foot booted, the other chained —that as we live truly, we get more freedom, and so on. I can't think there was a special opening of the heavens to Christ. Each man's measure of ability is special, and for him; but the use thereof subject to general laws. Inspiration, I think, comes by universal laws. Just as we obey the laws of our being, *we get inspiration,* it seems to me; a little being *less,* the larger being *more.* I look on Jesus as the *celestial blossoming of man,* the highest fact in our story.

It seems to me there is a progress of man's capabilities here on earth. I don't mean that man changes in his essence, but practically in his potency. We don't find Waldo Emersons among the Choctaws, but among the Yankees. Let the world have peace for 500 years, the aristocracy of blood will have gone, the aristocracy of gold has come and gone, that of talent will have also come and gone, and the aristocracy of goodness, which is the democracy of man, the government *of* all, *for* all, *by* all, will be the power that is. Then what may we not look for? Hitherto our hero has been of force, his symbol the sword or the sceptre of command. It will not always be so. We are now developing the hand, and shall one day the head, and then the heart. All this is conformable to Christianity.

I think Jesus saw the great law of man's nature and taught absolute religion, *i.e.,* religion with no limitations; free goodness,

free piety, free thought, and free development of man's consciousness. By the reception of that are we to be *"saved,"* and the world
saved, and by that process alone.

What men and women shall we not raise up? In prospect of
that how little seem all the "sects," from the "Catholic" to the
"Unitarian," and how melancholy all the swelling insolence of
some hero of a coterie—a saint in long-clothes—a demi-god, who
at best can fill a surplice! But how encouraging is it to work! Men
tell me of the littleness of men—I see it, feel it; of their folly, stu-
pidity, sin—I feel that, and know it well enough. But I say, Well,
we have had a Jesus, and see what comes of that Jesus! I am full
of hope; I see each day more good in man than I knew of before,
and trust *men* more than ever, and am less often deceived. God is
in history, slowly getting incarnated.

TO A FRIEND IN GERMANY

Boston, June 8, 1847

I had formerly a small parish in Roxbury, but abandoned
that a couple of years ago and came to Boston, where I have a
large audience of intelligent and noble men and women. I send
you a little tract published by the Unitarians themselves, which
gives some account of them. What I must add is not much in their
favour. They started originally with a protest against the doctrine
of the Trinity. They denied the divinity of Christ, but they did not
declare the humanity of Christ. So they only affirmed a negative;
their history was but the development of a negation, and little
more; the protest began amongst a class of cultivated men in the
most cultivated part of America; with men who had not the religious element developed in proportion to the intellectual or the
æsthetic element. Therefore, they had not the element of piety in
their preaching to the same extent as their opponents. Unitarianism
always had a worldly character; gradually the opposition of the
Trinitarians grew less and less, though the name of Christian is
still wickedly denied to the Unitarians by their opponents. The
Unitarians formed themselves into a sect, with the regular machinery of a theological party, *i.e.,* officers and missionaries,
money and tracts. Then it was necessary for them to publish their
symbolical books. But they have not ideas enough to form a
theological party; the development of their negations is all that

is left for them distinctively as a party. If they would affirm the humanity of Christ, they might become a great sect; but they do not see far enough for that. They declare the paternal character of God, but yet do not (as the Universalists) declare the eternal salvation of all men. They are not now making any advances towards a liberal theology; they stand still, and become more and more narrow and bigoted from year to year.

Yet, among them there are some very noble men who are entirely free, and desirous of further progress. From them as individuals much is to be hoped, but from the sect, as a sect, nothing must be looked for. It is curious to see the distinguished men who have once been Unitarian preachers, but who now preach no longer. Andrews Norton, the best scholar of the party, who, however, devotes himself exclusively to theological pursuits, is narrow, bigoted, and sectarian, but an able man. His chief work is "A Defence of the Genuineness of the Gospels," 4 vols. 8vo. Jared Sparks, eminent as an historian and editor of American State Papers; Edward Everett, formerly Governor of Massachusetts, and American Ambassador to England, now President of Harvard University; George Bancroft, now Ambassador to England, the historian of the United States, a man of great ability and genius as an historical writer; R. W. Emerson, the most original author we have produced in America, a man of wonderful gifts, and the author of some volumes of Essays, which I wish might be translated into German; John G. Palfrey, now a member of Congress, and Secretary of the State of Massachusetts; George Ripley, a sound and philosophical man, who is devoting himself to the doctrines of Fourier. All these men have left the pulpits of the Unitarians. The most prominent scholars in the denomination are Dr. James Walker, Professor of Intellectual Philosophy at Harvard University; Dr. Convers Francis, Professor of Theology at the Unitarian Theological Seminary; Dr. George R. Noyes, also Professor of Theology at the same place; Dr. Lamson; Dr. Gannett; Dr. Dewey, a showy but superficial writer; Dr. Putnam, an eloquent preacher, but nothing more. There is little scholarship and less philosophical thinking among the Unitarians. Some of their members engage in the great moral movements of the day, such as the Temperance Reform, and the Anti-Slavery movement. But the sect as such is opposed to all reforms. However, it has already done a great work in liberalizing the minds of men; the misfortune is that it is not disposed to go on further. However, *"non omnia possumus omnes,"* and others are rising up with nobler ideas than the Unitarians, who go more profoundly to work, and preach absolute religion, not controlled by the traditional authority of men, but resting in the instincts of man, and the primeval revelation which God makes to mankind. The triumph of this liberal movement, I think, is certain; for every year the people become more and more emancipated from authority, and disposed to think freely, and to allow all others to do the same. Some of the most liberal theologians in the country are not in the Unitarian ranks, but are men of enlarged minds and generous culture. I think the destiny of the sect is to liberalize the mind of the nation in some measure, and then gradually to decay and perish. There is now a powerful movement going on in favour of the most *entire freedom of thought*. This will sweep away all the absurdities of tradition. Some valuable things of tradition will likewise be dropped, and then we must wait till some one goes back and gathers them up. Hitherto our *political* and *industrial* progress has been greater than our advance in literature and philosophy. That was unavoidable. But now intellectual things are getting attended to.

TO A SOUTHERN SLAVEHOLDER

Boston, February 2, 1848

SIR,—Your letter of January last has just come to hand, and I hasten to reply. I thank you for your frankness, and will reply as plainly and openly as you write to me. You need not suppose that I have any spite against the slaveholders; I wish them well not less than their slaves. I think they are doing a great wrong to themselves, to their slaves, and to mankind. I think slave-holding is a wrong in itself, and, therefore, a sin; but I cannot say that this or that particular slave-holder is a sinner because he holds slaves. I know what sin is—God only knows who is a sinner. I hope I have not said anything harsh in my letter, or anything not true. I certainly wrote with no ill-feeling towards any one.

You seem to think that the Old Testament and New Testament are just alike, that Christianity and Judaism are, therefore, the same. So, as a Christian, you appeal to the Old Testament for your authority to hold slaves. Now, look a little at the matter, and see the difference between the Old Testament and New Testament. The Old Testament *demands* circumcision, a peculiar priest-hood, the sacrifice of certain animals, the observance of certain fast-days, full-moon days, new-moon days, the seventh day, and the like. It demands them all in the *name of a Lord.* Yet you do not observe any of them. Now, you say, I suppose, that the ritual laws of the Old Testament came from God, but were repealed by Christ, who also spoke by the command of God. If that were so, then it would appear that God had repealed His own commands. You say, God could not change. So I say. I do not think God ever makes laws and then changes them; but if the Bible, as a whole, as you say, is the Word of God, then it is plain that in the New Testament He takes back what He commanded in the Old Testa-ment. In the Old Testament a man is allowed to put away his wife for any cause, or none at all; but you know that Christ said *Moses* gave that command on account of the hardness of men's hearts. In Exodus xxxv. 2, 3, it is forbidden to kindle a fire on Saturday —Sabbath—on pain of death. In Numbers xv. 32-36, it is said, the Lord commanded a man to be *stoned to death* because he picked up sticks on Saturday; yet, I suppose you have a fire in your house Saturday and Sunday, too, and, perhaps would not think it wicked to bring in an armful of wood to make a fire on either of those days. Now, I do not think God changes; therefore, I don't believe He ever uttered those dreadful commands in the Old Testament. I believe that God has the attributes of universal jus-tice and universal love. Doubtless, you will call me an "Infidel," but that makes no odds; I try to be a Christian, but do not begin by discarding conscience, reason, and common-sense. I think Saint Paul was a Christian, and you know what he says about the law, that is, the *Law of Moses,* as recorded in the Old Testament.

Now, let us look at the case of the negroes. You think the children of Ham are under a perpetual curse, and that the negroes are the children of Ham. The tenth chapter of Genesis treats of the descendants of Ham, but it does not mention among them a single tribe of negroes. I don't think the writer of that account knew even of the existence of the peculiar race of men that we call negroes. He mentions the *Egyptians,* it is true, and other *North African people,* but it is well known that they were not negroes. But even if some of the descendants of Ham were ne-groes, though it is plain from Genesis x. they were not, still, that does not bring them under the curse of Noah, for Noah does not curse *Ham and all his children,* but only *Canaan.* Now, the de-scendants of Canaan are mentioned in Gen. x. 15-19; not one of them was ever an *African people;* they all dwelt in the *western part of Asia,* and are the nations with whom the Hebrews were often at war. The Hebrews conquered many of these tribes, seized their country, and often their persons. Many of them fled, and I think, settled in *North Africa;* the Berbers, and, in part, the Moors are of that race, *perhaps,* but none of them are negroes.

But even if the negroes were the children of Canaan, as it is plain they were not, what title could you make out to hold them by? It would be this:—4000 years ago Noah cursed Canaan, and, therefore, you hold one of Canaan's children as a slave. Now, do you think a *man* has power to curse so far off as that? But you will say, God gave the curse; well, the Bible does not say so. You say, Canaan and his posterity were "constitutionally unworthy," but you don't know that. On the contrary, the Sidonians, who were the descendants of Canaan, were a very illustrious people of antiquity—a good deal like the English and Americans at this day—and actually held great quantities of the Jews in slavery. Before you can hold a single negro under that clause in Gen. ix. 25, you must make out—1. That the negro is descended from Canaan; 2. That the curse was actually uttered as related; 3. That it announces personal slavery for more than 4000 years; 4. That the curse was authorized by God Himself. Now, there is not one of these four propositions which ever has been made out or ever can be. My dear sir, I am really surprised that an intelligent man, in the nineteenth century, a *Christian man—a Republican of Georgia*—could seriously rely a moment on such an argument as that. Fie on such solemn trifling about matters so important as the life of two or three millions of men! For my own part, I don't believe the story of Noah cursing his grandson for his father's fault. I think it all a foolish story got up to satisfy the hatred which the Jews felt against the Canaanites. I know Bryant's book and Faber's, but never use either now-a-days. B. had more fancy than philosophy, it always seemed to me. I may be as "confident" as you think me, but don't call myself a learned man, though I have read about all the valuable works ever written on that matter of Noah's curse.

You ask if I could not propose some good to be done to the slaves now. Certainly; their marriage and family rights might be made secure, their work easier, their food and clothing better, they might not be beaten. Pains might be taken to educate them. But all that is very little, so long as you keep the man from his natural liberty. You would not be happy if a slave, would not think it right for a Christian man to hold you in bondage, even if one of your ancestors but fifty years ago, had cursed you, still less if 4000 years ago. If I were a slave-holder I would do this—I would say, "Come, now, you are free, go to work and I will pay you what you can earn." I think, in ten years' time, you would be a richer man, and in two hours' time, a far happier one, a more Christian one.

Dear sir, Christianity does not consist in believing stories in the Old Testament, about Noah's curse and all that, but in loving your brother as yourself, and God with your whole heart. Do not think that I *covet* your slaves. No consideration would induce me to become a slave-holder. *I* should be a *sinner,* though God grant that you are not one for that act! Let me ask you, *while you take from a man his liberty, his person, do you not violate that command,* "Thou shalt not covet anything that is thy neighbour's"? *Do you not break that golden rule,* "Whatsoever you would that men should do unto you, do ye even so unto them"?

I do not think you feel easy about this matter. What you say about colonization convinces me that you do not believe slavery is a Christian institution; that you are not very angry with me, after all. Do not think that I assume any airs of superiority over you because I am not a slave-holder. I have never had that temptation; perhaps if born in Georgia, I should not have seen the evil and the sin of slavery. I may be blind to a thousand evils and sins at home which I commit myself. If so, I will thank you to point them out. I hope you will write me again as frankly as before. I wish I could see Este's book. I will look for it, and study it, for I am working for the truth and the right. I have nothing to gain personally by the abolition of slavery, and have, by opposing that institution, got nothing but a bad name. I shall not count you my enemy, but am

Truly your friend.

TO ROBERT WHITE

Boston, February 11, 1848

DEAR FRIEND,—Your letter of the 25th ult. came to me a few days ago, accompanied by J. Dunlary's manifesto. I feel glad that you can approve something which I have written about religion, and also I rejoice to hear of another man who loves the freedom of the truth. I think I understand the doctrines of the Shakers. I am not wholly ignorant of the books they have issued, which set forth their history and their opinions. I have always admired the order, the neatness, the economy, the plenty, and the peace which are so noticeable in their establishments. I rejoice to confess that they have solved the problem of association, at least so far as to show that men can live harmoniously in a community, and thereby make a great saving of time, labor, and all the material things which help to make up the comforts of life. But you will excuse me for my frankness when I say that I think they have made a capital mistake in attempting to nullify the distinction of sex: that is not a distinction of man's making, but of man's finding as God made it. From that distinction there comes the union of one man and one woman, united by the most sacred and most beautiful and endearing ties. Each is a complement to the other. Out of their union grows up the family—each new-born child to them a new Messiah, a new revelation from God. I admire the wondrous ways of God. I reverence his wisdom, I love his love, as I find this everywhere. But I see nowhere more lovely instances thereof than in the very distinction of sex, and the effects which grow out of that cause; yet I think I see the causes which led the founders of the Shakers to renounce all this. I know, too, the history of similar parties in other days, and the doctrine which led them also to renounce marriage.

One thing more let me mention, and that is, the neglect of education in the establishments of your friends. You are a man of cultivation: it is evident the men who transact the business of the societies, and come in contact with the world likewise get some culture. But I have looked with great pain on the countenances of the young men and women that I have seen in Shaker settlements; they look so ignorant, so undeveloped, so clownish, and sometimes stupid and almost animal. Excuse me, my friend, for mentioning these things; think not that I do not honor the much of good that is in your friends, because I point out what seem to me the evils. God gave us many faculties, all good in their place; certainly all good when acting in harmony, and each in its proportion. The problem of life is to tune all these strings to harmony. Now I think the Shakers found one or two strings a little difficult to tune, and so they broke them off; then they tuned the rest quite well. Still the cords broken off were wanted. So the Shaker music is not yet *the whole human hymn.* Excuse me for writing this long letter, and believe me, truly your friend,

TO DR. R. L. HOWARD

Boston, April 30, 1849

DEAR SIR,—Your letter reached me to-day. I cannot suffer any business or any weariness to prevent me from answering it before I sleep. I thank you for the candor with which you write. I confess my work seems to me somewhat fearful; it did so when I began it, and I was often tempted to be silent, for I saw what a revolution would take place, suddenly or slowly, in the popular theology. If my principles were true, I saw that a mountain of rubbish must be swept away; that many reputations, many hopes, many institutions, likewise, were based on that mountain of rubbish, and of course must perish with their foundation. I saw that many men would look on me as the enemy of religion, and so as the enemy of mankind; that some would think that, while I opposed the folly of so much which men had believed in as religion, there was no reality at all for religion. But, at the same time, I had a strong confidence that what was true was also safe; that falsehood was not safe. I thought I could show men that the popular theology had no natural, at least no indissoluble, connection with true religion; that underneath the shifting sands of sectarian theology there lay the eternal rock of religion. I have never been sorry that I undertook the work; indeed, I could not have forborne if I would. I have felt the loneliness which you speak of; that comes from breaking away from early associations and tender ties. But that has long since passed away; still, I do not like to be hated, as I sometimes have been.

I have been compelled to pull down; but I have no delight in that work. It has always been painful. I did it only that something better might be built up in place of what but cumbered the ground before. I saw that religion was natural to man; the infinite goodness of God I could never doubt; the connection between God and man seemed to me so obvious, so essential to the nature of each, that I wondered any man could doubt of these facts. The more I live, the greater religion appears, the more attractive, the more satisfying, the more beautiful. But it seems plainer and plainer that religion is one thing, and the books written about it quite a different thing. At one time the Bible rested on me like a nightmare; I could not bear it nor get rid of it; now that I take a different view of it, the imperfections which I find in both the Testaments no longer disturb me, and the truths I find in both are the more welcome, because I feel free to come and to go, free to examine and satisfy my own mind and conscience, before I accept the conclusions of men who lived in another age and wrote from a different point of view.

I think I understand the circumstances in which you are placed. It requires not a little heroism to do as you seem disposed to do. But who can be contented with a divided heart? You do not lose your sympathy with the religion of your old associates, only with their theology. In all that is real piety, love of God, or real goodness, love of man, you will sympathise with them the more. Still, I suppose men not much enlightened will think ill of you, and speak harshly of your name. Sometimes it requires a little charity to be just to men who, from their ignorance, are unjust to us, but such charity is twice blessed. I hope my poor book will do no harm, but some little good to mankind. It would be a comfort to think that I had helped men in the way to religion, and all it brings; even to have helped a little. I have no doubt committed many errors, which, of course, must do harm. I hope they will be exposed, and left to perish. Now and then, some one writes me a letter like yours, which shows me that I have not spoken in vain; altogether, we may all be grateful for the liberal spirit of this age, which allows men to keep their heads on their shoulders, while these heads are full of thoughts which must work a revolution in the world. But let me not weary a busy man with a letter over-long. I will send the *Review,* as you suggest, and such of my sermons as are still on hand, though I lament that some which I value most are out of print. If I can ever be of service to you I shall be glad, and am,

Truly your friend,

TO REV. JAMES MARTINEAU

Boston, November 11, 1850

DEAR FRIEND,—I take this opportunity to write you a brief note to interest you in a couple of my parishioners who are about to visit England under quite remarkable circumstances. They are two fugitive slaves,—William Craft and his wife Ellen Craft. Perhaps you have heard their story: if you have not, you will, before long, learn of their wonderful flight from Macon in Georgia to Philadelphia,—a distance of more than nine hundred miles through the enemy's country. . . .

The Crafts have been in Boston nearly two years; are sober and industrious people. She is a seamstress: he is a cabinet-maker.

They are members of my parish. But, a few weeks ago, there came a ruffian from Macon in Georgia, by the name of Hughes,—he is a *jailer* at home,—with authority to seize and carry off the two fugitives. He applied to the proper officer, got his warrant, and secured the services of the marshal. All was ready for the seizure; but William armed himself with two revolvers and a substantial dirk, and was ready to kill any one who should attempt to kidnap him. His wife was concealed by some friends, who kept her safe and sound. I will tell you more of her concealment at some future time; but it is not safe now.

The slave-hunters remained in Boston more than a week. There was a "vigilance committee" appointed by a meeting of citizens; and they kept the slave-hunters in a state of disturbance all the time they remained here, and finally frightened them so, that they were glad to sneak out of the city. After the danger was over, Craft's friends thought it was wiser for them to go to England, that you may see what sort of men and women we make slaves of in "the model republic." They need no *pecuniary* aid; but if you will tell their story to your friends, and draw public attention to the fact that such persons are not safe in Boston, you may help the great cause of humanity in a new mode. . . .

I keep in my study two trophies of the American Revolution: one is a musket which my grandfather fought with at the battle of Lexington (April 19, 1775) against the "British;" the other is a great gun which he captured in that battle. He was the captain of the Lexington soldiers, and took the first prisoner, and the first musket taken in war for independence and the rights of man. But now I am obliged to look to "the British" for protection for the liberty of two of my own parishioners who have committed no wrong against any one. Well, so it is; and I thank God that Old England, with all her sins and shames, allows no slave-hunter to set foot on her soil.

I have written you a long letter, when I intended to write only a short note. I am glad to learn from my friend Sargent what a pleasant time he had with you in North Wales and elsewhere. I wish I had been of the party. Remember me kindly to Mrs. Martineau and the children. I know not how many there are now; but there was a houseful of them once. Give my kindest regards to Mr. and Mrs. Thom. I wish you would show him this letter; for I think his great heart will be interested in the case of these poor fugitives. With many and affectionate regards, believe me

Truly your friend,

TO HON. CHARLES SUMNER

Boston, April 26, 1851

DEAR SUMNER,—I have not been able to come and offer you my congratulations on your election. I was almost at your office this morning, when I met some one who told me you were not there, so you will accept my written congratulations instead of the spoken, and let me read you a little bit of a sermon. Perhaps you had better lay this away till Sunday, for I am going to preach. You told me once that you were in morals, not in politics. Now I hope you will show that you are still in morals although in politics. I hope you will be the senator *with a conscience*. The capital error of all our politicians is this: with understanding and practical sagacity, with cunning and power to manage men in the heroic degree, in moral power, in desire of the true and the right, "first good, first perfect, and first fair," they are behind the carpenters and blacksmiths. Look at Cass, Woodbury, Webster, Clay, Calhoun—nay, even at J. Q. Adams. The majority of the shoemakers in Norfolk County had a love of justice which bore a greater proportion to their whole being than Adams's to his. He never *led* in any moral movement.

Now, I look to you to be a leader in this matter; to represent justice, *"quæ semper et ubique eadem est."* If you do not do this, you will woefully disappoint the expectations of the people in the country. It is a strange sight to find men as much inferior in moral power as they are superior in intellectual power; as much inferior in willingness to make a sacrifice for their country, as they are superior in station! I expect you to make mistakes, blunders; I hope they will be intellectual and not moral; that you will never miss the Right, however you may miss the Expedient.

Then, you told me once that you should never find it more difficult to make a personal sacrifice for the True or the Right than in 1845. It seems to me that just as you take a high office in the State, you are bound more and more to perfect yourself for the sake of the State; to deny yourself for the sake of the State. I consider that Massachusetts has put you where you have no right to consult for the ease or the reputation of yourself, but for the eternal Right. All of our statesmen build, on the opinion of to-day, a house that is to be admired to-morrow, and the next day to be torn down with hootings. I hope you will build on the Rock of Ages, and look to eternity for your justification.

You see, my dear Sumner, that I expect much of you, that I

expect heroism of the most heroic kind. The moral and manly excellence of all our prominent men is greatly over-rated by the mass of men. I hope you will never be over-rated by the people, but will overshoot their estimate of you. Yours is a place of great honor, of great trust, but of prodigious peril, and of that there will be few to warn you, as I do now; few to encourage you as I gladly would. You see I try you by a difficult standard, and that I am not easily pleased. I hope some years hence to say, "You have done better than I advised!" I hope you will believe me what I am, sincerely your friend.

TO MISS ————

Boston, June 6, 1851

DEAR OLD LADYE,—. . . I have finished the Life of Wordsworth, and got a straw hat—manilla—just like the old one raised from the dead; and that is all I have done this week. Wordsworth was a dear old granny, with a most hearty love of mankind, especially of the least attractive portions of it,—*beggars* and *fools,* and Bishop Doane, who he thinks was a great and good man. Wordsworth heard him preach once at London; saw him at his (Wordsworth's) house, and liked him much. If Wordsworth had lived a little in London, and felt the presence of some one who was manly and differed from him, it would have done him service. He runs in a narrow round of objects, ideas, and sentiments; is humane (and means to be so in his penal sonnets), devout, self-denying, and genial: but he lived too much in solitude, was too much with his worshippers, and limited himself in his reading. He loved his neighbors and their little bits o' blossoms. His domestics he treated in the most Christian way,—like his own sisters. I love the man the more after reading all the twaddle of his letters and talk. He was like Dr. Channing and William Silsbee united. But he was the most self-conscious poet I remember to have read or read of: he knows the anatomy of his own mind as if he took himself to pieces. There was more of *will* in his poetry than you commonly find. Things were so because William Wordsworth would have them so. They grew out of his will more than out of his whole nature. But I love the dear old poetical Betty more after reading his Life than before. You will rejoice in the book, which will wait for you when you return.

West Newton, August 9, 1852

There are left two great families,—the Teutonic and the Sclavic. In Scandinavia and the Alps, I take it, they will keep up liberal governments, and become progressively more liberal; but in the centre of Europe, it seems to me, this family will continually retreat before the Slâves. Then England, with her immense practical talent, energy, and materialism, seems to me likely to become more and more powerful, more and more liberal. This is a remarkable peculiarity of the Anglo-Saxon race: they never fight for glory, but for gain. France is poorer for all her "glorious" victories: England is richer. Then France covets *old* countries: England covets *new ones*. Look at her possessions now,—Great Britain, Gibraltar, Malta, Greek Islands, a footing in Greece, right of way in Egypt, little bits of land all along the Gulf of Guinea, South Africa (and is now fighting the Caffres, and will soon have all the east of Africa), India, a footing in Siam (and is marching by that route to China), a footing in China, New Holland, New Zealand, a footing in Borneo, multitudes of islands in the Pacific Ocean, Jamaica, Bermudas, half of North America. She has now a hundred and fifty millions of subjects, and is horribly rich and formidably wise. Then there is the Anglo-Saxon American, just like his mother, with the same materialism, the same vulgarity, the same lust for land, and longing for individual freedom. I take it that, a hundred years hence, there will be only two great factors in the civilization of Christendom; viz., the Anglo-Saxon family (in two divisions,—the Anglo-Saxon Briton and the Anglo-Saxon American) and the Sclavic family. The history of mankind is getting simplified. It would not be surprising if these two tribes, then, should conquer all the globe. In due time, I trust, a nobler race of men will spring up, with higher notions, to establish a higher civilization. We Anglo-Saxons are *Romans of industry,* as the Romans were *Anglo-Saxons of war.* See how we invade nations with our *peddlers* and *workmen!* True, England and America are just alike in this.

I expect a good deal from the Sclavic family. Look at their great territorial possessions!—half Europe, half Asia, a big piece of North America. Look at their language, with every sound of all the alphabets of the race except the *th;* at their large heads, the biggest in the world; at their power in diplomacy, ruling all the courts of Europe for fifty years! Note the steady advance of the race in territory, in internal civilization, and all art. I think it will not be long before Russia is at Constantinople, and then at Athens. Let England go to Naples, to Rome, to Thebes, and Russia may go to Byzantium and Smyrna.

TO H. C. BOSTON

West Newton, August 31, 1852

The Law has these disadvantages:—1. That it exercises and develops the intellectual to the detriment of the other and higher faculties; 2. That it does not allow a very complete and generous development of the intellect itself, especially of the higher departments thereof,—say the reason and imagination,—but only of the understanding. Most of the lawyers that I have known are examples of this defective and vicious development. Indeed, most of the lawyers that I know make a mere money getting trade of their profession, and no science at all; so that with them law is not a *liberal* pursuit, only a head-craft, and they are only *Mechanics at Law,* with little more elevation, and sometimes less than is law to a handicraft. . . .

The same onesidedness which keeps lawyers from the study of the permanent-abstract of metaphysics deters them from the permanent-concrete of natural science. So they look on the arbitrary statutes of man, which are only a temporary accident of development, as if they were absolute and fixed, as much as the permanent-abstract or the permanent-concrete mentioned above. A statute is a temporary rule of conduct devised to suit the passing emergency. The metaphysician and the naturalist deal with natural laws, which are the constant modes of operation of the forces of the universe; the lawyer deals with those statutes which are the variables of man, while the philosopher deals with these laws which are the constants of God. But the misfortune of the lawyer is that he looks on his human variables as if they were as permanent and as absolutely imperative as the divine constant, the laws of matter or of mind. Hence he loses his natural conscience and gets a fictitious and artificial conscience; loses the conscience of Nature and gets the conscience of Doctors' Commons or of the Old Bailey or of the Supreme Court. The study of science helps to correct this. Yet I fear few lawyers care much for science. Judge Parsons was a man of large scientific attainments. John Pickering also—a quite uncommon man in many respects —was familiar with the highest results of science. Both of these were better lawyers, as well as more complete men, for this scientific development. I know a young lawyer who had to manage a case of damages for injury done to cows by water artificially contaminated, who in preparing for the case set himself to study the entire physiology of the cow, and so understand the effect of poisons upon her. That was the true way for a scientific lawyer to go to work; the rule applies everywhere.

I would not waste my time on mean authors. I would study the masters of poetry before I played with their apprentices, and still more before I played with the lackeys of the apprentices. You see uneducated persons waste a whole evening in silly talk about silly men or women. It is yet worse for an "educated man" to waste his time on silly books; they are always bad company. The books of great men will be good companions.

You need not fear that you shall suffer as a lawyer for what you gain as a man. Reputation for strict veracity, integrity, and honesty would be most eminently valuable to you as a lawyer. It would give you the best kind of business of the best men. I am glad you are to study with Mr. Charles G. Loring,—for I take it his moral character is loftier than that of any lawyer, of his age, in Boston. His personal influence will be good and greatly good. I need not say to you that I think there is no real nobleness of manly character without manly religion—the love of God and the love of man.

TO MISS ———

West Newton, September 15, 1852

POOR OLD LADYE,—Presently after reading the Life and Letters of Byron and Goethe, I read also that of Admiral Robert Blake. You know he was first a Puritan soldier, and held out the town of Lyme against Prince Rupert, and subsequently the city of Taunton (if *city* it were), both in a most extraordinary and successful manner; next he was admiral, and such an admiral! Cromwell on the land was the equal of Blake on the sea. He fought the Dutch, and swept the famous and formidable Van

Tromp out of the Channel. He went off to the Mediterranean, and levied contributions on the cities of Italy, Genoa, Leghorn, Rome, Naples, and on Tunis. He humbled the Spaniards in the Old World and the New. A man of not many words; a compact, resolute man, of the most formidable action. Well, Goethe's and Byron's lives seem little, mean, and trifling, after such a man, and more wicked; for, in all Blake's dreadful slaughters, there was conscience and humanity at the bottom of the man. I should rather be Blake sweeping Tromp out of the Channel for the nation's sake, and (as he thought) for *justice'* sake, than Byron sending for the police to turn the Venetian woman out of his house, or Goethe breaking the heart (so cruelly and wantonly) of pure, good Frederika von Sesenheim. It seems to me less to answer for before man and God. Then the lives of these literary men seem to me intensely *frivolous*, and scarred all over with egotism and selfishness. Goethe wastes how much time in nonsensical study of form, and in vain dramas, *Grosskophtas*, &c.! I felt often a great disgust at the sight of so much *génie* directed to such trifles as he spent much of his time upon. After all, Goethe was less of a man than Voltaire. Both wrought wholly by the pen,—or *chiefly*. Voltaire influenced his own age vastly more than Goethe, and will reach much farther into the future. His influence was better in kind, as well as greater. As a *philosopher,* Voltaire was more, more as a *poet,* and, including prose as well as rhythmic works, more as a *man*. I suppose it would be thought treason to say this; but it is true.

TO PROFESSOR EDWARD DESOR

Indianapolis, October 18, 1854

DEAR DESOR,—Here I am a thousand miles from dear old sedate Boston. I am on a lecturing-expedition. I am to lecture eleven times, and to preach once, in Indiana, Michigan, Ohio, and Pennsylvania. I have many things to say about the country and the people. I wish I had you to help me observe, and to generalize after the facts are known. The WEST, which I have now visited three times, impresses me much with the *width of all things*. There is a certain *largeness* to every thing,—streams, plains, trees, pumpkins, apples, swine (a hog in Ohio, 1854, weighed, alive, 1,980 *pounds;* another, 2,150), and men. But there is a certain *coarse-*

ness of fibre also noticeable in all things. The wood is coarse-grained; the nuts are big and fat, not nice and sweet; the apples have a coarse texture, all the vegetables, and all the fruits. Did you ever see the fishes of the Ohio? They are the most uncouth-looking monsters I ever saw, save the Roman fishes in the market at Rome,—the CATFISH, an ugly-looking devil, with a face like an owl; the SPOON-BILLED CATFISH (here is a picture of the "Spoon-bill Cat:" he weighed about eighty pounds: his spoon-bill was *two feet eight inches:* he looked like Dr. F——r), looking yet worse; the BUFFALO (an overgrown *sculpin*), the RED HORSE, and the SUCKER. One must be hard pushed to eat one of these wretches. Then men look sickly, yellow, and flabby. In Indiana I saw but one rosy-cheeked girl, about eighteen or nineteen. "Were you born here?"—"No, sir: in New Hampshire."—"I thought so." I saw three or four hundred children in the schools at Indianapolis; not a rosy cheek. The women have *no bosoms,* or, as "the professor" would say, "a very imperfect development of the *glandular* formation." They are tall and bony, their hair lank, their faces thin and flabby-cheeked.

What effect is this Western climate to have on the human race? It must check the intensity of the Anglo-Saxon character. The fertility of the soil, the dulness of the air, the general enervating influence of the physical circumstances, must deteriorate the human being for a long time to come. Health is poor; activity small, in comparison with New England. You are right in your estimate of American climate on Europeans. When Dr. F. the pachyderm came here, he weighed 293 *pounds:* he has *lost 80 pounds,*—over twenty-seven per cent. But I fear the West deteriorates Americans quite as much. It is too early to undertake to determine the future character of the Westerners; but this is pretty plain,—they will no more have the same energy as the New-Englanders than the Britons have the same as the Norsemen and Danes who went from Scandinavia to England.

There has been a great *baby-show* in Ohio. One hundred and twenty-seven babies were offered for prizes. One received three hundred dollars; one, two hundred dollars; one, one hundred dollars; and, besides, several gratuities were given to others. The prize, of course, was given to the mother. I think Jonathan is the first to offer *prizes to the best baby.* An agricultural society in England, a few years ago, gave twenty-five pounds for the prize ox, and *five shillings* for the *model peasant.* But you will see an account of the baby-show in "The New-York Tribune."

TO HON. HENRY WILSON

Boston, February 15, 1855

DEAR MR. WILSON,—Ever since your election I have been trying to write you a long letter, but found no minute till now. Let me tell you frankly just how I feel about your election and your future prospects. If I had the power to put whom I would in the Senate, my first choice would have been C. F. Adams or S. C. Phillips—though for either I have not half the personal friendship I feel for you. After them you would have been my man before all others in the State. Besides, there is one reason why I wanted you before even either of them, viz. I wanted to see a shoemaker get right up off his bench and go to the Senate, and that from Massachusetts. I wish you had never been to any but a common school, for I want the nation to see what men we can train up in the public institutions of education which stand open for all.

You have done more than any political man in Massachusetts or New England—in the last ten years perhaps, certainly in the last seven—to liberalize and harmonize the actions of the political parties. We must thank you for much of the organization of the Free-Soil party; for the revolution of the fogyism of Harvard College; for the election of Charles Sumner, and for the Constitutional Convention, which was worth all the time, and toil, and money which it cost. There is only one thing which made me prefer C. F. A. or S. C. P. to you—here it is. You have been seeking for office with all your might. What makes it appear worse is, you have no mean thing or secretiveness, and so your efforts for office are obvious to all men. Now I don't like this hunting for office in foes; and yet less in my friends. But for this, you would always have been my first choice for the senatorship. As it is—I have seen many men friendly and hostile in all parts of the State, and done what I could to promote your election—for I know the others are out of the question. No man rejoices more in your success. Now let me tell you what I think are the dangers of your position, and also what noble things I expect of you.

1. Your success has been rapid and brilliant. If you do not become a little giddy and conceited, a little overbearing and disposed to swagger, then you resist the temptation which so mars almost all men who have a similar history. Look at almost all the rich men in Boston who started poor or obscure and became famous!

2. You are to live by politics—a costly life with little direct or honest pay, but with manifold opportunities to gain by fraud—private gifts, &c., &c. I think the peril of such a position is very great. See how Webster went to the ground in that way! "A gift perverteth judgment." "Constructive mileage," and such things, are tempting and ruinous.

3. You are popular and successful. You will perhaps look for office above office—for the highest: for nothing American is beyond American hope. Then come the dangers of compromise with your own sense of right, and of all the evils which follow from that, crouching to the meanness of a party, or the whim of the moment.

It seems to me these are real dangers—and as a real friend I wish to point them out to you at the risk even of hurting your feelings. But it is better that I should tell you, than that you should not heed the peril till too late. Remember, besides, that I am a minister and must be allowed to *preach*.

Now for the noble things which I expect of you. By nature you are a very generous man, sympathizing with mankind in all lofty aspirations—a man of the people—with the popular instincts warm and powerful in you. I look to you as a champion of justice to all men; especially to the feeblest and most oppressed. I know you cannot fail to be faithful to this great question of Slavery. But your connection with the Know-Nothings makes me fear for other forms of justice. The Catholics are also men, the foreigners are men, and the world of America is wide and waste enough for them all. I hope you will never "give up to Know-Nothings what was meant for mankind." What a noble stand Sumner has taken and kept in the Senate! He is one of the few who have grown morally as well as intellectually by his position in Congress. But his example shows that politics do not necessarily debase a man in two years. I hope the office may do as much for you as for your noble and generous colleague.

I hope, my dear Mr. Wilson, you will take this long sermon in the same friendly spirit it has been written in, and believe me now and ever,

Respectfully and truly yours,

TO MR. JAMES ORTON

Boston, February 23, 1855

DEAR SIR,—I have not time to write at length as the theme demands. But it seems to me the American party rests on a very narrow foundation. I have no blood in my veins which did not come here between 1620 and 1640, but it is no better than if it had come between 1820 and 1840. Democracy must rest on humanity, not mere nationality or on modes of religion. I am as far removed from Catholicism as any man in America; but I should be ashamed to ask any religious privilege which I would not grant to any other man in the country. I would never exclude any man from office on account of his birth or religious creed; only for his character. Surely I should prefer a higher law Catholic, to a lower law Protestant; and a noble man born in Scotland, England, Ireland, to a mean man born on Plymouth rock.

The new party has done good things:—

(1.) It has rebuked the insolence of the Bishops and Archbishops of the Catholic Church—who required a severe chastisement.

(2.) It has shown American politicians that they cannot use the foreign population as before; that was sadly needed in Boston as well as elsewhere.

(3.) It has checked the administration and beaten them sorely.

(4.) It is knocking the old political parties to pieces with great rapidity.

All that is good work; but it is not done in the spirit of democracy, which allows every man his natural rights because he is a man—not a red-man, or a white-man, or an American man, &c. It is an important question how long a man ought to be here before he should vote, &c. Five years may not be long enough, or it may be—I have not made up my mind about that. But I would welcome the foreigners, they add to our riches and our national prosperity in general; and it is well that America should be the asylum of humanity for this century as for the seventeenth.

Hastily, but truly yours,

TO HON. HORACE MANN

Boston, June 27, 1856

MY DEAR MR. MANN,—Don't think that your labors are obscure or likely to be forgotten in this generation, or for many that are to come. Your works are written all over the commonwealth of Massachusetts, and are in no danger of being forgotten. I know how arduous your position is, also how unpleasant much of the work must be. I fancy you now and then feel a little longing after the well-cultured men and women whom you left behind at the East, and find none to supply in Ohio. But the fresh presence of young people is a compensation.

What a state of things we have now in politics! The beginning of the end! I take it we can elect Fremont; if so, the battle is fought and the worst part of the contest is over. If Buchanan is chosen, see what follows. The principles of the Administration will be the same as now; the measures the same; the mode of applying the principles and executing the measures will be slightly altered—no more. It is plain that another such Administration would ruin the country for men like those of Middlesex County, Massachusetts. I don't think the people will see themselves conquered by 350,000 slaveholders, headed by an old bachelor! If Buchanan is elected, I don't believe the Union holds out three years. I shall go for dissolution.

I wish I could go to the Lakes with you; but a family of most intimate friends will sail for Europe the 23rd of August, to be absent for three years. I want to see them all I can this summer; so we shall all go to Newton Corner, and live near by. Else I should do up my "unpretending luggage," and be off to Lake Superior with you.

I sent you a little sermon for the Sunday after Mr. Brooks struck Sumner, and have another pamphlet in press, containing two speeches made at New York a month ago, which please accept. On the 6th of July I shall preach on "The Prospect before us," and perhaps print.

July 8th, I go to "New York Central University." Such is the "high-phaluting" style and title of a college at Macgrawville, somewhere in New York, and deliver an address on the "Function of the Scholar in a Democracy."

I wish I was where I could see you often, but am glad to know that you are well.

Truly yours,

TO PROFESSOR EDWARD DESOR

Staten Island, August 24, 1856

MY VERY DEAR DESOR,—I am forty-six years old this day, and no wiser, no better, have done no more! But I have a fondness for dear old Desor, who is yet not so old as I, but an old friend. So I must gratify my inclination, and begin a letter here and to-day, but which will not get finished for some time to come. First, let me tell you about myself. I fear you would hardly know me, I am grown so old in look. My head is bald, and my beard is gray. I have a full beard, excepting the moustache. (Beards are common now in Boston as in Berne or in Wien.) I have grown very old within the last three years; too much work and too many cares have done this for me. But I shall mend one day when I take a little leisure, and you and I run down to the tropics and see the Orinoco; I shall recruit straightway, and become young once more. Here and now my life has not enough of sociality, of conversation, and joy in it. What you Germans call *Heiterkeit,* I have too little of. I mix with men chiefly as a teacher, to preach, lecture, or harangue. If I had at twenty-five joined some club of good fellows, and met with them to talk, laugh, dance, bowl, or play billiards once a fortnight ever since, I should be a wiser and a happier man. But let me mend for the future.

I look back with great pleasure on the happy times I have had with you when you used to come to our house. I was a little afraid of you at first, thinking it would not do for me to visit such a *savant* and *Gelehrte* as "M. Desor." But Cabot took me over to East Boston and I saw the crabs and the Echinoderms, and got acquainted with you right well. Few men ever stimulated my mind so much as you, for you not only had the knowledge of details in your sciences, but also the comprehensive generalizations which I value much more, and which so many naturalists lack. From my earliest recollections I have always had a tendency to make general rules and find out universal laws. I remember one example, when I was not quite seven years old. I looked over the lichens on a rock, and the reindeer-moss which grew close by it, and the huckleberry bushes, and then at the nut-trees, which were not far off, and said, "Here, now is a regular ascent, the rock, the lichen, the moss, the grass, the bush, the tree; and it is so everywhere." I went in and told my mother of my discovery of the scale of things, from the rock to the tree. Gradation seems a general law, *nihil per saltum,* though I had no Latin and hardly English to say it in. Dear me, I *am* growing old, talking so much about myself; but as it is a birthday letter you will forgive its *egotism*.

Well: you had a grand talent for generalization—and helped me much in many things. Now, I miss you greatly, not only affectionately, *as dear, good Desor,* but scientifically, as "Wise Mr. Desor, who looks so deep into things, and so wide too." Well: do you never mean to come back? To live with us, I suppose, never; but surely to visit us?

TO MISS ———

Galesburg, October 21, 1856

It is a good old ladye; only it is a good ways off,—twelve hundred miles by the shortest cut. To-morrow night (at Jacksonville) it will be thirteen or fourteen hundred. Don't like it to be so far away. What a country it is out here! Between this place and Chicago there is not a hill fifteen feet high, no undulations, only little ripples of land in this great sea of earth. There are few trees. You go many miles, and find none. The ground, where it is ploughed, is black as coal-dust, and fertile as Egypt. The natural wealth of Illinois exceeds belief. The rapid growth of population, too, seems fabulous, a miracle. Thus, seven years ago, Galesburg had six hundred inhabitants; now about seven thousand. One Judge Hale of Kenosha told me, on the 3d of July, 1835, he was following an Indian path through the Wisconsin Territory, and at night slept with only the sky above and the ground under him. There was not a house within many miles: only one woodsman was just beginning his log-cabin, chopping the trees for it. Last July 3 he went to the same spot (by railroad), and there was the city of Janesville, with nine thousand inhabitants; and he slept in a hotel not ten rods from the old spot where he encamped in 1835!

Quantity is immense out here. Bulk is the word to describe with: quality will come later. Quantity is the great burly brother; quality the nice, dainty little sister; but both of the same father and mother. Babies!—why, they are universal; babies in all the moods and tenses,—babies indicative, subjunctive, potential, imperative, and also infinitive; babies present, imperfect, perfect, pluperfect, and in the first (or obvious) and second (or potential) future; babies in the taverns, in the lecture-rooms, in the meeting-houses; in the cars, babies. Here they are stationary; there locomotive. I no more expect to see a woman without a baby than a man without tobacco. They are not only an "institution," but also a nuisance.

Preached at Waukegan Sunday forenoon, in a public hall, to about eight hundred or a thousand people. Our hymn-book in the desk. I sent them the hymn-books years ago. We had live singing too.

It is a dark day for America; but she has seen dark *years* before. Tories are nothing new. Reading Washington's Life again. I wonder that we ever got through the Revolution, so heedless are individuals of the welfare of the whole, so many are only particular, so few universal or national. There is something radically wrong in our civilization, which leads men to neglect their country. The pulpit is partly to blame; for while it is pounding away all the time on matters of individual, private concernment,—patience, prudence, prayer, benevolence, &c., in its best endeavors,—it seldom touches the great political duties which men owe to man as divine service of God. But politics is the religion of a nation, just as individual daily life is that of Peter and Rebecca. But how few ministers do (or can) look beyond mere individuals—in the "church on church green" and its Sunday school! But it is not worth while to scold men, only to mend 'em.

Love to all. It must be the best old ladye that ever was in all the world.

Good-by!

TO HON. JOHN PARKER HALE
Galesburg, October 21, 1856

I am glad I am not a senator this year. You win your "Hon." pretty dear this season. Stumping is no joke. I heard your opponent, Douglas, this afternoon. He . . . made one of the most sophisticated and deceitful speeches I ever listened to. It was mere brutality in respect of morals, and sophistry for logic, in the style and manner of a low blackguard. His enemies said he seldom or never did so ill. But there is a good deal of rough power in his evil face. I never saw him before.

I don't know how you *think* the election will turn out; but I look for defeat. I *hope* otherwise, but still *think* so. The battle is not won by our carrying the electoral tickets by popular vote. If Buchanan gets 148 electors, one million dollars, I think, might be raised to buy the 149th. I think there are thirty men in Boston who would give five thousand dollars apiece to see it done. It is the most important crisis in our national history. No Presidential election ever turned on such great questions. It is despotism or democracy which the people vote for. I wish the true issue was represented by the banners and mottoes. Buchanan's friends would bear this in front of all, "No unalienable rights to life, liberty, and the pursuit of happiness," "The Declaration of Independence a Lie," "No higher law." Then might follow, in historical order, "Slavery in Kansas," "Slavery in Cuba," "Slavery in all the Territories," "Slavery in all the Free States," "Bondage for niggers," "Bondage for poor whites," "Slavery for *greasy mechanics,*" "No free schools," "No free press," "No free pulpit," "No free speech," "No free men."

If Buchanan is President, I think the Union does not hold out his four years. It must end in civil war, which I have been preparing for these six months past. I buy no books, except for pressing need. Last year I bought fifteen hundred dollars' worth. This year I shall not order two hundred dollars' worth. I may want the money for cannons.

Have you any plan, in case we are defeated? Of course the principles and measures of the administration will remain unchanged, and the mode of execution will be more intense and rapid.

God save the United States of America!

Yours faithfully,

TO MISS SARAH HUNT . . . .

December 17, 1856

I am as busy as the apostle who had "no leisure; no, not so much as to eat." I wonder if St. Peter had not some dear little family off in Siberia or Australia, with a hippopotamus in it, which he must write to by the next steamer from Joppa, or by the Turkish mail-line, or the Jerusalem and Kamtschatka express?

I am lecturing all the time: twenty-five lectures since the 1st of November, and perhaps fifty more under contract. All this keeps me up late, and makes me work hard, which you know I dislike. In January and February I shall go several times to New-York State, having some twenty or more applications. So, perhaps, I shall continue to do till I am *fifty;* and after August, 1860, I intend no longer to live such an apostolical, nomadic, and unchristian life, but to sit down and write my books, which cry out for me to make them ready. But who knows? It is not in man that walketh to direct his steps. Some accident may stop the lecturing to-day, or something else make it necessary to continue the toil till I am a hundred. Poverty, like an armed man, may come upon me in my old age as on Pierpont, and stir me up to work when I would rather lie down and sleep. But, as the sky now promises no such storm (I should have said *threatens*), I lay plans of a different sort. "There's nothing sure but death and rates," say the Scotch: so who knows that 1860 will bring the long-coveted opportunity to write my books?

TO MRS. APTHORP

December 1857

The little class of well-educated men, by falseness to their position, have lost the confidence of the people; and a few men with more conscience, though often with less culture, command the homage of the very crowds which educated hypocrisy in vain attempted to cajole and win. See what reception is given to Beecher and Chapin!—men of not great intellect or great knowledge, but inspired with the progressive spirit of the age, and so standing in intimate relations with the people.

See the success of Sumner and Phillips! the triumph of Emerson, who has a more glorious history than any American of this generation! Prescott has changed no man's opinion. Bancroft has elevated no man. Irving has made men laugh at his fun, and rejoice in the precious beauty which blossoms in his field and his garden: that is all. Webster has connected himself with nothing except hunkerism: his symbol is his plaster bust; but his calf-bound volumes of speeches are as dead as the brass of the Colossus at Rhodes, which an earthquake threw down, and a Jew bought,—a load also for nine hundred camels: he affects no man's opinion. Clay was the tariff, which is now dead,—an obsolete idea, but a curse, while it lived, to the manufacturers who bought it of him. Calhoun was slavery: the greatest sophist the nation ever knew was properly devoted to the worst institution now in the growing world. The dead tariff will soon be buried also, and on top of Henry Clay; slavery will go to the Devil, and take with it the memory of John C. Calhoun, a great sophist, and of many little sophists at the same time: but Emerson has touched the deepest strings on the human harp, and, ten centuries after he is immortal, will wake music which he first waked.

Boston, April 9, 1858

DEAR MADAM,—I am much obliged to you for the interest you take in my spiritual welfare, and obliged to you for the letter which has just come to hand. I gather from it that you wish me to believe the theological opinions which you entertain and refer to. I don't find that you desire any thing more.

I make no doubt the persons who pray for my conversion to the common ecclesiastical theology, and those who pray for my death, are equally sincere and honest. I don't envy them their idea of God when they ask him to come into my study and confound me, or to put a hook into my jaws so that I cannot speak. Several persons have come to "labor with me," or have written me letters to convert me. They were commonly persons quite ignorant of the very things they tried to teach me. They claimed a divine illumination which I saw no proofs of in them, in their lives or their doctrines. But I soon found it was with them as it is with you: they did not seek to teach me either piety (which is the love of God) or morality (which is the keeping of the natural laws he has written in the constitution of man), but only to induce me to believe their catechism, and join their church. I see no reason for doing either.

I try to use what talents and opportunities God has given me in the best way I can. I don't think it is my fault that I reject the absurd doctrines which I find in the creed of these people who wish to instruct me on matters of which they are profoundly ignorant.

But the Catholics treated the Protestants in the same way, and the Jews and the Heathens thus treated the Christians. I find good and religious men among all classes of men,—Trinitarians, Unitarians, Salvationists and Damnationists, Protestants, Catholics, Jews, Mahometans, Heathen. There is one God for us all; and I have such perfect love for him, that it long since cast out all fear.
                                        Believe me yours truly,

TO JOHN PARKER HALE

Boston, May 12, 1858

Now a word about Kansas. There are two modes of action for Kansas independence. I. The political course: to accept the Lecompton Constitution, with its bribes; organize under it, but with free State men for its officers. They are in the Union. Next, repudiate that constitution, and make a new one. I find that recommended, but I object to it. 1. It is fraudulent. 2. It can't succeed, as there are seven chances against it to three in its favor (the Government will declare the slavery men elected, &c.). 3. It is false to the friends of Kansas, who have reported her as a virtuous young lady in love with a nice young man, and hostile to the miserable old curmudgeon, her guardian has tried to coax, and then to drive, and finally to bully her into marrying. Now, if both suitors come with her into the meeting-house, and then she chooses the old rich miser, consummates the marriage, gets the settlements fixed as her absolute and exclusive property as *femme sole,* and then runs off with her "nice young man," and squats on the estate conveyed to her by the defrauded husband, I think her reputation is gone, and won't come back "till the kye come home," and her family will be blown upon.

II. The moral course: to accept the new Leavenworth Constitution; organize under it, repudiate the Lecompton and all its works; drill their soldiers, cast their bullets, shoot at targets with "Lecompton" on them, painted either as Old Nick, or Old Buck, and be ready. There will be no fighting, or need of it; only need to be ready to fight, though Kansas will not come into the Union in 1858, or in the winter of 1860. But next autumn a new House of Representatives must be chosen. The Lecompton men of the North will go where the Kansas-Nebraska men went in 1854 and 1856. The defeated and outgoing Administration will not have the means to bribe as in 1857-8. The House will let in Kansas, with yet more generous grants than the Democrats have offered her as bribe for slavery. The Presidential and Senatorial Executive will be glad to get rid of the mischief, and have a clear field for the election battle in the autumn of 1860. So Kansas may be in the Union before Christmas, 1859. She must say "No" to the old lecher who wants to add her to his harem; "Yes" to the young man whom she loves (and he loves her); she will have fortune enough by-and-bye. I meant to have said that in a speech at New York, but rheumatism hindered. I will let it off at Boston in the Anti-Slavery Convention.

Faithfully yours,

TO MISS SARAH HUNT

Boston, June 3, 1858

DEAR SARAH,—I have just read your sweet little letter of May 13, full of profound and just remarks on English and American people. I quite assent to all you say of the English. Their national pride is *immense;* so is their *personal* pride: but, unlike the French and the Americans, they have little national vanity, little personal. *Insolent* they truly are as a nation and as individuals, *incapable of appreciating other nationalities and individualities.*

But, with all the faults of the Islanders, I like the creatures. We are of the same stock, and have the same great problems to work out in the civilization of mankind; viz.: 1. To organize the powers of Nature for the service of man; 2. To organize the social powers of humanity, so as to have national unity of action; 3. To develop the individual man into a great variety of forms. These are the three great problems of civilization. England and America work thereat side by side, both unconscious that they are factors in this great product of humanity. I love the Germans. As a family of men, they do immense service to mankind. They are not diffusive, but deep,—wells dark, cool, mysterious (you can see stars from their bottom at noonday), never-failing; while the English are a wide lake, full of green islands, varied in form, green with life, but *not deep;* and the Americans are a river, never still, noisy and turbulent, dirty, but bearing fertility in this very mud which troubles the stream; now spreading into rich lakes bigger than the island which holds that British pond; now laughing in waterfalls, which one day will turn the mills of all the world; then flattening out into dull lagunes, where only the alligator and the snapping-turtle can live, and watering marshes which reek with slavery; then, anon, gathering its waters into one deep, wide channel, where, laden with the fleets of commerce going out and coming in, it flows tranquil on to the ocean, whence all wells, lakes, and rivers are at first supplied, and whither they all at last return.

TO REV. JAMES FREEMAN CLARK

Rome, 1859

Now a word about *sin.* It is a theological word, and is commonly pronounced *ngsin-n-n-n!* But I think the thing which ministers mean by *ngsin-n-n-n* has no more existence than *phlogiston,* which was once adopted to explain combustion. I find *sins,* i.e., *conscious violations of natural right,* but no *sin,* i.e. no conscious and intentional preference of wrong (as such) to right (as such); no condition of "enmity against God." I seldom use the word sin —it is damaged phraseology, tainted by contact with infamous notions of man and God. I have some sermons *of sin* and of *sins,* which I may live long enough to prepare for printing, but also may not.

Deacon Wryface, of the Hellfire Church, says, "Oh, I am a great sinner; I am one mass of sin all over; the whole head is sick, and the whole heart faint. In me there dwelleth no good thing. There is no health in me." "Well," *you* say to him, "for once, Deacon, I think you pretty near right; but you are not yet quite so bad as you talk."

"Why—what have *you* got against me—what do *you* know against my character?" says the Hellfire Church deacon.

"If you want a bill of particulars, here goes," say you; "just answer as I call them off.

"1. You will lie!" " *'Tain't true.*"

"2. You cheat in your trade, and lately wronged Widow Crosby out of her house and land?" "That's a lie—I never cheat!"

"3. You get drunk—on other men's wine—and were boosy only day before yesterday, and had to be helped up-stairs." "That's a slander."

"4. You are inhuman, and have got ships in the Coolie trade, and I think in the African slave-trade besides?" "Well—there's no wrong in that—the niggers are the descendants of Ham, of whom God said, 'Cursed be Canaan.' I do this to bring the benighted heathen under Christian influences."

"5. You are avaricious, and dodge all the charities. You put your name at the head of subscriptions to decoy others, and then never pay up." "That's a lie!"

"6. You are a consummate hypocrite, pretending to all the virtues of humanity, while you practise only the vices." "It is all a lie."

"Well then," say you, "what *are* the special sins you do commit?"

"Oh, *there ain't any.* I hain't got a bad habit in the world— no, not one!"

"Then what did you mean by saying just now that you were such a sinner?"

"Oh, I referred to my *natur':* it is all *ngsin-n-n-n.*"

That is the short of it—all men are created equal in *ngsin-n-n-n*. Dr. Channing was as great a sinner—in the theological sense—as ————: it is his *fallen nature*—his will can never clean him from that o-d-i-o-u-s gall.

Oh, James, I think the Christian (!) doctrine of sin is the Devil's own, and I hate it—hate it utterly. Orthodox scholars say, "in the heathen classics you find no consciousness of sin." It is very true—God be thanked for it! They were conscious of wrath, of cruelty, avarice, drunkenness, lust, sloth, cowardice, and other actual vices, and struggled, and got rid of the deformities, but they were not conscious of "enmity against God," and did not sit down and whine and groan about non-existent evil. I have done wrong things enough in my life, and do them now; I miss the mark (ἁμαζτανῶ), draw bow and try again. But I am not conscious of hating God, or man, or right, or love, and I know there is much "health in me;" and in "my body," even now, when it is really not worth much, there dwelleth many a "good thing," spite of consumption and St. Paul.

Here at Rome you see the odds between the old classic conception of man, and the modern Christian (!) conception. The heathen men and their gods, &c., are represented as stout able-bodied fellows, who did their work manfully, ate their dinners, married their wives, and begat sons and daughters with thankfulness of heart. But the statues and paintings of the Christian heroes hang their heads, and wring their hands, and draw down the corners of their mouth, and go without their breakfast; they don't sleep well o' nights, they make "a covenant with their eyes not to look upon a maid," and are always making a fuss about their s-o-u-l. I would rather have a good, plump, hearty heathen, like Aristotle, or Demosthenes, or Fabius Maximus than all the saints from Peter, James, and John (δοχοῦωτες στυλοι εἶναι) down to the last one manufactured by the Roman Church—I mean as those creatures are represented in art; for the actual men I have a reasonable respect—they had some spunk in them, while the statues even of Paul represent him "as mean as a *yaller* dog." But let *ngsin-n-n-n* go—I will turn to something else.

TO GEORGE RIPLEY

Rome, October 29, 1859

Here I am booked for six months—if I live so long—having paid my board for that time. I have a deal of work to do, as follows:—(1,) to study the geology of Rome; (2,) its flora and fauna; (3,) its archæology: (4,) its architecture. I have begun already, though I have been here but a few days. This work will keep me out of doors all the pleasant weather, and turn my mind off from myself, one of the most disagreeable subjects of contemplation. I can't attend much to the fine arts, painting and sculpture, which require a man to be in doors. And, by the way, the fine arts do not interest me so much as the coarse arts which feed, clothe, house, and comfort a people. I should rather be such a great man as Franklin than a Michael Angelo; nay, if I had a son, I should rather see him a great mechanic, who organized use, like the late George Stephenson in England, than a great painter like Rubens, who only copied beauty. In short, I take more interest in a cattle-show than in a picture-show, and feel more sympathy with the Pope's bull than his *bullum*. Men talk to me about the "absence of art" in America (you remember the stuff which Margaret Fuller used to twaddle forth on that theme, and what transcendental nonsense got delivered from gawky girls and long-haired young men); I tell them we have cattle-shows, and mechanics' fairs, and ploughs and harrows, and saw-mills; sowing machines, and reaping machines; thrashing machines, planing machines, &c. There is not a saw-mill in Rome; I doubt if there is in the Pontifical States. All the timber is sawed by hand! Mr. Toysawyer stands on the log, Mr. Pitsawyer stands underneath; all the stone they veneer their houses with, is sawed by hand! At the revival of letters the Italian people turned to the arts of beauty, the Teutonic people to science and the arts of use. What an odds between the Italians in 1450 and the English! What a different odds to-day! I love beauty—beauty in nature, in art, in the dear face of man and woman; but when a nation runs after beauty to the neglect of use—alas! for that people. The assembly of Roman cardinals, in full costume, all of those "educated men," all riding to council in great red coaches, and with their big-calved servants, is a grand sight; while the Senate of Massachusetts, shoemakers, farmers, storekeepers, lawyers, knowing small Latin and less Greek, walking through the crooked streets of Boston as they go to council, has a rough look. But which has the spirit of legislation?

TO MRS. ELIZA F. EDDY
Rome, November 19, 1859

Your son has *fallen a martyr in a cause not less holy,* and *much more philanthropic.* He sought to deliver his own country-men from domestic misrule and oppression incomparably greater than what your fathers fought against. Don't think his young life was wasted and thrown away because the expedition [with John Brown at Harper's Ferry] failed of its immediate object: it will help obtain its ultimate object; will strike terror into the hearts of all slaveholders, and so weaken the bonds which now hold the slave. Every victory we rejoice in has been bought with the blood of men. Such as died had mother and sisters, often wives and chil-dren, to mourn the private cost at which the public benefit was bought. To the emancipation of American bondmen you have contributed your first-born son: not a drop of his blood is wasted. He himself is immortal, and has passed to that higher world we shall all enter on before long. He is a gainer by the change; and though his second birth took place in such terrible scenes, and he was delivered from the mortal flesh with such dreadful instruments, not the less does he pass into that glorious life "which eye hath not seen, nor ear heard, nor the heart of man conceived." I know what you lose; but I think of no cause in which I should rather one of my friends would lay down his mortal life. Surely the blessing of men ready to perish will fall on him. Here is your consolation on earth; and, beyond the earth, it will not be long before there is another meeting of souls widowed and orphaned here below. . . .

I know nothing of the details of your son's departure, only what "The Standard" briefly told. The last time I saw him, he came to consult me about another enterprise, which yet looked to the same end, only by means apparently more fearful. I could not fail to honor the motives which prompted him then: not less do I honor him now; nay, far more.

Your family have been always in the first rank of the oppo-nents of slavery, continually making sacrifices for the slave. It is not inappropriate that the crown of martyrdom should be set on one of the members of the same family,—a crown of thorns, in-deed, but also a crown of glory. I have been with you in other troubles terrible to bear. I think I know with what religious forti-tude you will endure this.

Oh that I were in Boston to give consolation in private, and in public to warn the young and wicked nation against the folly which now threatens to ruin us! I would prove that the slaves have a *natural right to destroy their oppressors,* and that it may be the duty of freemen to help them. This is only the beginning. Nine experiments will seem to fail: the tenth will succeed, and pay for all the previous mistakes. The defeats in the early part of the American Revolution were essential to the great victory at last; part of the battle in which we were conquerors. My dear Mrs. Eddy, accept again my heartiest sympathy: would I had more to offer! Tell your father I shall write him soon as I have news of the trial and fate of Capt. Brown. God bless you all!

Believe me ever faithfully yours and affectionately,

TO DR. FLINT

Rome, December 31, 1859

I think Massachusetts is the foremost State in the world—spite of the two hundred thousand Paddies and children of Paddies, whose poverty, ignorance, nastiness, superstition and crime lower the general average. She is in advance of every other 1,200,000 people in industry, intelligence, and virtue. Boston too is the noblest of cities, and the seed of religious fire never is quenched out from her venerable hearth; it is the home of great ideas, sure one day to be great facts. But after all this she can't say to Virginia "let me pull out the mote out of thine eye." So I was glad the Legislature, though in love with its own extra-session, was modest enough to refuse to adjourn on the day her sister hanged one of the noblest of New England's patriots. Let us work, and pray, trust in God, and keep our powder dry; but not say to Virginia, "Massachusetts is faithful." She is *not* faithful—one day she will be. It was a good while from the Boston massacre to the evacuation of Boston.

We sometimes do a little injustice to our own State and the slow way we have of doing great things. In the South there is no respect for personal freedom; hence the slavery of the negroes; hence the enormous tyranny of public opinion over the minority; hence men like Mr. Helper, Mr. Underwood, and many more, are driven out of the country because they favour democratic institutions. Neither Washington nor Jefferson would be suffered to live in Virginia to-day. There is as little respect in the South for general law, either local or Federal. Hence the continual interruptions of the regular course of judicial proceedings to get at the end more swiftly. I refer to the *lynchings* that are so common. Hence, too, the violations of positive law—not to serve the higher law of justice, which all statutes in general are supposed to aim at, but to carry out the purposes of selfish passion or selfish calculation. Hence came the importation of slaves from Africa, the fillibustering against Cuba, &c., and the threat to dissolve the Union. These things being so, philanthropic Northerners—impatient of process, but greedy of result—praise the "courage" and "determination" of the South in adhering to her idea. It is quite foolish—at least, short-sighted. Look here! In the North, especially in New England, there is a profound respect for personal freedom, represented by INDIVIDUAL LIBERTY. Hence any man is free till he commits a crime, and is punished for it by law made beforehand and made known. Hence industry is free, opinion free, the press free, and the tongue! The atheist is free to attack all religion, the bigot to denounce the wrath of God against all who doubt the bigot's stupid creed. On the 4th of July, at Salem, twenty or thirty years ago, R. H. D. delivered the address before the town of Salem, and attempted to show that democracy was a mistake, we ought to have a limited monarchy, &c. (this is after the best of my recollection). His right to deliver his opinion in a 4th of July oration was held sacred. Webster, Choate, and shoals of the "democratic" small-fry, have opposed the most valued institutions and ideas of New England; ministers preached the most ghastly doctrines, which would make democracy impossible. Nobody questions their right; their worst enemies would defend their right to speak and print, and would never seek to abridge it: so profound is this respect for personal freedom of body and of spirit. But along with this, there is also a profound respect for social unity, represented by GENERAL LAW. Hence we obey laws we know to be unjust; obey them at first or allow them to be enforced, simply because they are laws; but, at the same time, go to work to rid ourselves of them in a regular legal way. (I know there are two exceptions to this, in the disobedience of the Usury Laws and the Maine Liquor Law; but these exceptions, when understood, don't detract much from what I said above.) The resistance Massachusetts makes to the Fugitive Slave Bill is an example of this. If Wendell Phillips could have got a scrap of law as big as a dollar, and a constable's pole to put in front, he could have had hundreds of men to follow and take Sims or Burns out of jail. But as that could not be done, these two victims went back to slavery. At this time we have thrown a few threads of law round the fugitive, and on them I think the people would lay hold, and rescue any runaway in these times.

But the New Englanders must do their work in regular manner and form—by due course of law. If a man commits a great crime—a fraud, for example—and there is no statute that will reach him, we never think of lynching the wretch; we make a law for the future and let the past go. Now this love of law gives us an immense advantage over the South in the long run, though they often get the start of us in carrying a special measure. No doubt we sometimes go too far, and allow the final purpose of law, which is the preservation of individual liberty, to be defeated. But in a democratic community, when the appeal to the people is so direct and comes so soon, even this failing leans to virtue's side. Soon as we get a little individual liberty, we hedge it round with general law. Hence the progress of Democracy in New England is continuous and certain. So we have social unity of action represented by law, and individual variety of action represented by liberty, and that to a degree no people ever had before.

In this particular affair Massachusetts has done admirably—never so well before. It is curious to see how even Boston makes progress in her hate against slavery. It is not thirty years since a mob of "respectable gentlemen" broke up a meeting of women, who came together to debate on slavery. Leverett Street Gaol was the only safe place for Garrison. When the Fugitive Slave Bill passed, the family of kidnappers fired one hundred cannons. Sims was taken off by them without much trouble, though at the darkest hours of the night. But in the Burns time, what a row there was! (If Captain Brown had been in Boston, there would have been a rescue. We had only miserable scholars for leaders—lawyers, ministers, doctors—not men with *fists*.) How the Kansas Bill and the Dred Scott decision thinned the ranks of the Hunkers! And now see how Massachusetts sympathises with John Brown—think of towns tolling their meeting-house bells for an hour on the day Virginia hung that milk-brother of Washington and Jefferson! Such things have not been done since the times of the Stamp Act. Think of the old South on the platform, with Emerson and Phillips. Think of such a sermon as Wheelock's, at the Music Hall. God bless the dear old State! God bless the dear old town! Massachusetts can't call Virginia hard names; she will do much better, will overpower her sister by the great truths which will hammer great institutions, and surpass her in respect for liberty and respect for law, which will mean reverence for the eternal right.

TO MISS FRANCES COBBE

Rome, 1860

MY VERY DEAR MISS COBBE,—My friends or foes could not have been further out of the way than in saying what you mention as to my opinion about divorce. I have preached on almost all matters of great public concern in America except this divorce question, on which I have never given any opinion in public, and never but twice, as I remember, touched it at all. Once, in a course of lectures on the New Testament, commenting on Jesus's opinion on marriage and divorce, I gave a history of both in the Jewish and the Christian Churches. Again, in a lecture on "The Savage, the Hebrew, the Classic, the Christian, and the Philosophic Idea of Woman," I spoke of marriage and divorce in heathen nations, of course briefly, and in a manner purely objective and historical. I have not touched this great matter for two reasons: (1) I don't feel quite competent to deal with it, and perhaps never shall, even if I live; and (2) things are going on very well without my interference, perhaps better without it. All the progressive States of America are changing their laws of divorce, and in New England they have altered much in fifty or even in twenty years. The instinct and reflection of the people demand a change. In the new Western States the alterations are very great and rapid. In private, I do *not* share the opinions attributed to me, and have painfully spent much time in attempting to reconcile married people who at first sought a divorce. Yet, out of many trials, I remember but *one* where the attempt was at all successful. I have small sympathy with men and women who would either make or break a marriage lightly; but I do not think material adultery is the only breach of marriage. I think I once petitioned the Massachusetts Legislature to make habitual drunkenness a ground for divorce, if the aggrieved party desired it. But proper notions of marriage, and so of divorce, can only come as the result of a slow but thorough revolution in the idea of woman. At present all is chaotic in the relation between her and man; hence the ghastly evils of involuntary celibacy, of unnatural marriage, and of that dreadful and many-formed vice which disgraces our civilization. But we shall gradually outgrow this feudalism of woman, and Kosmos will come where Chaos was. I have few things more at heart than the elevation of woman, and have written much on that theme which may never yet see the light.

VII

Poems

27. Poems

The Gospel of Love

"O Brother, who for us didst meekly wear.
The crown of thorns about thy radiant brow!
What gospel from the Father didst thou bear
Our hearts to cheer, making us happy now?"
" 'Tis this alone," the immortal Saviour cries:
"To fill thy heart with ever-active love,—
Love for the wicked as in sin he lies,
Love for thy brother here, thy God above.
Fear nothing ill; 'twill vanish in its day:
Live for the good, taking the ill thou must;
Toil with thy might; with manly labor pray;
Living and loving, learn thy God to trust,
And he will shed upon thy soul the blessings of the just."

Sons of Men . . .

Sons of men who dared be free
For truth and right, who cross'd the sea,
Hide the trembling poor that flee
    From the land of slaves!

Men that love your fathers' name,
Ye who prize your country's fame,
Wipe away the public shame
    From your native land!

Men that know the mightiest Might,
Ye who serve the eternal Right,
Change the darkness into light—
    Let it shine for all!

Now's the day, and now's the hour;
See the front of thraldom lower,
See advance the Southern power,
    Chains and slavery!

See! the kidnappers have come!
Southern chains surround your home;
Will you wait for harsher doom?
    Will you wear the chain?

By yon sea that freely waves,
By your fathers' honored graves,
Swear you never will be slaves,
    Nor steal your fellow-man!

By the heaven whose breath you draw,
By the God whose higher law
Fills the heaven of heavens with awe;
    Swear for freedom now!

Men whose hearts with pity move,
Men that trust in God above,
Who stoutly follow Christ in love,
    Save your brother men!

In Darker Days . . .

In darker days and night of storm,
Men knew Thee but to fear Thy form;
And in the reddest lightnings saw
Thine arm avenge insulted law.

In brighter days, we read Thy love
In flowers beneath, in stars above;
And in the track of every storm
Behold Thy beauty's rainbow form.

And in the reddest lightnings' path
We see no vestiges of wrath,
But always wisdom—perfect love,
From flowers beneath to stars above.

See, from on high sweet influence rains
On palace, cottage, mountains, plains!
No hour of wrath shall mortals fear,
For their Almighty Love is here.

Sonnets

FROM THE LIBERTY BELL, 1846

I

JESUS, there is no name so dear as thine
  Which Time has blazon'd on his ample scroll;
No wreaths nor garlands ever did entwine
  So fair a temple of so vast a soul;
There every angel set his triumph seal,
  Wisdom combined with strength and radiant grace
In a sweet copy Heaven to reveal,
  And stamp perfection on a mortal face:
Once on the Earth wert thou before men's eyes,
  That could not half thy beauteous brightness see,
E'en as the emmet cannot read the skies,
  Nor our weak orbs look through immensity;
Once on the Earth wert thou—a living shrine,
Wherein conjoining dwelt—the Good, the Lovely, the
    Divine.

II

OH thou great Friend to all the sons of men,
  Who once appear'd in humblest guise below,
Sin to rebuke and break the captive's chain,
  To call thy brethren forth from want and woe,—
Thee would I sing. Thy Truth is still the Light
  Which guides the nations—groping on their way,
Stumbling and falling in disastrous night,
  Yet hoping ever for the perfect day;
Yes! thou art still the Life; thou art the Way
  The holiest know,—Light, Life, and Way of Heaven!
And they who dearest hope and deepest pray,
  Toil by the Light, Life, Way, which thou hast given.
And by thy Truth aspiring mortals trust
T' uplift their faint and bleeding brothers rescued from
    the dust.

III

DEAR Jesus, were thy spirit now on earth
  Where thou has pray'd and toil'd a world to win,—
What vast ideas would sudden rise to birth,
  What strong endeavours 'gainst o'er-mastering Sin!
Thy blest beatitudes again thou'dst speak;
  But with deep-hearted words that scorch like fire,
Wouldst thou rebuke the oppressors of the weak:
  Or, turning thence to Prophets that aspire,
How wouldst thou cheer the men who toil to save
  Their brothers smarting 'neath a despot's rod,
To lift the Poor, the Fallen, and the Slave,
  And lead them all alive to worship God!
Bigots wouldst thou rebuke—that idle stand,
But send thy Gospel-fraught Apostles conquering through
    the land.

VIII

"I Have Finished the Course"

28. Experience as a Minister

1859

Parker was endowed with a rugged constitution, but with a disposition to consumption as well. Had he nursed his health carefully, he might have had a long life, devoting himself to scholarship and the not-too-exacting demands of a country parish. Instead, from his earliest youth he used, and abused, his physical and intellectual resources—working sixteen or eighteen hours a day; travelling incessantly on cold, uncomfortable trains or over country roads; never pausing for rest or vacation; exhausting himself intellectually in his prodigious scholarly labors and emotionally in his activities in the reform and the antislavery crusades. There was a series of warnings in the mid-fifties. Then . . .

On the first Sunday of 1859, Parker preached a sermon on *What Religion May Do for a Man*. He planned to follow it the next Sunday with a sermon on *The Religion of Jesus and the Christianity of the Church, or the Superiority of Good Will to Man over Theological Fancies*. This would have been the summation of a lifetime of preaching. But on the morning of January 9, Parker suffered a hemorrhage of the lungs and sent word that he would be unable to preach then—or later. His doctors told him he had one chance in ten. Those were the odds he was used to, he said, and early in February he set off for Santa Cruz in the West Indies to see what sunshine and rest would do for him. He hoped to recover and devote his remaining years to scholarship. But he was desperately tired. "Sometimes I think of knocking at Earth's gate with my staff, saying Liebe Mutter, let me in," he wrote, and again: "When I see the inevitable I fall in love with it."

During the sea-voyage on the *Karnac*, Parker planned a letter to his beloved congregation which would review his religious and ministerial career: *Theodore Parker's Experience as a Minister*, he would call it. Once settled at Fredericksted in Santa Cruz, he set to work with almost his customary enthusiasm, scrawling page after page in that impossible handwriting which only his wife, Lydia, and his devoted secretary-assistant, Hanna Stevenson, could read. By April 19 (a date he always liked to signalize in some way) he had finished this forty-thousand-word letter—not bad for a sick man—and sent it off to his church. It was an account of the work he had done and had meant to do; of the obstacles he had met and overcome, or failed to overcome. It was a picture of religious and intellectual Boston in the second quarter of the century, a philosophical history of a whole generation. Nothing quite as good had been written by any contemporary.

It is presented here in almost complete form. Only those passages have been omitted which seem to be duplicated in Parker's
writings elsewhere in this anthology.

MY DEAR AND VALUED FRIENDS,— ... In my early boyhood
I *felt* I was to be a minister, and looked forward with eager long-
ings for the work to which I still think my nature itself an "effectual call," certainly a deep one, and a continuous. Few men have
ever been more fortunate than I in having pains judiciously taken
with their intellectual culture.

My early education was not costly, as men count expense
by dollars; it was exceeding precious, as they might reckon outlay
by the fitness of the process to secure a development of natural
powers. By father and mother, yes, even by brothers and sisters,
great and unceasing care was taken to secure power of observation, that the senses might grasp their natural objects; of voluntary
attention, fixed, continuous, and exact, which, despite of appear-
ances, sees the fact just as it is, no more, no less; of memory, that
holds all things firm as gravitation, and yet, like that, keeps them
unmixed, not confusing the most delicate outline, and reproduces
them at will, complete in the whole, and perfect in each part;
much stress was also laid on judgment and inventive imagination.
It was a great game they set me to play; it was also an advantage
that the counters cost little money, but were common things,
picked up daily on a farm, in a kitchen, or a mechanic's thoughtful shop. But still more pains were taken with my moral and religious culture. In my earliest boyhood I was taught to respect the
instinctive promptings of conscience, regarding it as the "voice of
God in the soul of man," which must always be obeyed; to speak
the truth without evasion or concealment; to love justice and conform to it; to reverence merit in all men, and that regardless of
their rank or reputation; and, above all things, I was taught to love
and trust the dear God. He was not presented to me as a great
King, with force for his chief quality, but rather as a Father, eminent for perfect justice, and complete and perfect love, alike the
parent of Jew and Gentile, Christian and non-Christian, dealing
with all, not according to the accident of their name and situation,
but to the real use each should make of his talents and opportunities, however little or great. I was taught self-reliance, intellectual,
moral, and of many another form; to investigate all things with

my own eyes; carefully to form opinions for myself, and while I believed them reasonable and just, to hold and defend them with modest firmness. Inquiry was encouraged in all directions. . . .

After my general preliminary education was pretty well ad-vanced, the hour came when I must decide on my profession for life. All about me there were ministers who had sufficient talents; now and then one admirably endowed with learning; devout and humane men, also, with no stain on their personal character. But I did not see much in their clerical profession to attract me thither; the notorious dulness of the Sunday services, their mechanical character, the poverty and insignficance of the sermons, the un-naturalness and uncertainty of the doctrines preached on the au-thority of a "divine and infallible revelation," the lifelessness of the public prayers, and the consequent heedlessness of the congre-gation, all tended to turn a young man off from becoming a minis-ter. Besides, it did not appear that the New-England clergy were leaders in the intellectual, moral, or religious progress of the people; if they tried to seem so, it was only the appearance which was kept up. "Do you think our minister would dare tell his audi-ence of their actual faults?"—so a rough blacksmith once asked me in my youth. "Certainly I do!" was the boyish answer. "Humph!" rejoined the smith, "I should like to have him begin, then!" The genius of Emerson soon moved from the clerical con-stellation, and stood forth alone, a fixed and solitary star. Dr. Channing was the only man in the New-England pulpit who to me seemed great. All my friends advised me against the ministry—it was "a narrow place, affording no opportunity to do much!" I thought it a wide place.

The legal profession seemed to have many attractions. There were eminent men in its ranks, rising to public honours, judicial or political; they seemed to have more freedom and individuality than the ministers. For some time I hesitated, inclined that way, and made preliminary studies in the law. But at length the perils of that profession seemed greater than I cared to rush upon. Mis-taking sound for sense, I thought the lawyer's moral tone was lower than the minister's, and dared not put myself under that temptation I prayed God not to lead me into. I could not make up my mind to defend a cause I knew to be wrong, using all my efforts to lead judge or jury to a decision I thought unjust. A powerful and successful practitioner told me "none could be a lawyer without doing so," and quoted the well-known words of Lord Brougham. I saw men of large talents yielding to this temptation, and counting as great success what to me even then seemed only great ruin. I could not decide to set up a law-mill beside the public road, to put my hand on the winch, and by turning one way, rob innocent men of their property, liberty, life; or, by reversing the motion, withdraw the guilty from just punishment, pecuniary or corporeal. Though I hesitated some time, soon as I got clearness of sight, I returned to my first love, for that seemed free from guile. I then asked myself these three questions:—

1. "Can you seek for what is eternally true, and not be blinded by the opinions of any sect, or of the Christian Church; and can you tell that truth you learn, even when it is unpopular and hated?" I answered, " I CAN!" Rash youth is ever confident.

2. "Can you seek the eternal right, and not be blinded by the statutes and customs of men, ecclesiastical, political, and social; and can you declare that eternal right you discover, applying it to the actual life of man, individual and associated, though it bring you into painful relations of men?" Again I swiftly answered, "I CAN."

3. "Can you represent in your life that truth of the intellect and that right of the conscience, and so not disgrace with your character what you preach with your lips?" I doubted of this more than the others; the temptation to personal wickedness seemed stronger than that to professional deceit—at least it was then better known; but I answered, "I CAN TRY, AND WILL!"

Alas! I little knew all that was involved in these three questions, and their prompt, youthful answers. I understand it better now.

So I determined to become a minister, hoping to help mankind in the most important of all human concerns, the development of man's highest powers.

Zealously I entered on my theological education, with many ill-defined doubts, and some distinct denials, of the chief doctrines of the ecclesiastical theology of Christendom.

1. In my early childhood, after a severe and silent struggle, I made way with the ghastly doctrine of Eternal Damnation and a wrathful God; this is the Goliath of that theology. From my seventh year I have had no *fear* of God, only an ever-greatening love and trust.

2. The doctrine of the Trinity, the "great mystery of Revelation," had long since gone the same road. For a year, though born and bred among Unitarians, I had attended the preachings of Dr. Lyman Beecher, the most powerful orthodox

minister in New-England, then in the full blaze of his talents and reputation, and stirred also with polemic zeal against "Unitarians, Universalists, Papists, and Infidels." I went through one of his "protracted meetings," listening to the fiery words of excited men, and hearing the most frightful doctrines set forth in sermon, song, and prayer. I greatly respected the talents, the zeal, and the enterprise of that able man, who certainly taught me much, but I came away with no confidence in his theology; the better I understood it, the more self-contradictory, unnatural, and hateful did it seem. A year of his preaching about finished all my respect for the Calvinistic scheme of theology.

3. I had found no evidence which to me could authorize a belief in the supernatural birth of Jesus of Nazareth. The two-fold Biblical testimony was all; that was contradictory and good for nothing; we had not the affidavit of the mother, the only competent human witness, nor even the declaration of the son; there was no circumstantial evidence to confirm the statement in the Gospels of a most improbable event.

4. Many miracles related in the Old and New Testament seemed incredible to me; some were clearly impossible, others ridiculous, and a few were wicked; such, of course, I rejected at once, while I still arbitrarily admitted others. The general question of miracles was one which gave me much uneasiness, for I had not learned carefully to examine evidence for alleged historical events, and had, besides, no clear conception of what is involved in the notion that God ever violates the else constant mode of operation of the universe. Of course I had not then that philosophical idea of God which makes a theological miracle as impossible as a round triangle, or any other self-evident contradiction.

5. I had no belief in the plenary, infallible, verbal inspiration of the whole Bible, and strong doubts as to the miraculous inspiration of any part of it. Some things were the opposite of divine; I could not put my finger on any great moral or religious truth taught by revelation in the New Testament, which had not previously been set forth by men for whom no miraculous help was ever claimed. But, on the whole matter of Inspiration, I lacked clear and definite ideas, and found neither friend nor book to help me.

In due time I entered the Theological School at Cambridge, then under the charge of the Unitarians, or "Liberal Christians." I found excellent opportunities for study: there were able and earnest professors, who laid no yoke on any neck, but left each man free to think for himself, and come to such conclusions as he must. Telling what they thought they knew, they never pretended they had learned all that may be known, or winnowed out all error from their creed. They were honest guides, with no more sophistry than is perhaps almost universal in that calling, and did not pretend to be masters. There, too, was a large library containing much valuable ancient lore, though, alas! almost none of the new theologic thought of the German masters. Besides, there was leisure, and unbounded freedom of research; and I could work as many hours in the study as a mechanic in his shop, or a farmer in his field. The pulpits of Boston were within an easy walk, and Dr. Channing drew near the zenith of his power.

Here, under these influences, I pursued the usual routine of theological reading, but yet, of course, had my own private studies, suited to my special wants. It is now easy to tell what I then attempted without always being conscious of my aim, and what results I gradually reached before I settled in the ministry.

I. I studied the Bible with much care. First, I wished to learn, What is the Bible—what books and words compose it? this is the question of criticism; next, What does the Bible mean—what sentiments and ideas do its words contain? this is the question of interpretation. I read the Bible critically, in its original tongues, the most important parts of it also in the early versions, and sought for the meaning early attributed to its words, and so studied the works of Jewish Rabbis on the Old Testament, and of the early Christian Fathers on both New and Old; besides, I studied carefully the latest critics and interpreters, especially the German.

I soon found that the Bible is a collection of quite heterogeneous books, most of them anonymous, or bearing names of doubtful authors, collected none knows how, or when, or by whom; united more by caprice than any philosophic or historic method, so that it is not easy to see why one ancient book is kept in the Canon and another kept out. I found no unity of doctrine in the several parts; the Old Testament "reveals" one form of religion, and the New Testament one directly its opposite; and in the New Testament itself, I found each writer had his own individuality, which appears not only in the style, the form of thought, but quite as much in the doctrines, the substance of thought, where no two are well agreed.

Connected with this Biblical study, came the question of inspiration and of miracles. I still inconsistently believed, or half believed, in the direct miraculous interposition of God, from time to time, to set things right which else went wrong, though I found no historic or philosophic reason for limiting it to the affairs of Jews and Christians, or the early ages of the Church. The whole matter of miracles was still a puzzle to me, and for a long time a source of anxiety; for I had not studied the principles of historic evidence, nor learned to identify and scrutinize the witnesses. But the problem of inspiration got sooner solved. I believed in the immanence of God in man, as well as matter, his activity in both; hence, that all men are inspired in proportion to their actual powers, and their normal use thereof; that truth is the test of intellectual inspiration, justice of moral, and so on. I did not find the Bible inspired, except in this general way, and in proportion to the truth and justice therein. It seemed to me that no part of the Old Testament or New could be called the "Word of God," save in the sense that all truth is God's word.

II. I studied the historical development of religion and theology amongst Jews and Christians, and saw the gradual formation of the great ecclesiastical doctrines which so domineered over the world. As I found the Bible was the work of men, so I also found that the Christian Church was no more divine than the British State, a Dutchman's shop, or an Austrian's farm. The miraculous, infallible Bible, and the miraculous, infallible Church, disappeared when they were closely looked at; and I found the fact of history quite different from the pretension of theology.

III. I studied the historical development of religion and theology amongst the nations not Jewish or Christian, and attended as well as I then could to the four other great religious sects—the Brahminic, the Buddhistic, the Classic, and the Mohammedan. As far as possible at that time, I studied the sacred books of mankind in their original tongues, and with the help of the most faithful interpreters. Here the Greek and Roman poets and philosophers came in for their place, there being no sacred books of the classic nations. I attended pretty carefully to the religion of savages and barbarians, and was thereby helped to the solution of many a difficult problem. I found no tribe of men destitute of religion who had attained power of articulate speech.

IV. I studied assiduously the metaphysics and psychology of religion. Religious consciousness was universal in human history. Was it then natural to man, inseparable from his essence, and so from his development? In my own consciousness I found it automatic and indispensable; was it really so likewise in the human race? The authority of Bibles and Churches was no answer to that question. I tried to make an analysis of humanity, and see if by psychologic science I could detect the special element which produced religious consciousness in me, and religious phenomena in mankind—seeking a cause adequate to the facts of experience and observation. The common books of philosophy seemed quite insufficient; the sensational system so ably presented by Locke in his masterly Essay, developed into various forms by Hobbes, Berkeley, Hume, Paley, and the French Materialists, and modified, but not much mended, by Reid and Stewart, gave little help; it could not legitimate my own religious instincts, nor explain the religious history of mankind, or even of the British people, to whom that philosophy is still so manifold a hindrance. Ecclesiastical writers, though able as Clarke and Butler, and learned also as Cudworth and Barrow, could not solve the difficulty; for the principle of authority, though more or less concealed, yet lay there, and, like buried iron, disturbed the free action of their magnetic genius, affecting its dip and inclination. The brilliant mosaic, which Cousin set before the world, was of great service, but not satisfactory. I found most help in the works of Immanuel Kant, one of the profoundest thinkers in the world, though one of the worst writers, even of Germany; if he did not always furnish conclusions I could rest in, he yet gave me the true method, and put me on the right road.

I found certain great primal intuitions of human nature, which depend on no logical process of demonstration, but are rather facts of consciousness given by the instinctive action of human nature itself. I will mention only the three most important which pertain to religion.

1. The instinctive intuition of the divine, the consciousness that there is a God.

2. The instinctive intuition of the just and right, a consciousness that there is a moral law, independent of our will, which we ought to keep.

3. The instinctive intuition of the immortal, a consciousness that the essential element of man, the principle of individuality, never dies.

Here, then, was the foundation of religion, laid in human nature itself, which neither the atheist nor the more pernicious bigot, with their sophisms of denial or affirmation, could move, or even shake. I had gone through the great spiritual trial of my life, telling no one of its hopes or fears; and I thought it a triumph that I had psychologically established these three things to my own satisfaction, and devised a scheme which to the scholar's mind, I thought, could legitimate what was spontaneously given to all, by the great primal instincts of mankind.

Then I proceeded to develope the contents of these instinctive intuitions of the divine, the just, and the immortal, and see what God actually is, what morality is, and what eternal life has to offer. In each case I pursued two methods—the inductive and deductive. . . .

I left the Theological School with reluctance, conscious of knowing so little of what I must presently teach, and wishing more years for research and thought. Of course my first sermons were only imitations; and even if the thought might, perhaps, be original, the form was old, the stereotype of the pulpit. I preached with fear and trembling, and wondered that old and mature persons, rich in the experience of life, should listen to a young man, who might, indeed, have read and thought, but yet had had no time to live much and know things by heart. I took all possible pains with the matter of the discourse, and always appealed to the religious instinct in mankind. At the beginning I resolved to preach the natural laws of man as they are writ in his constitution, no less and no more. After preaching a few months in various places, and feeling my way into the consciousness of men, I determined to preach nothing as religion which I had not experienced inwardly, and made my own, knowing it by heart. Thus, not only the intellectual, but also the religious part of my sermons would rest on facts that I was sure of, and not on the words of another. I was indebted to another young candidate for the hint. I hope I have not been faithless to the early vow. A study of the English State Trials, and a careful analysis of the arguments of the great speeches therein, helped me to clearness of arrangement, and distinctness in the use of terms. Here and in the Greek and Latin orations I got the best part of my rhetorical culture.

On the longest day of 1837, I was ordained Minister of the Unitarian Church and Congregation at West Roxbury, a little village near Boston, one of the smallest societies in New-England, where I found men and women whose friendship is still dear and instructive. I had thought freely, and freely preached what I thought; none had ever questioned my right. At the Theological School, the professors were then teachers to instruct, not also inquisitors to torture and to damn; satisfied of the religious character of the pupils, they left each to develope his own free spiritual individuality, responsible only to his own conscience and his God. It was then the boast of the little Unitarian party that it respected individuality, freedom of thought, and freedom of speech, and had neither Inquisitors nor Pope. Great diversity of opinion prevailed amongst Unitarians, ministers and laymen, but the unity or religion was more thought of than the variety of theology. At ordinations, for some years, their councils had ceased to inquire into the special opinions of the candidate, leaving him and the society electing to settle the matter. The first principle of congregationalism certainly requires this course. As a sect, the Unitarians had but one distinctive doctrine—the unity of God without the Trinity of Persons. Christendom said, "Jesus of Nazareth is Jehovah of Hosts!" The Unitarians answered, "He is not!" At my ordination, none of the council offered to catechise me, or wished to interfere with what belonged to me and the congregation, and they probably thought of my piety and morality more than of the special theology which even then rode therewith in the same panniers. The able and earnest ministers who preached the sermon, delivered the charge, and gave me the right-hand of fellowship, all recommended study, investigation, originality, freedom of thought and openness of speech, as well as humanity, and a life of personal religiousness. One, in his ordaining prayer, his hand on my head, put up the petition, "that no fondness for literature or science, and no favourite studies, may ever lead this young man from learning the true religion, and preaching it for the salvation of mankind!" Most heartily did I say "Amen!" to this supplication.

For the first year or two the congregation did not exceed seventy persons, including the children. I soon became well acquainted with all in the little parish, where I found some men of rare enlightenment, some truly generous and noble souls. I knew the characters of all, and the thoughts of such as had them. I took great pains with the composition of my sermons; they were never out of my mind. I had an intense delight in writing and preaching; but I was a learner quite as much as a teacher, and was feeling my way forward and upward with one hand, while I tried to lead men with the other. I preached natural laws, nothing on the authority of any church, any tradition, any sect, though I sought illustration and confirmation from all these sources. For historical things, I told the historical evidence; for spiritual things, I found ready proof in the primal instincts of the soul, and confirmation in the life of religious men. The simple life of the farmers, mechanics, and milk-men, about me, of its own accord, turned into a sort of poetry, and re-appeared in the sermons, as the green woods, not far off, looked in at the windows of the meeting-house. I think I preached only what I had experienced in my own inward consciousness, which widened and grew richer as I came into practical contact with living men, turned time into life, and mere thought became character.

But I had much leisure for my private humanitarian and philosophic studies. One of the professors in the Theological School had advised against my settling "in so small a place," and warned me against "the seductions of an easy-chair," telling me I must become a "minister at large for all mankind," and do with the pen what I could not with the voice. I devoted my spare time to hard study. To work ten or fifteen hours a day in my literary labours, was not only a habit, but a pleasure; with zeal and delight I applied myself anew to the great theological problems of the age.

Many circumstances favoured both studious pursuits and the formation of an independent character. The years of my preliminary theological study, and of my early ministry, fell in the most interesting period of New-England's spiritual history, when a great revolution went on—so silent that few men knew it was taking place, and none then understood its whither or its whence.

The Unitarians, after a long and bitter controversy, in which they were often shamelessly ill-treated by the "orthodox," had conquered, and secured their ecclesiastical right to deny the Trinity, "the Achilles of dogmas;" they had won the respect of the New-England public; had absorbed most of the religious talent of Massachusetts, founded many churches, and possessed and liberally administered the oldest and richest college in America. Not yet petrified into a sect, they rejoiced in the large liberty of "the children of God," and, owning neither racks nor dungeons, "did not covet any of those things that were their neighbours'." With less education and literary skill, the Universalists had fought manfully against eternal damnation—the foulest doctrine which defiles the pages of man's theologic history—secured their ecclesiastical position, wiping malignant statutes from the law books, and, though in a poor and vulgar way, were popularizing the great truth that God's chief attribute is LOVE, which is extended to all men. Alone of all Christian sects, they professedly taught the immortality of man in such a form that it is no curse to the race to find it true! But, though departing from those doctrines which are essential to the Christian ecclesiastic scheme, neither Universalist nor Unitarian had broken with the authority of Revelation, the word of the Bible, but still professed a willingness to believe both Trinity and Damnation, could they be found in the miraculous and infallible Scripture.

Mr. Garrison, with his friends, inheriting what was best in the Puritan founders of New-England, fired with the zeal of the Hebrew prophets and Christian martyrs, while they were animated with a spirit of humanity rarely found in any of the three, was beginning his noble work, but in a style so humble that, after much search, the police of Boston discovered there was nothing dangerous in it, for "his only visible auxiliary was a negro boy." Dr. Channing was in the full maturity of his powers, and after long preaching the dignity of man as an abstraction, and piety as a purely inward life, with rare and winsome eloquence, and ever progressive humanity, began to apply his sublime doctrines to actual life in the individual, the state, and the church. In the name of Christianity, the great American Unitarian called for the reform of the drunkard, the elevation of the poor, the instruction of the ignorant, and, above all, for the liberation of the American slave. A remarkable man, his instinct of progress grew stronger the more he travelled and the further he went, for he surrounded himself with young life. Horace Mann, with his coadjutors, began a great movement, to improve the public education of the people. Pierpont, single-handed, was fighting a grand and two-fold battle —against drunkenness in the street, and for righteousness in the pulpit—against fearful ecclesiastic odds, maintaining a minister's right and duty to oppose actual wickedness, however popular and destructive. The brilliant genius of Emerson rose in the winter nights, and hung over Boston, drawing the eyes of ingenuous young people to look up to that great, new star, a beauty and a mystery, which charmed for the moment, while it gave also perennial inspiration, as it led them forward along new paths, and toward new hopes. America had seen no such sight before; it is not less a blessed wonder now.

Besides, the Phrenologists, so ably represented by Spurzheim and Combe, were weakening the power of the old supernaturalism, leading men to study the constitution of man more wisely than before, and laying the foundation on which many a beneficent structure was soon to rise. The writings of Wordsworth were becoming familiar to the thoughtful lovers of nature and of man, and drawing men to natural piety. Carlyle's works got reprinted at Boston, diffusing a strong, and then, also, a healthy influence on old and young. The writings of Coleridge were re-printed in America, all of them "aids to reflection," and brilliant with the scattered sparks of genius; they incited many to think, more especially young Trinitarian ministers; and, spite of the lack of both historic and philosophic accuracy, and the utter absence of all proportion in his writings; spite of his haste, his vanity, prejudice, sophistry, confusion, and opium—he yet did great serv-ice in New-England, helping to emancipate enthralled minds. The works of Cousin, more systematic, and more profound as a whole, and far more catholic and comprehensive, continental, not insular, in his range, also became familiar to the Americans—reviews and translations going where the eloquent original was not heard—and helped to free the young mind from the gross sensationalism of the academic philosophy on one side, and the grosser super-naturalism of the ecclesiastic theology on the other.

The German language, hitherto the priceless treasure of a few, was becoming well known, and many were thereby made acquainted with the most original, deep, bold, comprehensive, and wealthy literature in the world, full of theologic and philosophic thought. Thus, a great storehouse was opened to such as were earnestly in quest of truth. Young Mr. Strauss, in whom genius for criticism was united with extraordinary learning and rare facility of philosophic speech, wrote his "Life of Jesus," where he rigidly scrutinized the genuineness of the Gospels and the authen-ticity of their contents, and, with scientific calmness, brought every statement to his steady scales, weighing it, not always justly, as I think, but impartially always, with philosophic coolness and deliberation. The most formidable assailant of the ecclesiastical theology of Christendom, he roused a host of foes, whose writings —mainly ill-tempered, insolent, and sophistical—it was very profitable for a young man to read.

The value of Christian miracles, not the question of fact, was discussed at Boston, as never before in America. Prophecy had been thought the Jachin, and miracles the Boaz, whereon alone Christianity could rest; but, said some, if both be shaken down, the Lord's house will not fall. The claims of ecclesiastical tradition came up to be settled anew; and young men, walking solitary through the moonlight, asked, "Which is to be permanent master—a single accident in human history, nay, perchance only the whim of some anonymous dreamer, or the substance of human nature, greatening with continual development, and

"Not without access of unexpected strength?"

The question was also its answer.

The rights of labour were discussed with deep philanthropic feeling, and sometimes with profound thought, metaphysic and economic both. The works of Charles Fourier—a strange, fantastic, visionary man, no doubt, but gifted also with amazing insight of the truths of social science—shed some light in these dark places of speculation. Mr. Ripley, a born Democrat, in the high sense of that abused word, and one of the best cultured and most enlightened men in America, made an attempt at Brookfarm in West Roxbury, so to organize society that the results of labour should remain in the workman's hand, and not slip thence to the trader's till; that there should be "no exploitation of man by man," but toil and thought, hard work and high culture, should be united in the same person.

The natural rights of women began to be inquired into, and publicly discussed; while in private, great pains were taken in the chief towns of New-England, to furnish a thorough and comprehensive education to such young maidens as were born with two talents, mind and money.

Of course, a strong reaction followed. At the Cambridge Divinity school, Professor Henry Ware, jun., told the young men, if there appeared to them any contradiction between the reason of man and the letter of the Bible, they "must follow the written word," "for you can never be so certain of the correctness of what takes place in your own mind, as of what is written in the Bible." In an ordination sermon, he told the young minister not to preach himself, but Christ; and not to appeal to human nature for proof of doctrines, but to the authority of revelation. Other Unitarian ministers declared, "There are limits to free inquiry:" and preached, "Reason must be put down, or she will soon ask terrible questions;" protested against the union of philosophy and religion, and assumed to "prohibit the banns" of marriage between the two. Mr. Norton—then a great name at Cambridge, a scholar of rare but contracted merit, a careful and exact writer, born for controversy, really learned and able in his special department, the interpretations of the New Testament—opened his mouth and spoke: the mass of men must accept the doctrines of religion solely on the authority of the learned, as they do the doctrines of mathematical astronomy; the miracles of Jesus—he made merry at those of the Old Testament—are the only evidence of the truth of Christianity; in the popular religion of the Greeks and Romans, there was no conception of God; the new philosophic attempts to explain the facts of religious consciousness were "the latest form of infidelity;" the great philosophical and theological thinkers of Germany were "all atheists;" "Schleiermacher was an atheist," as was also Spinoza, his master, before him; and Cousin, who was only "that Frenchman," was no better; the study of philosophy, and the neglect of "Biblical criticism," were leading mankind to ruin—everywhere was instability and insecurity!

Of course, this reaction was supported by the ministers in the great churches of commerce, and by the old literary periodicals, which never knew a star was risen till men wondered at it in the zenith; the Unitarian journals gradually went over to the opponents of freedom and progress, with lofty scorn rejecting their former principles, and repeating the conduct they had once complained of; Cambridge and Princeton seemed to be interchanging cards. From such hands Cousin and Emerson could not receive needed criticism, but only vulgar abuse. Dr. Channing could "not draw a long breath in Boston," where he found the successors of Paul trembling bofore the successors of Felix. Even Trinitarian Moses Stuart seemed scarcely safe in his hard-bottomed Hopkinsian chair, at Andover. The Trinitarian ministers and city schoolmasters galled Horace Mann with continual assaults on his measures for educating the people. Unitarian ministers struck hands with wealthy liquor dealers to drive Mr. Pierpont from his pulpit, where he valiantly preached "temperance, righteousness, and judgment to come," appealing to "a day after to-day." Prominent anti-slavery men were dropped out of all wealthy society in Boston, their former friends not knowing them in the streets; Mr. Garrison was mobbed by men in handsome coats, and found defence from their fury only in a jail; an assembly of women, consulting for the liberation of their darker sisters, was driven with hootings into the street. The Attorney-General of Massachusetts brought an indictment for blasphemy against a country minister, one of the most learned Biblical scholars in America, for publicly proving that none of the "Messianic prophecies" of the Old Testament was ever fulfilled by Jesus of Nazareth, who accordingly was not the expected Christ of the Jews. Abner Kneeland, editor of a newspaper, in which he boasted of the name "Infidel," was clapped in jail for writing against the ecclesiastical notion of God, the last man ever punished for blasphemy in the State. At the beck of a Virginian slave-holder, the Governor of

Massachusetts suggested to the legislature the expediency of abridging the old New-England liberty of speech.

The movement party established a new quarterly, the *Dial,* wherein their wisdom and their folly rode together on the same saddle, to the amazement of lookers-on. The short-lived journal had a narrow circulation, but its most significant papers were scattered wide by newspapers which copied them. A *Quarterly Review* was also established by Mr. Brownson, then a Unitarian minister and "sceptical democrat" of the most extravagant class, but now a Catholic, a powerful advocate of material and spiritual despotism, and perhaps the ablest writer in America against the rights of man and the welfare of his race. In this he diffused important philosophic ideas, displayed and disciplined his own extraordinary talents for philosophic thought and popular writings, and directed them towards Democracy, Transcendentalism, "New Views," and the "Progress of the Species."

I count it a piece of good fortune that I was a young man when these things were taking place, when great questions were discussed, and the public had not yet taken sides.

After I became a minister I laid out an extensive plan of study, a continuation of previous work. I intended to write a "History of the Progressive Development of Religion among the leading Races of Mankind," and attended at once to certain preliminaries. I studied the Bible more carefully and comprehensively than before, both the criticism and interpretation; and, in six or seven years, prepared an "Introduction to the Canonical Scriptures of the Old Testament," translated from the German of Dr. De Wette, the ablest writer in the world on that theme; the book as published was partly his and partly mine. This work led me to a careful study of the Christian Fathers of the first five centuries, and of most of the great works written about the Bible and Christianity. I intended to prepare a similar work on the New Testament, and the Apocrypha of both Old and New. I studied the philosophers, theologians, and Biblical critics of Germany, the only land where theology was then studied as a science, and developed with scientific freedom. I was much helped by the large learning and nice analysis of these great thinkers, who have done as much for the history of the Christian movement as Niebuhr for that of the Roman State. But as I studied the profound works of Catholic and Protestant, the regressive and the progressive men, and got instruction from all, I did not feel inclined to accept any one as my master, thinking it lawful to ride on their horses without being myself either saddled or bridled.

The critical study of the Bible only enhanced my reverence for the great and good things I found in the Old Testament and New. They were not the less valuable because they were not the work of "miraculous and infallible inspiration," and because I found them mixed with some of the worst doctrines ever taught by men; it was no strange thing to find pearls surrounded by sand, and roses beset with thorns. I liked the Bible better when I could consciously take its contradictory books each for what it is, and felt nothing commanding me to accept it for what it is not; and could freely use it as a help, not slavishly serve it as a master, or worship it as an idol. I took no doctrine for true, simply because it was in the Bible; what therein seemed false or wrong, I rejected as freely as if I had found it in the sacred books of the Buddhists or Mormons.

I had not preached long before I found, as never before, that practically, the ecclesiastical worship of the Bible hindered the religious welfare and progress of the Christians more than any other cause.

With doctors, the traditionary drug was once a fetish, which they reverenced and administered without much inquiring whether it would kill or cure. But now, fortunately, they are divided into so many sects, each terribly criticising the other, the spirit of philosophic scepticism and inquiry by experiment has so entered the profession, that many have broken with that authority, and ask freely, "How can the sick man recover?" The worship of the traditionary drug is getting ended.

With lawyers, the law of the land, custom, or promulgated statute, is also a fetish. They do not ask, "Is the statute right?— will its application promote justice?" which is the common interest of all men; but only, "Is it law?" To this the judge and advocate must prostitute their conscience; hence the personal ruin which so often is mistaken for personal success.

With Protestant ministers, the Bible is a fetish; it is so with Catholic priests likewise, only to them the Roman Church is the master-fetish, the "big thunder," while the Bible is but an inferior and subservient idol. For ultimate authority, the minister does not appeal to God, manifesting himself in the world of matter and the world of man, but only to the Bible; to that he prostitutes his mind and conscience, heart and soul; on the authority of an anonymous Hebrew book, he will justify the slaughter of innocent men, women, and children, by the thousand; and, on that of an anonymous Greek book, he will believe, or at least command others to believe, that man is born totally depraved, and God will perpetually slaughter men in hell by the million though they had committed no fault, except that of not believing an absurd doctrine they had never heard of. . . .

I had not been long a minister, before I found this worship of the Bible as a fetish hindering me at each progressive step. If I wished to teach the nobleness of man, the Old Testament and New were there with dreadful condemnations of human nature; did I speak of God's love for all men, the Bible was full of ghastly things—chosen people, hell, devil, damnation—to prove that He loved only a few, and them not overmuch; did I encourage free individuality of soul, such as the great Bible-men themselves had, asking all to be Christians as Jesus was a Christ, there were texts of bondage, commanding a belief in this or that absurdity. There was no virtue, but the Scriptures could furnish an argument against it. I could not deny the existence of ghosts and witches, devils and demons, haunting the earth, but revelation could be quoted against me. Nay, if I declared the constancy of nature's laws, and sought therein great argument for the constancy of God, all the miracles came and held their mythologic finger up. Even slavery was "of God," for the "divine statutes" in the Old Testament admitted the principle that man might own a man as well as a garden or an ox, and provided for the measure. Moses and the prophets were on its side, and neither Paul of Tarsus nor Jesus of Nazareth uttered a direct word against it. The best thing in the Bible is the free genius for religion, which is itself inspiration, and not only learns particular truths through its direct normal intercourse with God, but creates new men in its own likeness, to lead every Israel out of his Egypt, and conduct all men to the Land of Promise: whoso worships the Bible loses this.

I set myself seriously to consider how I could best oppose this monstrous evil: it required great caution. I feared lest I should weaken men's natural trust in God, and their respect for true religion, by rudely showing them that they worshipped an idol, and were misled into gross superstition. This fear did not come from my nature, but from ecclesiastical tradition, and the vice of a New-England theologic culture. . . .

But the whole matter must be treated more philosophically, and set on its true foundation. So, designing to save men's reverence for the grand truths of the Bible, while I should wean them away from worshipping it, I soon laboriously wrote two sermons on the contradictions in the Scripture—treating of historic contradictions, where one part is at variance with another, or with actual facts, authenticated by other witnesses; of scientific contradictions, passages at open variance with the facts of the material universe; and of moral and religious contradictions, passages which were hostile to the highest intuitions and reflections of human nature. . . .

I kept my sermons more than a year, doubting whether the little congregation would be able to choose between truth and error when both were set before them, and fearing lest I should weaken their faith in pure religion, when I showed it was not responsible for the contradictions in the Hebrew and Greek Scripture! But at length I could wait no longer; and to ease my own conscience, I preached the two sermons, yet not venturing to look the audience in the face and see the immediate result. In the course of the week, men and women of the commonest education, but of earnest character and profound religious feeling, took pains to tell me of the great comfort I had given them by showing, what they had long felt, that the Bible is one thing and religion another; that the two had no necessary connection: that the faults of the Old Testament or the New need not hinder any man from religious development; and that he never need try to believe a statement in the Bible which was at variance with his reason and his conscience. They thanked me for the attempt to apply common sense to religion and the Bible. The most thoughtful and religious seemed the most instructed. I could not learn that any one felt less reverence for God, or less love for piety and morality. It was plain I had removed a stone of stumbling from the public path. The scales of ecclesiastical tradition fell from my eyes; by this crucial experiment, this guide-board instance, I learned that the mass of men need not be led blind-fold by clerical authority, but had competent power of self-direction, and while they needed the scholar as their help, had no need of a self-appointed master. It was clear that a teacher of religion and theology should tell the world all he knew thereunto appertaining, as all teachers of mathematics or of chemistry are expected to do in their profession.

I had once felt very happy, when I could legitimate these three great primal instinctive intuitions, of the divine, the just, and the immortal; I now felt equally joyous at finding I might safely appeal to the same instincts in the mass of New-England men, and build religion on that imperishable foundation.

I continued my humble studies, philosophical and theological; and as fast as I found a new truth, I preached it to gladden other hearts in my own parish, and elsewhere, when I spoke in the pulpits of my friends. The neighbouring ministers became familiar with my opinions and my practice, but seldom uttered a reproach. At length, on the 19th of May, 1841, at the ordination of Mr. Shackford, a thoughtful and promising young man, at South Boston, I preached a "Discourse of the Transient and Permanent in Christianity." The Trinitarian ministers who were present joined in a public protest; a great outcry was raised against the sermon and its author. Theological and commercial newspapers rang with animadversions against its wickedness. "Unbeliever," "Infidel," "Atheist," were the titles bestowed on me by my brothers in the Christian ministry; a venerable minister, who heard the report in an adjoining county, printed his letter in one of the most widely circulated journals of New-England, calling on the Attorney-General to prosecute, the grand jury to indict, and the judge to sentence me to three years' confinement in the State prison for blasphemy!

I printed the sermon, but no bookseller in Boston would put his name to the title-page—Unitarian ministers had been busy with their advice. The Swedenborgian printers volunteered the protection of their name; the little pamphlet was thus published, sold, and vehemently denounced. Most of my clerical friends fell off; some would not speak to me in the street, and refused to take me by the hand; in their public meetings they left the sofas or benches when I sat down, and withdrew from me as Jews from contact with a leper. In a few months most of my former ministerial coadjutors forsook me, and there were only six who would allow me to enter their pulpits. But yet one Unitarian minister, Rev. John L. Russell, though a stranger till then, presently after came and offered me his help in my time of need! The controlling men of the denomination determined, "This young man must be silenced!" The Unitarian periodicals were shut against me and my friends—the public must not read what I wrote. Attempts were secretly made to alienate my little congregation, and expel me from my obscure station at West Roxbury. But I had not gone to war without counting the cost. I well knew beforehand what awaited me, and had determined to fight the battle through, and never thought of yielding or being silenced. I told my opponents the only man who could "put me down" was myself, and I trusted I should do nothing to bring about that result. If thrust out of my own pulpit, I made up my mind to lecture from city to city, from town to town, from village to village, nay, if need were, from house to house, well assured that I should not thus go over the hamlets of New-England till something was come. But the little society came generously to my support and defence, giving me the heartiest sympathy, and offered me all the indulgence in their power. Some ministers and generous-minded laymen stood up on my side, and preached or wrote in defence of free thought and free speech, even in the pulpit. Friendly persons, both men and women, wrote me letters to cheer and encourage, also to warn— this against fear, that against excess and violence; some of them never gave me their names, and I have only this late opportunity to thank them for their anonymous kindness. Of course scurrilous and abusive letters did not fail to appear.

Five or six men in Boston thought this treatment was not quite fair; they wished to judge neither a man nor his doctrines unheard, but to know at length what I had to say; so they asked me to deliver a course of five lectures in your city, on religious matters. I consented, and in the autumn of 1841 delivered five lectures on "Matters pertaining to Religion;" they were reported in some of the newspapers, most ably and fully in the *New York Tribune,* not then the famous and powerful sheet it has since become. I delivered the lectures several times that winter in New-England towns, and published them in a volume the next spring. I thought no bookseller would put his name to the title-page; but when the work was ready for the public eye, my friend, the late Mr. James Brown, perhaps the most eminent man in the American book trade, volunteered to take charge of it, and the book appeared with the advantage of issuing from one of the most respectable publishing-houses in the United States. Years afterwards he told me that two "rich and highly-respectable gentlemen of Boston" begged him to have nothing to do with it; "we wish," said they, "to render it impossible for him to publish his work!" But the bookseller wanted fair play.

The next autumn I delivered in Boston six "Sermons for the Times," treating of theology, of religion, and of its application to life. These also were repeated in several other places. But, weary with anxiety and excess of work, both public and private, my health began to be seriously impaired; and in September, 1843, I fled off to Europe, to spend a year in recovery, observation, and thought. I had there an opportunity to study nations I had previously known only by their literature, and by other men's words; to see the effect which despotic, monarchic, and aristocratic institutions have on multitudes of men, who, from gereration to generation, had lived under them; to study the effect of those forms of religion which are enforced by the inquisitor or the constable; and, in many forms, to see the difference between freedom and bondage. In their architecture, painting, and sculpture, the European cities afforded me a new world of art, while the heterogeneous crowds which throng the streets of those vast ancient capitals, so rich in their historic monuments, presented human life in forms I had not known before. It is only in the low parts of London, Paris, and Naples, that an American learns what the ancients meant by the "people," the "populace," and sees what barbarism may exist in the midst of wealth, culture, refinement, and manly virtue. There I could learn what warning and what guidance the Old World had to offer to the New. Visiting some of the seats of learning, which, in Europe, are also sometimes the citadel of new thought and homes of genius, I had an opportunity of conversing with eminent men, and comparing their schemes for improving mankind with my own. Still more, I had an entire year, free from all practical duties, for revising my own philosophy and theology, and laying out plans for future work. My involuntary year of rest and inaction turned out, perhaps, the most profitable in my life, up to that time, in the acquisition of knowledge, and in preparing for much that was to follow.

Coming home the next September, with more physical strength than ever before, I found a hearty welcome from the many friends who crowded the little meeting-house to welcome my return—as before to bid me God-speed—and resumed my usual labours, public and private. In my absence my theological foes had contented themselves with declaring that my doctrines had taken no root in America, and my personal friends were turning off from the error of their ways; but the sound of my voice roused my opponents to new activity, and ere long the pulpits and newspapers rang with the accustomed warfare. But even in Boston there were earnest ministers who lifted up their voices in behalf of freedom of thought in the study, and free speech in the pulpit. I shall never cease to be grateful to Mr. Pierpont, Mr. Sargent, and James Freeman Clarke, "friends in need, and friends in deed." They defended the principle of religious freedom, though they did not share the opinions it led me to, nor always approve of the manner in which I set them forth. It was zeal for the true and the right, not special personal friendship for me, which moved them to this manly course. In the most important orthodox Quarterly in America, a young Trinitarian minister, Rev. Mr. Porter, reviewed by "Discourse of Religion," not doing injustice to author or work, while he stoutly opposed both. A few other friendly words were also spoken; but what were these among so many!

Under these circumstances you formed your society. A few earnest men thought the great principle of religious freedom was in danger; for, indeed, it was ecclesiastically repudiated, and that too with scorn and hissing by the Unitarians—the "liberal Christians!" the "party of progress"—not less than by the orthodox. Some of you came together, privately at first, and then in public, to look matters in the face, and consider what ought to be done. A young man proposed this resolution: *"Resolved,* That the Rev. Theodore Parker shall have a chance to be heard in Boston." That motion prevailed, and measures were soon taken to make the resolution an event. But, so low was our reputation, that, though payment was offered in advance, of all the unoccupied halls in Boston, only one could be hired for our purpose; but that was the largest and most central. So, one rainy Sunday, the streets full of snow, on the 16th of February, 1845, for the first time, I stood before you to preach and pray: we were strangers then! I spoke of the "Indispensableness of True Religion for Man's Welfare in his Individual and his Social Life." I came to build up piety and morality; to pull down only what cumbered the ground. I was then in my thirty-fifth year, and had some knowledge of the historical development of religion in the Christian world. I knew that I came to a "thirty years' war," and I had enlisted for the whole, should life hold out so long. . . .

Let me arrange, under three heads, some of the most important doctrines I have aimed to set forth.

I. THE INFINITE PERFECTION OF GOD.—This doctrine is the corner-stone of all my theological and religious teaching—the foundation, perhaps, of all that is peculiar in my system. It is not known to the Old Testament or the New; it has never been accepted by any sect in the Christian world; for, though it be equally claimed by all, from the Catholic to the Mormon, none has ever consistently developed it, even in theory, but all continually limit God in power, in wisdom, and still more eminently in justice and in love. The idea of God's imperfection has been carried out with dreadful logic in the "Christian Scheme." Thus it is commonly taught, in all the great theologies, that, at the crucifixion of Jesus, "the Creator of the universe was put to death, and his own creatures were his executioners." Besides, in the ecclesiastic conception of Deity, there is a fourth person to the Godhead—namely, the devil, an outlying member, unacknowledged, indeed, the complex of all evil, but as much a part of Deity as either Son or Holy Ghost, and far more powerful than all the rest, who seem but jackals to provide for this "roaring lion," which devours what the others but create, die for, inspire, and fill. I know this statement is ghastly—the theologic notion it sets forth to me seems far more so. While the Christians accept the Bible as the "Word of God," direct, miraculous, infallible, containing a complete and perfect "revelation" of His nature, His character, and conduct, it is quite impossible for them to accept, or even tolerate, the infinite perfection of God. The imperfect and cruel character attributed to God rejoicing in His hell and its legions of devils, is the fundamental vice of the ecclesiastical theology, which so many accept as their "religion," and name the hideous thing "Christianity!" They cannot escape the consequence of their first principle; their gate must turn on its own hinge.

I have taught that God contains all possible and conceivable perfection:—the perfection of being, self-subsistence, conditioned only by itself; the perfection of power, all-mightiness; of mind, all-knowingness; of conscience, all-righteousness; of affection, all-lovingness; and the perfection of that innermost element, which in finite man is personality, all-holiness, faithfulness to Himself.

The infinitely perfect God is immanent in the world of matter, and in the world of spirit, the two hemispheres which to us make up the universe; each particle thereof is inseparable from Him, while He yet transcends both, is limited by neither, but in Himself is complete and perfect.

I have not taught that the special qualities I find in the Deity are all that are actually there; higher and more must doubtless appear to beings of larger powers than man's. My definition distinguishes God from all other beings; it does not limit Him to the details of my conception. I only tell what I know, not what others may know, which lies beyond my present consciousness.

He is a perfect Creator, making all from a perfect motive, for a perfect purpose, of perfect substance, and as a perfect means; none other are conceivable with a perfect God. The motive must be love, the purpose welfare, the means the constitution of the universe itself, as a whole and in parts—for each great or little thing coming from Him must be perfectly adapted to secure the purpose it was intended for, and achieve the end it was meant to serve, and represent the casual motive which brought it forth. So there must be a complete solidarity between God and the two-fold universe which He creates. The perfect Creator is thus also a perfect providence; indeed, creation and providence are not objective accidents of Deity, nor subjective caprices, but the development of the perfect motive to its perfect purpose, love becoming a universe of perfect welfare.

I have called God Father, but also Mother, not by this figure implying that the Divine Being has the limitations of the female figure—as some ministers deceitfully allege of late, who might have been supposed to know better than thus to pervert plain speech—but to express more sensibly the quality of tender and unselfish love, which mankind associates more with Mother than aught else beside.

II. THE ADEQUACY OF MAN FOR ALL HIS FUNCTIONS.—From the infinite perfection of God there follows unavoidably the relative perfection of all that He creates. So, the nature of man, tending to a progressive development of all his manifold powers, must be the best possible nature, most fit for the perfect accomplishment of the perfect purpose, and the attainment of the perfect end, which God designs for the race and the individual. It is not difficult in this general way to show the relative perfection of human nature, deducing this from the infinite perfection of God; but I think it impossible to prove it by the inductive process of reasoning from concrete facts of external observation, of which we know not yet the entire sum, nor any one, perhaps, completely. Yet I have travelled also this inductive road, as far as it reaches, and tried to show the constitution of man's body, with its adaptation to the surrounding world of matter, and the constitution of his spirit, with its intellectual, moral, affectional, and religious powers, and its harmonious relation with the world of matter, which affords them a playground, a school, and a workshop. So I have continually taught that man has in himself all the faculties he needs to accomplish his high destination, and in the world of matter finds, one by one, all the material helps he requires.

We all see the unity of life in the individual; his gradual growth from merely sentient and passive babyhood, up to thoughtful, self-directing manhood. I have tried to show there was a similar unity of life in the human race, pointing out the analogous progressive development of mankind, from the state of ignorance, poverty, and utter nakedness of soul and sense, the necessary primitive conditions of the race, up to the present civilization of the leading nations. The primitive is a wild man, who gradually grows up to civilization. To me, the notorious facts of human history, the condition of language, art, industry, and the foot-prints of man left all over the torrid and temperate lands, admit of no other interpretation. Of course it must have required many a thousand years for Divine Providence to bring this child from his mute, naked, ignorant poverty, up to the many-voiced, many-coloured civilization of these times; and, as in the strata of mountain and plain, on the shores of the sea, and under "the bottom of the monstrous world," the geologist finds proof of time immense, wherein this material Cosmos assumed its present form, so in ruins of cities, in the weapons of iron, bronze, or stone, found in Scandinavian swamps, on the sub-aquatic enclosures of the Swiss lakes, in the remains of Egyptian industry, which the holy Nile, "mother of blessings"—now spiritual to us, as once material to those whose flesh she fed—has covered with many folds of earth and kept for us; and still more in the history of art, science, war, industry, and the structure of language itself, a slow-growing plant, do I find proof of time immense, wherein man, this spiritual Cosmos, has been assuming his present condition, individual, domestic, social, and national, and accumulating that wealth of things and thoughts which is the mark of civilization. I have tried to show by history the progressive development of industry and wealth, of mind and knowledge, of conscience and justice, of the affections and philanthropy, of the soul and true religion; the many forms of the family, the community, state, and church, I look on as so many "experiments in living," all useful, each, perhaps, in its time and place, as indispensable as the various geological changes. But this progressive development does not end with us; we have seen only the beginning; the future triumphs of the race must be vastly greater than all accomplished yet. In the primal instincts and automatic desires of man, I have found a prophecy that what he wants is possible, and shall one day be actual. It is a glorious future on earth which I have set before your eyes and hopes, thereby stimulating both your patience to bear now what is inevitable, and your thought and toil to secure a future triumph to be had on no other terms. What good is not with us is before, to be attained by toil and thought, and religious life.

III. ABSOLUTE OR NATURAL RELIGION.—In its complete

and perfect form, this is the normal development, use, discipline, and enjoyment of every part of the body, and every faculty of the spirit; the direction of all natural powers to their natural purposes. I have taught that there were three parts which make up the sum of true religion; the emotional part, of right feelings, where religion at first begins in the automatic, primal instinct; the intellectual part, of true ideas, which either directly represent the primitive, instinctive feelings of whoso holds them, or else produce a kindred, secondary, and derivative feeling in whoso receives them; and the practical part, of just actions, which correspond to the feelings and the ideas, and make the mere thought or emotion into a concrete deed. So, the true religion which comes from the nature of man, consists of normal feelings towards God and man, of correct thoughts about God, man, and the relation between them, and of actions corresponding to the natural conscience when developed in harmony with the entire constitution of man.

But this religion which begins in the instinctive feelings, and thence advances to reflective ideas, assumes its ultimate form in the character of men, and so appears in their actions, individual, domestic, social, national, ecclesiastical, and general—human; it builds manifold institutions like itself, wherein it rears up men in its own image. All the six great historic forms of religion—the Brahmanic, Hebrew, Classic, Buddhistic, Christian, Mohammedan—profess to have come miraculously from God, not normally from man; and, spite of the excellence which they contain, and the vast service the humblest of them has done, yet each must ere long prove a hindrance to human welfare, for it claims to be a finality, and makes the whole of human nature wait upon an accident of human history—and that accident the whim of some single man. The absolute religion which belongs to man's nature, and is gradually unfolded thence, like the high achievements of art, science, literature, and politics, is only distinctly conceived of in an advanced stage of man's growth; to make its idea a fact, is the highest triumph of the human race. This is the idea of humanity, dimly seen but clearly felt, which has flitted before the pious eyes of men in all lands and many an age, and been prayed for as the "Kingdom of Heaven." The religious history of the race is the record of man's continual but unconscious efforts to attain this "desire of all nations;" poetic stories of the "golden age," or of man in the garden of Eden, are but this natural wish looking back and fondly dreaming that "the former days were better than these." But while all the other forms of religion must ultimately fail before this, fading as it flowers, each one of them has yet been a help towards it, probably indispensable to the development of mankind. For each has grown out of the condition of some people, as naturally as the wild primitive flora of Santa Cruz has come from the state of this island—its geologic structure and chemical composition, its tropic heat, and its special situation amid the great currents of water and of air; as naturally as the dependent fauna of the place comes from its flora. Thus in the religions of mankind, as in the various governments, nay, as in the different geologic periods, there is diversity of form, but unity of aim; destruction is only to create; earthquakes, which submerged the sunken continents whose former mountains are but islands now, and revolutions, in which the Hebrew and Classic religions went under, their poetic summits only visible, have analogous functions to perform—handmaids of creation both.

For these three great doctrines—of God, of Man, of Religion—I have depended on no church and no scripture; yet have I found things to serve me in all scriptures and every church. I have sought my authority in the nature of man—in facts of consciousness within me, and facts of observation in the human world without. To me the material world and the outward history of man do not supply a sufficient revelation of God, nor warrant me to speak of infinite perfection. It is only from the nature of man, from facts of intuition, that I can gather this greatest of all truths, as I find it in my consciousness reflected back from Deity itself. . . .

These three great doctrines I have preached positively, as abstract truth, representing facts of the universe; that might be peaceful work. But they must take a concrete form, and be applied to the actual life of the individual family, community, state, and church; this would have a less peaceful look; for I must examine actual institutions, and criticise their aim, their mode of operation, and their result. The great obvious social forces in America may be thus summed up:—

1. There is the organized trading power—having its home in the great towns, which seeks gain with small regard to that large justice which represents alike the mutual interests and duties of all men, and to that humanity which interposes the affectional instinct when conscience is asleep. This power seems to control all things, amenable only to the all-mighty dollar.

2. The organized political power, the parties in office, or seeking to become so. This makes the statutes, but is commonly controlled by the trading power, and has all of its faults often

intensified; yet it seems amenable to the instincts of the people, who, on great occasions, sometimes interfere and change the trader's rule.

3. The organized ecclesiastical power, the various sects which, though quite unlike, yet all mainly agree in their fundamental principle of vicariousness—an alleged revelation, instead of actual human faculties, salvation from God's wrath and eternal ruin, by the atoning blood of crucified God. This is more able than either of the others; and though often despised, in a few years can control them both. In this generation no American politician dares affront it.

4. The organized literary power, the endowed colleges, the periodical press, with its triple multitude of journals—commercial, political, theological—and sectarian tracts. This has no original ideas, but diffuses the opinion of the other powers whom it represents, whose will it serves, and whose kaleidoscope it is.

I must examine these four great social forces, and show what was good in them, and what was ill; ascertain what natural religion demanded of each, and what was the true function of trade, government, a church, and a literature. When I came to a distinct consciousness of my own first principle, and my consequent relation to what was about me, spite of the good they contained, I found myself greatly at variance with all the four. They had one principle, and I another; of course, our aim and direction were commonly different and often opposite. Soon I found that I was not welcome to the American market, state, church, nor press. It could not be otherwise; yet I confess I had not anticipated so thorough a separation betwixt me and these forces which control society, but had laid out work I could not execute alone, nor perhaps without the aid of all the four.

It is not now, my friends, worth while for me to enter on the details of these plans which have come to nothing, and which I shall probably never work out; but I ought at least to name some of the most important things I hoped to do. When I first came to Boston I intended to do something for the perishing and dangerous classes in our great towns. The amount of poverty and consequent immorality in Boston is terrible to think of, while you remember the warning of other nations, and look to the day after to-day! Yet it seemed to me the money given by public and private charity—two fountains that never fail in Puritanic Boston—was more than sufficient to relieve it all, and gradually remove the deep-seated and unseen cause which, in the hurry of business and of money, is not attended to. There is a hole in the dim-lit public bridge, where many fall through and perish! Our mercy pulls a few out of the water; it does not stop the hole, nor light the bridge, nor warn men of the peril. We need the great charity that palliates effects of wrong, and the greater justice which removes the cause.

Then there was drunkenness, which is the greatest concrete curse of the labouring Protestant population of the North, working most hideous and wide-extended desolation. It is as fatal as starvation to the Irish Catholic. None of the four great social forces is its foe. There, too, was prostitution; men and women mutually polluted and polluting, blackening the face of society with dreadful woe. Besides, in our great towns, I found thousands, especially the poorer Irish, oppression driving them to us, who, save the discipline of occasional work, got no education here, except what the streets taught them in childhood, or the Popish priest and the American demagogue—their two worst foes—noisily offered in their adult years; it seemed to me not difficult for the vast charity of Boston to furnish instruction and guidance to this class of the American people, both in their childhood and their later youth. That admirable institution, the Warren Street Chapel —well-nigh the most Christian public thing in Boston—and the Children's Aid Society at New York, with its kindred, abundantly show how much can be done, and at how little cost.

Still more, I learned early in life that the criminal is often the victim of society, rather than its foe, and that our penal law belongs to the dark ages of brute force, and aims only to protect society by vengeance on the felon, not also to elevate mankind by refining him. In my boyhood I knew a man, the last result of generations of ancestral crime, who spent more than twenty years in our State Prison, and died there, under sentence for life, whose entire illegal thefts did not amount to twenty dollars! and another, not better born, who lawfully stole houses and farms, lived a "gentleman," and at death left a considerable estate, and the name of Land-shark. While a theological student, I taught a class in the Sunday School of the State Prison, often saw my fellow-townsman, became well acquainted with several convicts, learned the mode of treatment, and heard the sermons and ghastly prayers which were let fly at the heads of the poor, unprotected wretches; I saw the "orthodox preachers and other helps," who gave them "spiritual instruction," and learned the utter insufficiency of our penal law to mend the felon or prevent his growth in wickedness. When

I became your minister I hoped to do something for this class of men, whose crimes are sometimes but a part of their congenital misfortune or social infamy, and who are bereft of the sympathy of mankind, and unconstitutionally beset with sectarian ministers, whose function is to torment them before their time.

For all these, the poor, the drunken, and the ignorant, for the prostitute, and the criminal, I meant to do something, under the guidance, perhaps, or certainly with the help, of the controlling men of the town or State; but, alas! I was then fourteen years younger than now, and did not quite understand all the consequences of my relation to these great social forces, or how much I had offended the religion of the state, the press, the market, and the church. The cry, "Destroyer," "Fanatic," "Infidel," "Atheist," "Enemy of Mankind," was so widely sounded forth that I soon found I could do little in these great philanthropies, where the evil lay at our own door. Many as you are for a religious society, you were too few and too poor to undertake what should be done; and outside of your ranks I could look for little help, even by words and counsel. Besides, I soon found my very name was enough to ruin any new good enterprise. I knew there were three periods in each great movement of mankind—that of sentiment, ideas, and action: I fondly hoped the last had come; but when I found I had reckoned without the host, I turned my attention to the two former, and sought to arouse the sentiment of justice and mercy, and to diffuse the ideas which belonged to this five-fold reformation. Hence I took pains to state the facts of poverty, drunkenness, ignorance, prostitution, crime; to show their cause, their effect, and their mode of cure, leaving it for others to do the practical work. So, if I wanted a measure carried in the Legislature of the town or State, or by some private benevolent society, I did my work by stealth. I sometimes saw my scheme prosper, and read my words in the public reports, while the whole enterprise had been ruined at once if my face or name had appeared in connection with it. I have often found it wise to withhold my name from petitions I have myself set agoing and found successful; I have got up conventions, or mass meetings, whose "managers" asked me not to show my face thereat.

This chronic and progressive unpopularity led to another change of my plans, not abating my activity, but turning it in another direction. To accomplish my work, I must spread my ideas as widely as possible, without resorting to that indencency of advertising so common in America. There was but one considerable publishing-house in the land that would continue to issue my works—this only at my own cost and risk. As it had only a pecuniary interest therein, and that so slight, in its enormous business, my books did not have the usual opportunity of getting known and circulated. They were seldom offered for sale, except in one book store in Boston; for other States, I must often be my own bookseller. None of the Quarterlies or Monthlies was friendly to me; most of the newspapers were hostile; the *New York Tribune* and *Evening Post* were almost the only exceptions. So my books had but a small circulation at home in comparison with their diffusion in England and Germany, where, also, they received not only hostile, but most kindly notice, and sometimes from a famous pen. But another opportunity for diffusing my thought offered itself in the Lyceum or public lecture. Opposed by these four great social forces at home, I was surprised to find myself becoming popular in the lecture hall. After a few trials I "got the *hang* of the new school-house," and set myself to serious work therein.

For a dozen years or more, I have done my share of lecturing in public, having many invitations more than I could accept. The task was always disagreeable, contrary to my natural disposition and my scholarly habits. But I saw the nation had reached an important crisis in its destination, and, though ignorant of the fact, yet stood hesitating between two principles. The one was slavery, which I knew leads at once to military despotism—political, ecclesiastical, social—and ends at last in utter and hopeless ruin; for no people fallen on that road has ever risen again; it is the path so many other republics have taken and finished their course, as Athens and the Ionian towns have done, as Rome and the commonwealths of the Middle Ages. The other was freedom, which leads at once to industrial democracy—respect for labour, government over all, by all, for the sake of all, rule after the eternal right as it is writ in the constitution of the universe—securing welfare and progress. I saw that these four social forces were advising, driving, coaxing, wheedling the people to take the road to ruin; that our "great men," in which "America is so rich beyond all other nations of the earth," went strutting along that path to show how safe it is, crying out "Democracy," "Constitution," "Washington," "Gospel," "Christianity," "Dollars," and the like, while the instincts of the people, the traditions of our history, and the rising genius of men and women well-born in these times of peril, with still, small voice, whispered something of self-evident truths and inalienable rights.

I knew the power of a great idea; and spite of the market, the State, the Church, the press, I thought a few earnest men in the lecture halls of the North, might yet incline the people's mind and heart to justice and the eternal law of God—the only safe rule of conduct for nations, as for you and me—and so make the American experiment a triumph and a joy for all humankind. Nay, I thought I could myself be of some service in that work; for the nation was yet so young, and the instinct of popular liberty so strong, it seemed to me a little added weight would turn the scale to freedom. So I appointed myself a home missionary for lectures.

Then, too, I found I could say what I pleased in the lecture room, so long as I did not professedly put my thought into a theologic or political shape; while I kept the form of literature or philosophy, I could discourse of what I thought most important, and men would listen one hour, two hours, nay, three hours: and the more significant the subject was, the more freely, profoundly, and fairly it was treated, the more would the people come, the more eagerly listen and enthusiastically accept. So I spared no labour in preparation or delivery, but took it for granted the humblest audience, in the least intelligent town or city, was quite worthy of my best efforts, and could understand my facts and metaphysic reasonings. I did not fear the people would be offended, though I hurt their feelings never so sore.

Besides, the work was well paid for in the large towns, while the small ones did all they could afford—giving the lecturer for a night more than the schoolmaster for a month. The money thus acquired enabled me to do four desirable things, which it is not needful to speak of here.

Since 1848 I have lectured eighty or a hundred times each year—in every Northern State east of the Mississippi, once also in a Slave State, and on slavery itself. I have taken most exciting and important subjects, of the greatest concern to the American people, and treated them independent of sect or party, street or press, and with what learning and talent I could command. I put the matter in quite various forms—for each audience is made up of many. For eight or ten years, on the average, I have spoken to sixty or a hundred thousand persons in each year, besides addressing you on Sundays, in the great hall you throw open to all comers.

Thus I have had a wide field of operation, where I might

rouse the sentiment of justice and mercy, diffuse such ideas as I thought needful for the welfare and progress of the people, and prepare for such action as the occasion might one day require. . . .

Still more, in the railroad cars and steamboats I travelled by, and the public or private houses I stopped at, when the lecture was over, strangers came to see me; they were generally marked men—intellectual, moral, philanthropic, at any rate, inquiring and attentive. We sometimes talked on great matters; I made many acquaintances, gained much miscellaneous information about men and things, the state of public opinion, and, perhaps, imparted something in return. So I studied while I taught. . . .

In the last dozen years, I think scarcely any American, not holding a political office, has touched the minds of so many men, by freely speaking on matters of the greatest importance, for this day and for ages to come. I am sure I have uttered great truths, and such are never spoken in vain; I know the effect a few great thoughts had on me in my youth, and judge others by what I experienced myself. Those ministers were in the right, who, years ago, said, "Keep that man out of the lecture room; don't let him be seen in public. Every word he speaks, on any subject, is a blow against our religion!" They meant, against their theology.

Such are the causes which brought me into the lecture room. I did not neglect serving YOU, while I seemed only to instruct other men; for every friend I made in Pennsylvania or Wisconsin became an auxiliary in that great cause, so dear to you and me. Nay, I did not abandon my scholarly work while travelling and lecturing. The motion of the railroad cars gave a pleasing and not harmful stimulus to thought, and so helped me to work out my difficult problems of many kinds. I always took a sack of books along with me, generally such as required little eyesight and much thought, and so was sure of good company; while travelling I could read and write all day long; but I would not advise others to do much of either; few bodies can endure the long-continued strain on eye and nerve. So, I lost little time, while I fancied I was doing a great and needful work.

When I first came before you to preach, carefully looking before and after, I was determined on my purpose, and had a pretty distinct conception of the mode of operation. It was not my design to found a sect, and merely build up a new ecclesiastical institution, but to produce a healthy development of the highest faculties of men, to furnish them the greatest possible amount of most needed instruction, and help them each to free spiritual individuality. The Church, the State, the community, were not ends, a finality of purpose, but means to bring forth and bring up individual men. To accomplish this purpose I aimed distinctly at two things: first, to produce the greatest possible healthy development of the religious faculty, acting in harmonious connection with the intellectual, moral, and affectional; and second, to lead you to help others in the same work. Let me say a word in detail of each part of my design.

I. According both to my experience and observation, the religious element is the strongest in the spiritual constitution of man, easily controlling all the rest for his good or ill. I wished to educate this faculty under the influence of the true idea of God, of man, and of their mutual relation. I was not content with producing morality alone—the normal action of the conscience and will, the voluntative keeping of the natural law of right: I saw the need also of piety—religious feeling toward the divine, that instinctive, purely internal love of God, which, I think, is not dependent on conscience. I was led to this aim partly by my own disposition, which, I confess, naturally inclined me to spontaneous pious feeling, my only youthful luxury, more than to voluntary moral action; partly by my early culture, which had given me much experience of religious emotions; and partly, also, by my wide and familiar acquaintance with the mystical writers, the voluptuaries of the soul, who dwelt in the world of pious feeling, heedless of life's practical duties, and caring little for science, literature, justice, or the dear charities of common life.

I count it a great good fortune that I was bred among religious Unitarians, and thereby escaped so much superstition. But I felt early that the "liberal" ministers did not do justice to simple religious feeling; to me their preaching seemed to relate too much to outward things, not enough to the inward pious life; their prayers felt cold; but certainly they preached the importance and the religious value of morality as no sect, I think, had done before. Good works, the test of true religion, noble character, the proof of salvation, if not spoken, were yet implied in their sermons, spite of their inconsistent and traditionary talk about "Atonement," "Redeemer," "Salvation by Christ," and their frequent resort to other pieces of damaged phraseology. The effect of this predominant morality was soon apparent. In Massachusetts, the headquarters of the Unitarians, not only did they gather most of the eminent intellect into their ranks, the original talent and genius

of the most intellectual of the States, but also a very large proportion of its moral talent and moral genius, most of the eminent
conscience and philanthropy. Leaving out of sight pecuniary gifts
for theological and denominational purposes, which come from
peculiar and well-known motives, where the Trinitarians are professedly superior, I think it will be found that all the great moral
and philanthropic movements in the State—social, ecclesiastical,
and political—from 1800 to 1840, have been chiefly begun and
conducted by the Unitarians. Even in the Anti-Slavery enterprise,
the most profound, unrespectable, and unpopular of them all, you
are surprised to see how many Unitarians—even ministers, a
timid race—have permanently taken an active and influential part.
The Unitarians certainly once had this moral superiority, before
the free, young, and growing party became a sect, hide-bound,
bridled with its creed, harnessed to an old, lumbering, and crazy
chariot, urged with sharp goads by near-sighted drivers, along the
dusty and broken pavement of tradition, noisy and shouting, but
going nowhere.

But yet, while they had this great practical excellence, so
obvious once, I thought they lacked the deep, internal feeling of
piety, which alone could make it lasting; certainly they had not
that most joyous of all delights. This fact seemed clear in their
sermons, their prayers, and even in the hymns they made, borrowed, or "adapted." Most powerfully preaching to the understanding, the conscience, and the will, the cry was ever, "duty,
duty! work, work!" They failed to address with equal power the
soul, and did not also shout "joy, joy! delight, delight!" "Rejoice
in God always, and again I say unto you, rejoice!" Their vessels
were full of water: it was all laboriously pumped up from deep
wells; it did not gush out, leaping from the great spring, that is
indeed on the surface of the sloping ground, feeding the little
streams that run among the hills, and both quenching the wild
asses' thirst, and watering also the meadows newly mown, but
which yet comes from the rock of ages, and is pressed out by the
cloud-compelling mountains that rest thereon—yes, by the gravitation of the earth itself.

This defect of the Unitarians was a profound one. Not actually, nor consciously, but by the logic of their conduct, they had
broke with the old ecclesiastic supernaturalism, that with its whip
of fear yet compelled a certain direct, though perverted, action
of the simple religious element in the Trinitarians: ceasing to fear
"the great and dreadful God" of the Old Testament, they had not

quite learned to love the all-beautiful and altogether lovely of the universe. But in general they had no theory which justified a more emotional experience of religion. Their philosophy, with many excellences, was sure of no great spiritual truth. To their metaphysics eternal life was only probable: the great argument for it came not from the substance of human nature, only from an accident in the personal history of a single man; its proof was not *intuitive*, from the primal instincts of mankind; nor *deductive*, from the nature of God; nor yet *inductive*, from the general phenomena of the two-fold universe; it was only *inferential*, from the "resurrection of Christ"—an exceptional fact, without parallel in the story of the race, and that resting on no evidence! Nay, in their chief periodical, when it represented only the opinions of the leaders of the sect, one of their most popular and powerful writers declared the existence of a God was not a certainty of metaphysical demonstration, nor even a fact of consciousness. So this great truth, fundamental to all forms of religion, has neither an objective, necessary, and ontological root in the metaphysics of the universe, nor yet a mere subjective, contingent, and psychological root in the consciousness of John and Jane, but, like the existence of "phlogiston" and "the celestial æther" of the interstellar spaces, it is a matter of conjecture, of inference from observed facts purely external and contingent; or, like the existence of the "Devil," is wholly dependent on the "miraculous and infallible revelation." Surely, a party with no better philosophy, and yet rejecting instinct for guide, breaking with the supernatural tradition at the Trinity, its most important link, could not produce a deep and continuous action of the religious element in the mass of its members, when left individually free; nor when organized into a sect, with the discipline of a close corporation, could it continue to advance, or even to hold its own, and live long on its "Statement of Reasons for not believing the Trinity." Exceptional men—like Henry Ware, jun., who leaned strongly towards the old supernaturalism, or like Dr. Channing, whose deeper reflection or reading supplied him with a more spiritual philosophy—might escape the misfortune of their party; but the majority must follow the logic of their principle. The leaders of the sect, their distinctive creed only a denial, always trembling before the orthodox, rejected the ablest, original talent born among them; nay, sometimes scornfully repudiated original genius, each offering a more spiritual philosophy, which they mocked at as "transcendental," and turned off to the noisy road of other sects, not grateful to feet trained in paths more natural. After denying the Trinity, and the Deity of Christ, they did not dare affirm the humanity of Jesus, the naturalness of religion to man, the actual or possible universality of inspiration, and declare that man is not amenable to ecclesiastic authority, either the oral Roman tradition, or the written Hebrew and Greek Scriptures: but naturally communing with God, through many faculties, by many elements, has in himself the divine well of water, springing up full of everlasting life, and sparkling with eternal truth, and so enjoys continuous revelation. . . .

Coming amongst you with some ministerial experience, and much study of the effect of doctrines, and ecclesiastical modes of procedure, I endeavoured to guard against the vices which so often attend the culture of this sentimental part of religion, and to prevent the fatal degeneracy that often attends it. When the religious element is actively excited under the control of the false theological ideas now so prevailing, it often takes one or both of these two misdirections:—

1. It tends to an unnatural mysticism, which dries up all the noble emotions that else would produce a great useful character. . . .

2. It leads to ecclesiastical ritualism. This is the more common form in New-England, especially in hard men and women. . . .

Mindful of these two vices, which are both diseases of the misdirected soul, and early aware that devoutness is by no means the highest expression of love for God, I have attempted not only to produce a normal development of religious feeling, but to give it the normal direction to the homely duties of common life, in the kitchen, the parlour, nursery, school-room, in the field, market, office, shop, or ship, or street, or wherever the lines of our lot have fallen to us; and to the "primal virtues," that shine aloft as stars which mariners catch glimpses of mid ocean's rack, and learn their course, and steer straight in to their desired haven; and also, to the "charities, that soothe, and heal, and bless," and which are scattered at mankind's feet like flowers, each one a beauty the bee sucks honey from, and a seed to sow the world with wholesome loveliness; for it is plain to me that the common duties of natural life are both the best school for the development of piety, and the best field for its exercise when grown to manly size.

II. Partly for your education in true religion, and partly to promote the welfare of your brother man, I have preached much on the great social duties of your time and place, recommending not only "palliative charity," but still more "remedial justice." So I have not only preached on the private individual virtues, which are, and ought to be, the most constant theme of all pulpits, but likewise on the public social virtues, that are also indispensable to the general welfare. This work brought me into direct relation with the chief social evils of our day. In treating these matters I have proceeded with much caution, beginning my attack a great way off. First of all, I endeavoured to establish philosophically the moral principle I should appeal to, and show its origin in the constitution of man, to lay down the natural law so plain that all might acknowledge and accept it; next, I attempted to show what welfare had followed in human history from keeping this law, and what misery from violating it; then I applied this moral principle of nature and the actual experience of history to the special public vice I wished to whelm over. Such a process may seem slow; I think it is the only one sure of permanent good effects. In this manner I have treated several prominent evils.

1. I have preached against intemperance, showing the monstrous evil of drunkenness, the material and moral ruin it works so widely. My first offence in preaching came when I first spoke on the misery occasioned by this ghastly vice. The victims of it sat before me, and were in great wrath; they never forgave me. Yet, I have not accepted the opinion of the leading temperance men, that the use of intoxicating drinks is in itself a moral or a physical evil. I found they had not only a medical, but also a dietetic use to serve, and in all stages of development above the savage, man resorts to some sort of stimulus as food for the nervous system: for a practice so nearly universal, I suppose there must be a cause in man's natural relation to the world of matter. Accordingly, I do not like the present legal mode of treating the vice, thinking it rests on a false principle which will not long work well; yet public opinion, now setting strong against this beastly vice, required the experiment, which could never be tried under better auspices than now. But I have gladly joined with all men to help to put down this frightful vice, which more than any other concrete cause hinders the welfare and progress of the working people of the North. It was the first public social evil I ever attacked. I have not ceased to warn old and young against this monstrous and ugly sin, and to call on the appointed magistrates to use all their official power to end so fatal a mischief. In a great trading town, of course, such calls are vain; the interest of the few is against the virtue of the people.

2. I have preached against covetousness—the abnormal desire of accumulating property. In the Northern States our civilization is based on respect for industry in both forms, toil and thought. Property is the product of the two: it is human power over nature, to make the material forces of the world supply the wants of man; its amount is always the test of civilization. Our political and social institutions do not favour the accumulation of wealth in a few men or a few families; no permanent entails are allowed; it follows the natural laws of distribution amongst all the owner's children, or according to his personal caprice; in a few generations a great estate is widely scattered abroad. But as we have no hereditary honours, office, or even title, and as wealth is all the parent can bequeath his child, it becomes not only a material power, but also a social distinction—the only one transmissible from sire to son. So wealth, and not birth from famous ancestors, is the thing most coveted; the stamp of the all-mighty dollar is the mark of social distinction; science may be accounted folly, and genius madness, in the paved or the furrowed towns, but money is power in each. American "aristocracy" rests on this movable basis; it is plutocracy: every poor white boy may hope to trundle its golden wheels on to his little patch of ground, for the millionnaire is not born, but self-made. Hence comes an intense desire of riches; a great amount of practical talent goes out in quest thereof. Besides its intrinsic character, respect for money is in America what loyalty to the crown and deference to feudal superiors is in England: "the ox knoweth his owner, and the ass his master's crib," and the Americans the millionnaire, the highest product of plutocracy. . . .

I have often spoken of the tyranny of the rich over the thriving and the poor—our country, State, and town all furnishing grievous examples of the fact. "As the lion eateth up the wild ass in the wilderness, so the rich eateth up the poor," is as true now in New-England as two thousand years ago in Egypt. But when I have seen a man with large talents for business helping others while he helped himself, enriching his workmen, promoting their education, their virtue, and self-respect, I have taken special delight in honouring such an act of practical humanity. Happily we need not go out of Boston to find examples of this rare philanthropy.

3. As I was a schoolmaster at seventeen, though more from necessity than early fitness, I fear, and chairman of a town school committee at twenty-two, I have naturally felt much interest in

the education of the people, and have often preached thereon. But I have seen the great defect of our culture, both in public and private schools; our education is almost entirely intellectual, not also moral, affectional, and religious. The Sunday-schools by no means remedy this evil, or attempt to mend it; they smartly exercise the devotional feelings, accustom their pupils to a certain ritualism, which is destined only to serve ecclesiastical, and not humane purposes; they teach some moral precepts of great value, but their chief function is to communicate theological doctrine, based on the alleged supernatural revelation, and confirmed by miracles, which often confound the intellect, and befool the conscience. They do not even attempt any development of the higher faculties to an original activity at all commensurate with the vigorous action of the understanding. In the public schools there are sometimes devotional exercises, good in themselves, but little pains is directly taken to educate or even instruct the deeper faculties of our nature. The evil seems to increase, for of late years many of the reading-books of our public and private schools seem to have been compiled by men with only the desire of gain for their motive, who have rejected those pieces of prose or poetry which appeal to what is deepest in human nature, rouse indignation against successful wrong, and fill the child with generous sentiments and great ideas. Sunday-school books seem yet worse, so loaded with the superstitions of the sects. The heroism of this age finds no voice nor language in our schools.

But this lack of morality in our schemes of culture appears most eminent in the superior education, in colleges, and other costly seminaries for maids and men. The higher you go up in the scale of institutions, the less proportionate pains is taken with the development of conscience, the affections, and the soul; in the dame school for infants, something is done to make the child "a good boy," or "a good girl," but almost nothing in the richest and most respectable colleges. They are commonly seats of an unprogressive and immoral conservatism, where the studious youth may learn many an important discipline—mathematical, philological, scientific, literary, metaphysical, and theologic—but is pretty sure to miss all effective instruction in the great art and science of personal or public humanity. Hence our colleges are institutions not only to teach the mind, but also for the general *hunkerization* of young men; and a professor is there sometimes unscrupulously appointed whose nature and character make it notorious that his chief function must necessarily be to poison the waters of life, which young men, from generation to generation, will be compelled to bow down at, and drink! In the last forty years I think no New-England college, collective faculty, or pupils, has shown sympathy with any of the great forward movements of mankind, which are indicated by some national outbreak, like the French Revolutions of 1830 or 1848!

From this fatal defect of our scheme of culture, it comes to pass that the class which has the superior education—ministers, professors, lawyers, doctors, and the like—is not only never a leader in any of the great humane movements of the age, where justice, philanthropy, or piety is the motive, but it continually retards all efforts to reform evil institutions, or otherwise directly increase the present welfare or the future progress of mankind. The scholars' culture has palsied their natural instincts of humanity, and gives them instead, neither the personal convictions of free, moral reflection, nor the traditional commands of church authority, but only the maxims of vulgar thrift, "get the most, and give the least; buy cheap, and sell dear!" Exceptional men, like Channing, Pierpont, Emerson, Ripley, Mann, Rantoul, Phillips, Sumner, and a few others, only confirm the general rule, that the educated is also a selfish class, morally not in advance of the mass of men. No thoughtful, innocent man, arraigned for treason, would like to put himself on the college, and be tried by a jury of twelve scholars; it were to trust in the prejudice and technic sophistry of a class, not to "put himself on the country," and be judged by the moral instincts of the people.

Knowing these facts—and I found them out pretty early—I have told them often in public, and shown the need of a thorough reform in our educational institutions. Still more have I preached on the necessity that YOU should do in private for your children what no school in this age is likely to attempt—secure such a great development of the moral, affectional, and religious powers, as shall preserve all the high instincts of nature, while it enriches every faculty by the information given. I need not now speak of what I had long since intended to do amongst you in this matter, when the opportunity should offer; for, alas, when it came, my power to serve you quickly went.

4. I have preached much on the condition of woman. I know the great, ineffaceable difference between the spiritual constitution of her and man, and the consequent difference in their individual, domestic, and social functions. But, examining the matter both philosophically and historically, it seems clear that woman is

man's equal, individually and socially entitled to the same rights. There is no conscious hostility or rivalry between the two, such as is often pretended; man naturally inclines to be a little more than just to her, she a little more than fair to him; a man would find most favour with a jury of women, as boys with nurses. But, certainly, her condition is sadly unfortunate; for, whether treated as a doll or drudge, she is practically regarded as man's inferior, intended by nature to be subordinate to him, subservient to his purposes; not a free spiritual individuality like him, but a dependent parasite or a commanded servant. This idea appears in all civilized legislation; and in the "revealed religion" of Jews and Christians, as well as in that of Brahmins and Mohammedans. Even in New-England no public provision is made to secure superior education for girls as for boys. Woman has no place in the superior industry—shut out from the legal, clerical, and medical professions, and the higher departments of trade, limited to domestic duties, and other callings which pay but little; when she does a man's service she has but half of his reward; no political rights are awarded to her; she is always taxed, but never represented. If married, her husband has legally an unnatural control over her property and her person, and, in case of separation, over her children. A young man with superior talents, born to no other heritage, can acquire wealth, or, unaided, obtain the best education this age makes possible to any one: but with a woman it is not so; if poor, she can only be enriched by marriage; hence mercantile wedlock is far more pardonable in her; no talents, no genius can secure a poor man's daughter her natural share in the high culture of the age. The condition of woman follows unavoidably from the popular idea, which she also shares often in the heroic degree, that she is by nature inferior to man: prostitution and its half-known evils come from this as naturally as crime and drunkenness from squalid want—as plants from seeds.

I have preached the equivalency of man and woman—that each in some particulars is inferior to the other, but, on the whole, mankind and womankind, though so diverse, are yet equal in their natural faculties; and have set forth the evils which come to both from her present inferior position, her exclusion from the high places of social or political trust. But I have thought she will generally prefer domestic to public functions, and have found no philosophic or historic argument for thinking she will ever incline much to the rough works of man, or take any considerable part in Republican politics; in a court like that of Louis XV., or Napoleon III., it might be different; but I have demanded that she should decide that question for herself, choose her own place of action, have her vote in all political matters, and be eligible to any office.

In special, I have urged on YOU the duty of attending to the education of young women, not only in accomplishments—which are so often laborious in the process, only to be ridiculous in the display, and idle in their results—but in the grave discipline of study, and for the practical duties of life. A woman voluntarily ignorant of household affairs and the management of a family, should be an object of pity or of contempt; while the women of New-England incline to despise the indispensable labour of house-keeping, and can neither make wearable garments, nor eatable bread, I have sometimes doubted whether the men of New-England, irritated with their sour fare, would think them quite fit to make laws for the State, or even for the Union. I have also called your attention to those most unfortunate outcasts, the friendless young girls in the streets of your own city, the most abandoned of the perishing class, who will soon become the most harmful of the dangerous class—for prostitution is always two-fold, male as well as female damnation.

It is delightful to see the change now taking place in the popular idea of woman, and the legislation of the Northern States. This reform at once will directly affect half the population, and soon also the other half. I am not alarmed at the evils which obviously attend this change—the growing dislike of maternal duties, the increase of divorces, the false theories of marriage, and the unhappy conduct which thence results; all these are transient things, and will soon be gone—the noise and dust of the waggon that brings the harvest home.

5. The American people are making one of the most important experiments ever attempted on earth, endeavouring to establish an industrial democracy, with the principle that all men are equal in their natural rights, which can be alienated only by the personal misconduct of their possessor; the great body of the people is the source of all political power, the maker of all laws, the ultimate arbiter of all measures; while the special magistrates, high and low, are but appointed agents, acting under the power of attorney the people intrust them with. This experiment was perhaps never tried before, certainly not on so large a scale, and with so fair an opportunity for success; but wise men have always foretold its utter failure, and pointed to the past as confirming this

prophecy. Certainly, we have human history against us, but I think human nature is on our side, and find no reason to doubt the triumph of the American idea. So I have taken a deep interest in politics, important not merely as representing the national housekeeping, but also the public morality, and so tending to help or hinder the people's success. Never failing to vote, I have yet kept myself out of the harness of every party; responsible to none and for none, I have been free to blame or praise the principles and the purposes of all, their measures and their men. Addressing such multitudes, most of them younger than I, in times like the last fourteen years, when such important interests came up for public adjudication, and when the great principles of all national morality have been solemnly denied by famous officials, men also of great personal power, who declared that human governments were amenable to no natural law of God, but subject only to the caprice of magistrate or elector—I have felt a profound sense of my responsibility to YOU as a teacher of religion. So I have preached many political sermons, examining the special measures proposed, exposing the principle they rested on, and the consequences they must produce, and applying the lessons of experience, the laws of human nature, the great doctrines of absolute religion, to the special conduct of the American people. No doubt I have often wounded the feelings of many of YOU. Pardon me, my friends! if I live long I doubt not I shall do so again and again. YOU never made me your minister to flatter, or merely to please, but to instruct and serve.

Treating of politics, I must speak of the conspicuous men engaged therein, when they come to die, for such are the idols of their respective parties. In America there are few objects of conventional respect—no permanent classes who are born to be reverenced; and as men love to look up and do homage to what seems superior, a man of vulgar greatness, who has more of the sort of talent all have much of, is sure to become an idol if he will but serve the passions of his worshippers: so with us, a great man of that stamp has a more irresponsible power than elsewhere among civilized men; for he takes the place of king, noble, and priest, and controls the public virtue more. The natural function of a great man is to help the little ones: by this test I have endeavoured to try such as I must needs speak of. Not responsible for their vice or virtue, I have sought to represent them exactly as I found them, and that, too, without regard to the opinion of men, who only looked up and worshipped, not asking what. If I were an assayer

of metals, I should feel bound to declare the character of the specimens brought before me, whether lead or silver; shall I be less
faithful in my survey of a great man, "more precious than the fine
gold of Ophir"? I am no flatterer, nor public liar-general; when
such a one is wanted he is easily found, and may be had cheap;
and I cannot treat great men like great babies. So, when I
preached on Mr. Adams, who had done the cause of freedom such
great service, on General Taylor and Mr. Webster, I aimed to
paint them exactly as they were, that their virtues might teach us,
and their vices warn. Still further to promote the higher education
of the people, and correct an idolatry as fatal as it is stupid, as dangerous to the public as it is immediately profitable to wily rhetori-
cians, I have prepared lectures on four great famous Americans—
Franklin, Washington, Adams, and Jefferson. The last, however,
was not delivered when my present illness laid me low. I wished to
daguerreotype these great, noble men, and place true pictures before the people.

Perhaps no part of my public labours has been condemned
with more noise and violence than this attempt at historic truth.
Certainly I did depart from the panegyrical custom of political and
clerical eulogizers of the famous or the wealthy dead; but I have
confidence enough in the people of the Northern States to believe
they will prefer plain truth to the most rhetorical lies.

I have not quite disdained to turn your eyes to little, mean
men, when set in high office, that you might get instruction from
their folly or wickedness. So, when the chief magistrate of the city
was notoriously the comrade of drunkards, and of the most infamous of humankind, and that of the State was celebrated chiefly
for public and private lying, and both abused their office to promote their own little purposes of mischief or of gain, debauching
the public virtue, as well as wasting the people's money—I did not
fail to advertise the fact, that YOU at least might learn by the lesson which cost the public so dear.

6. I have preached against war, showing its enormous cost
in money and men, and the havoc it makes of public and private
virtue. A national occasion was not wanting; for obedient to the
whip of the slave-power, which hagrides the nation still, the
American Government—not the people, nor even Congress—
plunged us into a wicked contest with Mexico, she clearly in the
right, we notoriously in the wrong. I have often spoken against
war, and tried to discourage that "excessive lust for land," that
aggressive and invasive spirit, which is characteristic of both the

American and British people. It is clear that the strongest races will ultimately supplant the feebler, and take their place, as the strong grasses outroot the weak from the farmer's meadow. I complain not of this just natural law, which indeed pervades the universe; but the work need not be done by violence, nor any form of wrong. So I have preached against the *fillibustering* of America, and the not less wicked *diplomatizing* and *soldiering* by which our parent across the sea accomplishes the same thing, though with even more harshness and cruelty.

Yet I have not preached the doctrine of the non-resistants, who never allow an individual to repel wrong by material violence; nor that of the ultra-peace men, who deny a nation's right to stave off an invader's wickedness with the people's bloody hand. The wrathful emotions are also an integral part of humanity, and with both nations and individuals have an indispensable function to perform, that of self-defence, which, in the present state of civilization, must sometimes be with violence, even with shedding aggressive blood. It is against needless and wicked wars—the vast majority are such—that I have preached; against the abuse ambitious rulers make of the soldier's trained art to kill, and of the wrathful, defensive instincts of the multitude. In this age I think the people do not make war against the peaceful people of another land; nay, in New-England, the most democratic country, we have too much neglected the miltary art, I fear—a mistake we may bitterly regret in that strife between the Southern habit of despotism, and the Northern principle of democracy, which any day may take the form of civil war, and one day must. For America will not always attempt to carry a pitcher of poison on her left shoulder, and one of pure water on her right; one or the other must soon go to the ground.

7. I have spoken against slavery more than any concrete wrong, because it is the greatest of all, "the sum of all villanies," and the most popular, the wanton darling of the Government. I became acquainted with it in my early childhood, and learned to hate it even then, when, though I might not comprehend the injustice of the principle, I could yet feel the cruelty of the fact. I began to preach against it early, but used the greatest circumspection, for I knew the vulgar prejudice in favour of all successful tyranny, and wished my few hearers thoroughly to accept the principle of justice, and apply it to this as to all wrongs. But even in the little meeting-house at West Roxbury, though some of the audience required no teaching in this matter, the very mention of

American slavery as wicked at first offended all my hearers who had any connection with the "democratic" party. Some said they could see no odds between claiming freedom for a negro slave, and "stealing one of our oxen," the right to own cattle including the right to own men; they thought slavery could ride behind them on the same pillion with "democracy," according to the custom of their masters. But, as little by little I developed the principle of true democracy, showing its root in that love of your neighbour as yourself, which Jesus both taught and lived, and of that eternal justice, which comes even to savage bosoms, and showed how repugnant slavery is to both—gradually all the more reflective and humane drew over to the side of freedom; and they who at first turned their faces to the floor of their pews when I announced slavery as the theme for that day's sermon, ere many years turned on me eyes flashing with indignation against wrong, when I told the tale of our national wickedness; they have since given me the heartiest sympathy in my humble efforts to moralize the opinions and practice of the people.

MY FRIENDS,—Since I have been your minister, I have preached much on this dreadful sin of the nation, which now threatens to be also its ruin; for, while in my youth slavery was admitted to be an evil, commercially profitable, but morally wrong, an exceptional measure, which only the necessity of habit might excuse, but which nothing could justify, of late years it is declared a "moral good," "the least objectionable form of labour," fit for Northern whites not less than African negroes, one of those guide-board instances which indicate the highway of national welfare. For some years slavery has been the actual first principle of each Federal Administration; to this all interests must bend, all customs and statutes conform, and the nation's two great documents, containing our programme of political principles and of political purposes, must be repudiated and practically annulled; the Supreme Court has become only the jesuitical propaganda of slavery.

For some years, while busied with theological matters, and with laying the metaphysic foundation of my own scheme, I took no public part in the anti-slavery movements outside of my own little village. But when I became your minister, and had a wider field to till, when the ambition of the slave power became more insolent by what it fed upon, and the North still tamer and more servile under the bridle and the whip of such as were horsed thereon, a different duty seemed quite clear to me. I have seldom

entered your pulpit without remembering that you and I lived in
a land whose church members are not more numerous than its
slaves, as many "communing with God" by bread and wine, so
many communing with man by chains and whips; and that not
only the State, press, and market, but also the Church takes a
"South-side view of slavery," as indeed she does of each other
wickedness presently popular, and "of good report!" Since 1845, I
have preached against all the great invasive measures of the slave
power, exposing their motive, the first principle they refer to, and
showing that they are utterly hostile to that democracy which is
justice; and all tend to establish a despotism, which at first may
be industrial and many-headed, as now in Louisiana, but next
must be single-headed and military, as already in France, and
finally must lead to national ruin, as in so many countries of the
old world.

In due time the Fugitive Slave Bill came up from seed which
wicked men had sown and harrowed into the Northern soil; Boston fired her hundred cannons with delight, and they awoke the
ministers, sitting drowsy in their churches of commerce, mid all
the pavements of the North, who thought an angel had spoke to
them. Then I preached against slavery as never before, and defied
the impudent statute, whereto you happily said *Amen* by the first
clapping of hands which for years had welcomed a sermon in Boston; how could you help the natural indecorum? When, roused by
these jubilant guns, one minister, so generous and self-devoted, too,
in many a noble work, called on his parishioners to enforce that
wicked act, which meant to kidnap mine, and declared that if a
fugitive sought shelter with him he would drive him away from his
own door; when another uttered words more notorious, and yet
more flagrant with avaricious inhumanity, which I care not now to
repeat again; and when the cry, "No higher law!" went down from
the market, and, intoned by the doctorial leaders of the sects, rang
through so many commercial churches throughout the Northern
land, I did not dare refuse to proclaim the monstrous fact as one
of the unavoidable effects of slavery, whose evil seed must bear
fruit after its kind, and to gibbet the wrong before the eyes of the
people, to whom I appealed for common justice and common humanity. When two men, holding mean offices under the Federal
Government, one of them not fit by nature to do a cruel deed,
actually stole and kidnapped two innocent inhabitants out from
your city of Franklin, and Hancock, and Adams, and attempted,
with their unclean, ravenous jaws, to seize yet others, and rend

the manhood out of them, I preached against these jackals of slavery and their unhuman work; and have now only to lament that my powers of thought and speech were no more adequate fitly to expose the dark infamy of that foul deed, against which I asked alike the people's justice and their wrath; I knew I should not ask in vain. And when a drunken bully from South Carolina, in Congress, fitly representing the first principle, if not the first persons of his State—where none can serve in even the Lower House of Assembly "unless he be seized in his own right of ten negro slaves"—made his assault, not less cowardly than brutal, on our noble Senator, wounding him with worse than death, and while the United States Attorney sought "to make murder safe and easy in the capital," not dreaming it would one day, unpunished, reach his own heart, I spoke of that matter, and showed it was the cowards of Massachusetts who drew the blow on her faithful champion, and that no "anodyne" could make them less than glad that it was struck!

But why speak more of those sad days? Others may come with sterner face, not black, but red! However, a blessed change in public opinion now goes calmly on in Massachusetts, in New-England, and all the North, spite of the sophistry and cunning of ambitious men smit with the Presidential fever. The death of a dozen leading anti-slavery men to-day would not much retard it, for the ground is full of such!

8. But I have preached against the errors of the ecclesiastic theology more than upon any other form of wrong, for they are the most fatal mischiefs in the land. The theological notion of God, man, and the relation between them, seems to me the greatest speculative error mankind has fallen into. Its gloomy consequences appear:—Christendom takes the Bible for God's word, His last word; nothing new or different can ever be expected from the source of all truth, all justice, and all love; the sun of righteousness will give no added light or heat on the cold darkness of the human world. From portions of this "infallible revelation," the Roman Church logically derives its despotic and hideous claim to bind and loose on earth, to honour dead men with sainthood, or to rack and burn with all the engines mechanic fancy can invent, or priestly cruelty apply; and hereafter to bless eternally, or else for ever damn. Hence, both Protestant and Catholic logically derive their imperfect, wrathful Deity, who creates men to torment them in an endless hell, "paved with the skulls of infants not a span long," whereinto the vast majority of men are, by the million, trodden

down for everlasting agony, at which the elect continually rejoice. Hence, they derive their Devil, absolutely evil, that ugly wolf whom God lets loose into his fold of lambs; hence their total depravity, and many another dreadful doctrine which now the best of men blind their brothers' eyes withal, and teach their children to distrust the infinite perfection which is nature's God, dear Father and Mother to all that is. Hence clerical sceptics learn to deny the validity of their own superior faculties, and spin out the cobwebs of sophistry, wherewith they surround the field of religion, and catch therein unwary men. Hence the Jews, the Mohammedans, the Mormons, draw their idea of woman, and their right to substitute such gross conjunctions for the natural marriage of one to one. There the slaveholder finds the chief argument for his ownership of men, and in Africa or New-England, kidnaps the weak, his mouth drooling with texts from "the authentic word of God;" nay, there the rhetorician finds reason for shooting an innocent man who but righteously seeks that freedom which nature declares the common birthright of mankind. It has grieved me tenderly to see all Christendom make the Bible its fetish, and so lose the priceless value of that free religious spirit, which communing at first hand with God, wrote its grand pages, or poured out its magnificent beatitudes.

Christendom contains the most intellectual nations of the earth, all of them belonging to the dominant Caucasian race, and most of them occupying regions very friendly to the development of the highest faculties of man. Theirs, too, is the superior machinery of civilization, political, ecclesiastical, domestic, social. Nowhere on earth does the clerical mass so connect itself with the innermost of man. Christendom is the bold leader in all intellectual affairs—arts of peace and war, science, literature, skill to organize and administer mankind. But yet the Christian has no moral superiority over the Jews, the Mohammedans, the Brahmins, the Buddhists, at all commensurate with this intellectual power. In the sum of private and public virtues, the Turk is before the Christian Greek. For 1500 years the Jews, a nation scattered and peeled, and exposed to most degrading influences, in true religion have been above the Christians! In temperance, chastity, honesty, justice, mercy, are the leading nations of Christendom before the South-Asiatics, the Chinese, the islanders of Japan? Perhaps so— but have these "Christians" a moral superiority over those "heathens" equal to their mental superiority? It is notorious they have not. Why is this so, when these Christians worship a man whose religion was love to God and love to men, and who would admit to heaven only for righteousness, and send to hell only for lack of it? Because they WORSHIP Him, reject the natural goodness He relied upon, and trust in the "blood of Christ which maketh free from all sin." It is this false theology, with its vicarious atonement, salvation without morality or piety, only by belief in absurd doctrines, which has bewitched the leading nations of the earth into such practical mischief. A false idea has controlled the strongest spiritual faculty, leading men to trust in "imputed righteousness," and undervalue personal virtue. Self-denying missionaries visit many a far-off land "to bring the heathens to Christ." Small good comes of it; but did they teach industry, thrift, letters, honesty, temperance, justice, mercy, with rational ideas of God and man, what a conversion there would be of the Gentiles! Two-and-thirty thousand Christian ministers are there in the United States, all "consecrated to Christ;" many of them are able men, earnest and devoted, but, their eyes hood-winked, and their hands chained by their theology, what do they bring to pass? They scarce lessen any vice of the State, the press, or the market. They are to "save souls from the wrath of God."

I have preached against the fundamental errors of this well-compacted theologic scheme, showing the consequences which follow thence, and seldom entered your pulpit without remembering slavery, the great sin of America, and these theological errors, the sacramental mistake of Christendom. But I have never forgotten the great truths this theology contains, invaluable to the intellect, the conscience, the heart and soul. I have tried to preserve them all, with each good institution which the Church, floating over the ruins of an elder world, has borne across that deluge, and set down for us where the dove of peace has found rest for the sole of her foot, and gathered her olive-branch to show that those devouring waters are dried up from the face of the earth. To me the name of Christianity is most exceeding dear, significant of so great a man and of such natural emotions, ideas, and actions, as are of priceless value to mankind. I know well the errors, also, of the doubters and deniers, who in all ages have waged war against the superstitious theology of their times, and pulled down what they could not replace with better. I have not sat in the seat of the scornful; and while I warned men against the snare of the priest, I would not suffer them to fall into the mocker's pit. I have taken exquisite delight in the grand words of the Bible, putting it before all other sacred literature of the whole ancient world; to me it is more dear when I regard them not as the miracles of God, but as the work of earnest men, who did their uttermost with holy heart. I love to read the great truths of religion set forth in the magnificent poetry of psalmist and prophet, and the humane lessons of the Hebrew peasant, who summed up the prophets and the law in one word of LOVE, and set forth man's daily duties in such true and simple speech! As a master, the Bible were a tyrant; as a help, I have not time to tell its worth; nor has a sick man speech for that, nor need I now for my public and private teachings sufficiently abound in such attempts. But yet, to me the great men of the Bible are worth more than all their words; he that was greater than the temple, whose soul burst out its walls, is also greater than the Testament, but yet no master over you or me, however humble men!

In theological matters my preaching has been positive, much more than negative, controversial only to create; I have tried to set forth the truths of natural religion, gathered from the world of matter and of spirit; I rely on these great ideas as the chief means for exciting the religious feelings, and promoting religious deeds; I have destroyed only what seemed pernicious, and that I might build a better structure in its place. . . .

To the success of the great truths I have taught, it is now but of the smallest consequence whether I preach in Boston and all the Lyceums of the North, or my body crumbles in some quiet, nameless grave. They are not MY truths! I am no great man whom the world hinges on; nor can I settle the fate of a single doctrine by my authority. Humanity is rich in personalities, and a man no larger than I will not long be missed in the wide field of theology and religion. For immediately carrying a special measure, and for helping this or that, a single man is sometimes of great value; the death of the general is the loss of the battle, perhaps the undoing of a state; but after a great truth of humanity is once set a-going, it is in the charge of mankind, through whom it first came from God; it cannot perish by any man's death. Neither State, nor press, nor market, nor Church, can ever put it down; it will drown the water men pour on it, and quench their hostile fire. Cannot the Bible teach its worshippers that a grave is no dungeon to shut up truth in; and that death, who slays alike the priest and the prophet, bows his head before her, and passes harmless by? To stone Stephen did not save the Church of the Pharisees. A live man may harm his own cause; a dead one cannot defile his clean immortal doctrines with unworthy hands.

In these tropic waters not far off, in time of strife, on a dark night, but towards morning, an English ship-of-war once drew near what seemed a hostile vessel under sail; she hailed the stranger, who answered not, then hailed again, no answer, then fired a shot across the saucy bows, but still there was no reply; next fired at her, amidships, but got not a word in return. Finally the man-of-war cleared for action, began battle in earnest, serving the guns with British vigour, but found no return, save the rattle of shot rebounding and falling back into the heedless sea. Daylight presently came with tropic suddenness, and the captain found he spent his powder in battering a great rock in the ocean! So many a man has fought long against a truth which he fancied was but a floating whim, bound to yield to his caprice; but, at last, the dawning light has shown him it was no passing ship, of timber and cordage and canvas, driven by the wind and tossed by the undulations of the sea, but a SAIL-ROCK, resting on the foundations of the world, and amenable neither to the men-of-war that sailed in the wind, not yet to the undulation of the sea whereon they came and went. It is one thing to rejoice at the sickness and death of a short-lived heretic, but it is another and a little different, to alter the constitution of the universe, and put down a fact of spontaneous human consciousness, which also is a truth of God.

When I first came amongst you, and lived in a trading town where a great variety of occupations lay spread out before me all the time, and preached to such crowds of men as offered a wide diversity of nature, character, and conduct, I found not only an opportunity to work, but also to learn and grow. You say I have taught you much; I hope it is so, but you have been a large part of your own schooling, for I have also learned much from you, the audience has always furnished a large part of the sermon and the prayer. I have received much direct instruction, and that in matters of deep concern, from some of you, by hearing your words and looking at your lives; the indirect help to my power of thought and speech, I fear you would hardly credit should I attempt to tell. It is enough to say now, that amongst you I have found men and women, often in quite humble stations, who have added new elements of both strength and beauty to my notion of what constitutes a "glorious human creature," in particular excellences their actual surpassing my ideal. I have been a learner quite as much as a teacher; indeed, out of nearly a thousand sermons I have written, I think there are not five-and-twenty which are not also steps in my own development, studies I have learned by, quite as much as lessons you have been taught with.

To me, human life in all its forms, individual and aggregate, is a perpetual wonder; the flora of the earth and sea is full of beauty and of mystery which science seeks to understand; the fauna of land and ocean is not less wonderful; the world which holds them both, and the great universe that folds it on every side, are still more wonderful, complex, and attractive, to the contemplating mind. But the universe of human life, with its peculiar worlds of outer sense and inner soul, the particular faunas and floras which therein find a home, are still more complex, wonderful, and attractive; and the laws which control it seem to me more amazing than the mathematic principles that explain the celestial mechanics of the outward world. The Cosmos of matter seems little compared to this Cosmos of immortal and progressive man; it is my continual study, discipline, and delight. Oh, that some young genius would devise the "novum organum" of humanity, determine the "principia" thereof, and with deeper than mathematic science, write out the formulas of the human universe, the celestial mechanics of mankind.

In your busy, bustling town, with its queerly mingled, heterogeneous population, and its great diversity of work, I soon learned to see the unity of human life under all this variety of circumstances and outward condition. It is easy for a simple-hearted man, standing on a central truth, to reduce them all to one common denomination of humanity, and ascertain the relative value of individuals in this comparative morality. The huckster, with a basket, where apples, pea-nuts, candy, and other miscellaneous small stores are huddled together, is a small merchant; the merchant with his warehouse, his factory, or bank, his ships on many a sea, is a great huckster; both buy to sell, and sell to gain; the odds is quantative, not in kind, but in bulk. The cunning lawyer, selling his legal knowledge and forensic skill to promote a client's gainful wickedness; the tricksy harlot, letting out her person to a stranger's unholy lust; the deceitful minister, prostituting his voice and ecclesiastical position to make some popular sin appear decent and Christian, "accordant with the revealed word of God"—all stand in the same column of my religious notation. In the street I see them all pass by, each walking in a vain show, in different directions, but all consilient to the same end!

So, the ambitious vanities of life all seem of nearly the same

value when laid side by side on this table of exchange. The poetess, proud of her superiority over other "silly women" in the "vision and the faculty divine," or in but the small "accomplishment
of verse;" the orator, glorying in his wondrous art, longer than
other men to hold the up-looking multitude with his thread of
speech, and thereby pour his thought or will into the narrow vials
of so many minds; and the scavenger, who boasts that he "can
sweep round a lamp-post better than any man in the gang"—all
seem alike to an eye that looks beneath and above the rippling
tide of phenomenal actions, learning its whither and its whence,
and knowing the unseen causes which control this many-billowed
sea of life. The diamonds of many-skirted Empress Eugénie at
Versailles, and the Attleborough jewellery of the bare-footed char-
woman Bridget, at Cove Place, are symbols of the same significance, and probably of the same value to their respective occcu-
pants. The man not winged with talent, whom a political party
cranes up to some official eminence he could not reach by the most
assiduous crawling; and the dawdling woman, who can make neither bread to eat nor clothes to wear, nor yet order any household even of only two, whom an idle hand, and a pinkish cheek,
and a lolling tongue, have fastened to another, but bearded
fool—these seem wonderfully alike to me; and I say to both, "May
God Almighty have mercy on your souls!" So, the effort after
nobleness of character is ever the same, clad in whatever dress;
the black washerwoman, on Negro Hill, as, with a frowzy broom,
a mob, and a tub or two, she keeps the wolf away from her un-
fathered babies, all fugitives from slavery, and thence looks up
to that dear God whom she so feels within her heart a very present
help in her hour of need, which is her every hour—to me seems
as grand as Paul preaching on Mars Hill to the Athenian senators;
nay, not less glorious than Jesus of Nazareth on his mountain,
uttering blessed beatitudes to those thousands who paused in their
pilgrimage towards Jerusalem, to look and listen to one greater
than the temple, and destined to control men's hearts when that
city, compactly built, has not stone left on stone. The thoughtful
eye, like the artistic hand, invests with the same magnificence the
Hebrew preachers and the negro washerwoman, borrowing the
outward purple from the glory within. It is the same great problem
of duty which is to be wrought out by all—huckster, merchant,
lawyer, harlot, minister, poetess, orator, Eugénie, and Bridget, unworthy officer, and idle, helpless wife, Dinah on Negro Hill, Paul at
the Areopagus, and Jesus on Mount Tabor; and it is not of such

future consequence to us as men fancy, whether the tools of our work be a basket or a warehouse, a mob or a cross; for the divine justice asks the same question of each, "What hast thou done with *thy* gifts and opportunities?" Feeling the democracy of mankind, and preaching it in many a form, I have learned to estimate the worth of men by the quality of their character, and the amount of their service rendered to mankind. So of each I ask but two questions, "What are you? What do you do?" The voluntary beggar in rags, and the voluntary beggar in ruffles, alike answer, "Nought."

In my preaching I have used plain, simple words, sometimes making what I could not find ready, and counted nothing unclean, because merely common. In philosophic terms, and in all which describes the inner consciousness, our Saxon speech is rather poor, and so I have been compelled to gather from the Greek or Roman stock forms of expressions which do not grow on our homely and familiar tree, and hence, perhaps, have sometimes scared you with "words of learned length." But I have always preferred to use, when fit, the every-day words in which men think and talk, scold, make love, and pray, so that generous-hearted philosophy, clad in a common dress, might more easily become familiar to plain-clad men. It is with customary tools that we work easiest and best, especially when use has made the handles smooth.

Illustrations I have drawn from most familiar things which are before all men's eyes, in the fields, the streets, the shop, the kitchen, parlour, nursery, or school; and from the literature best known to all—the Bible, the newspapers, the transient speech of eminent men, the talk of common people in the streets, from popular stories, school-books, and nursery rhymes. Some of you have censured me for this freedom and homeliness, alike in illustration and in forms of speech, desiring "more elegant and sonorous language," "illustrations derived from elevated and conspicuous objects," "from dignified personalities." A good man, who was a farmer in fair weather and a shoemaker in foul, could not bear to have a plough or a lapstone mentioned in my sermon—to me picturesque and poetic objects, as well as familiar—but wanted "kings and knights," which I also quickly pleased him with. But for this I must not only plead the necessity of my nature, delighting in common things, trees, grass, oxen, and stars, moonlight on the water, the falling rain, the ducks and hens at this moment noisy under my window, the gambols and prattle of children, and the common work of blacksmiths, wheelwrights, painters, hucksters, and traders of all sorts; but I have also on my side the example of all the great masters of speech—save only the French, who disdain all common things, as their aristocratic but elegant literature was bred in a court, though rudely cradled elsewhere, nay, born of rough loins—of poets like Homer, Dante, Shakspeare, Goethe, of Hebrew David, and of Roman Horace; of philosophers like Socrates and Locke; of preachers like Luther, Latimer, Barrow, Butler, and South; nay, elegant Jeremy Taylor, "the Shakspeare of divines" owes half his beauty to these weeds of nature, which are choicest flowers when set in his artistic garden. But one need not go beyond Jesus of Nazareth and the first three Gospels to learn great lessons in the art of speech; for in him you not only reverence the genius for religion, which intuitively sees divine truth and human duty, but wonder also at the power of speech that tells its tale as deliverly as the blackbird sings or the water runs down-hill. Besides, to me common life is full of poetry and pictorial loveliness; spontaneously portrayed, its events will fill my mind as one by one the stars come out upon the evening sky, like them each one "a beauty and a mystery." It is therefore a necessity of my nature that the sermon should publicly reflect to you what privately hangs over it with me, and the waters rained out of my sky when cloudy, should give back its ordinary stars when clear. Yet, for the same reason, I have also fetched illustrations from paths of literature and science, less familiar perhaps to most of you, when they, better than aught else, would clear a troubled thought; so, in my rosary of familiar beads, I have sometimes strung a pearl or two which science brought from oceanic depths, or fixed thereon the costly gems where ancient or modern art has wrought devices dearer than the precious stone itself.

Using plain words and familiar illustrations, and preaching also on the greatest themes, I have not feared to treat philosophic matters with the rigour of science, and never thought I should scare you with statistic facts, which are the ultimate expression of a great principle doing its work by a constant mode of operation, nor by psychologic analysis, or metaphysical demonstration. Ministers told me I was "preaching over the heads of the people;" I only feared to preach below their feet, or else aside from their ears. Thus handling great themes before attentive men, I have also dared to treat them long, for I read the time not on the dial, but the audience. I trust you will pardon the offence, which I perhaps shall not repeat. . . .

When a young man, it was a part of my original plan to leave the practical work of continual preaching, a little before

I should be fifty years old, and devote the residue of my life to publishing works which I hoped might be of permanent value, separating the two periods by a year or two of travel in the American tropics and the Mediterranean countries of the Old World; so I thought I might be most useful to mankind, for I did not anticipate or desire long life, and did not originally rate very high my ability to affect the mass of men by direct word of mouth, and made no pretensions to that most popular of intellectual attainments, that eloquence, which, like other beauty, is at once a pleasure and a power, delighting whom it compels. But, when I found the scholarly class more unfriendly than the multitude, I began to think I had chosen the wrong audience to address; that it was the people, not the scholars, who were to lead in philosophic thought; and when you gave me a chance to be heard in Boston, and I preached on from year to year, great crowds of men, who were not readers but workers in the week, coming and continuing to listen to the longest of sermons, wherein great subjects were treated without respect to popular prejudice, ecclesiastical, political, or social, and that, too, without sparing the severest attention of the hearers; when I found these multitudes seemed to comprehend the abstractest reasoning, and truths most universal, and appeared to be instructed, set free, and even elevated to higher hopes both here and hereafter, and to noble character; when, with all my directness of homely speech, I found myself welcome in most of the lecture halls between the Mississippi and the Penobscot, and even beyond them, having thence two or three hundred invitations a year; when the national crisis became nearer and more threatening, and I saw my sentiments and ideas visibly passing into the opinion and the literature of the people, and thence coming out in the legislation of New-England and the other Northern States—I thought it not quite time to withdraw, and my early purposes were a little shaken. I intended to continue some ten years more in severe practical work, till about sixty, then retire, not to lie down in the grave like a camel under his load at night, but hoping to enjoy a long, quiet autumn of twenty years or so, when I might accomplish my philosophic and literary works, and mow up as provender for future time what I had first raised as green grass, and then mowed down to make into sound hay, but have now left, alas! either strewn where it grew, or but loosely raked together, not yet carted into safe barns for the long winter, or even stacked up and sheltered against immediate spoiling by a sudden rain in harvest.

Besides, I felt quickened for practical work by the great exigencies of the nation, the importance of the fight already going on between despotism on one side, with its fugitive slave bills, New-England kidnappers and sophists, in bar or pulpit, and democracy on the other, with its self-evident truths, inalienable rights, and vast industrial and educational developments—a battle not yet understood, but destined to grow hot and red ere long—and by the confidence I have always felt in the ultimate triumph of the right and true, the beautiful and good. Moreover, I was encouraged in my course by the soundness and vigour of my bodily frame, not stout, perhaps, and strong, but capable of much and long-continued work of the most various kinds, not tiring soon, nor easily made ill, but quick recovering from both fatigue and sickness; and by the long average life of six generations of American fathers and mothers. But I have now learned by experience that it is not wise to cherish wide personal hopes in a narrow life, or seek to make an apple-tree larger than the orchard.

For some years, I have been warned that I was not only spending the full income of life, but encroaching a little on the capital stock. But what wise man even is always wise? The duties were so urgent, the call for help so imploring, the labour at once so delightful in its process and so prophetic of good results, and I felt such confidence in my bodily power and ancestral longevity, that I did not sufficiently heed the gentle admonition; till, last year, in March, nature at once gave way, and I was compelled to yield to a necessity above my will. I need not tell the fluctuations in my health since then, rather, my friends, let me again thank YOU for the prompt and generous sympathy you gave then and ever since.

Immediately after my present illness, I left your pulpit empty for a day. YOU wrote me a letter signed by many a dear familiar name, and but for the haste, I know it had been enriched with the signatures of all; it was dated at Boston, January 11th. Your affection wrote the lines, and a kindred wisdom kept them from me till I was able to bear this unexpected testimonial of your sympathy and love. On Sunday, the 6th of March, while you were listening to—alas! I know not whom you looked to then—my eyes filled with tears as I first read your words of delicate appreciation and esteem. My friends, I wish I were worthy of such reverence and love; that my service were equal to your gratitude. I have had more than sufficient reward for my labours with you; not only have I seen a good work and a great prosper in my hands as you held them up, but in public, and still more in private, you have given me the sweetest, best of outward consolations—the grateful sympathy of earnest, thoughtful, and religious men. If my public life has been a battle, wherein my head grows bald, my beard turns grey, and my arm becomes feeble, before their time, it has been also a triumph, whose crown is not woven of the red-flowered laurels of war, but of the olive, the lily, the violet, and the white rose of peace. I have no delight in controversy; when assailed, I have never returned the assault; and though continually fired upon for many years from the bar-room and the pulpit, and many another "coigne of vantage" betwixt the two, I never in return shot back an arrow, in private or public, until in the United States Court I was arraigned for the "misdemeanor" of making a speech in Faneuil Hall against that kidnapping in Boston, perpetrated by the public guardian of widows and orphans; then I prepared my *Defence,* which had been abler were I more a lawyer, though less a minister.

To compose sermons, and preach them to multitudes of men of one sort but many conditions, thereto setting forth the great truths of absolute religion, and applying them to the various events of this wondrous human life, trying to make the constitution of the universe the common law of men, illustrating my thought with all that I can gather from the world of matter, its use and beauty both, and from the world of man, from human labours, sorrows, joys, and everlasting hopes—this has been my great delight. Your pulpit has been my joy and my throne. Though press and state, market and meeting-house, have been hostile to us, YOU have yet given me the largest Protestant audience in America, save that which orthodox Mr. Beecher, who breaks with no theologic tradition of the New-England Church, inspires with his deep emotional nature, so devout and so humane, and charms with his poetic eloquence, that is akin to both the sweet-briar and the rose, and all the beauty which springs up wild amid New-England hills, and to the loveliness of common life; I have given you my sermons in return, at once my labour and delight. My life is in them, and all my character, its good and ill; thereby you know me better than I, perhaps, myself—for a man's words and his face when excited in sermon and in prayer tell all he is, the reflection of what he has done. Sermons are never out of my mind; and when sickness brings on me the consciousness that I have nought to do, its most painful part, still by long habit all things will take this form; and the gorgeous vegetation of the tropics, their fiery skies so brilliant all the day, and starlit too with such exceeding beauty all the night; the glittering fishes in the market, as many-coloured as a gardener's show, these Josephs of the sea; the silent pelicans, flying forth at morning and back again at night; the strange, fantastic trees, the dry pods rattling their historic bones all day, while the new bloom comes fragrant out beside, a noiseless prophecy; the ducks rejoicing in the long-expected rain; a negro on an ambling pad; the slender-legged, half-naked negro children in the street, playing their languid games, or oftener screaming 'neath their mother's blows, amid black swine, hens, and un-counted dogs; the never-ceasing clack of women's tongues, more shrewd than female in their shrill violence; the unceasing, multi-farious kindness of our hostess; and, overtowering all, the self-sufficient, West Indian Creole pride, alike contemptuous of toil, and ignorant and impotent of thought—all these common things turn into poetry as I look on or am compelled to hear, and then transfigure into sermons, which come also spontaneously by night and give themselves to me, and even in my sleep say they are meant for YOU. Shall they ever be more than the walking of

> "A sick man in his sleep,
> Three paces and then faltering?"

The doctors cannot tell; I also know not, but hope and strive to live a little longer, that I may work much more. Oh, that the truths of absolute religion, which human nature demands, and offers, too, from the infinitely perfect God who dwells therein, while He transcends the universe; oh, that these were an idea enlightening all men's minds, a feeling in their hearts, and action in their outward life! Oh, that America's two-and-thirty thousand ministers, Hebrew, Christian, Mormon, knew these truths, and to mankind preached piety and morality, and that theology which is the science of God and his twofold universe, and forgot their mythologic and misguiding dreams! Then what a new world were ours! Sure I would gladly live to work for this.

I may recover entirely, and stand before you full of brown health, equal to the manifold labours of that position, live to the long period of some of my fathers, and at last die naturally of old age. This to me seems most desirable, though certainly not most probable.

Or, I may so far recover, that I shall falter on a score of years or so, one eye on my work, the other on my body, which refuses to do it, and so urge my weak and balky horse along a miry, broken road. If this be so, then, in some still, little rural nook, in sight of town, but not too nigh, I may finish some of the many things I have begun, and left for the afternoon or evening of my days; and yet, also, from time to time, meet you again, and, with words of lofty cheer, look on the inspiring face of a great congregation. With this I should be well content; once it was the ideal of my hope.

In either of these cases, I see how the time of this illness, and the discipline alike of disappointment and recovery, would furnish me new power. Several times in my life has it happened that I have met with what seemed worse than death, and, in my short-sighted folly, I said, "Oh, that I had wings like a dove! for then would I fly away and be at rest!" Yet my griefs all turned into blessings; the joyous seed I planted came up discipline, and I wished to tear it from the ground; but it flowered fair, and bore a sweeter, sounder fruit than I expected from what I set in earth. As I look over my life, I find no disappointment and no sorrow I could afford to lose; the cloudy morning has turned out the fairer day; the wounds of my enemies have done me good. So wondrous is this human life, not ruled by fate, but Providence, which is Wisdom married unto Love, each infinite! What has been, may be. If I recover wholly, or but in part, I see new sources of power beside these waters of affliction I have stooped at; I shall not think I have gone through "the valley of Baca" in vain, nor begrudge the time that I have lingered there, seeming idle; rainy days also help to seed the ground. One thing I am sure of: I have learned the wealth and power of the grateful, generous feelings of men, as I knew them not before, nor hoped on earth to find so rich. High as I have thought of human nature, I had not quite done justice to the present growth of these beautiful faculties. Here and now, as so oft before, I have found more treasure than I dreamed lay hidden where I looked.

But if neither of these hopes becomes a fact, if the silver cord part soon above the fountain, and the golden bowl be broke, let not us complain; a new bowl and a stronger cord shall serve the well of life for you. Though quite aware how probable this seems, believe me, I have not yet had a single hour of sadness; trust me, I shall not. True, it is not pleasant to leave the plough broken in the furrow just begun, while the seed-corn smiles in the open sack, impatient to be sown, and the whole field promises such liberal return. To say farewell to the thousands I have been wont to preach to, and pray with, now joyous, and tearful now—it has its bitterness to one not eighty-four but forty-eight. To undo the natural ties more intimately knit of long-continued friendship and of love—this is the bitter part. But if it be my lot, let not you nor me complain. Death comes to none except to bring a blessing; it is no misfortune to lay aside these well-loved weeds of earth, and be immortal. To YOU, as a congregation, my loss may be easily supplied; and to me it is an added consolation to know that, however long and tenderly remembered, I should not long be missed; some other will come in my place, perhaps without my defects, possessed of nobler gifts, and certainly not hindered by the ecclesiastical and social hostility which needs must oppose a man who has lived and wrought as I. It will not always be unpopular justly to seek the welfare of all men. Let us rejoice that others may easily reap golden corn where we have but scared the wild beasts away, or hewn down the savage woods, burning them with dangerous fire, and made the rich, rough ground smooth for culture. It was with grimmer fight, with sourer sweat, and blacker smoke, and redder fire, that the fields were cleared where you and I now win a sweet and easy bread.

What more shall I say to sweeten words of farewell, which must have a bitter taste. If I have taught you any great religious truths, or roused therewith emotions that are good, apply them to your life, however humble or however high and wide; convert them into deeds, that your superior religion may appear in your superior industry, your justice, and your charity, coming out in your housekeeping and all manner of work. So when your

> "Course
> Is run, some faithful eulogist may say,
> He sought not praise, and praise did overlook
> His unobtrusive merit; but his life,
> Sweet to himself, was exercised in good,
> That shall survive his name and memory."

Let no fondness for me, now heightened by my illness, and my absence too, blind your eyes to errors which may be in my doctrine, which must be in my life; I am content to serve by warning, where I cannot guide by example. Mortal, or entered on immortal life, still let me be your minister, to serve, never your master, to hinder and command. Do not stop where I could go no further, for, after so long teaching, I feel that I have just begun to learn, begun my work. "No man can feed us always;" welcome, then, each wiser guide who points you out a better way. On earth I shall not cease to be thankful for your patience, which has borne with me so much and long; for your sympathy, nearest when needed most, and the examples of noble Christian life, which I have found in some of you,

"To whom is given
The joy that mixes man with Heaven:
Who, rowing hard against the stream,
See distant gates of Eden gleam,
And never dream it is a dream;
But hear, by secret transport led,
Even in the charnels of the dead,
The murmur of the fountain-head:
Who will accomplish high desire,
Bear and forbear, and never tire—
Like Stephen, an unquenchèd fire,
As looking upward, full of grace,
He prayed, and from a happy place
God's glory smote him on the face!"

Here they add to my joy; perhaps their remembrance will add to my delight in Heaven.

May you be faithful to your own souls; train up your sons and daughters to lofty character, most fit for humble duty; and to far cathedral heights of excellence, build up the being that you are, with feelings, thoughts, and actions, that become "a glorious human creature," by greatly doing the common work of life, heedful of all the charities, which are twice blest, both by their gifts and their forgiveness too. And the Infinite Perfection, the Cause and Providence of all that is, the Absolute Love, transcending the time and space it fills, OUR FATHER, and OUR MOTHER too, will bless you each beyond your prayer, for ever and for ever. Bodily absent, though present still with you by the immortal part, so hopes and prays

Your Minister and Friend,

Fredericksted, West-End, Santa Cruz,
April 19th, 1859.

Sources

Key

Centenary: Centenary Edition of the Writings of Theodore Parker. 15 vols. Boston: American Unitarian Association, 1907.

Cobbe: Frances Power Cobbe: *The Collected Works of Theodore Parker.* 14 vols. London: Trübner & Co., 1863, 1864, 1865, 1867, 1871, 1872, 1875, 1876.

Frothingham: Octavius Brooks Frothingham: *Theodore Parker: A Biography.* Boston: James R. Osgood and Company, 1874.

Trial: Theodore Parker: *The Trial of Theodore Parker for the "Misdemeanor" of a Speech in Faneuil Hall against Kidnapping Before the Circuit Court of the United States at Boston, April 3, 1855, with the Defence.* Boston: Published for the Author, 1855.

Weiss: John Weiss: *Life and Correspondence of Theodore Parker.* 2 vols. New York: D. Appleton & Company, 1864.

1. *Recollections of Boyhood*
   From a memoir begun at Rome on March 16, 1860. In Weiss, I, pp. 17 ff.

2. *Autobiographical Fragments*
   I. Weiss, I, p. 40.
   II. *Trial,* pp. 220-21.
   III. Frothingham, pp. 330-31.
   IV. Weiss, I, p. 50.
   V. Weiss, I, p. 61.
   VI. Weiss, I, pp. 67-68.
   VII. Weiss, I, p. 75.
   VIII. From *A Discourse of the Relation Between the Ecclesiastical Insti-*
   tutions and the Religious Consciousness of the American People. In Cobbe, III, pp. 207-8.

3. *The Transient and Permanent in Christianity*
   Cobbe, VIII, pp. 1 ff.

4. *A Crusading Clergyman and a Conservative Church*
   I. From an article, "Hollis Street Council," in *The Dial,* October 1842 (Vol. III, No. II), pp. 212-19.
   II. Frothingham, pp. 276-77.

5. *William Ellery Channing*
   From a pamphlet, *An Humble Tribute to the Memory of William Ellery Channing,* preached October 9, 1842, pp. 8-31.

6. *The True Idea of a Christian Church*
   From *The True Idea of a Christian Church.* In Cobbe, III, pp. 43-54.

7. *Transcendentalism*
   I. From *The World of Matter and the Spirit of Man.* In Centenary, VI, pp. 6-7, 23-32, 37-38.
   II. From *The Function and Place of Conscience, in Relation to the Laws of Men.* In Cobbe, V, pp. 134-36.

8. *The Position and Duty of a Minister*
   From "Of the Position and Duty of a Minister" in *Some Account of My Ministry.* In Cobbe, XII, pp. 223-26, 229.

Sumner: Weiss, II, p. 111.
Miss ————: Frothingham, pp. 297-98.
Desor: Frothingham, pp. 319-20.
Boston: Weiss, I, pp. 377-78.
Miss ————: Frothingham, pp. 298-99.
Desor: Frothingham, pp. 316-17.
Wilson: Weiss, II, pp. 209-10.
Orton: Weiss, II, p. 238.
Mann: Weiss, II, p. 188.
Desor: Weiss, I, pp. 330-31.
Miss ————: Frothingham, pp. 307-8.
Hale: Weiss, II, p. 187.
Hunt: Frothingham, pp. 483-84.
Apthorp: Frothingham, pp. 441-42.
Bridges: Frothingham, pp. 277-78.
Hale: Weiss, II, p. 225.

Hunt: Frothingham, pp. 470-71.
Clark: Weiss, I, pp. 151-52.
Ripley: Weiss, II, pp. 376-77.
Eddy: Frothingham, pp. 278-80.
Flint: Weiss, II, pp. 397-99.
Cobbe: Weiss, II, pp. 418-19.

27. *Poems*
    The Gospel of Love: Frothingham, p. 331.
    Sons of Men . . . : Weiss, II, p. 109.
    In Darker Days . . . : Weiss, II, p. 39.
    Sonnets: Cobbe, X, pp. 78-80.

28. *Experience as a Minister*
    From *Theodore Parker's Experience as a Minister, with Some Account of His Early Life, and Education for the Ministry.* In Cobbe, XII, pp. 262 ff.